SHAKESPEARE SURVEY

ADVISORY BOARD

Assistant to the Editor: ANN THOMPSON

SHAKESPEARE SURVEY

AN ANNUAL SURVEY OF
SHAKESPEARIAN STUDY AND PRODUCTION

33

EDITED BY
KENNETH MUIR

CAMBRIDGE UNIVERSITY PRESS

CAMBRIDGE
LONDON   NEW YORK   NEW ROCHELLE
MELBOURNE   SYDNEY

Published by the Press Syndicate of the University of Cambridge
The Pitt Building, Trumpington Street, Cambridge CB2 1RP
32 East 57th Street, New York, NY 10022, USA
296 Beaconsfield Parade, Middle Park, Melbourne 3206, Australia

First published 1980

Shakespeare Survey was first published in 1948. For the first
eighteen volumes it was edited by Allardyce Nicoll under the
sponsorship of the University of Birmingham, the University
of Manchester, the Royal Shakespeare Theatre and the
Shakespeare Birthplace Trust

Printed in Great Britain
at the University Press, Cambridge

British Library Cataloguing in Publication Data
Shakespeare Survey.
33
1. Shakespeare, William – Societies,
periodicals, etc.
I. Muir, Kenneth
822.3'3   PR2885   49–1639
ISBN 0 521 23249 X

EDITOR'S NOTE

Allardyce Nicoll, in introducing the first volume of *Shakespeare Survey*, said that it aimed 'at appealing to the scholar, the theatre-worker and the archivist, while at the same time presenting material likely to be of value to a wider public generally interested in Shakespeare'; and he hoped that opportunity would be 'found for the reproduction of documentary material, either new or difficult of access'.

The retiring editor has pursued the same aims. Apart from a variety of articles on theatrical and dramatic topics, we have been able to publish in the last few years documents relating to George Wilkins, the Bankside, the Globe Theatre, the Cockpit, and a theatre at Gdansk similar to the Fortune; and in the present issue we print some unpublished documents about English actors abroad.

As already announced, the central theme of *Shakespeare Survey 34*, already in the press, will be 'Characterization in Shakespeare'. It will include some papers from the 1980 International Shakespeare Conference at Stratford-upon-Avon. The theme of volume 35 will be 'Shakespeare in the Nineteenth Century'. Contributions on that, or on other topics, should reach the new editor, Dr Stanley Wells (40 Walton Crescent, Oxford OX1 2JQ) by 1 September 1981 at the latest. As many articles are accepted before the deadline those that arrive earlier have a greater chance of acceptance. Contributors should leave generous margins, use double spacing, and follow the style and lay-out of articles in the current issue. A style-sheet is available on request. Contributions should not normally exceed 5,000 words.

Books for review should be sent to the Editor at the above address, *not* to the publisher. The Editor will also be glad to receive offprints of articles, as our reviewers may easily miss those which appear in journals not primarily concerned with Shakespeare.

K.M.

Volume 36 will have as its theme 'Shakespeare in the Twentieth Century', with a deadline of 1 September 1982.

CONTRIBUTORS

ROY BATTENHOUSE, *Professor of English, University of Indiana*

JAMES BLACK, *Professor of English, University of Alberta, Calgary*

ANDREW FICHTER, *Assistant Professor of English, Princeton University*

HARRIETT HAWKINS, *Oxford*

G. R. HIBBARD, *Professor of English, University of Waterloo, Ontario*

ARTHUR F. KINNEY, *Professor of English, University of Massachusetts, Amherst*

FRANK MCCOMBIE, *Newcastle-upon-Tyne*

J. W. R. MEADOWCROFT, *Lecturer in English, Concordia University, Montreal*

JOHN ORRELL, *Professor of English, University of Alberta, Edmonton*

DEREK PEAT, *Lecturer in Adult Education, University of Sydney*

GĀMINI SALGĀDO, *Professor of English, University of Exeter*

WILLEM SCHRICKX, *Professor of English and American Literature, University of Ghent*

ALAN SINFIELD, *Lecturer in the School of English and American Studies, University of Sussex*

SUSAN SNYDER, *Professor of English, Swarthmore College, Pennsylvania*

GARY TAYLOR, *Associate Editor, Shakespeare Department, Oxford University Press*

ROGER WARREN, *Lecturer in English, University of Leicester*

STANLEY WELLS, *General Editor, Shakespeare Department, Oxford University Press*

GEORGE WALTON WILLIAMS, *Professor of English, Duke University*

CONTENTS

PLATES

'KING LEAR': A RETROSPECT, 1939-79

G. R. HIBBARD

Throughout the period under review there has been a wide measure of agreement that *King Lear* is the greatest of all the plays, and, perhaps as a consequence, an equally wide measure of disagreement about what it says. In the course of the many scrutinies it has been subjected to, almost every significant word in it has been examined with minute care, as though the drama were an extended metaphysical poem; yet, paradoxically enough, there is no general consensus among editors as to what Shakespeare actually wrote; and editions differ greatly from one another in the texts they offer. G. K. Hunter, for example, in his New Penguin edition first published in 1972, lists well over a hundred readings in which his text does not concur with those of Peter Alexander (1951), Kenneth Muir (1952), and Dover Wilson and G. I. Duthie (1960).[1] The prime cause of the variations is, of course, that there are two substantive texts not one: the Quarto of 1608, containing some 300 lines not found in the Folio, and the Folio itself, containing 100 lines not found in the Quarto. The editor must, therefore, or has hitherto felt that he must, make use of both while knowing full well, to complicate his task still further, that neither of them was set up from a manuscript in Shakespeare's hand. Nevertheless, one great advance has been made. In a classic study, published in 1940,[2] W. W. Greg established conclusively that the Quarto of 1608, in a copy which, like all extant copies, was made up of both corrected and uncorrected sheets, was used for setting the Folio text. He also showed that the copy of the Quarto employed for this purpose had been collated with a text from the playhouse, in all probability the prompt-copy, and much altered in the process. His findings on this score have won general acceptance, though both G. I. Duthie, in the New Cambridge edition of the play, and G. Blakemore Evans, in the Riverside edition of Shakespeare (1974), agree with A. S. Cairncross[3] that the Folio also had some recourse to the second Quarto of 1619, a view that has been vigorously challenged and repudiated by J. K. Walton, who asserts categorically that it is 'of no value'.[4]

As well as defining the relationship between the two substantive texts, Greg's investigation also brought into sharp focus the major problem that every editor has to face, for in the course of it he discovered clear evidence 'that the folio has in some instances inadvertently reproduced errors of the quarto in place of what we must assume to have been the readings of the playhouse manuscript'. It therefore follows that 'where the folio differs from the quarto its readings...must be derived from the authoritative playhouse manuscript, whereas where the two agree we can never be certain

[1] *King Lear*, ed. G. K. Hunter (Harmondsworth, 1972), pp. 331–5.
[2] *The Variants in the First Quarto of 'King Lear'* (1940).
[3] 'The Quartos and the First Folio Text of *King Lear*', *Review of English Studies*, n.s. VI (1955), 252–8.
[4] *The Quarto Copy for the First Folio of Shakespeare* (Dublin, 1971), pp. 282–7.

that the folio has not carelessly reproduced an error of the quarto' (p. 187). Since then Charlton Hinman[1] has given editors yet another reason for treating the Folio text with some caution by demonstrating that it was not set by one compositor, B, as Alice Walker had suggested,[2] but by two, B and E, and that E, probably an apprentice and the least skilled member of Jaggard's team, was responsible for more than half of it.

In these circumstances, the nature and origin of the copy used for the 1608 Quarto has become an issue of the first importance, and has proved an extremely recalcitrant one. In 1940 Greg thought the copy had probably been obtained 'from actual performance by some method of shorthand' (p. 138). By 1955, however, he had been persuaded by G. I. Duthie[3] that shorthand was not the answer.[4] Less convinced by Duthie's theory that the copy-text was dictated to a scribe by the cast relying on their memories,[5] he found himself attracted by the freshness and ingenuity of Alice Walker's hypothesis, advanced in her *Textual Problems* (pp. 37–67), that it was derived from, as he puts it, 'a surreptitious transcript of the foul papers by two boy actors, "Goneril" dictating to "Regan", who in their haste contaminated the written text by recollections of what they were accustomed to speak and hear on the stage' (p. 382). All the same, he still had his doubts, especially about the identification of the two boys as the culprits. This last doubt was shared by Duthie, who, in his final words on a subject to which he had devoted so much of his life, accepted Miss Walker's general theory but modified it to read: 'transcription from foul papers, the persons involved having had some memorial knowledge of the play, seems the most convincing solution'.[6] J. K. Walton, however, argues that Duthie was wrong to abandon his original theory, and that memorial reconstruction still remains the likeliest answer to the question of the origin of the copy employed by the printer of the 1608 Quarto.[7] In doing so Walton does not mention the indirect support Miss Walker's theory has received from E. A. J. Honigmann, who, pointing to the occasional greater metrical regularity of the Quarto, makes an interesting case for the idea that some of the variants between the two texts can best be explained as representing first thoughts (the Quarto) and second thoughts (the Folio) on the part of Shakespeare himself.[8] More recently still, Michael J. Warren, resorting to literary rather than bibliographical criteria, has boldly attacked the whole assumption, hitherto the basis of editorial endeavour, that there is or ever was such a thing as the ideal text of the tragedy. He holds 'that Q and F *King Lear* are sufficiently dissimilar that they should not be conflated, but should be treated as two versions of a single play, both having authority'.[9]

Greg concluded *The Variants in the First Quarto of 'King Lear'* on an optimistic and hortatory note: 'I believe that now the whole of the information needed is at the disposal of editors, and it appears to be high time that they set about the job of preparing a text of the play

[1] 'The Prentice Hand in the Tragedies of the Shakespeare First Folio: Compositor E', *Studies in Bibliography*, IX (1957); and *The Printing and Proof-Reading of the First Folio of Shakespeare* (Oxford, 1963), I, 212.

[2] *Textual Problems of the First Folio* (Cambridge, 1953), pp. 62–3.

[3] *Elizabethan Shorthand and the First Quarto of 'King Lear'* (Oxford, 1949).

[4] *The Shakespeare First Folio* (Oxford, 1955), p. 380.

[5] *King Lear*, ed. G. I. Duthie (Oxford, 1949), pp. 19–116.

[6] *King Lear*, ed. G. I. Duthie and J. Dover Wilson (Cambridge, 1960), pp. 132–5.

[7] *The Quarto Copy*, pp. 269–81.

[8] *The Stability of Shakespeare's Text* (1965), pp. 121–8.

[9] 'Quarto and Folio *King Lear* and the Interpretation of Albany and Edgar', in *Shakespeare: Pattern of Excelling Nature*, ed. David Bevington and Jay Halio (Newark, N. J., and London, 1978), p. 97.

that shall be based upon a properly reasoned estimate of the evidence' (p. 190). In 1955, when he published *The Shakespeare First Folio*, the optimism had disappeared. Summing up what had been done in the interim, which had, in fact, seen the publication of Duthie's edition of 1949, the most scholarly we have, and of Kenneth Muir's New Arden edition of 1952, the most commonly used by literary critics, he wrote: 'It is to be feared that a consideration of the various theories [about the origin of the copy for the Quarto] so far advanced can only lead to the conclusion...that *King Lear* still offers a problem for investigation' (p. 383). Nothing has been discovered since then to alter that verdict. For the editor the play remains a nightmare – and her nine-fold.

The uncertainties about the text have in no way inhibited the activity of aesthetic criticism. The last forty years have produced a formidable – one is sorely tempted to say, daunting – outpouring of studies and interpretations of the most diverse kind. The very nature of the world we live in has much to do with the interest the play excites. Shot through with hints and fears of Doomsday, *King Lear* has taken on a peculiar immediacy and urgency. It speaks to our condition. What it says varies from critic to critic for two main reasons. First, as Helen Gardner acutely observes, no one can write about *King Lear* today without, at the same time, writing about himself and 'interpreting its design in the terms of his own conception of the mystery of things';[1] and, secondly, the clear-cut conflict in it between good and evil holds out an almost irresistible invitation to ideological readings, especially in a world where Shakespeare has, to quote Harry Levin, become 'a sort of lay religion'.[2] Like the story of the Fall of the Angels, *King Lear* 'has been adopted by both parties', and has undergone, on occasions, some strange metamorphoses in the process. Paul N. Siegel, for example, improving the ending in a manner that did not

occur to Nahum Tate, assures us that Lear and Cordelia 'become reunited in eternal bliss';[3] while Jan Kott sweeps all attempts to find some positive meaning in the tragedy into the dustbins of *Endgame* thus:

In Shakespeare's play there is neither Christian heaven, nor the heaven predicted and believed in by humanists. *King Lear* makes a tragic mockery of all eschatologies; of the heaven promised on earth, and the heaven promised after death; in fact – of both Christian and secular theodicies; of cosmogony, and of the rational view of history; of the gods and natural goodness, of man made in the 'image and likeness'. In *King Lear*, both the medieval and the renaissance orders of established values disintegrate. All that remains at the end of this gigantic pantomime is the earth – empty and bleeding.[4]

Which of the two are we to accept? 'Both? one? or neither?' Confronted by Edmund's dilemma, the sensible man will, surely, opt for the last of the three possibilities, and look for guidance elsewhere.

Between these two extremes of sentimental wishful thinking and reductive nihilistic rant there is no shortage of such guidance, sometimes brilliantly illuminating, sometimes tendentiously misleading, and sometimes painfully and painstakingly moralizing and repetitious. I shall, therefore, attempt no more than to distinguish some of the main trends and major issues.

L. C. Knights, writing some twenty years ago, observed that 'the appreciation of Shakespeare, the kind of thing men have got from Shakespeare, has varied enormously at different periods'. He then went on to say:

from time to time major shifts of attention occur, and not the least significant and fruitful of these is the one that has taken place in our time, and that scholars and critics of very different kinds have helped to bring

---

[1] *King Lear* (1967), p. 4.
[2] *Shakespeare and the Revolution of the Times* (Oxford, 1976), p. 6.
[3] *Shakespearean Tragedy and the Elizabethan Compromise* (New York, 1957), p. 186.
[4] *Shakespeare Our Contemporary* (1964), p. 118.

about. Conceptions of the nature and function of poetic drama have been radically revised; the essential structure of the plays has been sought in the poetry rather than in the more easily extractable elements of 'plot' and 'character'.[1]

If such is indeed the case, then the new trend should be most obvious over the period in question (c. 1930–59) in what was written about King Lear, for, as Wolfgang Clemen assures us, 'An attempt to interpret a Shakespearian play solely on the basis of its imagery – a risky undertaking – would have the greatest chance of success if King Lear were the play in question.'[2] In fact, three years before Clemen's book came out but too late for him to make use of it, such an attempt had been made. R. B. Heilman's This Great Stage,[3] significantly subtitled 'Image and Structure in King Lear', is based on the assertion that 'In its fullness the structure [of the play] can be set forth only by means of the patterns of imagery' (p. 32). The use of 'only' there was, not surprisingly, very strongly objected to by, among others, W. R. Keast, who condemned the work out of hand as 'in almost all respects a bad book'.[4] Yet, once the initial fuss had died down, Heilman's main findings were absorbed into the critical bloodstream with great rapidity, and have persisted there ever since. They could not be rejected because he had pointed to a feature of the play which is demonstrably there but had not been properly noticed before: the presence in it of elaborate verbal patterns made up of references to sight, smell, clothes, sex, animals, and justice, and, behind them all, the striking paradoxes of madness in reason and reason in madness. It is significant that the one serious attack on the work in more recent years, Paul J. Alpers's 'King Lear and the Theory of the "Sight Pattern"',[5] does not deny that the sight pattern is there; instead, it argues that Heilman and those who have followed him have mistaken its import. It is also worth noting that Heilman did his work so thoroughly that little

has been added to it. William Empson examines the use of the word 'fool' in the play, but ingeniously counterpoints the approach through 'pattern' with an approach through 'character' in order to bring out the different results they can give;[6] and Rosalie Colie puts some of Heilman's discoveries into a larger historical context in the chapter on King Lear in her Paradoxia Epidemica,[7] where she relates the paradoxes in the tragedy to the Renaissance tradition of paradox in general, and shows how they are closely interwoven with one another, much as his patterns are.

Yet, exciting and important as Heilman's book was and remains, it did little to alter existing judgements on the play's larger significances, though it did add an extra dimension to one's sense of Shakespeare's artistry in conveying them. His final conclusions about what King Lear says do not differ greatly from Bradley's. In revealing what a close study of the imagery could accomplish he had also, unintentionally, revealed what it could not. At this point I turn to Knights's own essay on the play. Its main contention is that King Lear is 'timeless and universal'.[8] It makes good this claim by concentrating, as D. A. Traversi had done,[9] on the conflict within the mind of the hero as the core of the tragedy, the focus from which everything else radiates. It is true that Knights uses the poetry to illustrate the points he makes; but the strength of the essay lies in its psychological penetration and imaginative grasp. In fact, the approach is,

[1] Some Shakespearean Themes (1959), pp. 13–14.
[2] The Development of Shakespeare's Imagery (1951), p. 133.
[3] Baton Rouge, 1948.
[4] 'Imagery and Meaning in the Interpretation of King Lear', Modern Philology, 47 (1949), 45.
[5] In Defense of Reading, ed. Reuben A. Brower and Richard Poirier (New York, 1962).
[6] The Structure of Complex Words (1951), pp. 125–57.
[7] Princeton, 1966.
[8] Some Shakespearean Themes, p. 84.
[9] 'King Lear', Scrutiny, XIX (1952–3).

in no small measure, traditional. By 1959, when *Some Shakespearean Themes* appeared, the idea that the 'poetry' alone could provide the master-key to understanding was losing its hold.

In the same essay Knights says that *King Lear* 'marks a moment of great importance in the changing consciousness of the civilization to which it belongs', and then proceeds to a short consideration of the way in which the connotations of the word 'Nature' were undergoing a radical shift at the time when the play was written. Here he is taking up a topic which had interested him for a long time and which had already affected the criticism of *King Lear*. He touches on it in 'How Many Children had Lady Macbeth?' (1933), where he links it to the idea of order; and the economic and social crisis of the early seventeenth century is very much to the fore in his *Drama and Society in the Age of Jonson* (1937). Somewhere at the back of it all lie the influence of R. H. Tawney, the preoccupation of the thirties and forties in England with social change, and the developing study, especially in the United States, of the history of ideas. The impact of the last on the interpretation of *King Lear* is evident in Theodore Spencer's treatment of the play, where much emphasis falls on microcosm and macrocosm: the connexions between family, state, and the gods.[1] Combining this kind of interest with a wide knowledge of medieval and sixteenth-century drama, S. L. Bethell distinguishes two meanings of 'Nature' in the tragedy: 'first, nature as opposed to supernature, or the realm of grace; and secondly, nature as opposed to civilisation' (p. 56). The second nature is, he suggests, incarnate in Edmund, who represents the 'new thought' of Machiavelli, while supernature appears as Cordelia, who is 'associated with theological terminology and Christian symbol' (p. 59).[2] A similar kind of thinking, at the political level, is present in Edwin Muir's *The Politics of 'King Lear'*, which envisages the action as a dramatization of the destruction of the Middle Ages by a gang of Renaissance adventurers.[3] The final step towards giving *King Lear* a significant place in the history of ideas and of social change was taken by John Danby in his *Shakespeare's Doctrine of Nature: A Study of 'King Lear'*.[4] In it he contends that the good characters in the play see Nature, much as Hooker saw it, as God-ordained, benignant, and ordered; while the bad characters see it as Machiavelli had done, and as Hobbes was soon to do. The action thus becomes a struggle between the Middle Ages and the Renaissance, and, more than that, between two forms of society: 'Edmund's is the society of the New Man and the New Age...Lear's is the feudal state in decomposition' (p. 138). Above and beyond both stands Cordelia, representing the ideal: 'Nature in its communal aspect'.

Making a good deal of play with traditions of Christian communism, this was an attractive thesis at the time when it appeared, particularly in an England where there was a strong feeling that 'distribution should undo excess,/And each man have enough', and it won many adherents. Since then it has come under fire from Robert Ornstein, who accuses Danby of oversimplifying and oversubtilizing Shakespeare's intention because 'the attempt to define Goneril, Regan, and Edmund ideologically merely diverts attention from the true philosophical drama of the play which is focused in Lear's mind'.[5] Nevertheless, the main thesis has continued to exert a strong appeal. It has been adopted by Nicholas Brooke and Maynard Mack, among others, while

[1] *Shakespeare and the Nature of Man* (New York, 1942).
[2] *Shakespeare and the Popular Dramatic Tradition* (1944).
[3] Glasgow, 1947.
[4] 1949.
[5] *The Moral Vision of Jacobean Tragedy* (Madison and Milwaukee, 1960; paperback edn 1965), p. 264.

Rosalie Colie has carried its social implications a stage further by seeking to relate some aspects of the play to the crisis of the aristocracy described by Lawrence Stone.[1] Its capacity to endure would seem to indicate that it was something more than a *King Lear* for the forties.

As well as bringing out the clash between the two ideas of Nature in the drama, Danby tries, much more questionably, to turn Shakespeare himself into a medieval poet, whose work can best be interpreted by medieval methods of exegesis. He writes of Cordelia: 'she is a figure comparable with that of Griselde or Beatrice: literally a woman; allegorically the root of individual and social sanity; tropologically Charity "that suffereth long and is kind"; anagogically the redemptive principle itself' (p. 125). Here his argument links up with and becomes part of the most important development of the forties: a strong trend towards making *King Lear* an explicitly Christian tragedy. Two tendencies, which might, on first sight, appear antagonistic, came together to assist in the process. On the one hand, there was, among some of Bradley's followers, an impulse to free some of his more hesitant insights from the cautions and reservations with which he had so carefully hedged them in; on the other, there was the growing reaction against his heavy reliance on character study, and the attempt to replace it by an approach through theme, imagery, and symbol, such as that which Wilson Knight had already employed, with fresh and illuminating results, in his *The Wheel of Fire*, where, incidentally, he says that Cordelia 'represents the principle of love' (p. 201).

In *Shakespearean Tragedy* Bradley tentatively suggests that *King Lear* might not unfittingly be called *The Redemption of King Lear*. He does this, startlingly and paradoxically enough, within the overall framework of his conviction that Shakespearean tragedy is secular, that any theological interpretation of the world by the author is excluded from it, and that the play, 'the most terrible picture that Shakespeare painted of the world', does not contain 'a revelation of righteous omnipotence or heavenly harmony, or even a promise of the reconciliation of mystery and justice'. Nevertheless, his alternative title is, he thinks, justified because the King's sufferings have the effect of 'reviving the greatness and eliciting the sweetness of [his] nature', and "the gods", who inflict these sufferings on him, do so in order to enable him to attain 'the very end and aim of life'. The Christian implications of that final remark are, despite Bradley's calculated retention of 'the gods', inescapable. The statement is inconsistent with everything he says at the end of his first chapter on the play; but the temptation it held out to others, especially when coupled with the word 'redemption', was too strong to be resisted.

Combining Bradley's alternative title with another of his more adventurous suggestions, to the effect that the tragedy, in its concern with the ultimate power in the universe, affects the imagination as the *Divine Comedy* does, though the two works are entirely different in kind, R. W. Chambers came to see *King Lear* as 'a vast poem on the victory of true love', moving from the *Purgatorio* to the *Paradiso*, where 'Lear, consoled, ends by teaching patience to Gloucester and to Cordelia'.[2] He was followed, in his optimistic reading, by S. L. Bethell, who views the world of the play as one without revelation but seeking for some sort of moral and religious order, which is symbolized by Cordelia, who is constantly associated with Christian doctrine;[3] by G. L. Bickersteth, for whom Cordelia is the symbol

[1] 'Reason and Need: *King Lear* and the "Crisis" of the Aristocracy', in *Some Facets of 'King Lear': Essays in Prismatic Criticism*, ed. Rosalie L. Colie and F. T. Flahiff (Toronto and Buffalo, 1974).

[2] *King Lear* (Glasgow, 1940), pp. 48–9.

[3] *Shakespeare and the Popular Dramatic Tradition*, pp. 54, 60.

of divine love in a pagan setting;[1] and, of course, by John Danby. All of them agree that Lear becomes a better man for his sufferings, and that the tragedy is, to quote J. C. Maxwell, 'a Christian play about a pagan world'.[2] The wide currency this view gained is evident from the prominence given to it in Kenneth Muir's introduction to his New Arden edition (1952).

Even in the forties, however, at least two powerful voices were raised in opposition. F. P. Wilson stated emphatically: 'No compensatory heaven is offered. Man has only himself and his own power and endurance to fall back on. These are very great, but when they fail only madness or death remains, and death is, if not nescience, escape into the unknown.'[3] George Orwell, characteristically going his own independent way, not only denied that the play is Christian but also disposed briskly of the idea that Lear is regenerated. The old King dies, he tells us, 'still cursing, still understanding nothing', having failed to recognize that 'If you live for others, you must live *for others*, and not as a roundabout way of getting an advantage for yourself', this being the true meaning of 'renunciation', which is, as Orwell sees it, what the play is really about.[4] In the early fifties more voices joined these two. Convinced that the tragic experience is not compatible 'with any form of religious belief that assumes the existence of a personal and kindly God' (p. 18), Clifford Leech contends that the comedy in *King Lear* helps us to accept the play's picture of life 'because it confirms our most private judgment, our deepest awareness of human folly' (p. 82);[5] and William Empson, also much preoccupied with folly, inclines to Orwell's view that the King does not become wise, and retorts to those who think he becomes patient: 'if Lear really seemed regenerated to the point of accepting his calamities (including the death of Cordelia) the play would become sickly'.[6]

A more sustained and damaging attack came from D. G. James, gathering weight from having behind it one of the most wide-ranging considerations of the play as a contribution to man's knowledge of himself in his world that the entire period has to offer. *The Dream of Learning*[7] is based on the idea that 'poetry... issues from a peculiar labour of knowing' (p. 78), different from but no less important than the labour that goes into scientific knowing, an idea that James attempts to establish by bringing together *Hamlet*, *The Advancement of Learning*, and *King Lear*. So far as the last is concerned, James contends that the drive of the play is an effort to penetrate to the limits of human experience. Consequently, while there are 'signs that Christian belief was moving in Shakespeare's mind in the course of its composition' (p. 119), 'what seems certain is that it was [his] fully conscious decision not to give the story any fraction of a Christian context. The play's action is terrible in all conscience; but there is no crumb of Christian comfort in it' (pp. 92–3). All the same, Lear emerges from his madness a changed man; and the tragedy makes its own non-doctrinal affirmation, because the good characters continue to act out of wholly disinterested motives right to the end. This conclusion is not dissimilar to that reached by Arthur Sewell, following a different route, in his *Character and Society in Shakespeare*.[8] Affirming that 'the Christian-allegorical interpretations recently placed upon certain of Shakespeare's works (especially *King Lear* and *The Winter's Tale*) are almost certainly in error' (p. 60), and rejecting outright Danby's identifi-

---

[1] *The Golden World of 'King Lear'* (1946).
[2] 'The Technique of Invocation in *King Lear*', *Modern Language Review*, 45 (1950).
[3] *Elizabethan and Jacobean* (Oxford, 1945), p. 121.
[4] 'Lear, Tolstoy and the Fool', *Shooting an Elephant* (1945).
[5] *Shakespeare's Tragedies and Other Studies in Seventeenth-Century Drama* (1950).
[6] *The Structure of Complex Words*, p. 154.
[7] Oxford, 1951.
[8] Oxford, 1951.

cation of Cordelia with Charity, Sewell finds that the distinctive feature of *King Lear* is that 'the characters are imagined not only as members of each other but also as members of a nature which is active both within themselves and throughout the circumambient universe. Man is nowhere so certainly exhibited as a member of all organic creation and of the elemental powers' (p. 117).

It is against this background, to which, by the time Barbara Everett wrote, Paul N. Siegel had added his thoroughgoing Christian version of the drama,[1] that one must set her astringent article 'The New *King Lear*'.[2] In it, making no mention of such allies as Orwell, James, and Sewell, she attacks what she calls the orthodox approach to the play, focusing her attention mainly on Muir's introduction to his edition, which she finds fault with for its excessive, as she sees it, emphasis on the Christian content of the drama at the expense of everything else. This is not strictly true, for one of the most valuable features of that introduction is its extensive treatment of the play's sources. This said, however, there is no denying that the essay is acute and very much to the point. It accuses the Christian allegorizers of attaching more importance to the 'poetry' than to the plot; of overlooking Bradley's honest doubts about his own transcendental reading of the ending; and, most importantly, of reducing the specific concerns of the play to a rather platitudinous moralizing, a charge that Keast had levelled at Heilman some ten years before. What matters is, she contends, less what Lear learns than that it is Lear, royal Lear with his demand for absolutes, who learns it, and learns it in a peculiarly direct and physical manner.

The article does not stand alone. The year in which it came out, 1960, also saw the appearance of other writings which move in the same general direction as it does. Robert Ornstein, too, rejected moralizing, saying rather neatly: 'One can of course read *Lear* as a warning against pride, wrath, or relatives. But I suspect that like all great tragedy *Lear* actually celebrates the vulnerability of man, the sublime folly of his "needs" and aspirations, the irrationality of his demands upon the vast inscrutable universe which surrounds him' (p. 273).[3] Two powerful and well reasoned essays in *Shakespeare Survey 13* took issue with Bradley's reading of the play's ending. J. Stampfer, noting that Lear's illusion that Cordelia lives is not confined to his last speech but recurs several times after he enters carrying her body, decides, in his 'The Catharsis of *King Lear*', that the tension in the King right up to the moment of his death is 'between an absolute knowledge that Cordelia is dead, and an absolute inability to accept it' (p. 2). J. K. Walton takes another road to a similar destination. The main experience of Lear in the latter half of the play is, he argues, a continuous enlargement of consciousness. So for him to believe, to the very end, that his daughter is still alive reverses 'the direction of the whole movement which has been taking place' (p. 17). Bradley is, therefore, wrong about 'Lear's Last Speech', as the essay is entitled. To these witnesses one must also add Maynard Mack, who, in his richly suggestive article 'The Jacobean Shakespeare',[4] writes of Lear at the end of the play:

the man before us...who sweeps Kent aside, rakes all who have helped him with grapeshot...exults in the revenge he has exacted for Cordelia's death, and dies self-deceived in the thought she still lives – this man is one of the most profoundly human figures ever created in a play; but he is not, certainly, the Platonic ideal laid up in heaven, or in critical schemes, of regenerate man. (p. 38)

[1] *Shakespearean Tragedy and the Elizabethan Compromise.*
[2] *Critical Quarterly*, 2 (1960).
[3] *The Moral Vision of Jacobean Tragedy.*
[4] *Jacobean Theatre*, ed. J. R. Brown and B. Harris (1960).

Looking back from the vantage-point of today, one can see, I think, that a crucial shift was taking place round about 1960, not only in the controversy as to whether *King Lear* is, or is not a Christian tragedy, but also in critical assumptions and methods. But the shift took time. Two works appearing in that year reassert the Christian reading in all its fullness. G. I. Duthie, in his introduction to the New Cambridge edition, says the play is 'about education...conversion, spiritual regeneration, the attainment of salvation' (p. xx); sees Cordelia and Kent as Christ-like figures; and finds a just and merciful, though, he feels constrained to add, inscrutable, God behind the entire action. Irving Ribner is no less assured. Combining his extensive knowledge of medieval and sixteenth-century drama with an almost indiscriminate resort to symbolism – 'All the characters perform symbolic functions' – in the chapter on the play in his *Patterns in Shakespearian Tragedy*,[1] he has no hesitation about saying that *King Lear* 'affirms justice in the world, which it sees as a harmonious system ruled by a benevolent God' (p. 117).

Few critics and scholars since then have gone quite so far as that, though many continue, as well they might, to see the Lear of the latter part of the play as a better man than the Lear of the first two acts. Chief among the few are Virgil K. Whitaker[2] and Roy W. Battenhouse.[3] Assuming that *King Lear* rests on 'the Christian concept that God permits suffering to try and refine the natures of men' (p. 210), Whitaker, unwittingly one trusts, reveals some of the grislier implications of that notion by telling us, for example, that Lear 'has been stretched long enough upon the rack of this tough world, not so much because he can endure no more as because he has become patient and resigned, perfected in the "ripeness" that is all. He is a higher kind of man for the stretching' (p. 227). Even the blinding of Gloucester is seen simply as an appropriate punishment for the lustful

man (p. 237). The fact that it is more immediately and more pressingly the ironical consequence of Gloucester's charity and heroism in helping the old King his master is conveniently overlooked. Battenhouse goes to work after another fashion. Calling typology to his aid, and taking it for granted that both Shakespeare and his audience were as well versed in the teachings of St Augustine as he is himself, he finds the play informed by 'a background sense of parable, which...turns about the possibilities for human progress under providence' (p. 301). There is immense learning behind the book, but one cannot but conclude that it has been misapplied.

Oddly enough Battenhouse makes no more than a passing reference to William Elton's *'King Lear' and the Gods* (1966),[4] which had come out three years before his own work, and in which the whole question of whether the play is an optimistically Christian drama receives the most thorough and scholarly examination it has ever been subjected to. Looking at the tragedy in the light of the religious beliefs, disbeliefs, and disputes of the time when it was written, Elton distinguishes four main attitudes towards the ultimate governance of the world and the operation of providence in it that are to be found in both Sidney's *Arcadia* and Shakespeare's play. They are: *prisca theologia*, the position of the virtuous heathens who were on the way, as it were, to Christian thinking; atheism; superstition; and *Deus absconditus*, the notion of an inscrutable providence. Having identified these positions, Elton equates the characters of the play with them. Cordelia and Edgar exemplify the first; Goneril, Regan, and Edmund, the second; Gloucester, the third; and Lear himself, the fourth. It all looks highly

---

[1] 1960.
[2] *The Mirror up to Nature* (San Marino, 1965).
[3] *Shakespearean Tragedy: Its Art and Its Christian Premises* (Bloomington and London, 1969).
[4] San Marino.

schematic, yet it does throw an enormous amount of fresh light on the question it attempts to answer. Elton's principal conclusions are: that it is to underestimate 'the complexity both of the play and of Lear's character' to say that he 'repents and attains humility and patience, thus becoming fit for heaven' (p. 283); that 'the double plot is an instrument of complexity, the assurance of a multifaceted ambivalence which, contrary to the salvation hypothesis, probes and tests, without finally resolving, its argument of mysterious human suffering' (*ibid.*); and that the play as a whole is best described as 'a syncretically pagan tragedy' (p. 338). Since those words were written, Robert G. Hunter has tackled the same problem by putting *King Lear* alongside the tragedies which have an undeniably Christian background – *Richard III*, *Hamlet*, *Othello*, and *Macbeth* – a procedure which leads him to the view that in *King Lear* 'Shakespeare dramatizes the final possibility: there is no God'.[1]

That verdict too will no doubt be contested, but in its seeming finality it sounds a suitable note on which to leave this particular topic. Before doing so, however, I must record two reflections which the story of this long-drawn-out controversy brings with it. On the one hand, the determination with which believers and unbelievers alike seek to annex (if that is not too strong a word) the tragedy to their cause is a tremendous tribute to its power and significance; on the other, the peripheral nature, as it seems to me, of much of the learning brought to bear on the issue suggests that there is a real danger that criticism of *King Lear* may degenerate into an arid kind of scholasticism.

Fortunately, that danger has been recognized by some students of the play for some time. The new direction which critical thinking begins to take around 1960, less concerned with ideological considerations and dwelling more on the poignantly human experience that *King Lear* embodies, becomes clear not only in Knights's essay but also in John Holloway's treatment of the tragedy in his *The Story of the Night* (1961).[2] In it he expresses his dissatisfaction with the view that the ending is an affirmation of the value of love, because the word 'love' is too vague to cope with 'the range, power and variety of the issues of life on which this incomparable work has touched'; what matters most is that Cordelia is not content to love, she seeks to do – to recover her father his right. This anticipates, in some ways, Paul J. Alpers's dismissal of the whole tendency to make Cordelia a symbolic figure, of which he says: 'Cordelia is Cordelia. Surely there is no need to identify her with the abstraction Love in order to say that she is extraordinarily loving.'[3] Moreover, he will have no truck with the kind of moralizing which, he asserts, falsifies the essential experience. He writes:

If we treat Lear's recognition of Cordelia as a moral awareness that gives him a new personal identity, we must claim that his suffering is a good. It seems to me that we must say that Lear's suffering is shocking and heartbreaking and also (not 'and yet') it enables him to say 'Thou art a soul in bliss' and then to recognize his daughter. (*Ibid.*)

This is the kind of response that leads on naturally to Nicholas Brooke's wonderfully economical and penetrating analysis of the drama in his *Shakespeare: King Lear*.[4] Working his way through the play as it unfolds, he finds the pattern of the action to be one in which hope after hope is raised only to be dashed, a process which reaches its culmination in Albany's speech about rewards and punishments, which is abruptly broken off and made

[1] *Shakespeare and the Mystery of God's Judgments* (Athens, Georgia, 1976).
[2] London.
[3] '*King Lear* and the Theory of the "Sight Pattern"', p. 152.
[4] 1963.

totally irrelevant by Lear's last speech.[1] Questioning the idea that a sense of 'affirmation' is the proper response to tragedy, and thus, by implication, the desire for 'affirmation' which led Bradley to the notion of redemption, Brooke sums up his final impression in these words: 'all moral structures, whether of natural order or Christian redemption, are invalidated by the naked fact of experience' (pp. 59–60). Within the context of his book, this appears as something he was led to, not something he hoped to find, still less set out to find.

Maynard Mack's 'King Lear' in Our Time,[2] though it sums up much that had gone before in an admirably lucid and readable manner, seems rather muted by comparison with his incisive and direct response to the play's ending in 'The Jacobean Shakespeare', too cluttered by references to the homiletic tradition; but we are back on what seems to me to be the high-road of more recent criticism with Helen Gardner's close-packed lecture on the tragedy,[3] where, in a very brief space, she does justice to its 'extraordinary unity of action, characterization, and language' by saying something significant about each without, I think, using the word 'symbol' at all. It is a far cry from this searching and elegant piece of condensation to Marvin Rosenberg's The Masks of King Lear,[4] which is anything but elegant. Nevertheless, the determination to approach the play without preconceptions as to what it means informs this work also. Rosenberg's concern is with King Lear not merely in the study or the classroom but in the theatre and the film studio also. As he painstakingly makes his way through the text scene by scene, almost line by line at times, considering one interpretation after another, one begins to ask what can come out of such a procedure, in which all witness seems to be equally valid. Is not this to trust the player rather than the play? The answer is a firm no. His report on what he finds is both convincing and helpful because he has done the necessary work before making it. After challenging one's ready-made responses on issue after issue, he writes: 'The dark, deadly, grimly comic world of Lear evokes so wide and intense a range of responses on so many levels of consciousness...that it must defeat any attempts to enclose its meaning in limited formulae such as redemption, retribution, endgame, morality, etc.' (p. 328).

The same distrust of formulas is evident in H. A. Mason's analysis of King Lear in his Shakespeare's Tragedies of Love[5] and in the writings of several more recent critics. Mason is astringent and stimulating in the way that Empson can be, especially in his questioning of the play's artistry. At other times he seems simply wrong-headed, as when he blames Gloucester for not intervening in I, i, where the decisive action takes place while Gloucester is off stage. But one cannot help but applaud the firmness with which he insists that in the middle of the play Gloucester 'rises in stature to a major figure' (p. 207) and the vigour with which he asserts, in his final sentence: 'Lear dies an obstinately unreconstructed rebel' (p. 226). A similar sense of the old King's heroic quality makes itself felt in Arthur G. Davis's The Royalty of Lear,[6] and in S. L. Goldberg's An Essay on 'King Lear',[7] though in each case one is left wondering whether the essay proper might not have served the author's purpose better than the book.

The contributions of philosophers and of critics with strong philosophical leanings, such

---

[1] This matter is pursued further and expanded by John D. Rosenberg in his 'King Lear and His Comforters', Essays in Criticism, XVI (1966), and by John Shaw in his 'King Lear: The Final Lines', ibid.
[2] Berkeley, Los Angeles, and London, 1965.
[3] King Lear.
[4] Berkeley, Los Angeles, and London, 1972.
[5] 1970.
[6] New York, 1974.
[7] Cambridge, 1974.

as Stanley Cavell[1] and Walter Stein,[2] to the understanding of *King Lear* will, one hopes, continue; and Emrys Jones's brilliant exposition of the play's structure in his *Scenic Form in Shakespeare*[3] deserves far more than a passing mention. So does much else. But, like time, that takes survey of all the world, this piece, that takes survey of forty years, must have a stop.

[1] 'The Avoidance of Love: A Reading of *King Lear*', in his *Must We Mean What We Say?* (New York, 1969).
[2] *Criticism as Dialogue* (Cambridge, 1969).
[3] Oxford, 1971.

© G. R. HIBBARD 1980

SOME CONJECTURES ON THE COMPOSITION OF 'KING LEAR'

ARTHUR F. KINNEY

I

Act III. [*A heath.*] The storm and king rage: the moment of greatest dramatic tension in *King Lear* comes precisely at the center of the play and remains the work's fulcrum, yet where did Shakespeare get the idea for it? We have dozens of possible sources for *Lear*,[1] yet none seems to yield sufficient clue. Lightning flashes twice in Shakespeare's most certain source, *The True Chronicle Historie of King Leir and His Three Daughters* (?1594; 1605), where it frightens the messenger who is sent by Ragan to murder Leir and Perillus in the thicket, but the lightning is seen there by the three men as a sign of heavenly judgement, as flashes of cosmic omen, not as a raging storm within the broader kingdom or the little mind of man.[2] Another likely source for Shakespeare, Book II, chapter 10 of Sir Philip Sidney's *Arcadia* (1590), provided the playwright with a foul storm which allows Sidney to tell the story of the Paphlagonian king overheard by Pyrocles and Musidorus and now accepted as the basis for the subplot of Gloucester, Edmund, and Edgar. Sidney's single Ciceronian sentence elongates the effectiveness of his description.

It was in the kingdome of *Galacia*, the season being (as in the depth of winter) very cold, and as then sodainely growne to so extreame and foule a storme, that never any winter (I thinke) brought foorth a fowler child: so that the Princes were even compelled by the haile, that the pride of the winde blew into their faces, to seeke some shrowding place within a certaine hollow rocke offering it unto them, they made it their shield against the tempests furie.[3]

The storm is common as well to another possible source, Samuel Harsnett's *Declaration of Egregious Popish Impostures* (1603) where one of the 'pittiful' creatures, like Edgar, lies 'abroade in the fieldes' and is 'scared with lightning and thunder, that happened in the night' (p. 24).[4] The repeated motif may have been what triggered Shakespeare's conception for much of act III, but there is at least as likely a fourth work, concerned with kingship, that he knew and had in mind, one extraordinarily popular work which holds as its fundamental principle the idea that right rule depends on the authority grounded in a combination of justice and clemency – a neat encapsulation of

---

[1] See, for example, Geoffrey Bullough, *Narrative and Dramatic Sources of Shakespeare*, 8 vols (London; New York, 1973), VII, 267–420; Kenneth Muir, *The Sources of Shakespeare's Plays* (New Haven, Conn., 1977); *A New Variorum of Shakespeare: King Lear*, ed. Horace Howard Furness (London; Philadelphia, 1880; 1908), pp. 383–407 and notes to the play; *King Lear* (New Arden edition), ed. Kenneth Muir (Cambridge, Mass., 1952; repr. 1959), pp. 211–56, and notes to the play; Joseph Satin, *Shakespeare and his Sources* (Boston, 1966), pp. 445–532.

[2] *Leir*, scene 19; in Bullough, *Narrative and Dramatic Sources*, pp. 373 ff.

[3] *The Prose Works of Sir Philip Sidney*, ed. Albert Feuillerat, 4 vols (Cambridge, 1912–26; repr. 1968), I, 206–7; quoted with some changes in Bullough, *Narrative and Dramatic Sources*, pp. 402–3.

[4] Quoted in Bullough, *Narrative and Dramatic Sources*, p. 300.

the understanding of kingship behind *Lear*. This work, *Six Bookes of Politickes or Civil Doctrine, Written in Latine by Iustus Lipsius*, translated into English by William Jones, entered in the *Stationers' Register* on three occasions in 1589 and 1590, and finally printed by Richard Field for William Ponsonby in 1594, was the chief book of political philosophy by one of three or four of the most renowned humanist scholars of Shakespeare's day, and the period's greatest Roman historian. There in Book II, chapter x, the linkage is made explicit:

Amongst the great lights [of virtue], I place *Iustice* and *Clemencie* whereof I account the first as the sun, the which except by the clearenesse thereof, it doth beautifie and enlighten the whole bodie of kingdoms, they remaine darkened and full of storms and tempest (sig. E2)[1]

– and, on the verso, a tag line from Book III of Cicero's *De Officiis* which is choric for Lipsius, '*Iustice is the foundation of eternall fame and renowne, without the which nothing can deserue to be praised and commended*' (E2v).

Of course we cannot know now, with such sparse biographical evidence, what books Shakespeare read; the problem is compounded when we recognize that the political thought in *Lear* – the need for an authoritative but sensitive ruler, the folly of dividing a kingdom, the irresponsibility inherent in a king's abdication – is so commonplace that Shakespeare needed no source at all. Moreover, he had Holinshed as always, and there the story of Leir was encased in the predictable perspective of the medieval world outlook with its emphasis on order and propriety. What is initially attractive about adding Lipsius to the list of nominations for authors Shakespeare knew, then, is the frequency with which his central observations resonate in the action and language of *King Lear*.

Lipsius's book is summary, a suitable manual for a writer. 'I intend', he promises at the outset, 'to instruct thee, how thou mayst safely set forward in the way of *Ciuill life*, and finish thy iourney without wandering, & that, not by my owne sayings, but by the precepts of ancient authors, deliuered also in their own wordes' (B1). The book, then, is a storehouse of ideas from Tacitus and Cicero, with infrequent attention to other Roman writers; it is a compendium of classical thought which might be considered to be contemporaneous with old Leir himself. Book IV, chapter ix – ten pages of Lipsius's text in the Jones translation – is dense with issues that find echoes in Shakespeare's play. Lipsius begins by positioning good rule in the full authority of a single ruler.

AMongst those vertues which help to conserue a kingdome, *Authoritie* beareth a place...I do againe define it to be *a reuerent opinion of the King and his estate, imprinted as well in his owne subiects, as in strangers*. It consisteth of admiration and feare, the temperature or mixture of both the which do make this vertue, which I confesse to be more readily obtayned of some people, for *in some Nations a reuerence towards their kings is ingendered by nature*, others are more hardly bent... (L3v)

'Seueritie' is proper to a rule because it keeps order, which is the correct end of right rule (L4). But the king is limited to maintaining a continuum with past tradition. He must preserve the ways of his forefathers.

The second thing I desire, is that the forme of gouernment may be constant, which I interpret to be, when it runneth after one and the same ancient tenour. What do you talke of change? heare the true opinion of *Alcybiades: Those men liue safest, who doe gouerne their common wealth, without altering awhit their present customes and lawes, albeit they be not altogether so good*. Heere like *Augustus* who did thus admonish the Senate: *Obserue constantly those lawes which are once established; neyther do thou alter any of them. For those things which remaine whole in their estate, and the same, although they be worser, yet are they more profitable to the common wealth, then those which are brought in by innouation, albeit they seeme better.* (L4v)

Yet so directed, kings must be absolute; their judgement should not be questioned – as Lear

---

[1] My text is the Houghton copy of STC 15701.

insists – and they are not, in making chief decisions, to be susceptible to advisors such as Kent. '*Kings are lords of times and seasons, and of the things that are handled in them, and they are leaders and not followers of counsell.* Doest thou yeeld any thing herein? then thou loosest all. For *the conditiō of bearing rule as a king is such, that it cannot otherwise stãd, but whē all authority is cōmitted to one*' (M1). Additionally, there are the instruments of power and what Lear terms 'the name and all th' addition to a king; the sway,/Revenue' (I, i, 136–7).[1]

Maiestie without force is unassured. I vnderstand power in this place to be *an abilitie of things competent and necessary, to conserue a mans owne, and to get more*: which these fiue instruments will purchase thee, *Wealth, Weapons, Counsell, Alliances,* and *Fortune*: so that thou vse them to the purpose, and after that manner that I will instruct thee. (M1v)

The king may seek support from the gods, as Lear does from Hecate in his wrath at Cordelia's obstinance, although Lipsius, in translating classical thought into terms congruent with Christianity, changes the deity.

Wherefore *Aristotle* did admonish, *that a Prince ought earnestly and aboue all things to haue care of things diuine.* He addeth in the reason hereof, *For the subiects do hope that they shall suffer lesse iniustice from that Prince, whom they deeme religious and who feareth God: and lesse conspiracies are complotted against him, as hauing euen God for his helpe and succour.* (M3v)

But still, he warns, 'We know *that the king lieth open to the trecherie euen of one person: that couetousnesse maketh no conscience of wickednesse*' (M4v).

Elsewhere, this compendium of classical thought glosses the subplot of *Lear*. Lipsius warns of the erroneous superstitions of both Gloucester and Edmund. 'And whereas some doe affirme that *Destinie is in the things themselues, which neuerthelesse haue their influence from the Planets,* and others do refer the same vnto the beginning and linking together of naturall causes, they do fouly erre . . .' (B3v). Moreover,

what is more harmful – because dangerous to the state – are those vices caused by pride that are figured by Edmund, Goneril, and Regan.

Vice, though it be longer a comming, . . . I define to be *An euill disposition of the King, or against him, hurtfull to the state.* This *Vice* is twofolde, *Hate,* and *Contempt,* which oppose themselues to as many vertues that establish a Kingdome: the one is a bad affection towards the King, the other an euill opinion of him. For *Hate, is an obstinate and harmeful malice and offence in the subiects, against the King and his estate.* (N3)

''Tis the infirmity of his age; yet he hath ever but slenderly known himself,' Regan says critically of her father the king, and Goneril matches her contempt: 'The best and soundest of his time hath been but rash' (I, i, 293–6).

A little further on, however, and the humanist Lipsius is preaching the king's possible need for dissimulation. 'They shall neuer gouerne well, who know not how to couer well, *and those to whome the charge of a common wealth is committed, must needs be tied to this.* And *to come to the effect of their determinations, they are constrained against their wils to faine, and dissemble many things with greefe*' (Q3). Indeed, the innocence of a Cordelia may be fatally dangerous.

They which are so open, so simple, *without any counterfeiting, without fraud,* who carrie their heart, as they say, *on their forehead,* shall neuer be fit to play their part vpon this stage: where in my iudgement *the dissembler of Afranius* holdeth the cheefe place. And yet in such sort, that thou play thy part comely, and with a good grace, *for they which vse to dissemble but a little, and in those things which are not seene and discouered, do appeare gratious.* (Q3-Q3v)

The advice which has seemed so appropriate for Lear is now better assigned to Goneril and Regan; 'Learne this once in all kind of dissimulation, *Deceipt is no deceipt, if it be not cunningly handled*' (Q3v).

As consequent, the guiding principles for successful rule become a coin with two sides, Lear / Cordelia / Gloucester; Regan / Goneril /

---

[1] Quotations from Shakespeare's play are taken from the New Arden edition.

Edmund. 'Take estimation away and take away the estate: *and all this webb of commaundement, will runne but into many thrids, and small peeces: this ancient maiestie of the royall throne and their scepters without it, will be soone ouerthrowne*' (P3). Yet Lear and Cordelia and Gloucester are the ones who, unaware of the need for dissembling and trustful in their own appearances, become aware of the inherent dangers to the king, of the fragility of his rule, and for two of them the self-awareness takes the form Lipsius recognizes as the most debilitating: 'to be ouerburdened with age' (P4v). The conceptual parabola that has veered so widely now comes back on a course towards *Lear* that is painfully accurate, the echo in the play from this possible source exact. 'Know that we have divided/In three our kingdom,' the aged Lear tells a stilled and anxious court, 'while we/Unburthen'd crawl toward death' (I, i, 37–8; 40–1).

II

'*King Lear* is unique among the plays in this volume,' Joseph Satin writes in *Shakespeare and His Sources*, 'in that the direct sources of its plot and subplot are each clearly defined and richly detailed' (p. 445).[1] The simple configurations of an old king and his three daughters are as old as fable and fairy tale[2] and as concrete as the histories of Welsh and English chroniclers.[3] The story is in the *Historia Anglicana* of Geoffrey of Monmouth and the *Brut* of Layamon, in Robert of Gloucester and Fabyan, in the *Mirour for Magistrates* and the *Gesta Romanorum*, Polydore Vergil's *Anglicae Historiae* and Warner's *Albions England*, in Holinshed's *Historie* and Spenser's *Faerie Queene* (two of the most probable of the remaining sources), and in two works of Stow, both his *Summarie of Englyshe Chronicles* of 1565 and his *Annales* of 1592. Percy's *Reliques of Ancient English Poetry* has a charming if doggerel ballad that is anonymous and of unknown date but perhaps before Shakespeare's play, 'King Leir and His Three Daughters', and Camden finds a remarkable parallel in Ina, King of the West Saxons, in his *Remaines Concerning Britaine* (1606). There is the anonymous yet perhaps popular play, *The True Chronicle Historie of King Leir*; in addition, there is a long oral tradition now classified as folktale Types 510 and 923.[4] From this rich embarrassment, however, scholars are generally agreed that Shakespeare turned as usual to Holinshed (who has Geoffrey behind him) and to Spenser.

Geoffrey Bullough counts about 170 extant MSS of Geoffrey of Monmouth's *Historia*, the Welshman's widespread chronicle first introduced to the Tudors when Henry VII appointed a commission to trace his British ancestry and provide it with respectable antiquity.[5] In recounting the Leir story, Geoffrey introduced the division of the kingdom, Cordeilla's honesty, the two ungrateful daughters and their progressive reduction of Leir's retinue, Leir's two loyal companions, Cordeilla's weeping and nursing Leir when he arrives in Gaul, and Leir's slow recovery. In all this Shakespeare agrees; he departs only with the historical ending Geoffrey provides in Leir's flight to Gaul (where he is reunited with Cordeilla) and in his restoration to the British throne; and it is this ceremonial conclusion in Geoffrey that strikes

---

[1] The plays which Satin uses in this comparison are *Richard III, Richard II, The Merchant of Venice, 1 Henry IV, 2 Henry IV, Henry V, Julius Caesar, Twelfth Night, Hamlet, Othello, Macbeth,* and *Antony and Cleopatra*.

[2] A relatively complete study – despite its early publication – is Wilfred Perrett, *The Story of King Lear From Geoffrey of Monmouth to Shakespeare* (Berlin, 1904). Cf. Emile Bode, *Die Learsage vor Shakespeare* (Halle, 1904), pp. 139–42; Alan R. Young, 'The Written and Oral Sources of *King Lear* and the Problem of Justice in the Play', *Studies in English Literature*, XV, 2 (1975), 309–19.

[3] In Bullough, Furness, Muir and Satin (see above p. 13 n. 1).

[4] Young, 'The Written and Oral Sources of *King Lear*', p. 310.

[5] Bullough, *Narrative and Dramatic Sources*, p. 272.

16

such odds with the Shakespearian version we know best. The more somber conclusion comes two chapters later – in chapter xv – which records the subsequent reign of Cordeilla, her imprisonment by her two nephews Margan and Cunedagius, and her suicide.

Holinshed's version in 1587 condenses this account and provides two additional details that are in Shakespeare – he has Leir say that he loves Cordeilla best and has the old king discover what will become thematic in Shakespeare's play, that the other two daughters are not so much *unkind* as *unnatural*.[1] Another key phrase in John Higgins's addition to the 1586 *Mirour for Magistrates* may suggest a source most scholars ignore; it is there Cordelia (speaking of Leire from her perspective) tells her father during the love-test that she has *no cause* to despise him.

> No cause (quoth I) there is I should your grace
>   despise:
> For nature so doth bind and dutie me compell,
> To loue you, as I ought my father, well.[2]

From Spenser, it is generally agreed, Shakespeare took his spelling of *Cordelia* and her manner of death, hanging (although Spenser may have originated that to complete his rhyme: 'And overcommen kept in prison long,/Till wearie of that wretched life, her selfe she hong').[3] Bullough notes this and another line in Spenser's text, 'But true it is, that when the oyle is spent,/The light goes out, and weeke is throwne away' (stanza 30) which may have suggested the Fool's line, 'So out went the candle, and we were left darkling' (I, iv, 226). Finally, Sackville's and Norton's *Gorboduc* also dramatizes ruin that follows the division of a kingdom, Gorboduc's complaint of old age, his rationale of observing his successors' rule before his death, and his petition to wrathful skies to send down a storm, as well as Eubulus's ignored counsel (resembling the warnings of Kent) with its own apocalyptic vision of wasted towns and infinite bloodshed.

I have placed this catalogue of possible sources alongside the quotations from Lipsius to show that there is not conclusive evidence that Shakespeare knew them; many of them, in fact, have less in common with the play than Lipsius's *Sixe Bookes of Politickes or Civil Doctrine*. It is otherwise with the anonymous *True Chronicle Historie of King Leir*. Romantic and tragicomic though that play may be, it too emphasizes the flattery of Ragan and Gonorill and Cordella's inability to imitate them; it makes Cordella's wedding to Gallia subsequent to the love test, the king marrying her without dowry; and in Skallinger, Perillus, Cornwall, and Cambria it provides the originals of Oswald, Kent, Albany, and Cornwall. Here too we find themes common to Shakespeare's tragedy – the union of divine and natural law, the choric concern with kindness and unkindness (playing on both meanings of *kind*), and the importance of grace (here preventing Ragan's messenger from killing Leir and Perillus; in Shakespeare, it will be Cordelia's power to promote Lear's recovery). There is, then, the frequency of carry-over from this play by an unknown playwright to Shakespeare's *Lear* as there is carry-over in political thinking from Lipsius. Additionally, verbal echoes abound in the plays; correspondences resonate: in Leir's pronouncement to resign (scene 1), in the exchange between Leir and Cordella in the love test (scene 3), in Perillus's interruption and Leir's reply (Scene 6), Gallia's suit for Cordella (Scene 7) and Perillus's soliloquy (Scene 8) and Leir's address to his daughter (Scene 10). I

---

[1] Muir also believes (*Shakespeare's Sources*, 1957; *The Sources of Shakespeare's Plays*, 1977) that the scene at Dover Cliff and Edgar's account of the imaginary fiend were taken from Corineus's fight with Gogmagog, two pages before the Lear story in Holinshed's account. See New Arden *Lear*, p. 258.

[2] 1586 edition quoted in Furness, *A New Variorum of Shakespeare*, p. 389.

[3] *Faerie Queene*, II, x, stanza 32; quoted in Bullough, *Narrative and Dramatic Sources*, p. 334; p. 276.

think a close relationship between these two plays indisputable; and it is far likelier that the more primitive version came first.

The anonymous play has found other proponents; by contrast, Dr Johnson now seems alone in his firm contention that the anonymous ballad of 'King Leir and His Three Daughters' in Percy's *Reliques* is still another source.[1] But Dr Johnson makes a telling point; this is the one known source where Leir 'Grew frantic mad';

for in his mind

> He bore the wounds of woe:
> Which made him rend his milk-white locks,
>   And tresses from his head,
> And all with blood bestain his cheeks,
>   With age and honour spread:
> To hills and woods, and watry founts,
>   He made his hourly moan,
> Till hills and woods, and senseless things,
>   Did seem to sigh and groan.

Here too is the only other identical death scene.

> But when he heard Cordelia's death,
>   Who died indeed for love
> Of her dear father, in whose cause
>   She did this battel move;
> He swooning fell upon her breast,
>   From whence he never parted;
> But on her bosom left his life,
>   That was so truly hearted.[2]

And there is one other possible source (although I prefer to think of it as an analogue): Klein in his *Geschichte des Italienischen Dramas* notes a trio of fools real, feigned, and professional in *Le Stravaganze d'Amore* of Cristoforo Castelletti (Rome, 1585).

In sum, I think the story of Lear so commonplace that all but the anonymous play (and possibly the ballad) can be questioned as *necessary* sources for the main plot, tempting as it is to locate ideas, motifs, and verbal echoes elsewhere. The same situation roughly prevails for the underplot. Ever since Mrs Lennox first discovered the similarities of the Paphlagonian king in Sidney's *Arcadia* in 1754,[3] we have been quick to see (besides the storm) all the similarities: the king with two sons, one legitimate (Leonatus) and one not (Plexirtus), who believes Plexirtus when he tricks him into trying to kill Leonatus; the good son's flight after which the evil son blinds his father and banishes him from court; the wandering, helpless king who meets his good son and, not recognizing him, asks to be led to a high rock from which he might commit suicide. Later the subjects of Paphlagonia revolt, and they win and recall Leonatus to be king while his father dies, 'his hart broken with unkindnes & affliction, stretched so farre beyond his limits with this excesse of cōfort, as it was able no longer to keep safe his roial spirits.'[4] To this episode, Bullough adds the account of Plangus (*Arcadia*, II, 15) in which Plangus's stepmother arranges for him to come armed, presumably against the King her husband, and has the King and nobility eavesdrop to prove the son's treachery; Plangus flees into voluntary exile.[5] Lastly, Bullough cites Pamela's reply to Cecropia in their philosophic

---

[1] So Dr Johnson: 'The story of this play is derived... perhaps immediately from an old historical ballad. My reason for believing that the play was posterior to the ballad, rather than the ballad to the play, is, that the ballad has nothing of Shakespeare's nocturnal tempest, which is too striking to have been omitted, and that it follows the chronicle; it has the rudiments of the play, but none of its amplifications; it first hinted Lear's madness, but did not array it in circumstances. The writer of the ballad added something to the history, which is a proof that he would have added more if it had occurred to his mind, and more must have occurred if he had seen Shakespeare.' Quoted in Furness, *A New Variorum of Shakespeare*, p. 402. A more recent influence not commonly accepted, which I also find doubtful, has been proposed by David Kaula in *Shakespeare and the Vestarian Controversy* (The Hague, 1971).

[2] My text is from Furness, *A New Variorum of Shakespeare*, pp. 406–7.

[3] *Shakespeare Illustrated*, III, 302; Furness, *A New Variorum of Shakespeare*, p. 383.

[4] *Arcadia* in *Prose Works*, ed. Feuillerat, I, 212.

[5] Sidney, ed. Feuillerat, I, 248–9; see also Bullough, *Narrative and Dramatic Sources*, pp. 410–11.

debate (*Arcadia*, III, 10) as the original of Gloucester's 'As flies to wanton boys' (IV, i, 36).[1] By comparison, the use Shakespeare may have made of Harsnett's *Declaration* for the names of devils (perhaps cant terms) seems minor indeed.

Still this tabulation – the most inclusive I know[2] – bewilders. It omits more from the *effect* of Shakespeare's tragedy than it supplies; we sympathize with Satin's own conclusion that '*King Lear* offers probably the most profound spiritual experience in all of Shakespeare, and its idea of the ennoblement achieved through repentance finds slight basis in the direct sources'.[3] What is lacking is the *mood* of *Lear* and its *informing sense of character* – its cycling inquiry into the need for human suffering, its exploration of the dignity of man even in grief, and its testament to man's ability to endure. And all of this, I want to suggest, is basic to the Christian humanism and Christian Stoicism that inform each page of Lipsius. His thought is far from foreign to Shakespeare's, as it is not distant from Shakespeare's habit of mind. For we know Shakespeare turned to two other writers of Stoic persuasion, to the classical Plutarch and the contemporary Montaigne. Lipsius, we learn, also made Plutarch one of his authorities – and he was a correspondent with Montaigne. Of the three, however, it is Lipsius whose pointed treatise on kingship comes closest to embodying the political and philosophic thought that figures forth in each scene of *King Lear*. So we return to where we began.

III

The heath again; the raging storm and king. 'Blow, winds, and crack your cheeks!' the agonized Lear commands; 'rage! blow! You cataracts and hurricanoes, spout/Till you have drench'd our steeples, drown'd the cocks!' and, analogizing his family to such splintering of the cosmos, 'Crack Nature's moulds, all

germens spill at once/That makes ingrateful man!' (III, ii, 1–3; 8–9). The Fool's reply startles with its own crazed disjunctiveness. 'O Nuncle, court holy-water in a dry house is better than this rain-water out o' door. Good Nuncle, in, ask thy daughters blessing; here's a night pities neither wise men nor Fools' (III, ii, 10–13). What does the Fool mean by 'court holy-water'? Does he allude to baptismal fonts with *holy-water*; does he see the rain as a blessing once they have gone indoors from the storm? Confronted with the necessity to gloss, Furness cites his predecessors, then admits in his modest brackets that the phrase, presumably from Florio's Montaigne where it means 'to soothe or flatter one', 'does not give "court holy-water"; instead it reads "to perswade one that the moone is made of greene cheese"'.[4] Muir is more confident in citing Florio and adds Eliot's *Ortho-Epia Gallica* (1593) where a definition is given, and notes 'Harsnett makes frequent mention of holy-water.'[5] The *OED* calls *court holy water* obsolete and finds only two instances of its use prior to *Lear* – in Golding's *Calvin on Deuteronomy* (1583) and in Florio's *Mantellizare* (1598), giving as its meaning 'A proverbial phrase for fair words or flattery without performance or sincere intention.'[6] Tilley cites neither source of this rare 'proverbial' phrasing, but offers two others – in William Horman's *Vulgaria* (1519) and the anonymous *Life and Death of Jack Straw*

[1] In Sidney, ed. Feuillerat, I, 406–7; see also Bullough, *Narrative and Dramatic Sources*, p. 412.

[2] I have omitted only Muir's citations from Florio's Montaigne (pp. 249–53). The word-borrowing Muir cites seems to me doubtful; I shall take up a discussion of the most telling phrase in the next section when I discuss Montaigne's *Essayes*.

[3] Satin, *Shakespeare and his Sources*, p. 447.

[4] Furness, *A New Variorum of Shakespeare*, p. 172n.

[5] Muir (ed.) *Lear*, p. 107n. J. W. Lever discusses John Eliot's influence on Shakespeare in 'Shakespeare's French Fruits', *Shakespeare Survey 6* (Cambridge, 1953), pp. 79–90.   [6] II, 1095:1.

(1593).[1] But such sources or analogues seem fairly obscure – even Horman's compendium of Latin sayings had passed out of common use for improved schoolroom texts by the time Shakespeare went to the grammar school at Stratford-upon-Avon. It seems to me at least as likely, therefore, that Shakespeare found the phrase (and found it puzzling enough to award to the Fool) in Lipsius where it occurs in a chapter on flattery that has a reasonably close alliance with the play. The passage is in Book III, chapter viii, '*How a Prince ought to behaue him selfe in hearing counsel. Certaine precepts concerning this matter*', and reads,

Yet let him auoide *Obstinacie*: For this is a diuine saying of the Prince *Marcus. It is more decent and conuenient that I should follow the aduise, of so many, and such worthy freinds, then that they should onely be ruled by my will.*

Let him keep secret his determinatiō, following this rule: *Deliberate with many what is best to be done, but what you intend to do with very fewe, or rather with thy selfe.* Surelie secrecie is the soule of *Consultations: & no counsels proue better then those, vvhich are hidden from the enemy before they come to action.*

Let him freelie permit his Counsellers, to speake their minde boldlie, not louing *this court holy vvater. Flattery doth more often subuert & ouerthrow the wealth of a kingdome, then an open enemie.*[2] *His estate is desperate, vvhose eares are so framed, that he cānot heare any thing but that which is pleasing, and turneth to his hurt, and doth reiect that vvhich is profitable, if it seeme any thing sharpe. That Emperour is miserable from vvhom the troth is hidden.*

Let him heare with indifferencie: and keepe this precept secret, that he geue no rewardes in regarde of anie good aduise, least some vnder hope of gaine do decline from the troth, *and to currie fauour, speake against their conscience.* But let him likewise take heede, that he do not on the other side punish those, which haue not hapned to geue good counsell. For *no man vvould vtter his opinion, if it should turne to a matter of danger, if the same chāunced to be disliked.* Neither ought he *to thinke them the trustier, that do geue the best counsell* (that is) *vvhose aduise prospereth best.* For it is certaine, that *many times, bad counsels haue better successe then good, because Fortune gouerneth diuers things, as it pleaseth her.*   (G2v)

Here, recast as practical political advice and enclosed within the predictable course of Fortune, is a variant description of *Lear*, I, i, of the sum and substance of the *donné* of *Lear*. Lipsius's position is clear; he wants the king to be self-sufficient, warns him that he can best trust only himself. His beliefs may or may not agree with the words of others, and words may in turn be true or false, reliable or not, valid or invalid. Two chapters later, in '*Precepts concerning Ministers*', he returns to this urgent consideration: '*the Prince as well as others, by a certaine destinie in his natiuitie*', Lipsius instructs in III, x, '*is inclined to these flatterers, and they that vtter their mind plainly, are hatefull to him*' (G4). This too sums the lesson of *Lear*.

I have called Lipsius a neo-Stoic, yet the passages for which we have had cause to refer do not sound especially neo-Stoic. This discrepancy is easily resolved; Lipsius grounds his manual in the Stoic sense of prudence as the chief virtue of the prince. This axiom is the title of the opening chapter of Book III; in that chapter, he remarks that '*Prudence oftentimes is of more might then much force*' (G1v), a lesson on which the Fool and Cordelia might concur. '*We ought with expedition to execute a thing once concluded on, but to conclude vvith deliberation*' (H2). '*Amongst the shallowes, stubburne selfe will* is one, against the which this ship of perswasion, hath oftentimes touched' (H1). Since pride is always a danger to the prince, he must couple patience and deliberation – the antitheses of rashness – if he hopes to deal with possible occasions of deceit and flattery. This conjunction of ideas, so similar to *Lear* I, i, is discussed two chapters later, in Book

[1] Morris Palmer Tilley, *A Dictionary of The Proverbs in England In the Sixteenth and Seventeenth Centuries* (Ann Arbor, 1950; 1966), H532 (p. 315); cf. C724.

[2] A marginal note here cites Plutarch's *Apology to Curtius*, Book VIII.

III, chapter xi, *'Certaine precepts set downe for Ministers themselues, as their safegard'*.

In generall, doest thou determine to liue euer in Court? then acquaint thy selfe with these two, 1. *Patience*, (by the ancient example of him, who being demaunded, *how he had attained to that great age in Court? (a thing which chaunceth verie sildome) answered, By suffering wrong and giuing thanks)* 2. And *Warie circumspection*, because many will seeke to entrap thee, *and deceipt beareth great sway in Princes courts*. There is the place, *where the mind of euerie one burneth with a desire to reprehend and controll the deeds and words of other men: to which end it seemeth, that neither their mouth is wide enough, nor their tongue readie enough*. There are secret spies and enemies, who *do priuily defame the poore soule, that knoweth nothing thereof, and to the end he may with more subtiltie be intrapped, they commend him openly*. Why should I abuse thee? *Albeit thou art able to gard thy selfe from all others, thou shalt notwithstanding be endangered by thine owne fauorits*. And though no man seeke thine ouerthrow, thou wilt fal of thine owne accord. For *there is nothing in the world, lesse firme, and more vnstable, then a power that is not able to support it selfe*.   (I1–I1v)

Antonomous to such self-sufficiency is pride; and for Lipsius the stubborn will is the greatest internal danger for the king. 'Many times their obstinat *Pride* is cause thereof [of excessive behavior]. *This indurat princely pride, resisting against the troth, will not be mollified nor bent to that which is right. Deeming it as foule a disgrace to yeeld, as to be ouercome'* (K4).

Lipsius agrees with Machiavelli only in this: the greatest evil to a state is civil war. In Book VI, *'the causes of Ciuill warre, which he maketh of two sorts, Remote, and neere at hand'*, Lipsius traces the edges of prudence in Destiny and Riot and, so doing, limns the precise dangers that threaten Lear's kingdom.

Now these are the two remote causes. But what remedie is there against them? Against one of them none at all: Thou doest in vaine striue with Destinie, that is, against the decree of God. *Such was the pleasure of destinie, that the prosperitie of any thing whatsoeuer, should neuer stand alwayes at one stay. Nothing is exempt*

from the danger of change, not the earth, not the heauens, not the whole frame of all things: For although it be guided by God, it shall not alwayes hold this order, but time will alter it from his course. All things runne on their prefixed time, they haue time to be borne, to growe vp, and to be extinguished. But concerning Riot (if thou looke thereunto in time) thou hast a sure remedy therefore, from our censuring of manners.   (Bb4)

The good king can try to prevent riot and civil disorder by planning an orderly succession; the election of a prince, like the appointment of a successor, 'is a let to commotions, when otherwise *the chaunge of things giueth oportunitie, to great and strange attempts*: For it is euident, *the dishonest hopes of ambitious disturbers, are cleane cut off, when it is certainly knowne who shall succeed*' (D3); 'We have this hour a constant will to publish/Our daughters' several dowers', Lear announces, 'that future strife/May be prevented now' (I, i, 43–5).

But even the most cautious plans of the most thoughtful rulers can be upset, Lipsius instructs us, by the ambitions of others (like Edmund). He lists three basic causes of civil war – faction, sedition, and tyranny (Bb4) – and remarks, *'All ambition hath this fault: It is not respectiue: which is the cause why they, like vnto waues, do driue one another: and from hence proceedeth strife, hate, warre'* (Bb4v). The configurations of Lipsius's thought outline Shakespeare's in *Lear*, if in generalities; but when he comes finally to anatomize the ambitious rebel, the language resonates from tractate to play as it did in the passage on court holy-water.

He whom the discord of the Citizens, their slaughter, whom ciuill warre delighteth, can beare no affection to his owne familie, nor to publicke lawes, nor to the statutes that concerne the common libertie: and I esteeme him vnworthie not to bee accoumpted amongst the number of men, but vtterlie to be banished from their companie. And in deed what mischiefe is there in the world that ciuill warre is exempt of? Or what diuine or humaine things are left vnpolluted? The armies are disposed the one against the other; and the fathers against their owne sonnes, and the sonnes against their fathers, haue sworne, the one to destroie another. What a horror is it, *to see neere kinsmen to become enemies, brother to fight against brother, and two armies ioine battaile, allied together in consanguinitie? What murther is there not heere committed? the condemnation of innocent persons to purchase their goods; the torture and torment of noble men, citties waste and desolate, by fight and slaughter, the goods of the miserable cittizens, either giuen or solde, as a pray of the enemie. It is permitted to kill any man openlie: and lawfull to pardon none, but to the end thou maiest further intrap them. Neither age, nor honour, can protect any, that rape be not mingled with murther, and murther with rape. The nobilitie goeth to wracke, with the common people, and warre is spread on euery side, neither is anie man exempt from the edge of the sword.* (Bb2–Bb2v)

'Love cools, friendship falls off, brothers divide: in cities, mutinies; in countries, discord; in palaces, treason; and the bond crack'd 'twixt son and father', Gloucester tells us. 'There's son against father: the King falls from bias of nature; there's father against child. We have seen the best of our time: machinations, hollowness, treachery, and all ruinous disorders follow us disquietly to our graves' (I, ii, 110–14; 115–20). 'Receaue old men willinglie', Lipsius had argued, *'for where the body is weakest, there vnderstanding and wisedome is strongest'* (G3v). Lipsius's philosophy reaches out to embrace the characters of Lear and Cordelia, Regan and Edmund, Gloucester and Kent, and links them philosophically. How can we not be tempted to think that Shakespeare would know so great an authority of his day as Justus Lipsius?

IV

In our past reliance on *The Elizabethan World Picture* and *Shakespeare and the Nature of Man*, in charting our course by Burckhardt or Bush, Cassirer or Kristeller, we have turned to Elyot and Ascham, to Machiavelli, Pico, and Montaigne, but we have somehow ignored other important Continental thinkers of Shakespeare's own age – Bruno, Casaubon, Scaliger, Lipsius. Of these, Lipsius was perhaps the most important, both in his thought (as the first neo-Stoic of the Renaissance) and in his writing (as the one who introduced Senecan rhetoric to replace Ciceronian). 'His works', Jason Lewis Saunders reminds us, 'especially the Stoic treatises, were translated into every major language of Europe, and the number of published editions is very great. His *De constantia* inspired Montaigne, du Vair and Pierre Charron; his *Politics* was familiar to Richelieu and Bossuet, and his Stoic treatises were influential in the thought of Francis Bacon and, later, Montesquieu.'[1] Lipsius corresponded with Montaigne who was 'greatly impressed with the *Politics*' which he received in 1589.[2] All of them found in Lipsius that unique combination of humanism (especially in his study of Tacitus and Seneca), Christianity, and Stoicism from which he built a philosophy in which human reason met the sublime tragedy of human existence. Lipsius conflated the Stoic notion of Fate with the Christian concept of Providence and maintained God's omnipotence by positing evil in men and matter, the Gonerils and Edmunds and the four elements. Bullough senses some affinity between Stoicism and *Lear* when he notes that both agree in equating the sickness of mind with poverty and misery and by relating madness and anger (the *brevis furor* in Seneca).[3]

Lipsius's first important book was his *De constantia libri duo* of 1584 which went through more than eighty editions in Latin and was translated into all the major European languages; it was translated into English by Sir John Stradling in 1595.[4] Lipsius argues

[1] *Justus Lipsius: The Philosophy of Renaissance Stoicism* (New York, 1955), p. 66.
[2] *Epistolarum selectarum centuria*, I, 43 in *Opera omnia* (Wesel, 1675), II, 54; Saunders, *Justus Lipsius*, p. 65.
[3] Bullough, *Narrative and Dramatic Sources*, p. 301; p. 298.
[4] STC 15694 (Latin), STC 15695 (Stradling); ed. Rudolf Kirk and Clayton Morris Hall (New Brunswick, N.J., 1939).

here for steadfastness; he defines constancy as *'a right and immoueable strength of the minde, neither lifted vp, nor pressed downe with externall or casuall accidentes'* (I, 4; sig. C1). The sources of constancy for Lipsius are patience and lowliness of mind, the latter regulated by right reason in turn defined as *'A true sense and iudgement of thinges humane and diuine'* (I, 4; C1). Reason is continually obscured, Lipsius teaches, by the 'smoake of OPINIONS' (I, 2; B2) which try to pull down the soul as reason tries to lift up the body. 'Out of this twofolde fountaine of OPINION and REASON, floweth not only *Hardinesse and Weaknesse* of mind, but all things that deserue either praise or dispraise in this life' (I, 5; C1v). Constancy is supported by virtue, a quality of mind (in this he agrees with his precursors Epictetus and Seneca); virtue is opposed by false goods – such as riches, honor, authority, health, long life – which bring to us desire and joy and false evils – such as poverty, infamy, lack of promotion, sickness, death of 'whatsoeuer els is accidentall and happeneth outwardlie and bring us fear and sorrow' (I, 7; C4). (Here Lipsius follows Zeno who called the four affections of joy, desire, fear, and sorrow those that do greatly disquiet the life of man, by which he meant the inner man, the mind.) In addition, the mind is afflicted by public evils – war, pestilence, famine, tyranny, slaughter – encouraged by dissimulation, piety (corrupted as chauvinism), and commiseration, which leads to sentimentality. In Book II, Lipsius argues that such afflictions and calamities may be profitable; since they originate with God they cannot be evil but instead strengthen character, chastise the wrongdoers, and set good examples for others. Yet God's ways of justice are not always clear; although Albany finds 'you are above,/You justicers' (IV, ii, 78–9), Lear invites Cordelia to join him as one of 'God's spies' to 'take upon 's the mystery of things'; 'Upon such sacrifices, my Cordelia,/The Gods themselves

throw incense' (v, iii, 17; 16; 20–1). Lipsius's treatise, sums Saunders, 'was a general introduction to Stoic philosophy, explaining some definitions of free will, providence, justice, certain notions of immortality and fate – as the Stoics understood them'.[1]

Lipsius began work on the *Politicorum, sive civilis doctrinae libri sex* in 1583, while still a professor at Leiden; it was his second important work, and it went through eighty editions by 1752.[2] This work, which draws on Aristotle, Xenophon, Diodorus Siculus, Tacitus, and Cicero, is abstracted in *'The Author his Epistle'*.

What is more magnificent amongst men, then for one, to haue authoritie ouer manie: to giue lawes, and commandements: to gouerne the sea, the land, peace, and warre? The dignitie seemeth a certaine kind of diuinitie, and so it is indeed, if it be exercised, for the profite, & good of the Common wealth. But how hard a thing it is, both reason, and examples, do teach vs. If we looke into reason: of what difficultie is it, for so many heads to be brideled by one head, and that vniuersall multitude, vnquiet, disunited, seditious, to be moderately brought vnder a certaine common yoke of obedience? If we regard examples, how few haue bene found, . . . Doth [the prince] leade vs the way to vertue? we followe. To vice? we encline thither. Liueth he an honest, and blessed life? we flourish. Is he vnfortunate? we decline, or runne to ruine with him. And as the light or darkenesse in this world below proceedeth frō the sunne: so the greater part of good or euill in the subiects, is deriued from the prince.

(A4v–A5)

So the ostensible purpose; the work which follows has frequent and particularized application to *Lear*.

Briefly, Lipsius urges *'A certaine order as well in commanding: as in obeying*, the power (or rather the necessitie wherof) is so great, that it is the onely stay of humane affaires' (C4v). He develops the idea negatively. 'For without gouernement, *no house, no citie, no nation,*

[1] Saunders, *Justus Lipsius*, p. 23.
[2] *Ibid.*, p. 27.

neither the whole state of mankind, nor the vniuersall nature of things, no nor the world it selfe can stand, and continue' (C4v). What supplies order is the ruler; 'Surely, *this is the chaine, by which the common wealth is linked together, this is the vitall spirit, which so many millions of men do breath, and were this soule of commanding taken away, the common wealth of it selfe should be nothing but a burthen, and open prey*' (C4v-D1). Much depends, then, on the qualities of the ruler.

A iust and good king, laboureth, watcheth, and knoweth that *the greatest Empire is accompanied with greatest cares. His vigilancie preserueth his subiects when they are asleepe, his labour giueth them their ease, his industrie and trauell, maintaineth their pleasures, his care in his charge, their rest and quiet.* (D4)

Of special interest for us, he argues that the double virtues for conserving the kingdom are just those qualities with which Lear is concerned in the opening scene of Shakespeare's play, the quality he wants and the one he has – love and authority.

Loue and *Authoritie*: trulie both of thē ought to spring frō and by the king, yet in such maner, that they haue their seate, and place of abode in the harts of the people. Loue, is an affectiō towards the king, Authoritie, an opinion they conceiue of him. (I2)

Lipsius expands on this by way of Plato who taught that the king should exemplify lenity, bountifulness, and indulgence.

Thou oughtest first to shew *Lenitie* in thy selfe, being of a milde speach and behauiour, *prouoking men to be officious vnto thee, by thy gentlenesse, and affabilitie.* And why *oughtest not thou to liue in such manner with thy subiects, as a father with his childrē?* yet with this prouiso, *that thy honour be not hurt hereby.* Wherein there ought to be great moderatiō: in such sort, that *neither thou purchase thee reuerence with terrour, nor loue with seruile humility.* This hapneth very seldom, as it deserueth great cōmendation, when *diuers vertues of a different qualitie, are thorow prudence ioyned together.* (I2)

Turn the coin of good rule over, and you have the wrong rule of tyrants or the evil subject, the rebel. Both are anxious creatures, within and without.

They are in continuall feare, and *amaʒed at euery suspition.* Therefore, *by spials they take away the vse both of speaking and talking.* They do not onely vvatch mens tongues, but *mens hands, and do imagine though there be no complot laid for them, that they are sought after, and they are no moment free from feare. This condition of life agreeth with tyrants: they enuie worthy men, murther those that are valiant, they liue garded with weapons: compassed about with poison: their places of defence are suspected of them, and trembling, they threaten.*

Adde hereunto their inward, vexation and torment. For *if the hearts of tyrants lay open to view; you might behold them torne and rent, vvith crueltie, vvith lusts, vvith vvicked determinations, as the bodie vvith stripes.* And *they do euen desire that they had neuer shined with their proud scepters. So that their wickednesse and mischiefe doth turne to their owne punishment.* But to conclude, what is their end? either they are depriued of their estate or murthered. For iust kings waxe olde, *and leaue their kingdomes to their children or their nephues.* But *the authoritie of tyrants is hatefull and short. Thales* being asked, *vvhat rare thing he had seene?* aunswered, *an old tyrant.* And our Poet said not in vaine: *that few kings come to their full age without murther, or wound, and tyrants without a drie death, that is, without their bloudshedding.* (Cc4–Cc4v)

It is, finally, in Lipsius alone of all the sources I have cited that the law of the king and the law of nature are brought together – and in an image of a storm, as on the heath.

And I do with *Fauonius* affirme, that *ciuill warre is worse and more miserable than tyrannie, or iniust gouernement.* Wherefore should it not be more praise worthy, to tollerate our Prince as hee is? *Wee ought to remember the time wherein we are borne, and to pray to God to send vs good Princes, and how soeuer they are, to beare with them. For such things come from God, and from aboue, and as we endure scarsitie, or tempestuous showres in great aboundance, and other euils coming from nature, so ought we to suffer riot, and the couetousnesse of such as beare rule ouer vs.* (Dd1)

The wheel with us, as with Lear and Edgar, has come full circle.

Perhaps it is temerarious to project a new book in Shakespeare's library, a new source for *Lear*. Surely it would be foolhardy to hope that any new source, as in this case with its compendium of ideas, motifs, and verbal echoes, would untangle and so make boldly plain and simple the wondrous rich fabric of Shakespeare's play. But to focus as I have on Lipsius at the very least does this: it heightens the importance of Cordelia's dignity and reserve, the Fool's cries for reasonableness, and Lear's yearning for patience (and the reverence he awards it), the value of Gloucester's eventual resignation to life (and later to death) and Lear's and Cordelia's acceptance of (and transcendence over) final imprisonment. There is, I mean to urge, a remarkably rich and pervasive strain of neo-Stoicism in *Lear* which Lipsius, like Montaigne, commands that we reconsider, a philosophic bent of mind which, after all, may well be Lear's last stay against mortality as it may be Edgar's last stay against futility, allowing the Lear-world to resist the storm and endure a while longer despite Lear's infernal visions.[1] 'Is this the promis'd end?' asks Kent confronted with the inverse Pieta, the dead daughter in her father's arms; 'Or image of that horror?' adds Edgar (v, iii, 263–4). The horror is painful; it cannot be obliterated or diminished. For Lear, the awareness of evil cannot be lessened either, is indefatigable. Yet such a terrifying vision is, in the end, endured by those of us lesser beings than the old king. 'He is gone, indeed', observes Edgar; 'The wonder is he hath endur'd so long' adds Kent (v, iii, 315–16). Their reconciliation with the gods and Fate reminds us of Horatio and Desdemona, of the Roman Antony and Caesar; it looks backward to the Elizabethan Seneca (and the Senecan Kyd) and forward to John Ford; there is a quiet but dazzling ability to suffer with dignity, with self-sufficiency.

> The weight of this sad time we must obey;
> Speak what we feel, not what we ought to say.
> The oldest hath borne most: we that are young
> Shall never see so much, nor live so long.
>
> (v, iii, 323–6)

Such a counterforce as Christian or pagan Stoicism makes the tragedy of *King Lear* at once more tragic yet more tragically bearable, rounds its grievous emotional parabola to incorporate us – and helps it, too, to *make sense*.

[1] Since writing this essay, I have found the same viewpoint argued by Hiram Haydn in *The Counter-Renaissance* (New York, 1950), pp. 107–8, 642–51.

© ARTHUR F. KINNEY 1980

THE WAR IN 'KING LEAR'

GARY TAYLOR

The battle in act v between Cordelia's army and the combined armies of Albany and Edmund must rank among the most important events in *King Lear*. Structurally, we have been led to expect such civil war from the very first scene of the play, when Lear divided his kingdom, and that expectation has been stoked by repeated allusions in the first two acts to 'likely wars toward, twixt the Dukes', and thereafter by news of and responses to the French invasion. Thematically that invasion is the dominant reaction to the main action of the play's first half, the rebellion of the children, the deposing of the parents; it represents what we are inclined and encouraged to regard as the inevitable recoil of the moral universe against the violation of its laws by Goneril, Regan, Edmund and Cornwall. Given the remarkable division of the characters into good and evil camps, the battle between them inevitably takes on apocalyptic overtones, and the play appears to be organizing itself around a familiar mythical pattern: the abdication of temporal order, followed by chaos and the reign of Antichrist, culminating in armageddon and the foundation of a new order, temporal and spiritual.[1] Causally, it is the defeat of Cordelia which leads to her own death (and subsequently Lear's), while at the same time, by removing the pressure of a common enemy, it allows the suppressed divisions between the victors to come explosively to the surface.

Yet the war in *King Lear* has received surprisingly little attention. Partly this is symptomatic of a more general neglect, for Shakespeare's battles are widely regarded, by both critics and producers, as an embarrassment, about which the less said the better. But in this case there are also more specific causes, not least of which is the short shrift given this all-important battle by the text itself.

> *Exit* [Edgar]
> *Alarum and Retreat within.*
> *Enter Edgar*

This is what we might call 'perfunctory, with a vengeance'. One need only compare the treatment of climactic battles in *Macbeth* or *Julius Caesar* or the Histories, or the complex and varied dramatization of war in *Coriolanus* and *Antony and Cleopatra*, to perceive that the anticlimax in *Lear* must be deliberate. Everything takes place offstage; the audience sees nothing; like Gloucester, it can only sit and listen. The playwright presents us, as the world presents his characters, with a *fait accompli*. The promised apocalypse does not materialize. Any attempt to minimize this anticlimax – like Spedding's proposal that the act-break should be moved so as to come between Edgar's exit and his re-entrance,[2] or Glen Byam Shaw's interpolated battle scene, or Macready's interpolated soliloquy for Gloucester (IV, vi, 279–84,

---

[1] For a wide-ranging analysis of this pattern and its permutations, see Frank Kermode's *The Sense of an Ending* (New York, 1967), esp. pp. 3–34.

[2] James Spedding, *New Shakspere Society Transactions* (1877), pp. 312 ff. A. C. Bradley discusses and rejects this proposal in one of the notorious notes to his *Shakespearean Tragedy* (1904).

'How stiff is my vile sense...'), or Kozintsev's expansive cinematography, with its ravaged countryside and burning towns, or the Royal Shakespeare Company's allusions in 1976 to World War I, the 'apocalyptic' conflict which brought to an end the Austro-Hungarian empire and the Edwardian era, in which the early acts had so clearly been set – any such attempt seems to me fundamentally misguided. The battle cannot be successfully inflated into the satisfying armageddon we are led to expect; it must work, if it is to work at all, as an aggressive disappointment: the author's defiant and conscious refusal to give us what we want.

But although our view of the battle is un-expectedly foreshortened, it would be mistaken to equate the battle with the war. War is a period of open hostility, initiated by mobiliza-tion and concluded by occupation or demobil-ization, but only occasionally punctuated by outbreaks of actual fighting. In this sense, the war in *King Lear* extends from the beginning of act III, with the first mention of a French invasion, to somewhere in the middle of the final scene, when Edmund's army has been demobilized and Albany is in complete military control of the stage and the kingdom. Obviously, the last three acts dramatize a good deal more than the military preparations for and immedi-ate military consequences of the decisive battle, but these preparations and consequences do constitute a significant, distinct, and relatively unexplored element of the last half of *King Lear*.

As yet, I have said nothing about the larger textual morass which engulfs all discussions of this play, because for the battle itself the Quarto and Folio present identical texts. But of the war as a whole the two texts present signifi-cantly different versions, and any critical discussion must take some account of these; indeed, this textual uncertainty may be one factor which has inhibited criticism of the war, for its presentation is radically affected by differences between the two texts, and by editorial attempts to conflate them. A number of the most striking differences between the Quarto and Folio cluster around this crucial strand of the plot, and all tend to demonstrate that the two early texts present coherent but distinct accounts of the action, which can only be muddied or confused by conflation.[1]

The apparent motive for many of the major Folio changes from the Quarto text is to strengthen the structure of act IV, in the inevitable anticlimax which follows Gloucester's blinding.[2] The Folio has done this by cutting superfluities (IV, iii, much of IV, ii, the ending of IV, vii) and strengthening the narrative line, largely by accelerating and clarifying the move-ment toward war. This process begins even before the end of act III. The Folio's omission of the mock trial (in III, vi) merits an essay in itself; but certainly one consequence of the omission, when combined with the omission of Edgar's soliloquy at the end of that scene, and of the dialogue of the two servants at the end of the next (after Gloucester's blinding), is to streamline the plot. In III, i we learn of division between the Dukes, and of French spies among their servants; in III, iii, this is confirmed, with

[1] As the remainder of this essay will make clear, I wholly support the efforts of recent scholars to dis-credit the traditional conflated text. See Michael J. Warren, 'Quarto and Folio *King Lear* and the Interpretation of Albany and Edgar', in *Shakespeare: Pattern of Excelling Nature*, ed. David Bevington and Jay L. Halio (Newark and London, 1978), pp. 95–107; Stephen Urkowitz, *Shakespeare's Revision of 'King Lear'* (Princeton, 1980); Peter W. M. Blayney, *The Texts of 'King Lear' and Their Origins*, 2 vols (forth-coming). An earlier, tentative statement of this view can be found in E. A. J. Honigmann's *The Stability of Shakespeare's Text* (1965), especially pp. 121–8. I am myself most indebted to Peter Blayney, who intro-duced me to the two-text hypothesis in 1977; but we differ on the relative merits of the two versions.

[2] For a typically astute analysis of the dramatic problem here, see Harley Granville-Barker, *Prefaces to Shakespeare*, 2 vols (1958), I, 274–5, 331–2. Bradley's criticisms of the structure, particularly of act IV, are well known (pp. 254–8).

the further news that 'there is part of a power already footed'; in III, v Edmund betrays his father, by informing Cornwall that Gloucester is 'an intelligent party to the advantages of France'. Up to this point, the Quarto and Folio are, for our purposes, identical. Then, after a much abbreviated III, vi, Gloucester in the Folio sends Lear and Kent to Dover, 'where thou shalt meet/Both welcome and protection' and where an invasion force from France might be presumed to have landed; the Folio, by omitting Edgar's subsequent soliloquy, goes directly from this hurried escape to Dover ('Come, come, away') to III, vii, where we hear that 'the army of France is landed'. Gloucester is interrogated about and then blinded for his knowledge of the invasion, and at scene's end is 'thrust...out at gates' to 'smell/His way to Dover'. By omitting the final duologue of the servants, the Folio goes straight from this (second) exit toward Dover and the morally (and politically) crucial discovery that Cornwall 'bleed[s] apace', into the next scene. Then, in IV, ii, the Folio omits the references to Lear's relationship with Goneril, thus putting the emphasis entirely on the preparations for war, on Goneril's developing alliance with Edmund, on the removal of Gloucester and Cornwall from the political map. Then, having omitted IV, iii, the Folio brings on Cordelia *with drum and colours... and soldiers*. The appearance of this army, so soon after the preparations for war in IV, ii, and immediately before we learn that Albany and Edmund are in the field, strongly establishes the narrative momentum, and helps sustain the play through the long, leisurely scenes at Dover.

Most of the Folio's changes here are simple omissions – although perhaps the word 'simple' prejudices the issue. Deciding to take something out may affect the structure and meaning of a play as drastically as deciding to put something in, and there is no reason to suppose that Shakespeare was preternaturally incapable of

reshaping his own work by the judicious exercise of a blue pencil. By increasing the narrative momentum and giving relatively more emphasis to the war theme the Folio strengthens an audience's expectations of armageddon, and thereby makes the anticlimax when it comes not only sharper but more unmistakably meaningful. It is, in any case, surely remarkable that, although the Folio text contains significant additions to the Quarto in I, i, I, iv, II, iv, and III, ii, between the beginning of III, vi and the end of IV, iii it omits 157 lines, while adding only seven.[1] To put it another way, the Folio cuts *one-third* of the Quarto text in these five scenes; *half* of the approximately three hundred lines omitted by the Folio are from these scenes. The concentration of these omissions in one part of the play is surely very difficult to disregard, especially when they are so clearly related to a major problem of narrative momentum and dramatic structure.

The structural value of these omissions can be simply stated: they clearly and strongly establish the narrative expectation of war, and they reduce the amount of time that Lear himself is offstage. The most important events in act IV – those which most interest an audience, and those most important to the meaning of the play – are the build-up toward war, the Goneril–Regan–Edmund intrigue, the return of Cordelia, the reunion of Lear and Gloucester, and the reunion of Lear and Cordelia. All of these are emphasized and brought forward by the Folio omissions.[2] And what the Folio sacrifices is for the most part eminently

[1] Line counts and references are taken from Kenneth Muir's New Arden edition (1952; rev. edn 1972).

[2] The only important development postponed by the Folio is Edgar's deepening moral consciousness, expressed in the Quarto by two soliloquies, one at the end of III, vi and another at the start of IV, i; the Folio omits the first of these, thereby – as Granville-Barker observed (I, 274, n. 7) – removing the impression of redundance and making this new development the starting-point for act IV.

dispensable. The narrative prelude to Cordelia's return (IV, iii) is hardly necessary; it is much more immediately satisfying to hear and see Cordelia than to be told about her. Elsewhere, the Folio consistently omits backward-looking reflection on what has happened, so as to throw the emphasis forward on to what will happen. We surely no longer need to be told, by Edgar or the two servants or Albany or Cordelia, what to think of the two sisters' treatment of Lear and Gloucester. Albany need not go on at such length in IV, ii in order to 'motivate' his eventual repudiation of his wife in V, iii; so horrendous are the events of acts II and III that we will easily infer that Albany's feelings are similar to our own. If Albany speaks so vehemently and at such length as he does in the Quarto, we may rightly object that his delay in changing sides becomes inexplicable. Likewise, to 'motivate' the French King's absence (IV, iii, 1–8) raises an awkward question which would be better left unasked. In this case, as often, no excuse at all is more plausible than a poor one.

The traditional conflated text retains all of these passages omitted by the Folio. In IV, iv, however, the Folio adds instead of omitting, and editors, having rejected the Folio's omissions, accept its addition. In the Quarto, Cordelia enters with *others*; in the Folio, with *drum and colours...and soldiers*. Nothing in the Quarto text suggests that Cordelia's *others* are an army; the speeches decidedly suggest a more intimate scene. Indeed, Cordelia's first words ('Alack, 'tis he') do not very naturally follow from an entry with drum and colours, even in the Folio. Nor does the Doctor's presence fit a military scene, for though we easily associate surgeons with armies, Shakespeare and his contemporaries did not, usually restricting their doctors to attendance upon royalty.[1] Perhaps partly or wholly for this reason, the Folio throughout turns the Quarto's *Doctor* into the vaguer, less anomalous *Gentle-man*, calling for an unspecified number of these to enter with Cordelia's army, as it does again for Edmund's (V, i).

The Quarto text thus seems to envision Cordelia in IV, iv in the company of several nondescript attendants; in the Folio she enters at the head of an army. The advantages of the Folio staging in forwarding the war theme and its relation to the Folio omissions already discussed are, I hope, self-evident. But the Folio arrangement also has the merit of establishing at once who leads the army which landed at Dover, a matter discussed at curious length in the preceding scene (IV, iii), which the Folio omits.

Who leads the invasion army is in fact a crucial issue, as a number of other Folio alterations make clear. Thus, in the exit to battle itself (V, ii), one small but fundamental detail has been altered: the Quarto's *Powers of France* become in the Folio simply *drum and colours... and soldiers*, without indication of nationality. Contemporary plays include directions for French, Dutch, Spanish, Irish, Polish, Bohemian, Danish, Armenian, and Portuguese armies. Some of these may be literary fantasies, but since such directions do occur in memorial texts (Quarto *3 Henry VI*), in promptbooks (*The Two Noble Ladies*), and in one of only two surviving plots (*The Battle of Alcaʒar*), evidently Elizabethan theatres could produce recognizably foreign armies, when asked to do so. The Folio, though deriving from theatrical

[1] Philip C. Kolin, *The Elizabethan Stage Doctor as a Dramatic Convention*, Salzburg Studies in English Literature (Salzburg, 1975). The other major convention, clearly irrelevant here, was of doctor as charlatan. Kolin also notes that a doctor would have been distinguished on stage by his conventional red costume. For medical figures accompanying armies, Shakespeare elsewhere always refers to *surgeons*, not *doctors* (*Hen. V*, IV, i, 139, *Mac.*, I, ii, 45, *TNK*, I, iv, 30), a distinction of terminology and function maintained in contemporary military and legal works – for which see C. G. Cruickshank, *Elizabeth's Army* (Oxford; 2nd edition, 1966), pp. 174–88.

copy, does *not* ask for one. This omission, moreover, seems clearly related to a number of others. Earlier, the Folio also omits Goneril's reference to French invasion (IV, ii, 56), the scene which includes discussion of French general La Far and of the king's absence from his army (IV, iii), and Albany's explanation that he takes arms against Lear only because 'France invades our land' (V, i, 25). Consequently, in the last two acts of the Folio there remains but one (indirect) allusion to French intervention, being in fact Cordelia's disclaimer of territorial ambitions: 'No blown ambition doth our arms incite,/But love, dear love, and our ag'd father's right' (IV, iv, 27–8). The Folio of course does retain references to France in act III, where they contribute to the sense of moral and political chaos, and to the accusation of Gloucester's treason; therefore, if audiences paused to reflect, they would realize that Cordelia's army may be primarily French. But while the Quarto keeps this fact prominent, making it unavoidable in the penultimate moments before the battle, when for the first and only time a French army marches across the stage, the Folio instead encourages an audience to forget it, systematically removing verbal and visual reminders of the French presence, so that Cordelia seems to lead not an invasion but a rebellion, like Bolingbroke's or Richmond's: 'the King is come to his daughter,/With others whom the rigour of our state/Forc'd to cry out' (V, i, 21–3). The Folio thus not only accelerates and intensifies the movement toward war, but clarifies and simplifies that movement as well, deliberately excising an extraneous political complication.

Some might object that the complication is not extraneous. Indeed, there is a school of criticism which regards any and every complication as virtuous *per se*. In this case, it has been claimed that the nationality of Cordelia's army 'explains' its defeat, by allowing her enemies an appeal to patriotism. Presumably this was why Shakespeare emphasized the army's nationality in the first place, in the Quarto. But good reasons must of force give place to better. The most remarkable event in act v of *King Lear* is the inexplicable defeat of the deserving: Cordelia's death. That death forces the audience, as it forces Lear, to ask, 'why?'. Critics continue to offer answers to this question, the most frequent candidate for their opprobrium being Albany, with his 'Great thing of us forgot'. But such attempts to discover a moral logic in the catastrophe are themselves simply another symptom of that desire for poetic justice which the very same critics so scorn in Albany or Edgar.[1] There is no satisfactory answer to Lear's agonized 'why?'. Likewise, by removing even the ghost of a reason for Cordelia's military defeat, Shakespeare asks the same question, and again refuses to answer it. Naturally, Cordelia's death makes the point much more powerfully and insistently, but the thematic relevance of the coincidence is surely hard to discount, as is the fact that the Folio, by removing the implicit explanation provided by the nationality of Cordelia's army, contributes directly to the sense of deliberately frustrated expectation and to the impression of a *fait accompli*, which are the only aesthetic justifications for Shakespeare's cursory treatment of the final battle. Surely it is also clear that the Quarto and Folio treat the nationality of Cordelia's army in consistently different ways, and that any conflation of the two produces incoherence.

Recognition that the Quarto and Folio consistently diverge in their treatment of the French presence also helps resolve a major textual tangle in III, i. In Kent's speech there to

[1] Among the most recent of Albany's accusers is Walter Forman, Jr, in *The Music of the Close: The Final Scenes of Shakespeare's Tragedies* (Lexington, 1979), pp. 113–58. The unconscious parallel between the critic's own appetite for poetic justice, and his scorn for Albany's identical appetite, is in Forman's case particularly striking.

the Gentleman, Q1 includes thirteen lines not in F1 (ll. 30–42), while F1 includes eight not in Q1 (ll. 22–9). Editors conflate the two, though the result is obscure and, as Dr Johnson observed, tedious. In the Quarto, Kent says,

> ...from France there comes a power
> Into this scattered kingdom; who already,
> Wise in our negligence, have secret feet
> In some of our best ports, and are at point
> To show their open banner,

and then tells the Gentleman to hurry to Dover, to report on the sisters' treatment of Lear. But in the Folio Kent merely says, not that a French invasion is afoot, but that Albany and Cornwall

> ...have...servants, who seem no less,
> Which are to France the spies and speculations
> Intelligent of our state.

In short, in the Quarto French military preparations are already far advanced, although Lear was sent into the storm only at the end of the preceding scene;[1] in the Folio, we are simply told that France *knows what is happening.* Moreover, in the Folio, Kent breaks or is broken off in mid-sentence, the Gentleman interjecting, ambiguously, 'I will talk further with you'; in the conflated text, this incomplete sentence occurs, inexplicably, in the middle of Kent's speech, where it contributes heavily to editorial suspicions of textual corruption. But the Quarto version is self-evidently coherent as it stands, and the only objection to the Folio alternative is that in it, though Kent does not dispatch the Gentleman to Dover, he still says later in this scene, 'If you shall see Cordelia – / As fear not but you shall – show her this ring' (ll. 46–7). Dr Johnson says 'The messenger is sent, he knows not why, he knows not whither.' But in fact Kent merely tells the Gentleman – and the audience – that he will see Cordelia, presumably soon, presumably nearby, presumably as she has made clear in her letter (II, ii). And when Cordelia does arrive, she enters in the presence of this Gentleman (instead of the Quarto's Doctor), in an unlocalized scene (IV, iv – traditionally, but unnecessarily, placed 'near Dover'). So, again, both texts offer coherent but incompatible alternatives, the Quarto beginning act III with the imminence of a dubiously motivated French invasion, the Folio with the news that France knows what is happening, and that Cordelia – and Cordelia alone – is already on her way, somehow. I need hardly say that the Folio produces a more benevolent impression, one more clearly personified by Cordelia herself, as the sole representative of that apocalyptic counter-movement which culminates, disastrously, in v, ii.

After that battle, Quarto Edmund enters *with Lear and Cordelia prisoners.* This stage direction implies the presence of a few guards, but no more. We imagine a deliberately secluded, secretive scene, Edmund dispatching his two prisoners. When Lear and Cordelia exit, the guards go with them, leaving Edmund alone with the Captain: concentrated at first wholly upon the two prisoners, the scene now dramatically shifts its focus to Edmund and the Captain. The Captain exits; Albany enters with the sisters and an indeterminate number of *others* (one of them a captain, who later says 'Sound, trumpet'). Albany's retinue does not include a drum, and need not include a trumpet. Everything about this scene suggests a *Counsel of War*, like Caesar's after his final victory in *Antony and Cleopatra* (v, i), with the armies nearby but offstage.

But in the Folio, Edmund enters at the beginning of v, iii *in conquest with Drums and Colours...Soldiers.* Visually and emphatically, Edmund here has reached the summit of his pyramid; by implication, he alone has won the battle. Edmund thus demands a much larger

[1] The difficulty raised by the time-scheme here is analyzed at some length by W. W. Greg in 'Time, Place, and Politics in *King Lear*', *Collected Papers*, ed. J. C. Maxwell (Oxford, 1966), pp. 322–40.

share of our attention from the very beginning of the scene, and when the prisoners and the army exit[1] the Folio produces a rather different effect than the Quarto: the image of a crowded stage suddenly almost empty, of a public scene suddenly confidential. The Captain exits; Albany, Goneril, and Regan enter, accompanied in the Folio by trumpet and soldiers, and perhaps a drum.[2] Edmund, who forty lines before entered in triumph, at the head of an army, his enemies in his power, stands now alone on the stage, surrounded by Albany's soldiers. Thus, within fifty lines the Folio gives us three dramatic entrances, visually mirroring one another: before the battle, Lear and Cordelia and their confident army; after the battle, Edmund and his victorious army; after Edmund's final treachery, Albany and his army. Between the first two entrances comes the *fait accompli* of the battle; between the second and third, another unexpected *fait accompli*, one engineered by Albany, which will seek to reverse the effect of the first.

The Folio's treatment of Edmund's and Albany's entrances crucially affects the structure and interpretation of the following scene. In the Quarto, as both he and Goneril say, Edmund might have refused or delayed Edgar's challenge, 'by right of knighthood', but he accepts it in a mood of overconfident bravado, which infects all his speeches in the scene. For in the Quarto he, not Albany, calls the Herald ('A herald ho, a herald'); he, not Regan, imperatively asserts his title ('Let the drum strike, and prove my title good'). The Quarto offers the spectacle of blind confidence hurrying to its destruction; the Folio instead presents a man who sees the trap closing, who stands surrounded by Albany's soldiers, and who must therefore accept any opportunity offered him. When Edmund says 'safe and nicely I might well delay', in the Folio, surrounded by Albany's army, his vaunt is hollow, and he knows it. The Folio's is an Edmund less flamboyant, but more

dangerous, because still clear-sighted: as in so many other scenes, he stands silent, watching, waiting, seeking his opportunity to strike. But this time the opportunity does not come.

In the Quarto Edmund is to a large extent the victim of his own *hubris*; this cannot explain why Edgar defeats him, but it does explain why he fights Edgar at all. In the Folio, Edmund, who dismisses his army so that he can plot with the Captain the murder of Lear and Cordelia, as a result finds himself tactically out-manoeuvred by Albany; he thus has no real choice but to fight. But because he is not self-deluded, the Folio Edmund becomes more

[1] It might be thought that, since Folio brings on the semblance of an army, some of it might remain on-stage after the prisoners leave, but this possibility is denied by the necessary intimacy of the interview with the Captain, and more specifically by Albany's later 'Trust to thy single virtue; for thy soldiers,/All levied in my name, have in my name/Took their discharge' — lines ludicrous if part of Edmund's army still stood onstage.

[2] The assertion that in the Folio Albany enters with trumpet, soldiers, and perhaps a drum calls for a word of explanation, since the stage direction only specifies *soldiers*. In the Folio, at the start of the scene Edmund enters with a full-scale army, which later exits; when, thirteen lines afterwards, Albany enters with soldiers, it would be most convenient if the same actors simply came back onstage, creating a similar stage picture, with the essential difference that now the army is under Albany's command. Albany's soldiers in any case must enter with trumpet(s). The Folio (unlike the Quarto) gives the Herald a definite and singular entry (v, iii, 106), and also (unlike the Quarto) gives him three commands to the trumpeter — which means that the trumpeter must be a different character from the Herald, and must already be onstage. Likewise, at play's end the Folio (unlike the Quarto) calls for a *dead march*, which usually implies drumming, but apparently could be performed by trumpets. (For drums in the dead march see *OED march* sb[4] 5, 6. But at the end of the action in Kyd's *Spanish Tragedy* 'The trumpets sound a dead march'.) The Folio variants therefore require, not only that Edmund's army re-enter as Albany's, but that it re-enter with trumpet(s), and probably a drum, properties entirely unnecessary to the Quarto staging. A handful of soldiers or attendants is theatrically metamorphosed into an army by just such properties.

dangerous, and the outcome less predictable. Equally important, by making Edmund the victim of a trick, a (theatrical as well as political) *coup*, the Folio makes him more sympathetic. He is, again, the underdog. Critics may disagree on the relative merits of these two treatments of the character; but I hope they would not dispute that there are two distinct treatments, which it would be wrong to mix or confuse.

The other Folio changes in this scene it is not my business here to discuss, but all seem to me designed (as these are) to reinforce an audience's interest in the long gap between Lear's exit with Cordelia and his entrance with her body. This is achieved by omissions, by clarifications and rearrangements of action and business, by interrelated changes in the presentation of Edmund, Albany, and Goneril.[1] The altered aftermath of the battle thus contributes to an altered dramatization of the play's most important hiatus.

The central difficulty, for a critic, is in trying to conjecture what the Quarto or Folio play would be like as a whole, on its own: we are all inured to an amalgam of the two. It is especially difficult to imagine the unity and wholeness of a *King Lear* which doesn't have in it scenes and speeches we expect it to have. What we need, ideally, is good productions of the separate texts. But in the meantime we can patch together, from many productions, illustrations and intimations of what those separate performances might be like. Peter Brook, notoriously, omitted the servants from the end of III, vii; IV, iii has often been omitted, or at least severely cut; Kozintsev's film gives no impression of a foreign invasion; Brook played the offstage battle without elaborations, leaving his audiences alone with a silent Gloucester,

'snuffing the air'.[2] And the 1959 Glen Byam Shaw production at Stratford, though unsatisfactory in many ways, followed most of the Folio cuts and omissions in the war sequence, resulting in a fourth act marked by 'narrative excitement...speed and a new kind of urgency ...the speed of forces marshalling for battle...'.[3] These are not the characteristics which spring first to mind from most performances or interpretations of the play.

The Folio changes in the preparation for and aftermath of the decisive battle in v, ii – however unfamiliar, however difficult for us to imagine whole – do tackle the two most serious structural difficulties in the entire play: the anticlimax in the first half of act IV, and the hiatus in the middle of the last scene. And almost all are directly related to the peculiar dramatization of the battle itself: strengthening the expectations which that battle deliberately frustrates, removing the only possible explanation for its inexplicable outcome, echoing in a visually striking and unmistakably significant way its central image of a *fait accompli*. It is hard to believe that such a succession of interrelated changes happened by accident, and it would be churlish (let alone unnecessary) to attribute them to anyone but Shakespeare. If Aristophanes could revise his *Clouds*, and Euripides his *Hippolytus*, why not Shakespeare his *King Lear*?

[1] For a full discussion of these other alterations see the studies by Warren, Urkowitz, and Blayney (see above p. 28 n. 1).

[2] Frank Kermode, *Shakespeare, Spenser, Donne* (1971), p. 172.

[3] Muriel St Clare Byrne, '*King Lear* at Stratford-upon-Avon', *Shakespeare Quarterly*, 11 (1960), 198–9.

© GARY TAYLOR 1980

'KING LEAR': ART UPSIDE-DOWN

JAMES BLACK

It is a truism that in *King Lear* Shakespeare takes us into a world which is upside-down. We enter a great and terrible feast of misrule where the king gives away his kingdom and becomes a subject, where parents become wards of their children, asses are borne on men's backs over the dirt, and one goes to supper in the morning and to bed at noon. This is 'the upheaval of all nature, the reversal of all histories'.[1] Approaching such a paradoxical and apparently sprawling piece of art, commentators generally have sought some kind of orientation through imposing a shape or schema on the play. The most recent emblem for *King Lear* is the prism — 'the multiply-shaped thing', as it is called in Rosalie Colie's and Leo Flahiff's book *Some Facets of 'King Lear': Essays in Prismatic Criticism*.[2] As a figure for the play the prism image certainly is superior to the very old-fashioned way of charting a drama as rising action, peak, falling action — the hunt-the-climax pattern which dates back to the 1860s and the German scholar Gustav Freytag.[3] Where, after all, is the 'climax' of *King Lear*? If we should begin to chart it as a 'rising action' we might simply find ourselves following it helplessly up and up and up . . .: this play after all qualifies as scene individable and poem unlimited. Another figure imposed on *King Lear* is of course that of revolutionary action, the turning wheel of fortune. In the play itself this figure is suggested, and a significant number of the 'prismatic' essayists in *Some Facets of 'King Lear'* keep coming back to the circle. Clearly the shape, schema or graph of *King Lear* is not easy to define. Nicholas Brooke has argued that in this tragedy Shakespeare's 'structural process' is to break through all conventional structures and to force the audience to face the play's events, and especially its ending, 'without any support from systems of moral or artistic belief at all'.[4] Like Brooke, I believe that inner clues to patterns such as that of the wheel are false trails, and I further think that in *King Lear* Shakespeare is deliberately breaking forms, purposely overturning conventions and received techniques and in many ways turning his own dramatic art upside-down.

The simplest aspect of this upside-down Shakespearian approach to convention is seen in the appearance of the play's chief villains, all of whom are physically very handsome. Kent comments that he cannot wish Gloucester's fault in having illegitimately fathered Edmund undone, 'the issue of it being so proper' (I, i, 17–18), and soon after Edmund speaks of his own dimensions being as well compact and his shape as true as honest madam's issue

[1] Edith Sitwell, quoted in Harry Levin, 'The Heights and the Depths: A Scene from *King Lear*', the Signet Classic *King Lear*, ed. Russell Fraser (1963), p. 264. All citations of *King Lear* in this essay are to the New Arden edition, ed. Kenneth Muir (1952; repr. 1963).

[2] Toronto and Buffalo, 1974. See esp. p. viii.

[3] In *The Technique of the Drama* (1863, trans. E. J. MacEwan 1896, Chicago). For Freytag's schematization of drama see pp. 114–40.

[4] *Shakespeare: 'King Lear'*, Studies in English Literature no. 15 (1963), p. 60.

(I, ii, 7–9). The physical attraction between Edmund, Goneril and Regan is morally deplorable but understandable: even when he is furious at his daughters Lear admits Goneril's beauty (II, iv, 167) and Regan's gorgeousness (II, iv, 265–72) – in stage appearance at least these daughters look attractive. Looking no farther than Shakespeare's own practice, we seem far from the world of *Richard III*, or of *Hamlet*, where evil reassuringly looks its part: where Richard is misshapen and therefore determined to be a villain and Claudius can appear like a mildewed ear blasting his wholesome brother.[1] In *King Lear* Shakespeare is of course working out the *Measure for Measure* question, 'What may man within him hide/ Though angel on the outward side?'[2] – in *The Tempest* the deformed Caliban will not be half as savage as the consummate evil which is embodied in people such as Antonio and Sebastian, who can pass for inhabitants of a brave new world and bring from Miranda the cry, 'How beauteous mankind is!'[3] Lear himself, as the evidence of Goneril's and Regan's viciousness grows, is perpetually baffled: why do not these monsters or villains look the part? Albany too is baffled and expresses his puzzlement and his fear in an oxymoron, 'proper deformity':

> Proper deformity shows not in the fiend
> So horrid as in woman.   (IV, ii, 60)

Lear and Albany have as it were come out of an older tradition where expectations are adhered to, where deformity conventionally 'shows'. The drama in which they find themselves has its conventions awry.

We might of course say (conventionally) that handsome is as handsome does. Yet as the play gathers momentum we find that not only do the good and evil characters *appear* indistinguishable, but in certain vital instances they also *do* the same things. Edmund sets out on his plan to fool Gloucester by hastily pocketing the false letter and saying to his father

precisely what Cordelia has just before said to hers: 'What paper were you reading?/Nothing, my Lord' (I, ii, 30–1). To deceive Edgar he takes as his disguise and cue 'villainous melancholy, with a sigh like Tom o' Bedlam' (I, ii, 142–3). In turn, when Edgar needs to adopt a disguise to preserve his life he takes on exactly the same role, the Bedlam beggar poor Tom. The role seems so natural to them both that they might be imagined playing it together as children: we might guess that if Edmund saw Edgar in the role (which he doesn't) he would recognize him at once. But of course the point is that Edmund and Edgar each plays the Bedlam for a terribly different reason, the one to cause harm and the other at least to escape that harm. When Edmund frames his brother by pretending that Edgar has treacherously attacked him, he decides that 'Some blood drawn on me would beget opinion/Of my more fierce endeavour', and having 'seen drunkards/Do more than this in sport', wounds himself on the arm (II, i, 34–6). Two scenes later when Edgar adopts the role of Bedlam, he emulates how they 'Strike in their numb'd and mortified bare arms/Pins, wooden pricks, nails...' (II, iii, 15–16). It is appropriate to point out here that in Edgar's act of disguising an Elizabethan stage convention again is turned upside-down. The adoption of a disguise is most usually thought of as change of clothing, dressing the part: male for female attire, say, or the coloured cloak of the gentleman Lucentio exchanged for the drab one of his servant Tranio,[4] or the addition of some distinctive mark such as Iago's telling Roderigo to defeat his favour with a usurped beard.[5] But in *King Lear*, II, iii as Edgar becomes Poor Tom – and I think he is *becoming* Tom as he speaks his

[1] See *Hamlet*, III, iv, 64–5.
[2] *Measure for Measure*, III, ii, 285–6.
[3] *The Tempest*, V, i, 183.
[4] *The Taming of the Shrew*, I, i, 211–12.
[5] *Othello*, I, iii, 345–6.

soliloquy: taking off his clothing, smearing himself with dirt, elfing his hair in knots and stabbing his own arm as his brother did before; becoming, that is, at the end of the scene 'this horrible object' – and as he strips down to 'the thing itself' we see that *taking off* garments is a disguise. In *King Lear* one undresses the part.

So, early in the play Edmund and Edgar have done similar things for opposite reasons. But there is a much more important instance of the confusion of convention and expectation, of good and bad characters acting alike. In II, iv Goneril and Regan find Lear confused, tiring and vulnerable – near the end of his tether, as we might say. Or as Regan puts it:

> O, Sir! you are old;
> Nature in you stands on the very verge
> Of her confine: you should be ruled and led
> By some discretion that discerns your state
> Better than you yourself.   (II, iv, 147–51)

Here of course is voiced one of the great symbols of the play, that of the man on a dangerous edge or verge. Seeing Lear on this verge, Goneril and Regan do not 'rule and lead' him to safety but instead work to dizzy him, to send him staggering, to tip him over the brink. They bombard him with rhetorical and apparently reasonable questions; no doubt they stand on either side of him so that he actually has to turn and look from one to the other, and as he turns to deal with one question another comes from the unguarded side. It is a rhetorical blind-man's buff where the victim is turned around until he is disoriented:

> *Regan.*   what! fifty followers?
>   Is it not well? What should you need of more?
>   Yea, or so many...?
> *Goneril.*
>   Why might not you, my Lord, receive attendance
>   From those that she calls servants, or from mine?
> *Regan.*
>   Why not, my Lord?...
> *Goneril.*
>   What need you five-and-twenty, ten, or five...?
> *gan.*   What need one?   (II, iv, 239–65)

Lear, trapped by his own wrong-headed premise that affection can be quantified ('Thy fifty yet doth double five-and-twenty/And thou art twice her love,' ll. 261–2), has no answer. As Edgar literally undressed himself in the previous scene so, metaphorically, Lear is stripped here, his 'folds of favour' (I, i, 218) are systematically dismantled. He tries for a moment to reply to their questions – 'O! reason not the need', and then to appeal to their generosity (II, iv, 266–72), but in seven lines he breaks, as they know he will, lurches over that verge of confine and self-control, and goes raging into the storm.

In prodding Lear over that verge Goneril and Regan have not, however, driven him mad. Madness is another verge or bourne which Lear himself recognizes and tries to avoid: 'My wits begin to turn' (III, ii, 67); 'This tempest in my mind' (III, iv, 12). He knows that obsession with his daughters' cruelty to him is the way to madness, and says 'Let me shun that' (III, iv, 19–20). But the dramatic rush from the hovel of Edgar as Bedlam marks the decisive stage in Lear's fall into obsession. As the madman possessed (which is what Edgar is pretending to be) springs wildly out of the shelter he is greeted by the madman obsessed, for Lear says:

> Didst thou give all to thy daughters?
> And art thou come to this?   (III, iv, 48–9)

It would seem that either the shock of Edgar's sudden and violent arrival triggers something in Lear's mind or the very sight of this apparently complete madman acts as a kind of model for Lear to emulate. In some way Edgar/Tom helps Lear to accept madness – as Lear's madness helps Edgar in turn to bear *his* pain:

> Who alone suffers, suffers most i' th' mind,
> Leaving free things and happy shows behind;
> But then the mind much suffering doth o'erskip,
> When grief hath mates, and bearing fellowship.
>   (III, vi, 107–10)

Whatever the case may be clinically, it is a fact that in the narrative of the play it is the appearance of Edgar as Tom which gives Lear the final touch which sends or takes him over the verge into madness. Unintentionally, Edgar has completed what Goneril and Regan began.

This theme of verges moves of course to a culmination at Dover, in the 'cliff' scene (IV, vi) about which Harry Levin has written so well. As Edgar has inadvertently taken Lear over a verge of confine, so will he with infinite care assist his blind father over another brink – will help him to 'fall' and be renewed after that fall, in counterpoint to Edmund's dismissal of Gloucester: 'The younger rises when the old doth fall' (III, iii, 27). I will return to the cliff, but in this context of the good and evil characters in *King Lear* doing exactly the same things I would also mention the parallel activity of conducting trials. In III, vi the Fool, Edgar and Lear 'arraign' Goneril. These three 'wise men' (who respectively embody the idea that some are born mad, some achieve madness and some have madness thrust upon them) can achieve only a pitiful parody of a trial. In the next scene a fearful parody of a trial is enacted as Regan and Cornwall examine Gloucester and blind him. The decent but weak and the evil but strong go through the same sets of motions: Cornwall says 'We may not pass upon [Gloucester's] life/Without the form of justice, yet our power/Shall do a court'sy to our wrath' (III, vii, 24–6), and 'the form of justice' is travestied by each, with terribly different results. Any expectations we may have that some opposing or counter measures to evil might be taken by the good characters are not answered in the first three acts. But perhaps by the middle of the play we should be recognizing that this is a work in which conventional expectations are being overturned. Lear becomes, not a Prodigal Son (that favourite frame of reference for Shakespeare) but a Prodigal Father; Cordelia, who calls him 'poor *perdu*',

asks 'Wast thou fain, poor father,/ To hovel thee with swine' (IV, vii, 35–9); and, bedecked with flowers, he is King, not Queen, of the May.[1] By the overturning of narrative conventions Lear might, in this story of blindness and deceiving females, be a helpless Samson – he knows about firing out foxes (V, iii, 22–3); but Goneril also could be a powerful female Samson – she sees the possibility of having 'All the building in my fancy [plucked]/Upon my hateful life' (IV, ii, 85–6). And we also have the reversal, in Edgar's conducting of Gloucester to an enactment (Shakespeare would call it a 'shadow') of death from which Gloucester will miraculously be delivered, of Isaac leading Abraham.

Even when we are attuned to capsized expectations, 'Dover Cliff' still is a great stroke. For a start, it is difficult for an audience not to go to Dover with Gloucester: that is, not to follow Gloucester in his perceptions of the situation. His pain and misery command our company, beginning with the ominous repetitions at his 'trial', 'Wherefore to Dover?', and taking hold of us through his terrible fixation and resolve:

Gloucester.   Dost thou know Dover?
Edgar.
   Ay, master.
Gloucester.
   There is a cliff, whose high and bending head
   Looks fearfully in the confined deep;
   Bring me but to the very brim of it,
   And I'll repair the misery thou dost bear
   With something rich about me; from that place
   I shall no leading need.   (IV, i, 71–8)

(It will of course be a splendid turnabout of logic that at Dover Gloucester, who has a jewel hidden on his person and thinks he is helping and rewarding the wretched beggar by handing it over, actually is the one who has his misery repaired by Edgar, who in worldly terms has nothing.)

[1] Cf. Nicholas Brooke, *Shakespeare: 'King Lear'*, pp. 36–7.

When we set off to Dover with Gloucester and Edgar we have no way of knowing whether they are headed for a real or a symbolic cliff. As Levin says, we are just as blind as Gloucester;[1] and to Gloucester the cliff that awaits him is real – though 'confined deep' and 'the very brim' in his description of it may remind us of the metaphorical place, 'the verge of. . . confine' where Goneril and Regan found Lear. At the supposed cliff Edgar will tell Gloucester that he is within a foot of the 'extreme verge'. But before we hear this echo of Regan describing her father's dangerous and exploitable position we have to walk with Gloucester to Dover. When we arrive at 'the place' (this is Edgar's designation of it) we hear from the stage the greatest passage of scene setting in Shakespeare and possibly in all literature:

Edgar.
> Come on, sir; here's the place: stand still.
> How fearful
> And dizzy 'tis to cast one's eyes so low!
> The crows and choughs that wing the midway air
> Show scarce so gross as beetles; half way down
> Hangs one that gathers sampire, dreadful trade!
> Methinks he seems no bigger than his head.
> The fishermen that walk upon the beach
> Appear like mice, and yond tall anchoring bark
> Diminish'd to her cock, her cock a buoy
> Almost too small for sight. The murmuring surge
> That on th' unnumber'd idle pebble chafes,
> Cannot be heard so high. I'll look no more,
> Lest my brain turn, and the deficient sight
> Topple down headlong.

Gloucester.   Set me where you stand.

Edgar.
> Give me your hand; you are now within a foot
> Of th'extreme verge: for all beneath the moon
> Would I not leap upright.   (IV, vi, 11–27)

'Theatrical convention', Levin correctly says, 'prescribes that we accept whatever is said on the subject of immediate place as the setting.'[2] In any other Elizabethan play – in any other of Shakespeare's plays – we are required, as Antipholus of Syracuse puts it, to 'entertain the offered fallacy':[3] 'This is the Forest of Arden'; 'This castle hath a pleasant seat'; 'Night's candles are burnt out'. When Dr Johnson rejected the effect of Edgar's description with 'It should be all precipice – all vacuum. The crows impede your fall', he was not repudiating Shakespeare's descriptive abilities but the literary game of his club in rating pieces of art as 'the best' or 'the greatest'. All our own conditioning and expectations should lead us to believe that Gloucester is on the edge of a cliff which Shakespeare has made to appear before our ears. We are disabused, or at least relieved of fear for Gloucester, only when Edgar addresses us directly:

> Why I do trifle thus with his despair
> Is done to cure it.   (IV, vi, 33–4)

This may be as much as to say, 'You should not have entertained the offered fallacy. There is no cliff'. Yet the fallacy has been offered with astonishing brilliance and with a prodigality comparable to that of Lear himself unnecessarily giving away his lands, or Antony dispensing a bounty that had no winter in it,[4] while the audience with Elizabethan theatrical pre-conditioning is required simply to resist the irresistible. Even when we know that Edgar has been 'trifling' it is hard to be proof against the renewed description of the supposed cliff, seen now from the bottom:

Edgar.
> Ten masts at each make not the altitude
> Which thou hast perpendicularly fell. . .

Gloucester.
> But have I fall'n, or no?

Edgar.
> From the dread summit of this chalky bourn.
> Look up a-height; the shrill-gorg'd lark so far
> Cannot be seen or heard: do but look up.
>   (IV, vi, 53–9)

---

[1] Levin, 'The Heights and the Depths', p. 272.
[2] *Ibid.*, p. 272.
[3] *The Comedy of Errors*, I, ii, 188.
[4] *Antony and Cleopatra*, V, ii, 86–8.

And Gloucester's fall itself has an overturning of conventional tragic expectations. He flings himself forward and clearly is brought up short rather quickly, somewhat after the manner of someone who steps down a stair that isn't there and gets an embarrassing and painful jar for his mistake. There is enormous comic potential – or comic risk – in this soon-interrupted fall at what should be Gloucester's most solemn moment.

In *King Lear*'s language there is another notable overturning of art. At the beginning of the play Lear is presented as a man who rejoices in real or assumed lordships. He is lord of space, in that he has vast lands to give away – needing a map to outline his holdings and donations. He thinks he also is lord of time, or certainly believes that title-time is real time: he tells Goneril, 'To thine and Albany's issues/Be this perpetual' (I, i, 66–7); and Goneril, 'To thee and thine, hereditary ever...' (I, i, 79); while Cordelia he will hold from his heart for ever (I, i, 116). And clearly, he *is* lord of language; as Winifred Nowottny has said, his domination of the play is a linguistic domination.[1] Out of his mouth come gifts, imprecations, curses and, eventually, a storm. As we become accustomed to Lear's facility in speech – and to Shakespeare's art in devising that speech – it is all the more striking that his reconciliation with Cordelia comes in such simple words, when he admits that he is a very foolish fond old man, fears that he is not in his perfect mind, admits to confusion and ignorance about where he finds himself on waking, and then

> Do not laugh at me;
> For as I am a man, I think this lady
> To be my child Cordelia.   (IV, vii, 68–70)

When last he saw Cordelia, his 'sometime daughter', Lear had an inexhaustible store of terrifying and marvellous words with which to reject her. Now it is simply, and completely, 'my child', to which comes the responding 'I am, I am' and, in a moment, 'No cause, no cause'.

Of course, we have been prepared for this linguistic renunciation, for in the preceding scene, just before Gloucester fell from the supposed cliff he spoke of Edgar, the son whom he had rejected, in the simplest of words, 'If Edgar live, O, bless him!' (IV, vi, 40) – this in Edgar's hearing. The moments of reconciliation correspond to one another: Lear does not yet completely recognize Cordelia when he calls her 'my child'; Gloucester does not know that Edgar is within earshot when he says 'O, bless him!' The repeated moment is like that in *The Rime of the Ancient Mariner* when the Mariner responds to the water creatures who formerly had disgusted him:

> O happy living things! no tongue
> Their beauty might declare:
> A spring of love gushed from my heart,
> And I blessed them unaware:
> Sure my kind saint took pity on me,
> And I blessed them unaware.   (ll. 282–8)

This 'blessing unaware' in the reconciliation scenes is of course indicative of the ability to 'Love, and be silent'. A phrase of Juliet's comes to mind, of being 'more rich in matter than in words'.[2] So again in that terrible moment when Lear enters with Cordelia dead in his arms, bearing matter more than words can wield, the only expression of what he feels is the terrible whirlwind which once more speaks out of him, 'Howl, howl, howl!' Whatever expectations we might have of Lear's (and Shakespeare's) eloquence, we are offered in these reconciliation and death scenes only unaccommodated language.

When Nahum Tate adapted *King Lear* to end happily what he did was make it conform to audiences' (and not only Restoration audiences') and readers' expectations and hopes of how the play might conclude. He said in the dedication to his version that he was fearful

---

[1] 'Some Aspects of the Style of *King Lear*', *Shakespeare Survey 13* (Cambridge, 1960), p. 51.

[2] *Romeo and Juliet*, II, vi, 30.

about what he had done but found it over-
whelmingly approved by his audiences. What
Tate did to the ending of the play was twofold:
he fulfilled the general hopes that audiences
have of virtue triumphing and vice (especially
such vice as is seen in Shakespeare's *King Lear*)
being punished; and he also answered the
expectations of poetic justice which Shakespeare himself teasingly encourages. We are,
after all, told in Edgar's soliloquy at the
beginning of act IV that the worst returns to
laughter.

After Gloucester's miraculous deliverance
and Lear's rescue by Cordelia there is every
reason to hope that such setbacks as the loss of
the battle, Lear's and Cordelia's imprisonment
and Edmund's designs on them can be overcome. When Edgar defeats and mortally
wounds Edmund such hope is further encouraged. Then there is a moment of terror
followed by overwhelming relief. Remember,
we know that Edmund ordered an officer to
dispose of Lear and Cordelia, but we do not
know *how* this is to be done. Therefore, when,
as Edmund lies dying and Edgar is telling his
all-too-circumstantial tale, there enters *A
Gentleman, with a bloody knife,* the most
terrible potentialities are present:

Gentleman. Help, help! O, help!
Edgar.　　　　　　What kind of help?
Albany.　　　　　　　　　　Speak, man.
Edgar.
　What means this bloody knife?
Gentleman.　　　　　　　　'Tis hot, it smokes;
　It came even from the heart of – O! she's
　　dead.
Albany.
　Who dead? speak, man.　　(v, iii, 222–5)

Who dead? Cordelia? For as long as the pause
lasts that forces Albany to urge 'speak, man'
we can think that the knife has come from *her*
heart. The overwhelming relief is to hear the
answer when it finally comes:

Your lady, sir, your lady: and her sister
By her is poison'd: she confesses it.

And the poetic justice is underlined by Albany:

This judgment of the heavens, that makes us
　tremble,
Touches us not with pity.　　(v, iii, 226–7, 231–2)

Then everyone remembers Lear and Cordelia
and there is the exciting and hope-raising
bustle to save them. *Now* we learn that Cordelia
was to be hanged (v, iii, 254); and Albany,
growing every minute in confidence and
authority, fervently says, 'The gods defend
her!'

But of course even as he is saying this there
comes the terrible howl from offstage and Lear
enters with Cordelia in his arms ('*dead* in his
arms' is Rowe's interpolation). Kent's response,
'Is this the promis'd end?' not only can refer
to the Last Judgement but also can speak to
dashed hopes for a different outcome – is this
what we have been led to expect? And even
now Cordelia might be alive. Lear is desperate:

If that her breath will mist or stain the stone,
Why, then she lives...
This feather stirs; she lives! if it be so
It is a chance that doth redeem all sorrows
That ever I have felt.　　(v, iii, 262–3, 265–7)

Perhaps this breath of hope is not much to
stand against that howl and the storm of
negatives which also come from Lear – 'She's
gone for ever', 'She's dead as earth', 'I might
have sav'd her; now she's gone for ever!' But
Albany still (with the audience) clings to a faith
in justice and reparation:

What comfort to this great decay may come
Shall be applied...
　　　　　　　All friends shall taste
The wages of their virtue, and all foes
The cup of their deservings.
　　　　　　　　　　(v, iii, 297–8, 302–4)

But then in the next half of that last line Albany
is forced to say, 'O! see, see!' and Lear begins

his final speech with 'And my poor fool is hang'd! No, no, no life!...', and dies on

> Do you see this? Look on her, look, her lips,
> Look there, look there!

When Cordelia saw her father coming to himself in IV, vii she said, 'O! look upon me, Sir,/ And hold your hand in benediction o'er me' (ll. 57–8). Now Lear does indeed look upon her. When Edgar assured Gloucester of his miraculous escape at Dover, among his words were 'Do but look up' (IV, vi, 59). He says here again to Lear, 'Look up, my Lord.' These repetitions of 'look' seem to mock all expectations of a bearable ending.

If *we* look back as far as the beginning of act IV we can see that in a series of half-lines hopes have been dashed. Edgar's opening speech in IV, i, full of relief at having escaped the pursuit and the storm, and full of assurance that things must get better, ends with a half-line:

> The wretch that thou hast blown unto the worst
> Owes nothing to thy blasts.

The next half of the metrical line is 'But who comes here?' as Gloucester is led in, blind. In the next scene Albany, hearing that Cornwall has been killed 'going to put out/The other eye of Gloucester', hails this death as a triumph for justice:

> This shows you are above,
> You justicers, that these our nether crimes
> So speedily can venge!   (IV, ii, 78–80)

But in the remainder of the line he comes abruptly down from this idealistic flight to question a terrible reality:

> But, O poor Gloucester!
> Lost he his other eye?

And the half-line answer brings him flatly to earth: 'Both, both, my Lord' (ll. 80–1). Likewise when in IV, vi Edgar preaches gently to his father, Gloucester promises henceforth to bear affliction and finally is enjoined by Edgar to 'Bear free and patient thoughts' (l. 80). These last words are the first half of a line, the second half of which is 'But who comes here?' as Lear enters, mad, completely unable to bear any sort of patient thoughts. So too as Albany speaks of comfort, restoration and poetic justice in the final scene his metrical line is completed by the 'O! see, see!' as Lear enters his last agony. In each of these lines there is a kind of hinge or trapdoor, a drop or verge. To go beyond the hope or comfort expressed up to halfway along the line is to fall sickeningly to a lower level of pain and despair. From Albany's hopeful 'The gods defend her!' we were pitched to the sight of Lear and his poor fool, hanged: hanging itself entails a drop. Thus as the play drives to its conclusion every hope is a verge from which all fall down.

Perhaps this, then, is the shape or pattern of *King Lear*: not the wheel, not rising action-peak-falling action, not even an up-up-up movement; but a pattern which overturning all conventions, justice, expectations and hopes takes us down and down and down.

© JAMES BLACK 1980

'AND THAT'S TRUE TOO': 'KING LEAR' AND THE TENSION OF UNCERTAINTY

DEREK PEAT

'By the end of *King Lear*, we should see that Cordelia possesses everything that is genuinely worth having.' This might be a quotation from *Shakespearean Tragedy*, but it comes from a recent book by John Reibetanz.[1] The approach is new, but the conclusions are familiar: 'through his sufferings Lear has won an enlightened soul'; 'we protest so strongly against Cordelia's death because we are not of her world'; 'Material goods are fetters and the body a husk to be discarded so that the fruit can be reached.'[2] Reibetanz acknowledges the obvious debt to Bradley, but he is no ordinary disciple. He admits his master's weaknesses, and emphasises them by considering precisely those areas Bradley ignored: the nature of the public and private theatres; Shakespeare's use and adaptation of contemporary stage tradition and the expectations of an audience moulded by regular playgoing. In the light of this, it is ironic that he reaches similar conclusions to the man who argued the play was 'too huge for the stage'.[3] Much less ironic is the fact that while I find most of Reibetanz's commentary thoroughly convincing, it leads me to an exactly opposite conclusion.

This is not so surprising; a survey of the criticism reveals it is in the nature of *King Lear* to stimulate contrary responses. There is a marked division between critics for whom the play makes an 'affirmation' and those who believe it does not.[4] Reibetanz, who argues that the play 'definitely points us to'[5] Christian doctrine, obviously belongs with the former

group, and I had better admit now that my own sympathies lie with the other side. This division of critical opinion is in itself, I believe, a direct result of the fact that *King Lear* forces every spectator to choose between the contrary possibilities it holds in unresolved opposition. Norman Rabkin's idea of the working of any Shakespearian play is an exact description of this particular one: 'the dramatic structure sets

[1] John Reibetanz, *The Lear World: A Study of King Lear in its Dramatic Context* (Toronto, 1977), p. 121.

[2] *Ibid.*, pp. 108, 122, 121.

[3] A. C. Bradley, *Shakespearean Tragedy* (1904; repr. 1969), p. 202.

[4] L. C. Knights uses the word 'affirmation' in the essay in *Some Shakespearean Themes* (London, 1959), but following Bradley's idea of '*The Redemption of King Lear*' (p. 235), many critics have argued that the ending is positive because Lear is redeemed through suffering. Several of these interpretations view *King Lear* as a 'Christian' play: Oscar James Campbell, 'The Salvation of Lear', *English Literary History*, 15 (1948); John F. Danby, *Shakespeare's Doctrine of Nature* (1949); Terence Hawkes, *Shakespeare and the Reason* (1964); R. B. Heilman, *This Great Stage* (Baton Rouge, 1948) and G. Wilson Knight, *The Wheel of Fire* (1959).

On the other side are those who find no evidence of redemption and who stress the horrors of the final scene. Among the most notable are: W. R. Elton, *King Lear and the Gods* (San Marino, Calif., 1966); Barbara Everett, 'The New *King Lear*', *Critical Quarterly*, 2 (1960); Helen Gardner, *King Lear* (John Coffin Memorial Lecture, 1967); S. L. Goldberg, *An Essay on King Lear* (Cambridge, 1974); John Holloway, *The Story of The Night* (1961) and Marvin Rosenberg, *The Masks of King Lear* (Berkeley, Los Angeles and London, 1972).

[5] Reibetanz, *The Lear World*, p. 120.

up opposed elements as equally valid...and equally destructive, so that the choice that the play forces the reader to make becomes impossible'.[1] Others have noticed this tension of irresolution. For J. D. Rosenberg 'each assertion in the play confronts a counter-assertion and all interpretations contain the seed of their refutation',[2] and S. L. Goldberg puts it this way: 'The outline of one thing is the boundary of its counterpart.'[3] The penultimate scene reveals the working of the play in microcosm:

Edgar.
Here, father, take the shadow of this tree
For your good host; pray that the right may thrive.
If ever I return to you again,
I'll bring you comfort.
Gloucester.   Grace go with you, sir! [*Exit Edgar.*
Alarum; afterwards a retreat. Re-enter Edgar.
Edgar.
Away, old man! give me thy hand: away!
King Lear hath lost, he and his daughter ta'en.
Give me thy hand; come on.
Gloucester.
No further, sir; a man may rot even here.
Edgar.
What! in ill thoughts again? Men must endure
Their going hence, even as their coming hither:
Ripeness is all.   Come on.
Gloucester.   And that's true too.   [*Exeunt.*
                                                  (v, ii, 1-11)[4]

Edgar asks for prayer and Gloucester gives his blessing, but 'the right' do not thrive. Before the battle Edgar is certain of victory and makes a strong assertion, only to have the action contradict him. The audience's expectation of a happy ending, fueled by the reconciliation between the King and his daughter (and for Shakespeare's contemporaries supported by memories of Leir and Cordella's victory in the old play) is abruptly reversed. Since the faked 'miracle' at Dover cliff, many of Gloucester's lines have indicated patient acceptance of his lot, yet here he reverts to despair. Most important of all, in a play which questions everything and depends upon right choice, is the way the

scene ends. Contrary positions are given equal validity and Gloucester's reply to Edgar's famous remark might stand as the epigraph for the play: 'And that's true too.'

The point at which this process of juxtaposition comes to its climax is, appropriately enough, the moment when Lear dies:

Why should a dog, a horse, a rat, have life,
And thou no breath at all? Thou'lt come no more,
Never, never, never, never, never!
Pray you, undo this button: thank you, Sir.
Do you see this? Look on her, look, her lips,
Look there, look there!   (v, iii, 306-11)

There are two distinct possibilities: either Lear dies believing Cordelia lives, or his heart breaks as he realises the shattering reality of her death. The possibilities open up a variety of interpretations. A Lear who believes Cordelia is alive may be transcending earthly limitations, suffering under the final self-deception of a man who still 'but slenderly' knows himself, or taking refuge from reality in madness. In contrast, an awareness of Cordelia's death may be the culmination of a process of deepening knowledge of the self and the world. There is, of course, a third possibility, that Lear dies uncertain whether his daughter is alive or dead.

The text supports all these possibilities. The five times repeated 'never' seems conclusive enough, but since his entrance with Cordelia in his arms, the king has had other speeches which move from statement through qualification to counter-statement:

She's dead as earth. Lend me a looking-glass;
If that her breath will mist or stain the stone,
Why, then she lives...
This feather stirs; she lives!   (v, iii, 261-3, 265)

[1] Norman Rabkin, *Shakespeare and the Common Understanding* (New York and London, 1967), p. 12.
[2] John D. Rosenberg, 'King Lear and his Comforters', *Essays in Criticism*, 16 (1966), 144.
[3] S. L. Goldberg, *An Essay on King Lear* (Cambridge, 1974), p. 163.
[4] References are to the New Arden edition, ed. Kenneth Muir (1952; repr. 1967).

His final lines can be read as a similar move from one certainty to another, or as another example of his uncertainty.

The contradictory nature of the text is mirrored in the original editions. My quotation is the Folio version, but the Quarto omits the last two lines and contains the printer's formula for a death cry, 'O,o,o,o.' which suggests the king howling in anguish at his daughter's death. In the absence of evidence showing which ending Shakespeare favoured (if, indeed, both are his) all we can say is that while the Quarto supports one reading, the Folio allows others.

J. K. Walton makes his decision about the final lines after an examination of Lear's character and the development of the play. He concludes: 'If we take it that Lear finally believes that Cordelia is alive, we alter the direction of the whole movement which has been taking place throughout the play, a movement by which he attains to an even greater consciousness.'[1] Quite so, but in this play of reversals is there any reason to suppose Shakespeare did not 'alter the direction' himself? In the penultimate scene Gloucester reverses a parallel 'movement' in the subplot, and in this play subplot often mirrors main plot. In fact, as J. Stampfer points out, Gloucester's death 'twixt two extremes of passion' can parallel Lear dying torn between his realisation of death and hope of life.[2] The play provides evidence to support conflicting interpretations of Lear's last lines and it is not putting the cart before the horse to suggest that the decision we make about those lines finally determines the 'direction of the whole movement' of the play.

In performance what the audience see during Lear's death speech plays a major part in determining this decision. The actor responds to the change of tone after the final sonorous 'never' and there is a moment's pause as the button is undone. If this button is at Cordelia's throat, it may open to reveal the lacerations of the noose. Perhaps her mouth, to which Lear draws attention, falls open and utters 'nothing', not as a word but as an enduring silence. The relative stage positions, with the three daughters again surrounding their father, may complete the connection with the opening scene.[3] Or the button may be at Lear's throat which makes his transition to Cordelia's body logical as the king, gasping for air, remembers his hanged daughter. Lear may remember something else. After his experience of 'unaccommodated man', the 'this' to which he draws attention may be his own flesh. If a supernumerary undoes the button, the king may appear subdued and clear-eyed, but if he addresses Kent as 'Sir', the audience may see a man losing his grip on reality. At this point blocking is of crucial importance. If Lear stands close to Cordelia, or kneels clasping her, his death is at the focus of the audience's attention, but the effect is quite different if he moves away to have the button undone. Then, his insistent commands turn the attention of all onstage, and of the audience, towards the body and away from himself. The shock of his death is far greater if, as he falls, heads are turned away. The final lines may not refer to Cordelia at all. In Peter Brook's production,[4] Paul Scofield sat staring out blankly into the auditorium on his last 'look there'. In death his eyes remained open.

In his study of the play,[5] Marvin Rosenberg describes several other ways in which the death has been portrayed, but even my simplified list

---

[1] J. K. Walton, 'Lear's Last Speech', *Shakespeare Survey 13* (Cambridge 1960), p. 14.

[2] J. Stampfer, 'The Catharsis of *King Lear*', *Shakespeare Survey 13* (Cambridge, 1960), p. 4.

[3] Harley Granville-Barker noted this connection in his Preface. See *Prefaces to Shakespeare* (1947; repr. Princeton, 1965), pp. 17–18.

[4] Stratford-upon-Avon, 1962. The treatment of this moment in Brook's film of *King Lear* was quite different.

[5] Rosenberg, *The Masks of King Lear*, pp. 318–21.

makes it clear that, working from the contrary possibilities of one key speech (and I've said nothing about *how* the lines are delivered) we can create several different plays. One of them was suggested by Bradley who believed an actor should 'express, in Lear's last accents and gestures and look, an unbearable *joy*' because he thought Cordelia alive: 'To us, perhaps, the knowledge that he is deceived may bring a culmination of pain: but, if it brings *only* that, I believe we are false to Shakespeare.'[1] Some years ago, Maynard Mack argued along similar lines: 'Lear's joy in thinking that his daughter lives (if this is what his words imply) is illusory, but it is one we need not begrudge him...in a similar instance among our acquaintances, we would regard the illusion as a godsend, or even, if we were believers, as God-sent.'[2] Bradley was a believer: 'Let us renounce the world, hate it, and lose it gladly. The only real thing in it is the soul, with its courage, patience and devotion. And nothing outward can touch that.'[3] This is magnificent, but it is essentially the response of a reader who has divorced the play's meaning from its immediate effect in the theatre. Despite his insistence on the dramatic context, Reibetanz does something similar when he states: 'we should see Cordelia possesses everything that is genuinely worth having'. Perhaps we 'should', but I can't believe many spectators do.

Bradley, Mack and Reibetanz all share an assumption vital for their readings of the play: that the audience view Lear's final moments from a position of relative detachment and are, therefore, fully aware of the true facts of the situation. But what if the audience share the king's uncertainty? If they too look at Cordelia expecting some sign of life and find none as Lear falls, they are unlikely to view his death as a 'godsend' or to acknowledge that Cordelia has 'everything'. The audience may feel *they* have nothing.

King Lear opens with a discussion about an impossible choice:

Kent. I thought the King had more affected the Duke of Albany than Cornwall.
Gloucester. It did always seem so to us; but now, in the division of the kingdom, it appears not which of the Dukes he values most; for equalities are so weigh'd that curiosity in neither can make choice of either's moiety. (I, i, 1-7)

Two possibilities are equalised and the play opens on a note of uncertainty. As the action develops, questions of 'choice' and 'value' become of paramount importance and the uncertainty intensifies, as Shakespeare leads the audience ever deeper into a world where they too must choose. Marvin Rosenberg suggests 'The *Lear* world is a world of uncertainties',[4] but these uncertainties do not just exist within the play, they are generated within the audience. Shakespeare continually confounds their expectations and, at times, makes it almost impossible for them to determine what is happening onstage and why. The uncertainty that results reaches its climax in the final moments of the play. A full substantiation of these claims would require a great deal more space than this essay permits, so I will limit myself to a detailed analysis of part of act IV scene vi, Gloucester's fall from Dover cliff, and then return to the moment of Lear's death to offer an alternative to Reibetanz's 'affirmative' reading.[5]

[1] Bradley, *Shakespearean Tragedy*, p. 241.
[2] Maynard Mack, *King Lear in Our Time* (1966), p. 116.
[3] Bradley, *Shakespearean Tragedy*, p. 273.
[4] Rosenberg, *The Masks of King Lear*, p. 6.
[5] In what follows I attempt to see the play from the viewpoint of a spectator who knows nothing of *King Lear* in order to recover something of its initial effect. I am indebted to Marvin Rosenberg's concept of the 'naive spectator' which he used in his work on the play, but did not describe in full until his recent study of *Macbeth* (*The Masks of Macbeth*, Berkeley, 1978). While I owe much to his insights and method, I think his approach holds some dangers – he stages the play before audiences who have never seen it before,

The scene on Dover cliff caused Bradley to make an uncharacteristic point: 'contrary to expectation, it is not, if properly acted, in the least absurd on the stage'. He added: 'The imagination and the feelings have been worked upon with such effect...that we are unconscious of the grotesqueness of the incident for common sense.'[1] Modern criticism has moved the other way. After G. Wilson Knight's formative essay 'King Lear and the Comedy of the Grotesque',[2] the elements Bradley denied, the grotesque and the absurd, are those that are emphasised. Jan Kott has even read the scene in terms of contemporary absurd drama.[3]

How does the scene affect an audience? Do the spectators believe Gloucester is at the edge of a cliff? Alan C. Dessen gives a representative answer: 'the fictional nature of the plummet from the cliff would be obvious to the audience'.[4] Admittedly, in performance, the fact that there is no cliff is usually made obvious, but it strikes me that the working of the scene depends on our remaining confused about the existence of cliff and sea.[5] Obviously, what the spectators see onstage is of primary importance. John Cranford Adams required some form of visual illusion and suggested that at the Globe Gloucester climbed a ramp – the property 'mossbank' – and several other critics have felt the need for a symbolic indication of height.[6] Jan Kott is content with a flat stage: 'Edgar...lifts his feet high pretending to walk uphill. Gloster too lifts his feet as if expecting the ground to rise, but underneath his foot there is only air.'[7] Neither the property nor the pantomime is necessary and without them the scene achieves a powerful ambivalence.

As it opens Gloucester poses the question about their true location:

Gloucester.
When shall I come to th' top of that same hill?
Edgar.
You do climb up it now; look how we labour.

Gloucester.
Methinks the ground is even.
Edgar.   Horrible steep:
Hark! do you hear the sea?
Gloucester.   No, truly.
Edgar.
Why, then your other senses grow imperfect
By your eyes' anguish.   (IV, vi, 1–6)

Of course, on the platform stage the 'ground' is 'even' and we could point to the exaggeration on 'horrible' as a clue that what Edgar states is untrue, but there is an obvious disagreement and, unless he is given some clear visual indication by the actor playing Edgar, a spectator unfamiliar with the play could not be

his 'naive spectators', and then questions them about their reactions. He probably takes into account changes in language, culture, theatrical traditions and architecture that all modify the play's effect, but even his word 'naive' is revealing. I assume the original spectators were far from this. I assume they recognised references to other plays and to contemporary events and that their expectations of the probable development of a play they were attending were moulded as much by their experience of similar plays, as by the play in hand. Shakespeare, like any dramatist working in a living tradition, could depend on this. He traded on their sophistication rather than their naivete.

[1] Bradley, *Shakespearean Tragedy*, p. 203.
[2] G. Wilson Knight, *The Wheel of Fire* (1930).
[3] Jan Kott, *Shakespeare Our Contemporary* (1967).
[4] Alan C. Dessen, 'Two Falls and a Trap', *English Literary Renaissance*, 5 (1975), pp. 291–307, p. 303.
[5] See my 'G. Wilson Knight and "Gloucester's Leap"', *Essays in Criticism*, 23 (1973), pp. 198–200.
[6] John Cranford Adams, 'The Original Staging of *King Lear*', *Folger Shakespeare Library Joseph Quincey Adams Memorial Studies* (1948), p. 330. Alvin B. Kernan favours a 'low step', 'Formalism and Realism in Elizabethan Drama: the Miracles of *King Lear*', *Renaissance Drama*, 9 (1966), p. 60. Waldo F. McNeir prefers a fall from 'a booth stage', 'The Staging of the Dover Cliff Scene in *King Lear*', *Studies in English Renaissance Drama*, ed. McNeir (Baton Rouge, 1962), p. 97. Harry Levin opts for 'a single step or a low platform', 'The Heights and the Depths: a scene from *King Lear*', *More Talking of Shakespeare*, ed. John Garrett (New York, 1959), p. 98. Dessen has a useful discussion of all these views and he favours a flat stage.
[7] Kott, *Shakespeare Our Contemporary*, pp. 112–13.

sure. Then follows Edgar's long and vividly descriptive speech on the view from the cliff. On the bare Jacobean stage with its scant properties, Shakespeare often sketches the scenery for the audience in a similar way. Normally, there is a consensus of opinion: what one character sees the others see and the audience therefore know the scene is as described. Here, Shakespeare uses the convention to secure a further effect, because Edgar describes the scene for a blind man who cannot corroborate the information. The audience are thus forced to make their own decision. Even Edgar's explanatory comment, 'Why I do trifle thus with his despair/Is done to cure it', gives no indication that the scene he described is not real, although it does raise other riddling questions. Just what is he up to? Does he intend to prevent Gloucester from jumping, or does he hope his father will change his mind if given enough time? An unfamiliar spectator may well think Edgar means to cast off his disguise at the last moment.[1] The text offers just such a possibility on Gloucester's final lines before the fall: 'If Edgar live, O, bless him!/Now, fellow, fare thee well.' Edgar remains disguised and Gloucester falls.

For Shakespeare's contemporaries the shock must have been immense, because nothing had prepared them to expect this. In the source story in Sidney's *Arcadia*, the Paphlagonian king's son refuses a request to lead his father to the edge of a cliff, and this cures the king's despair for a time. Shakespeare reverses the source and this is not the only reversal here. Would the spectators recognise in Edgar and Gloucester an emblem of the Devil tempting Christ to leap down from the pinnacle of the Temple? If they did not think of this initially, they surely would later when Edgar suggests 'It was some fiend' that led Gloucester to the edge. In the Bible, the Devil promises that Christ will be unharmed if he jumps, but the whole point of the story is that Christ refuses

the temptation. This is by no means the only reversal of a religious image in the play. The greatest of them all is the reversed Pieta after Lear enters with Cordelia in his arms (the daughter has earlier associated herself with 'the Son' in an echo of Luke, ii, 49: 'O dear father,/It is thy business that I go about'). For the contemporary audience, the sight of a man damning his soul with a blessing on his lips must have had an impact it is hard for us to imagine.

At this point, then, perhaps the spectators are not struck by the 'grotesque comedy', but terrified by the possibility that Gloucester has actually fallen from a cliff. It is only now, *after the event*, that Edgar reveals it is all an illusion:

> And yet I know not how conceit may rob
> The treasury of life when life itself
> Yields to the theft; had he been where he thought
> By this had thought been past. (IV, vi, 42–5)

As Edgar has trifled with Gloucester, so Shakespeare has trifled with his audience. What he presents is so ambiguous that, to an extent, they are placed in Gloucester's situation: they too must trust the eyes and word of another, because they can't see for themselves.

Edgar's lines resolve the uncertainty about the cliff, but how are they spoken? Does he look on impassively as his father attempts suicide (did he expect him to jump?), or even though there is no real danger is he aware that he gambles with a human life? His next lines suggest the latter, as Shakespeare makes everything uncertain once more. Perhaps a man may die if he merely believes he has fallen from a cliff: 'Alive or dead?/Ho, you sir! friend! Hear you, sir! speak!' (ll. 45–6). For a moment the audience share the mounting anxiety evident in the broken rhythm, but Gloucester is not dead: 'Thus might he pass indeed; yet he revives.'

[1] Rosenberg, *The Masks of King Lear*, p. 264.

The scene is obviously a great theatrical *tour de force*, perfectly geared to the stage for which Shakespeare wrote: an open stage surrounded by the audience, on which illusion was created by the actors not by scenery. The proscenium stage is so much a part of the theatre of visual illusion that I suspect the scene can never attain its full power upon it. This may be why John D. Rosenberg finds it 'a remarkable piece of virtuoso stagecraft that does not quite come off'.[1] I don't agree, but I think his uncertainty is a direct response to Shakespeare's creation, because this scene exhibits precisely that tension created by contrary possibilities of which I spoke earlier. It strains the resources of the theatrical illusion to breaking point and there are few moments when our 'willing suspension of disbelief' is challenged so directly. How can an audience believe a flat stage is a hill? How can they believe Edgar when they know he is already involved in a deception? They are reminded of this at the scene's beginning and Gloucester's suspicion might well suggest that all Edgar states is untrue:

Edgar.
   ...your other senses grow imperfect
   By your eyes' anguish.
Gloucester.   So may it be, indeed.
   Methinks thy voice is alter'd, and thou speak'st
   In better phrase and matter than thou didst.
Edgar.
   You're much deceiv'd; in nothing am I chang'd
   But in my garments.
Gloucester.   Methinks you're better spoken.
                   (IV, vi, 5–10)

Then, as Gloucester seems on the point of some discovery, Edgar describes the view from the cliff. If his father hears the change in Edgar's voice, but doesn't hear the sea, then the sea doesn't exist. Or does it? The audience's attitude shares something of the duality of Gloucester's 'And that's true too': they half believe the cliff is real while half suspecting it is all an illusion. John Cranford Adams comes close to my perception of their double-vision: 'listening with Gloucester's ears the audience will share his illusion...Looking with Edgar's eyes, however, they will know that no precipice exists.' This expresses something of the tension I find in the scene, but for Adams the balance has already settled: 'Never for a moment is the audience expected to believe that Edgar has brought Gloucester to the edge of the Cliffs.'[2] My point is that the scene precludes such certainty. Until after the fall, Shakespeare does not allow the audience to make up their minds.

The *tour de force* continues as Edgar convinces his father that everything the audience suspected was real, is real indeed. There is much more that could be said of this amazing piece of theatre, but I want especially to note the way Shakespeare leaves the audience in uncertainty for so long and then allows them to witness a character who seemed dead return to life.

The final appearance of Lear with his daughter in his arms is an enormously powerful image. It has become a theatrical tradition that the severed noose hangs from Cordelia's neck, but the tradition begs the question: do the audience believe she is dead? The direction in both Quarto and Folio, 'Enter Lear with Cordelia in his arms', leaves this question open, but the reader of a modern edition may find the issue prejudiced by editors who follow Rowe and insert the word 'dead' after 'Cordelia'. In the theatre there are no such signposts.

The preparations for Lear's last entrance have been carefully made. Edgar's return from the battle (v, ii) is the first of a series of shock entrances that culminate in the king's final appearance. From this point, Shakespeare creates tension between an awareness of impending catastrophe and the possibility of a 'happy' resolution. As John Reibetanz suggests, the audience are 'suspended between hope and

[1] Rosenberg, 'King Lear and his Comforters', p. 142.
[2] Adams, 'The Original Staging of *King Lear*', p. 330.

despair' because 'Shakespeare invites a kind of double perspective: we follow the action as it progresses towards both its actual and its possible conclusions.' This seems to me exactly right, but Reibetanz adds: 'and we wait with some anxiety for the final stroke that will determine the shape of the whole'.[1] No audience in the theatre remains so detached: during this scene of mounting suspense, their emotion is intense. At the end, detachment is precisely what they are denied.

As the last scene opens, Shakespeare establishes the dual response the action will continue to evoke. Lear's 'birds i' th' cage' speech inspires hope, but while they respond to the beauty of the words, the audience remain aware of another listener, Edmund. His presence casts doubt on Lear's vision – he has already announced that the king 'Shall never see' Albany's pardon (v, i, 65–8) – and he interrupts with the voice of stark reality: 'Take them away' (v, iii, 19). Tension mounts throughout the scene as the pendulum swings between hope and despair. Immediately after Edmund despatches the murderer, hopes revive when Albany demands the captives, only to be damned again by Edmund's politic answer:

> . . . they are ready
> To-morrow, or at further space, t'appear
> Where you shall hold your session. At this time
> We sweat and bleed . . .   (v, iii, 53–6)

and the Captain has instructions to act 'instantly'. Albany maintains the possibility that 'right may thrive' by arresting Edmund and offering to fight himself, if the challenger fails to appear. As he predicted, the forces of evil begin to prey on one another as Regan succumbs to Goneril's poison, but what has happened to Lear and Cordelia? The question remains unanswered as Shakespeare creates other sources of suspense and uncertainty. The challenger must 'appear *by* the third sound of the trumpet'.[2] The trumpet sounds, but no one appears. As Albany is about

to step forward, a trumpet sounds within and a man in armour enters. A spectator unfamiliar with the play may guess this is Edgar, but he cannot be sure, even when he hears this master-of-many-voices speak. After Lear's unexpected defeat, the audience must wonder whether the challenger can win. In his film version, Peter Brook imaged the uncertainty by dressing the brothers in identical armour, so it was impossible to distinguish which was which. Albany's cry 'Save him! save him!' (l. 151) is certainly given point if he cannot determine who is down.

Edgar's victory boosts the audience's hopes, but the unrepentant Edmund tips the balance the other way:

> What you have charg'd me with, that have I done,
> And more, much more; the time will bring it out:
> 'Tis past, and so am I.   (v, iii, 162–4)

Perhaps it is already too late. The possibility of salvation recedes during Edgar's long explanatory speech, and the audience are torn 'twixt two extremes of passion' as they hear Edmund's tantalising response to the news of Gloucester's death:

> This speech of yours has mov'd me,
> And shall perchance do good; but speak you on;
> You look as you had something more to say.
>   (v, iii, 199–201)

Edgar seems to be about to announce the king's fate:

> This would have seem'd a period
> To such as love not sorrow; but another,
> To amplify too much, would make much more,
> And top extremity.
> Whilst I was big in clamour came there in a man
>   (v, iii, 204–8)

but he brought no news of Lear. It was Kent who, like Gloucester, breaks under the power of emotion: 'His grief grew puissant, and the strings of life/Began to crack' (ll. 216–17).

---

[1] Reibetanz, *The Lear World*, p. 115.

[2] The Folio reading. In the Quarto, no trumpet answers within and Edgar enters '*at* the third sound'. The business recorded in Folio seems calculated to increase suspense.

Edgar 'left him tranc'd' and the audience suspect he has joined the growing ranks of death. Suddenly a man rushes on with a bloody knife and Shakespeare engineers the moment so the audience think Cordelia is dead, but it is Goneril's death he announces, so hope remains. Then comes an even more startling entrance: Kent appears. As the climax approaches, hope and despair are held in almost simultaneous opposition and Kent's entrance is a case in point. It promotes hope because he has returned from the brink of death, and if he can others may, but his words provoke despair because he has only returned to die: 'I am come/To bid my king and master aye good night.' Albany remembers what the audience have never forgotten, but there is a pause while the bodies of Goneril and Regan are brought on and then continuing confusion and delay:

Edmund.   Quickly send,
   Be brief in it, to th' castle; for my writ
   Is on the life of Lear and on Cordelia.
   Nay, send in time.
Albany.   Run, run! O, run!
Edgar.
   To who, my Lord? Who has the office? send
   Thy token of reprieve.
Edmund.
   Well thought on: take my sword,
   Give it the captain.
Edgar.   Haste thee, for thy life.
                (v, iii, 244–51)

Just when it seems Lear and Cordelia will be saved, the king makes his final entrance. John Reibetanz believes: 'Shakespeare has... prepared us for the play's final, pitiful tableau by associating Cordelia with Christ: the mortal result of "my father's business" was the best known fact of Renaissance spiritual life.'[1] I would have thought the best known fact of spiritual life was the resurrection rather than the crucifixion. Christianity depends upon the fact that the dead Christ in Mary's arms will rise again. I am not suggesting that Cordelia is a

Christ-figure, merely that the tension created by the reversed Pieta stems from an emblem of death that contains a promise of rebirth. The audience are reminded of this when Lear says, if Cordelia lives 'It is a chance which does redeem all sorrows' (l. 266). Reibetanz locates many elements from Romance literature which relate *King Lear* to the Last Plays, and the possibility of a return to life, which is realised in those plays, is precisely the connection. Throughout the remainder of the scene, the possibility that Cordelia lives remains open and the audience continue to alternate between hope and despair. In this world of uncertainty, this is the greatest uncertainty of all. As I suggested earlier, Lear's speeches reveal a pattern of assertions, qualifications and contradictions (a familiar pattern in this play of reversed expectations) and this creates the audience's ambivalent response. Shakespeare's contemporaries must have wondered whether Cordelia would revive for a moment as Desdemona had done. In this play there are two precedents for a return to life: Gloucester's revival from a state resembling death,[2] and Kent's recovery from his trance.

The counter-argument is that Lear's confusion is not shared by the audience, because they do not view the scene through his eyes. However, the onlooker's comments provide little guidance. Kent and Edgar voice the audience's confusion: 'Is this the promis'd end?' 'Or image of that horror?' Albany is almost speechless: 'Fall and cease' and after this no one except Lear comments on Cordelia. During the dialogue between Kent and Lear, references to death accumulate: Lear 'kill'd the slave' who was hanging his daughter; Caius is 'dead and

---

[1] Reibetanz, *The Lear World*, p. 111.
[2] Notably Lear's awaking in the 'reconciliation scene' echoes Gloucester's words at Dover: *Gloucester*. 'Away, and let me die.' (IV, vi, 48); *Lear*. 'You do me wrong to take me out o' th' grave' (IV, vii, 45), so we might cite this as yet another precedent for a return to life.

rotten' (but no, he has returned from the grave as Kent); Goneril and Regan are dead and so is Edmund. At exactly the point where the spectators decide it is all over and Cordelia is dead, there is, as John Shaw suggests, a typical concluding speech. 'The wheel has come full circle' as Albany resigns the crown with an echo of Lear's opening words. The speech appears to move towards the concluding couplet:

> All friends shall taste
> The wages of their virtue, and all foes
> The cup of their deservings *bitter woes*[1]

but the couplet is broken: 'O! see, see!' and Lear delivers his final shattering speech with its unbearable, unanswerable, question: 'Why should a dog, a horse, a rat, have life,/And thou no breath at all?' (ll. 306–7). As I suggested in the beginning, again he moves from certainty to uncertainty, from despair to hope. For an audience who have been involved in a similar process, his death is a moment of absolute confusion. Even as they direct their attention to Cordelia, Lear falls. If for a second their hopes of life were reviving, this is the cruelest reversal in the play. Reibetanz believes they view 'Lear's final moments' 'through the steady eyes of Edgar', but the only steady eyes, as it turns out, belong to Kent. Edgar does not believe Lear is dead and his impulse is to hope for life: Kent on the contrary prays for death. The opposition is typical of the play. While the audience agree with Kent that Lear has suffered enough, they share Edgar's hopes and may even hear echoes of his words over Gloucester at Dover (the stage positions may complete the connection):

Edgar.   He faints! My Lord, my Lord!
Kent.
    Break, heart; I prithee, break!
Edgar.   Look up, my Lord.
Kent.
    Vex not his ghost: O! let him pass; he hates him
    That would on the rack of this tough world
    Stretch him out longer.   (v, iii, 311–15)

When Edgar decides 'He is gone, indeed' and Albany gives the order 'Bear them from hence', the audience are finally certain: it is finished. They are wrong. Shakespeare creates one last vivid image. Albany removes the crown from his head (this is Marvin Rosenberg's fine reading)[2] and says: 'Friends of my soul, you twain/Rule in this realm, and the gor'd state sustain.' Do Kent and Edgar stand each with a hand on the crown in a repetition of the moment in scene one (l. 139) when Albany and Cornwall did likewise? The play has demonstrated the terrible results of that first division of power and now there is a second. Or is there? Kent's final speech is usually played as his refusal of the crown (after all, he opposed the original division of power) and Edgar's speech is often a reluctant acceptance. There is a marked contrast between Kent's thoughts on death and Edgar's on youth, but the young man's words may imply he also refuses. The play ends as it began on a note of uncertainty:

Kent.
    I have a journey, sir, shortly to go;
    My master calls me, I must not say no.
Edgar.
    The weight of this sad time we must obey;
    Speak what we feel, not what we ought to say.
    The oldest hath borne most: we that are young
    Shall never see so much, nor live so long.

                      (v, iii, 321–6)

There is no emphasis on the restoration of order and no expressed hope in the future. On the contrary, the lines emphasise a general sense of diminution. With Lear's death something irreplaceable has gone out of the world and those who remain are smaller beings who can 'never see so much, nor live so long'. As the death march sounds, death finally holds dominion over all.

John Reibetanz believes: 'Edgar's desire to "Speak what we feel, not what we ought to

---

[1] John Shaw, '*King Lear:* The Final Lines', *Essays in Criticism*, 16 (1966), pp. 261–7, p. 264.
[2] Rosenberg, *The Masks of King Lear*, p. 322.

say"...shows that he has recognized the great value that resides in Cordelia's plainness, as opposed to her sisters' pleasing surfaces; and his words bring us to the same recognition.'[1] It would be remarkable if Edgar reached such a conclusion, since he has neither heard Cordelia speak nor occupied the stage with her until the final scene. The idea that any audience can sit back and respond with such 'clear-eyed moral insight and judgement'[2] strikes me as equally remarkable. Dr Johnson offers an excellent description of what happens at a performance of *King Lear* and it is ironic that he is describing the effect on a reader. The play, he says, 'fill[s] the mind with a perpetual tumult of indignation, pity, and hope...So powerful is the current of the poet's imagination that the mind which once ventures within it is hurried irresistibly along.'[3] The comment seems particularly applicable to the final scene, and it is this 'tumult' that precludes the affirmation for which some critics argue.

Bradley concluded that we realise 'our whole attitude in asking or expecting that goodness should be prosperous is wrong; that, if only we could see things as they are, we should see that the outward is nothing and the inward is all.'[4] Fine sentiments, but the audience can't 'see things as they are', can't even determine whether or not Cordelia lives, so how can they feel she is 'set free from life'?[5] For Bradley (and Reibetanz who follows him almost exactly) 'what happens to such a being does not matter; all that matters is what she is'.[6] This distinction is crucial to both critics' arguments, but it is one no spectator makes. For Bradley, Cordelia is 'a *thing* enskyed and sainted' (my emphasis),[7] but the dramatic structure Shakespeare creates ensures that the audience care intensely about what happens to her.

In an excellent essay, Nicholas Brooke accounts for the response of the affirming critics in terms of the kind of duality I've explored: 'Action and reaction are equal and opposite...

the sense of life in the presentation of death is the source of all this impulse to affirm.'[8] I would rather say 'the *possibility* of *continuing* life', because it is precisely because Shakespeare never takes up this possibility that some critics (like Tate before them) feel they must. As Brooke suggests: 'Hope springs eternal. It had better.'[9]

In the face of the uncertainty generated by the ending, it is natural to seek refuge in a dependable personal value, and it is because the play leaves the contraries unresolved that it forces us to look within ourselves and find there what we can. John Reibetanz believes '*King Lear* directs us to a realm of meaning that exists outside the *Lear* world'[10] and for him this meaning is Christian, but where the play directs us depends upon where we have the desire and the capacity to go. Shakespeare has left us with no single signpost. The play provokes a choice, but it makes none. However, while we may argue that the contraries remain unresolved and the questions unanswered, we should beware of suggesting that *King Lear* is, in our modern sense, 'open-ended'. Even Bradley admitted that pessimism is 'what we feel at times in reading'[11] and in performance this feeling is a great deal more pronounced because of the tension of uncertainty.

---

[1] Reibetanz, *The Lear World*, p. 121.

[2] Goldberg's comment on those who ignore the effects of performance and stress 'self-knowledge attained through suffering', p. 156.

[3] *Dr Johnson on Shakespeare*, ed. W. K. Wimsatt (Harmondsworth, 1969), p. 125.

[4] Bradley, *Shakespearean Tragedy*, p. 272.

[5] *Ibid.*, p. 270.

[6] *Ibid.*, pp. 271–2.

[7] *Ibid.*, p. 264.

[8] Nicholas Brooke, 'The Ending of *King Lear*', in *Shakespeare 1564–1964*, ed. E. A. Bloom (Providence, R. I., 1964), p. 87.

[9] *Ibid.*, p. 87.

[10] Reibetanz, *The Lear World*, p. 120.

[11] Bradley, *Shakespearean Tragedy*, p. 228.

'THE TAMING OF THE SHREW' AND 'KING LEAR': A STRUCTURAL COMPARISON

STANLEY WELLS

In this essay, I wish to suggest that, in writing two of his plays, Shakespeare was more than usually aware of the sometimes complementary, sometimes opposing functions of the mind and the body in human life; and that this awareness may be discerned in the layout of the narrative – the overall design – in the characterisation, and in the language: not simply the diction, but also the choice of sentiments to be uttered. I do not suggest that a reliance on these concepts accounts for every aspect of the plays' structure, nor that Shakespeare may not have had other guiding principles, too. But I hope that an analysis of the plays with these ideas in mind may tell us something about how they are made; I hope, too, that the juxtaposition of two essentially very different plays may also be fruitful.

The relationship between mind, or soul, and body was a common topic in Renaissance writings about religion, philosophy, morality, and physiology.[1] There is, to give just one example, an essay about it in Plutarch's *Moralia* which, interestingly enough, first appeared in English translation (by Philemon Holland) in 1603, shortly before the composition of *King Lear*, though I can find no evidence of direct relationship. Shakespeare has many glancing references to the theme, and some longer treatments of it. The plays with which I am concerned are not the only ones to which, I believe, it can provide a useful critical approach. I have chosen them for two main reasons. One is that in them the theme is exceptionally

evident in verbal details, so that the critic is less susceptible to the charge of reading between the lines; the other is that the juxtaposition of an early play in which design is relatively close to the surface, and a late one, in which the technique is far less readily apparent, seems to me to provide an insight into Shakespeare's creative processes.

In writing of *The Taming of the Shrew*, I shall be concerned with a fairly simple dualism of mind and body. But in *King Lear*, though 'body' will remain more or less constant, 'mind' will need to be extended to a range of meanings stretching as far as those usually signified by 'soul'. This appears to be justified by Shakespeare's own usage. Sometimes in him, as in other writers, we can discern a clear distinction between 'mind' referring to purely intellectual powers, and 'soul' referring to purely spiritual ones. But at other times the concepts merge: one of *OED*'s definitions of 'mind' is 'the soul as distinguished from the body' (III, 17), and one of its definitions of 'soul' is 'Intellectual insight or spiritual development; high development of the mental faculties', with a first quotation from *Othello* ('these fellows have some soul': I, i, 54). So in *Love's Labour's Lost* – which, indeed, might be regarded as an extended treatment of the topos – we have 'The mind shall banquet, though the body pine' (I, i, 25), a statement which has its spiritual counterpart in

[1] See e.g. chapter 14, 'Body and Soul', of Paul H. Kocher's *Science and Religion in Elizabethan England* (New York, 1953).

the metaphysical Sonnet 146: 'Then, soul, live thou upon thy servant's [that is, the body's] loss,/And let that *pine* to aggravate thy store'. But in the grossly physical Sonnet 151, *soul* seems to encompass intellectual as well as spiritual powers: 'My soul doth tell my body that he may/Triumph in love; flesh stays no farther reason...'. And in *2 Henry IV*, 'soul' could be substituted for 'mind' in the lines

> ...the Bishop
> Turns insurrection to religion.
> Suppos'd sincere and holy in his thoughts,
> He's follow'd both with body and with mind.
>
> (I, i, 200–3)[1]

Of all Shakespeare's plays the early comedies are those in which structural patterns can be most readily discerned. We think of the double quartets of lovers in *Love's Labour's Lost*, the two pairs of twins in *The Comedy of Errors*, the master–servant juxtapositions of *The Two Gentlemen of Verona*, and the double pairs of lovers in *A Midsummer Night's Dream*. *The Taming of the Shrew* is a little more difficult to discuss in these terms because of a textual problem. We cannot be certain whether the episodes involving Christopher Sly form a framework enveloping the main action, or whether that action emerges from them, like a butterfly from a chrysalis, never to return. But in any case, there is undoubtedly a relationship between these episodes and the play proper. Let us look at this for a moment in the light of the concepts of the mind and the body. These concepts are very prominent in the opening action. Initially, Christopher Sly is seen very much as a body, unanimated by a mind, scarcely even by breath:

> What's here? One dead, or drunk? See, doth
>   he breathe?   (Induction, i, 29)

The trick that the Lord devises to play upon him will work, by means of mainly physical properties, upon his mind. 'The beggar' will then be made to 'forget himself', to suppose that the body which he inhabits belongs in fact to someone else, 'a mighty lord'. The actors who help to put the trick into execution are, in doing so, obliged to exercise their own minds to control their bodies; indeed, as their leader reminds the Lord, they make a speciality of this:

> Fear not, my Lord; we can contain ourselves,
> Were he the veriest antic in the world.
>
> (Induction, i, 98–9)

They are professionals. Bartholomew, the Lord's page, is only an amateur. In case his mind cannot produce the requisite changes in his behaviour and appearance, he is to have external help:

> An onion will do well for such a shift,
> Which, in a napkin being close conveyed,
> Shall in despite enforce a watery eye.
>
> (Induction, i, 124–6)

In these episodes we are shown something of the power of art to deceive the mind and thus to influence the body, and this underlying basis of the action is made explicit in a curious image. The Lord and his servingmen offer to show Sly pictures which will seem like reality. All will be 'As lively painted as the deed was done'; indeed, it seems, the reality of the painting will not merely deceive Sly, but will affect the characters within the paintings themselves; they will show Sly

> ...Daphne roaming through a thorny wood,
> Scratching her legs, that one shall swear she bleeds
> And at that sight shall sad Apollo weep,
> So workmanly the blood and tears are drawn.
>
> (Induction, ii, 55–8)

Once Sly's metamorphosis is complete, the transition to the play proper is made in terms which again emphasise the power of mind over matter: Sly's doctors think it proper for him to see a comedy.

[1] All references are to the *Complete Works*, ed. Peter Alexander (London and Glasgow, 1951).

Seeing too much sadness hath congeal'd your blood,
And melancholy is the nurse of frenzy.
Therefore they thought it good you hear a play
And frame your mind to mirth and merriment,
Which bars a thousand harms and lengthens life.

(Induction, ii, 129–33)

These terms are interestingly like the claims made in preliminaries to Elizabethan works, such as the Epistle to Dekker's *The Shoemaker's Holiday*, in which, it is said, 'nothing is purposed but mirth. Mirth lengtheneth long life...'. So, perhaps consciously, we are prepared to see what follows as a work of art in itself. At any rate, the power of art to work on the body as well as the mind is re-stated at the beginning of the play-within-the-play, when Tranio advises Lucentio that, while it is all very well to 'admire/This virtue and this moral discipline', he should also use 'music and poesy' to 'quicken' him (I, i, 29–30, 36).

It is, however, in the 'taming' plot itself that the concepts of mind and body are most clearly of structural importance. Petruchio is mentally independent, so confident in his self-knowledge that he declares himself impervious to physical imperfections in his wife:

Be she as foul as was Florentius' love,
As old as Sibyl, and as curst and shrewd
As Socrates' Xanthippe or a worse –
She moves me not, or not removes, at least,
Affection's edge in me, were she as rough
As are the swelling Adriatic seas.   (I, ii, 67–72)

(The same idea is reinforced, in more generalised metaphors, at I, ii, 196 ff.: 'Think you a little din can daunt my ears...'). But Petruchio, in approaching Baptista with his request for permission to woo Kate, claims that he is moved mostly by mental qualities:

I am a gentleman of Verona, sir,
That, hearing of her beauty and her wit,
Her affability and bashful modesty,
Her wondrous qualities and mild behaviour,
Am bold to show myself a forward guest
Within your house...   (II, i, 47–52)

And initially, in soliloquy, he announces his determination to overcome her expected resistance to him through an exercise of his mind:

Say that she rail; why, then I'll tell her plain
She sings as sweetly as a nightingale.
Say that she frown; I'll say she looks as clear
As morning roses newly wash'd with dew.
Say she be mute, and will not speak a word;
Then I'll commend her volubility,
And say she uttereth piercing eloquence.

(II, i, 169–75)

This is, I take it, a key speech, placed as it is immediately before the first of the wooing scenes, and giving the audience insight into the way that Petruchio's mind is working. It provides an important perspective on the action, inclining us to see the taming process primarily from his point of view. And at this stage there is no suggestion that he will work on Kate by physical means. Except for a mild scuffle or two, his wooing is carried out in a combat of wits. Kate succumbs to it with unexplained ease – again the dramatic perspective favours Petruchio – and not until he is in church does he begin to exercise physical violence, as we hear in Gremio's description of the wedding. By now it is, surely, not merely easy but essential for the audience to understand that this is part of an act that Petruchio is putting on, just as the Lord and his gentlemen had put on an act to transmogrify Christopher Sly, and as the Lord had instructed the actors to behave before Sly. This it is that enables Petruchio to retain our sympathy. The physically aggressive behaviour stems from mental calculation of a good-humoured and benevolent kind.

The taming process itself, which begins with the marriage, takes place in two major stages, one of them aimed at subduing Kate's body, the second at taming her mind. That this has, so far as I can tell, been little remarked may be simply because it surely needs little demonstration. In the first stage, Petruchio carries Kate bodily away from her father's home; he causes her to undergo the physical tribulations, memorably catalogued by Grumio, of the journey to his home; and he knocks his servants around in her presence, throwing food and dishes at them. Again, the action is put in a perspective favourable to Petruchio by a soliloquy – or more properly, perhaps, a monologue addressed to the audience – in which he reminds us of the calculatedness of his behaviour – 'Thus have I politicly begun my reign' (IV, i, 172–95) – in which he compares Kate to a falcon which he is taming, outlines the next stage of his campaign, and claims the audience's sympathy by saying

> . . . amid this hurly I intend
> that all is done in reverend care of her

and by asking, disarmingly,

> He that knows better how to tame a shrew
> Now let him speak; 'tis charity to show.

The next stage of the taming story continues the physical process. Kate ruefully sums up the technique before it begins:

> . . . I . . .
> Am starv'd for meat, giddy for lack of sleep;
> With oaths kept waking, and with brawling fed;
> And that which spites me more than all these wants –
> He does it under name of perfect love.
>
> (IV, iii, 7–12)

After these recapitulatory and anticipatory passages, the taming begins again, as Kate is deprived first of food, then of new clothes; and this stage in the process comes almost to its end with the long speech of Petruchio, addressed to Kate, in which he draws a moral in terms which bring the ideas that I have been tracing explicitly to the play's surface:

> Well, come, my Kate; we will unto your father's
> Even in these honest mean habiliments;
> Our purses shall be proud, our garments poor;
> For 'tis the mind that makes the body rich;
> And as the sun breaks through the darkest clouds,
> So honour peereth in the meanest habit.
>
> (IV, iii, 165–70)

The tone is different from Sonnet 146, but the idea is the same: 'Within be fed, without be rich no more.'

Petruchio continues in this vein at some length, stressing the importance of inherent qualities rather than superficial ones. His long speech marks a turn in both the action and Petruchio's technique. In the coda of the scene, Shakespeare gently prefigures the next stage, as Kate contradicts Petruchio's statement that ''tis now some seven o'clock', and receives her warning from him:

> I will not go to-day; and ere I do,
> It shall be what o'clock I say it is.
>
> (IV, iii, 190–1)

Hortensio's closing line – 'Why, so this gallant will command the sun' – is also deliberately anticipatory. Now Petruchio is to work on Kate's mind and, even more importantly, on her imagination. He calls the sun the moon, Kate contradicts him, and he gives orders to return; but Kate is beginning to learn how to deal with him:

> Forward, I pray, since we have come so far,
> And be it moon, or sun, or what you please;
> And if you please to call it a rush-candle,
> Henceforth I vow it shall be so for me.
>
> (IV, v, 12–15)

It is a spirited reply, in its acknowledgement of absurdity. Petruchio puts her through her paces:

Petruchio.
  I say it is the moon.
Katherina.   I know it is the moon.
Petruchio.
  Nay, then you lie. It is the blessed sun.
Katherina.
  Then, God be bless'd, it is the blessed sun;
  But sun it is not, when you say it is not;
  And the moon changes even as your mind.
  What you will have it nam'd, even that it is,
  And so it shall be so for Katherine. (IV, v, 16–22)

There is a new-found articulacy in Kate's style here; and is there not something of a dig, not wholly submissive, at Petruchio in 'the moon changes even as your mind'? – it was, after all, women's minds that were proverbially as changeable as the moon.[1]

But Hortensio, at least, feels confident enough to congratulate Petruchio – 'the field is won' – and the next episode reveals Kate not merely concurring with her husband in patent absurdity, but entering with full imaginative commitment into what now seems more like a game than a display of the results of brainwashing, as she addresses old Vincentio as 'Young budding virgin, fair and fresh and sweet...' (IV, v, 36). This time she agrees immediately when Petruchio contradicts her, claiming that she has been 'bedazzled with the sun', and the episode passes off harmoniously. It remains simply for Kate to demonstrate her affection for her husband in public, and this she does, after a momentary flinching, with 'Nay, I will give thee a kiss; now pray thee, love, stay' (v, i, 133).

Behind my remarks lies a purpose which is to some degree secondary; to demonstrate that the 'taming' process is one which brings Katherine to a full realisation of her potentialities as a woman[2] rather than, as some interpreters would have it, being analogous to a process of brainwashing, crushing her into cowed submission. But my primary purpose has been, perhaps, a simpler one, a demonstration of what may well seem entirely obvious: that the structuring of this process can objectively be stated to be based on a design which has as its basic components the body and the mind, and that this finds its reflection also in other parts of the play.

I move with trepidation from the relatively simple pattern of The Taming of the Shrew to the far more complex structure which is King Lear; but I take encouragement from the fact that the tragedy has generally been thought to be exceptionally schematic, at least by comparison with most of Shakespeare's other, later plays. It is, we are often told, his only tragedy to have a fully-developed subplot; the action is stylised; the characters divide with unusual patness into the good and the bad. A. C. Bradley summed it up by saying that in King Lear Shakespeare's imagination tended 'to analyse and abstract, to decompose human nature into its constituent factors, and then to construct beings in whom one or more of these factors is absent...' This is, as he says, 'a tendency which produces symbols, allegories, personifications of qualities and abstract ideas; and we are accustomed to think it quite foreign to Shakespeare's genius, which was in the highest degree concrete. No doubt in the main we are right here; but it is hazardous to set limits to that genius.' Bradley is here commenting on the bases of Shakespeare's portrayal of character in this play, but he goes on to extend his observation to refer to the imagery, in particular to 'the idea of monstrosity' and to 'the incessant references to the lower animals and man's likeness to them'. The influence of such a technique is, says Bradley, 'to convey to us... the wider or universal significance of the spectacle presented to the inward eye'.[3] In suggesting that in King Lear, as in The Taming of the Shrew, Shakespeare was exceptionally aware of the dualism of mind and body, I am pointing to another manifestation of the same overall tendency that Bradley discerned in this play, and one that has the same overall effect.

The presence of the dualism in the play has been often enough remarked. Richard David, for example, states it as a commonplace: 'Lear, who has erred in judgment, loses in consequence his reason, the light of his mind, while Gloucester, whose error was physical and sensual, loses his

---

[1] Cf. Love's Labour's Lost, v, ii, 212.

[2] This is well argued by Cecil C. Seronsy, '"Supposes" as the Unifying Theme in The Taming of the Shrew', Shakespeare Quarterly, XIV (1963), 15–30.

[3] Shakespearean Tragedy (1904; repr. 1957), pp. 216–20.

eyes, the light of his body'.[1] That is an acknowledgement of the importance of Shakespeare's basic decision to juxtapose the story of a man who goes mad with one who is blinded; and it was, we must feel, a decision made with a purpose. W. R. Elton, discussing the double plot, lays more emphasis on character than action: 'Among...explanations for the double plot is that which identifies in Lear and Gloucester traditional aspects of the sensitive soul: the irascible and the concupiscible matching the protagonists' anger and lechery.' He points to examples of this dualism in some of Shakespeare's immediate predecessors, and finds that Lear and Gloucester receive traditional forms of punishment: 'Lear's intellectual error of anger receives the conventional punishment of madness (*ira furor brevis*), and Gloucester's physical sin of lechery the conventional retribution of blindness.'[2]

Clearly, then, the fact that 'Gloucester's struggles are largely physical, in contrast to Lear's 'spiritual trials' is 'a commonplace',[3] and the contrast-within-resemblance between them is very apparent in the fact that the crisis of Gloucester's suffering comes when he is blinded, of Lear's, when he goes mad. I want to suggest that the contrast evident in these facets of the play's action is merely the most obvious aspect of an exploration of the relationship between mind and body which may be held to underpin the structures of the entire play. I should say immediately that the connotations of these terms are enormously greater in *King Lear* than they were in *The Taming of the Shrew*. In particular, they expand into their moral counterparts, so that the body becomes associated with the values of sensuality and materialism, and the mind with virtue and spirituality. So in speaking of this play I shall use these and similar terms without feeling a need on every occasion to refer back to my basic terminology.

The play's opening lines emphasise Glouces-ter's physicality in the chatting about the 'whoreson', Edmund. Lear, too, in his opening speech, is concerned with the body, in his case, with its decay – he is dividing the kingdom that he may 'Unburdened crawl toward death.' In the love-contest that follows there is a juxta-position of material and spiritual values in which we see that the mind needs to find expression through the body, and that in the process, the truth may be distorted: Cordelia's 'love's/More ponderous than [her] tongue', – she cannot 'heave/[her] heart into [her] mouth' – that is, her body is an inadequate repre-sentative of her mind, yet she is glad not to have her sisters' 'still-soliciting eye' and tongues; and Kent wishes that her sisters' tongues may utter 'large speeches' which their 'deeds' will 'approve', while obviously fearing that they will not; here 'deeds', physical in their action, are seen nevertheless as reflections of the mind's truth. Lear condemns Cordelia to receive her 'truth' as her 'dower': an ironical betrayal of the falseness of his own scale of values, since, as the play is to show, in spiritual terms, this is the best dowry she could have. The King of France understands this – Cordelia 'is herself' – that is, without the material bounty that her sisters have gained – 'a dowry', so, he says, 'Thee and thy virtues here I seize upon.'

The first scene thus establishes an opposition between material and spiritual values, the false and the true. Of course, Shakespeare is not portraying a total opposition between mind and body, because the mind, whether virtuous

---

[1] *Shakespeare in the Theatre* (Cambridge, 1978), p. 25.

[2] *King Lear and the Gods* (San Marino, Calif., 1966), pp. 267, 270. While identifying non-Shakespear-ian treatments of the topic, including an interesting discussion of mind and body which occurs in Chap-man's *Sir Giles Goosecap* (v, ii, 1–50), Elton does not remark its appearance in earlier plays by Shakespeare.

[3] John Reibetanz, *The Lear World* (Toronto, 1977), p. 77.

or not, must operate through the body. This is, and is seen to be, one of man's basic limitations. What Shakespeare can do, and does, is to suggest a possible disjunction between mind and body, so that some people consciously make the body's functions misrepresent their mental attitudes – they are hypocritical – and other people may be more or less successful in discerning this. Goneril and Regan exercise their tongues to misrepresent their mind's truth; Cordelia finds her tongue inadequate to represent her mind's truth; she cannot heave her heart into her mouth. Lear fails to discern the mind through the body; the Duke of Burgundy cares more for material than for spiritual good; but Kent and the King of France can see through the body's false appearances to the truth that lies within. It is perhaps a paradox that Goneril and Regan, too, can see where truth lies; indeed, this completes our sense of the consciousness of their evil: 'He always lov'd our sister most,' says Goneril, 'and with what poor judgment he hath now cast her off appears too grossly.' And Regan replies: ''Tis the infirmity of his age; yet he hath ever but slenderly known himself'. (I, i, 287–93)

Lear's confusion of values in relation to his daughters is mirrored in Gloucester's attitude to his sons, and in similar terms. Reading the letter purporting to be written by Edgar, Gloucester asks 'Had he a hand to write this? a heart and brain to breed it in?', and Edmund says 'It is his hand, my lord; but I hope his heart is not in the contents' (I, ii, 53–4, 64–5). It is a complex variation on the situation in the first scene; for Edmund, pretending to hope that Edgar's hand does not convey the truth of his heart, is in fact himself dissimulating in a manner that causes us to associate him with Goneril and Regan, Edgar with Cordelia. And Edmund's rationality, too, in his denial of supernatural influence on man's actions, also aligns him with the wicked sisters, whereas Gloucester's attribution of significance to

'These late eclipses in the sun and moon' (I, ii, 99), though naively superstitious in tone, at least suggests a mind open to persuasion.

The short first movement of the play is over by the end of the third scene. This is the exposition, of ideas as well as action. With the fourth scene, Lear's troubles begin. They seem trivial at first, merely the insolence of the servant, Oswald. But as Lear's sense of outrage increases, two characters emerge as important to him. One is Kent, his body now disguised, and determined to 'serve' where he does 'stand condemn'd'. The idea of relationship between the heart, or mind, or intention, whatever we like to call it, and the body's appearance is taken a step further. Though Kent wishes to act as his mind prompts him – that is, virtuously – he can do so only by disguising his body's reality. Goneril and Regan had looked other than they were for evil purposes; Kent does so for good. It is significant to the play's design that Kent offers practical services: 'I can keep honest counsel, ride, run, mar a curious tale in telling it, and deliver a plain message bluntly' (I, iv, 32–3). Kent, we may say without excessive over-simplification, offers Lear bodily help; and, before long, he performs it in tripping up and beating Oswald. As soon as this is established, the next phase of the scene begins, with the entrance of the Fool, the paradoxically intellectual character who works entirely through his mind, who refers to himself as 'Truth' – a 'dog' that 'must to kennel' (I, iv, 110) – and who immediately gives an extended demonstration of his ability to work obliquely, through parable and paradox, on Lear's mind.

Shakespeare's conscious design is apparent behind the scene's vivacious naturalism. The design is related to that of The Taming of the Shrew, but it is subtler and more complex. The influences on body and mind are present simultaneously, not consecutively; and Lear's problems are greater than Kate's.

An early reaction of Lear's to the discovery that his daughters may use against him the power with which he has endowed them is the suspicion that either his mind or his body is beginning to fail him; he says of himself,

> Either his notion weakens, or his discernings
> Are lethargied. (I, iv, 227–8)

In fact, of course, his mind is being forced into unaccustomed activity. The effort to restrain his anger against Cornwall and Regan pushes him to suppose that Cornwall may be unwell, and here he explicitly uses the terms with which I am concerned:

> . . . we are not ourselves
> When nature, being oppress'd, commands the mind
> To suffer with the body. (II, iv, 105–7)

The statement is more interesting in relation to the man who makes it than to its subject. Lear is beginning to learn about man's limitations, the inevitable interdependence of mind and body – a lesson that is rubbed harshly home by Regan:

> O, sir, you are old;
> Nature in you stands on the very verge
> Of her confine. (II, iv, 144–6)

But his self-control is short-lived, and in the curses into which he erupts, his images are again of different parts of the body: Goneril had 'struck' him 'with her tongue. . . upon the very heart'; her 'eyes are fierce', but Regan's 'Do comfort and not burn.' He is astonished that his body can contain his emotion: 'O sides, you are too tough' (II, iv, 158–9, 171–2, 196). Nevertheless, he will commit himself to his emotion, even though to do so also means that he must make great demands upon his body; he will

> . . . abjure all roofs and choose
> To wage against the enmity o' th' air,
> To be a comrade with the wolf and owl
> (II, iv, 207–9)

rather than betray his mind's truth by returning with Goneril. His intransigence, which is in some ways deplorable but is seen nevertheless as an essential facet of his integrity – as Cordelia's had been – resembles that of an even more fixedly intransigent character, Coriolanus, who expresses his refusal to compromise in terms of a conflict between mind and body:

> . . . I will not do't,
> Lest I surcease to honour mine own truth,
> And by my body's action teach my mind
> A most inherent baseness. (III, ii, 120–3)

The result of Coriolanus's intransigence is that for a while he lives 'Under the canopy. . . I' th' city of kites and crows' (IV, v, 38–42). Lear, too, is forced, by both external and internal pressures, to ever-increasing dependence on his own body, uncushioned by ritual, ceremony, and the comforts of the court. The process makes him question the need for such 'superfluity' – Goneril's gorgeous clothing, for instance. (Kate had been subjected to similar criticisms.) But his reiterated expressions of fear that he will go mad show his concern that the body shall continue to be guided by the mind.

Though his hundred knights melt away, Lear is never destitute of loving companionship. We could if we wished see Kent and the Fool as projections of two aspects of Lear himself: his physical strength and his striving after the truth; but to do so would reduce the play's humanity, for Kent and the Fool are individuals whose loyalty to their master shows some of the better aspects of human nature. So on the heath they remain true to their natures, and thus to Lear, the Fool labouring 'to out-jest/ His heart-struck injuries' (III, i, 16–17), Kent offering more practical help. The Fool has the more difficult task: for though Lear suffers in body, his mental anguish is greater and, paradoxically, reduces his physical pain:

> . . . When the mind's free
> The body's delicate –

that is, when one has an untroubled mind one is particularly conscious of bodily sensation – but

> ... this tempest in my mind
> Doth from my senses take all feeling else
> Save what beats there. Filial ingratitude!

Again, the offence is imaged through parts of the body:

> Is it not as this mouth should tear this hand
> For lifting food to't?

Lear's sense of having been wronged increases his determination not to submit:

> ...In such a night,
> To shut me out! Pour on; I will endure.
>
> (III, iv, 17–18)

And he is brought to a feeling of kinship with the 'Poor naked wretches' who depend on body alone. His exposure has taught him to 'feel what wretches feel' – bodily sensation is affecting the imagination – and he recognises the need for a fairer distribution of 'the super-flux'.

Plot and subplot begin to merge with the reappearance of Edgar, whose physical disguise for good motives parallels Kent's, whom he also resembles in his ingenious practicality. The Fool prophesies that bodily suffering will afflict their minds: 'This cold night will turn us all to fools and madmen' (III, iv, 77) – and although Lear strives to retain his grasp upon reality in his contemplation of Edgar's 'uncover'd body' it is at the moment that he determines to become, like Edgar, 'the thing itself', 'a poor, bare, forked animal' (III, iv, 101, 105–7), that his mind deserts him. Now he can receive only physical help, so the Fool fades out of the play. Kent's comment implies that the mind has been to some extent dependent upon the body:

> ...Oppressed nature sleeps.
> This rest might yet have balm'd thy broken sinews,
> Which, if convenience will not allow,
> Stand in hard cure.   (III, vi, 97–100)

And Lear is taken to Dover, by Gloucester, Kent and the Fool. As they go out, Edgar comments, in gnomic couplets that draw attention to their own function, on the relativeness of mental suffering, and on the fact that it can be alleviated by companionship and by comparison:

> When we our betters see bearing our woes,
> We scarcely think our miseries our foes.
> Who alone suffers suffers most i' th' mind,
> Leaving free things and happy shows behind;
> But then the mind much sufferance doth o'erskip
> When grief hath mates, and bearing fellowship.
> How light and portable my pain seems now,
> When that which makes me bend makes the King bow.
>
> (III, vi, 102–9)

The action turns immediately from the mental to the physical; from the maddening of Lear to the blinding of Gloucester. This is the area of the play in which the dualism of mind and body is most readily apparent. Paradox, so prevalent in *King Lear*, is dominant here. As soon as Gloucester loses the power to see literally, he begins to do so metaphorically. The fact that he learns the truth about his sons immediately his second eye has been put out makes Shakespeare's intention transparently obvious. Like Lear, Gloucester is learning through deprivation:

> Our means secure us, and our mere defects
> Prove our commodities.   (IV, i, 21–2)

Like Lear's, his new knowledge extends from the particular to the general. Lear had learnt to 'feel what wretches feel' and wished to 'shake the superflux to them'; Gloucester, in lines of complex nuance, expresses the need in man for a proper balance of physical and mental qualities: the 'superfluous and lust-dieted man' – he who is excessive in both material possessions and sensual gratification – is he who 'will not see/Because he does not feel' (IV, i, 69–70): the complexity lies in the pun on 'see', coming from the newly blinded man who would still have been able to see literally if through proper feeling he had been able to recognise truth, followed by the use of 'feel' in a metaphorical sense rather than the literal one that might be expected to follow from 'see'.

Of course, Shakespeare's design is not so crude that Gloucester's suffering is merely physical; otherwise he would be no more than one of the animals so frequently evoked in the play's language. The physical and mental suffering that lead him to attempt suicide do not, however, drive him to madness; indeed, he wishes they had:

> The King is mad; how stiff is my vile sense,
> That I stand up, and have ingenious feeling
> Of my huge sorrows! Better I were distract;
> So should my thoughts be sever'd from my griefs,
> And woes by wrong imaginations lose
> The knowledge of themselves.   (IV, vi, 279–84)

The idea that physical suffering can bring mental revelation – that people will not begin to see until they learn to feel – is repeated by Lear in his madness, in vividly physical terms: 'When the rain came to wet me once, and the wind to make me chatter; when the thunder would not peace at my bidding; there I found 'em, there I smelt 'em out' (IV, vi, 100–3). And Gloucester's paradox is repeated, too, as if to drive it home:

> Lear.... Your eyes are in a heavy case, your purse in a light; yet you see how this world goes.
> Gloucester. I see it feelingly.
> Lear. What, art mad? A man may see how this world goes with no eyes.   (IV, vi, 146–51)

The Dover beach scene shows the play's central characters at the nadir of their fortunes; yet it shows them, too, in spite of their afflictions, as in some senses wiser and better men than they had been at the beginning of the action. Wretched though their state is, Shakespeare has already shown us a counter-action designed to alleviate it. Cordelia's return to the play is reported before we see her, in a scene (IV, iii) omitted in the Folio text and sometimes accounted unnecessary and sentimental. Certainly it presents Cordelia as a radiantly idealised figure. In her reactions to the letter bearing news of her father, she has displayed an ideal balance between mental control and physical response:

> ...It seem'd she was a queen
> Over her passion, who, most rebel-like,
> Sought to be king o'er her.   (IV, iii, 13–15)

And the idealisation is reinforced by what follows. As the play enters its last phase, its polarities become more extreme. Cordelia's virtues take on something of a transcendental quality. She herself associates her compassion with

> All blest secrets,
> All you unpublish'd virtues of the earth,

asking that they may

> Spring with [her] tears; be aidant and remediate
> In the good man's distress.   (IV, iv, 15–18)

(The unobtrusive adjective 'good' there is one of the subtle ways in which Shakespeare is guiding us towards total sympathy with Lear himself.) Lear, awaking from sleep and madness, sees her as 'a soul in bliss' and 'a spirit'; he speaks of them both as if they were somehow untouchable by time:

> [We'll] take upon's the mystery of things
> As if we were God's spies; and we'll wear out
> In a wall'd prison[1] packs and sects of great ones
> That ebb and flow by th'moon.   (V, iii, 16–19)

Kent and Edgar are seen as entirely selfless and compassionate; Albany develops from weakness into a strong upholder of the right, and speaks of the surviving characters of the play in morally absolute terms:

> ...All friends shall taste
> The wages of their virtue, and all foes
> The cup of their deservings.   (V, iii, 302–4)

[1] It is perhaps relevant that the idea of the body as a prison for the soul, memorably enshrined by Marvell in his 'Dialogue between the Soul and Body', was commonplace; cf. K. S. Datta, 'New Light on Marvell's "A Dialogue between the Soul and Body"', *Renaissance Quarterly*, 22 (1969), 242–55.

If 'mind' seems only vaguely appropriate as a term for one of the polarities in the last phase of the play, it surely can be claimed that 'body' is entirely appropriate for the other, in two of its important aspects. One is the sensual. The scene in which the virtuous Cordelia reappears is preceded and followed by ones in which Edmund's physical involvement with both Goneril and Regan is made known to us. Lear, in his madness, speaks of adultery, copulation, and luxury in a terrible diatribe against female sexuality. Goneril and Regan's competition for Edmund becomes increasingly sordid, and causes Goneril to encourage Edmund to kill Albany. Edgar, speaking to the defeated Edmund, attributes their father's suffering to his sensuality: 'The dark and vicious place where thee he got/Cost him his eyes': a moralisation which, though Edgar's tone is conciliatory – 'Let's exchange charity' – also invites us to link Edmund's present plight with *his* moral crimes.

Even more prominent in the play's closing passages is the sense and sight of a body as a corpse. Edgar kills Oswald; Lear believes that he has been taken from a grave; we are reminded of Cornwall's death; Regan is poisoned by Goneril; Edgar describes Gloucester's death; we hear that Kent is near to death; a Gentleman enters with the 'bloody knife' which Goneril has used to stab herself; her body and Regan's are brought on to the stage; Lear carries in the dead Cordelia, and boasts 'I kill'd the slave that was a-hanging thee'; we hear of Edmund's death; and Lear dies.

The play's closing moments throw an appalling emphasis on the dead human body. Granville-Barker's comment on Lear's entry 'with Cordelia in his arms' is often quoted. 'What fitter ending to the history of the two of them, which began for us with Lear on his throne, conscious of all eyes on him, while she shamed and angered him by her silence? The same company are here, or all but the same,

and they await his pleasure. Even Regan and Goneril are here to pay him a ghastly homage. But he knows none of them – save for a blurred moment Kent whom he banished – none but Cordelia. And again he reproaches her silence, for

...Her voice was ever soft,
Gentle and low, an excellent thing in woman.

Then his heart breaks.'[1]

That is a fine perception. But is it positive enough? Does Lear do no more than reproach Cordelia for her silence? Is it not important that now, in a total reversal of the crisis of the first scene, all his attention and all his love are focused upon Cordelia, that now he truly sees and acknowledges the beauty of her truth? And would it be entirely far-fetched to suggest that Lear's self-fulfilment is like Kate's in that both have been brought about through a complementary interaction of bodily and mental influences?

The intensity of his emotion over her body is the play's final paradox. Bewildered, despairing, nakedly true to his emotions, giving out pure and merited love, he is at his best; he is, if we wish to use the theological term, redeemed. Through feeling, he has been brought to see. 'Look there, look there.' Whether or not it is expressive of delusion, it shows sight well directed, and reminds us of what goodness has achieved. Fully human, Lear dies. The play ends by asserting the spiritual values which human beings can enshrine while also acknowledging the frailty of the individual human body. Thus, it seems to me, Shakespeare brings to a culmination his exploration within the fabric of this play of the relationship between mind, or soul, and body, and does so in action which has sometimes been thought to go distastefully beyond the requirements of plot, but which is essential to its structure of ideas.

[1] 'King Lear', *Prefaces to Shakespeare* (1930; repr. 1958), I, 277–8.

In emphasising the ideas of *King Lear*, I hope I have not seemed to undervalue its plot or its characters. I hope, indeed, that I have shown that I think them inseparable: that they must have evolved together in Shakespeare's imagina- in an organic relationship, a vital fusion which ultimately defies analysis. The figures in the carpet of *King Lear* are far more complex than those in *The Taming of the Shrew*, but one of them, I suggest, is woven of the same thread.

© STANLEY WELLS 1980

MEDIUM AND MESSAGE IN
'AS YOU LIKE IT' AND 'KING LEAR'

FRANK McCOMBIE

It is not surprising that in the constant talk of Shakespeare's 'tragic vision' and 'comic vision' the fact that 'vision', properly speaking, denotes not what is seen, but the process of seeing, should frequently have been overlooked: but it is much to be regretted that it has.[1] If we are persuaded that *King Lear* is the bleakest of the tragedies, it is tempting for us to accept it as a testament of bleakness, taking 'tragedy' to be the denotation not simply of the artistic medium employed by Shakespeare in this play, but also of the quality of life he is describing. To do so is, of course, to confuse what is seen with the manner in which it is revealed, the object with the medium or filter through which it is viewed. It is more than forty years since Sisson attacked some of the cruder precipitations of this confusion,[2] insisting that for criticism, 'it is in the main a question of the artistic problems which Shakespeare set himself, not of the problems which life set Shakespeare' (p. 24). That was well said, but unfortunately Sisson's admiration of the tragedies led him to a conclusion in which there is a good deal more faith and speculation than objective assessment. The fact that tragedy has nearly always made the greatest theatrical impact tends to blind us to the fact that Shakespeare himself did not consistently regard it as the best medium for what he wanted to say, and that eventually he seems to have found tragic form too constricting, and perhaps even reductive. It may be argued further that there was no inevitability of choice when Shakespeare decided in what form to 'make his statement', and that he was sometimes curious to see how the same 'statement' might be altered by the choice of another medium: in McLuhan's phrase, to see how the medium might alter the message.

Perhaps the most commonly recognised instance of this kind of relationship between two of Shakespeare's plays is provided by *Richard III* and *Macbeth*, but it could scarcely be thought the most striking. The diversity of genre was minimal, Shakespeare having very seriously considered, and in a significant degree explored, the potential for tragedy in *Richard III*. More striking altogether, but (unfortunately, in the present context) much more controversial, is the relationship between *Measure for Measure* and *Othello*, both written, probably, within a twelvemonth, though not necessarily in that order. What must be discovered is a pair of plays in which Shakespeare demonstrably takes as nearly as possible the same 'statement', and presents it first through one medium and then through another. The

[1] A regret apparently shared by Rosalie Colie. In concluding the last of the four lectures published as *The Resources of Kind: Genre-Theory in the Renaissance*, ed. Barbara K. Lewalski (Berkeley, 1973), Professor Colie observes (p. 127): 'Genres may be conservative, but they *are* the craftsman's tools, by which, in addition to effecting cultural transfer, even *nova reperta* may be made.' With the notion of *nova reperta* this paper will be much concerned.

[2] 'The Mythical Sorrows of Shakespeare', *Studies in Shakespeare: British Academy Lectures*, selected and introduced by Peter Alexander (1964), pp. 9–32.

plays will look very different, and must be very different in the experience of them; and, so McLuhan would say, must be very different in meaning, even though the authorial purpose and authorial statement are the same in each.

Two such plays are *As You Like It* and *King Lear*. Each is as nearly perfect as need be for the purpose of the discussion, so that we need not be distracted by failures of realisation. What I want to argue is that in deciding to write *King Lear*, Shakespeare knew very well that what he wanted to say he had said before: but then he had said it through comedy – and now he would say it again, through tragedy. Clearly, he felt it important enough to warrant re-presentation, re-filtering. In a fairly obvious way, the plays would be complementary. In the years between, he had shown no rooted assurance that tragedy could always say all he wanted it to say: far from it. But now, perhaps in a spirit of discovery, in order to determine, perhaps, exactly how much one's 'message' took new shape, became distorted, or heightened, or just got lost, in the alteration of the medium, Shakespeare set out to write another version of *As You Like It*. It was a version the eighteenth century, and most of the nineteenth, was more than ready to consider *As You Like It Not*, and altered it to bring its conclusion remarkably into line with that of the earlier version. That Shakespeare did so re-present the earlier play, and in what degree of consciousness he did so, it will be the first object of this paper to show. The second will be to consider some of the implications of this experiment for Shakespearian comedy and Shakespearian tragedy.

The broad affinities between *As You Like It* and *King Lear* are obvious enough, have often been noted,[1] and need not be laboured. Both plays are concerned with a casting out into the wilderness,[2] and, taking the forest of Arden to be the Ardennes – as Shakespeare did – there is a closer similarity between the two versions

of wilderness than used often to be acknowledged. In each play a prince has been cast out into an essentially uncomfortable situation, in which a very similar kind of experience is made available. It may be argued that there is an essential difference in that Lear undergoes a purgatorial process, a purging, while Duke Senior goes through a process of learning in which there is little sense of purging. Too much can be made of this: apart from the fact that it depends upon a restricted view of Arden, the sort of purging implied by the traditional doctrine of purgatory is fundamentally a learning, a readjustment of perspectives and values, and we have to take into account the fact that Shakespeare was in general much closer in his thinking to the central Christian traditions than are many of us.

If the central plot of each play may be said to concern a ruler and his daughter, the subplot concerns a faithful follower and his sons; and in neither play is the subplot something detached and simply running parallel to the central plot: the integration of the two is complete. In the central plot of the earlier play, the focus is much more upon the daughter than upon the father, but the relationship between the two of them is strikingly similar to that of the later pair. The subplots are in many respects almost identical. The plot against Orlando by his brother Oliver foreshadows in some detail the plotting against Edgar by

[1] Significantly by Maynard Mack, *King Lear in our Time* (1966), pp. 64–5. He draws some broad parallels as a prelude to his contention that *King Lear* is 'the greatest anti-pastoral ever penned'. This essay offers, *inter alia*, a modification of this view different from that argued by Rosalie L. Colie, *Shakespeare's Living Art* (Princeton, 1974), pp. 302ff.

[2] Neither, primarily, is a pastoral, though each owes much to the genre. What must be said of *As You Like It* as pastoral has been eloquently said by Professor Colie (*Shakespeare's Living Art*, especially pp. 243ff.). But her honest disclaimer ('the playwright's uncompromising insistence upon the problematical within pastoral thematics', p. 261) points the dangers of seeing it simply as an exercise in the genre.

Edmund; and while in *As You Like It* it reflects the plot of brother against brother at a higher level, in *King Lear* it reflects the inner turmoils of the two fathers in a more subtle way. Duke Frederick and his capricious evil-doing fore-shadows the unregenerate Lear of the first part of the play; Duke Senior, cast into the wilder-ness with a few followers, foreshadows Lear as victim. The similarities are emphasised by the fact that Shakespeare obviously has the two dukes only just separate in his mind, and never has them onstage together, so that both parts can easily be played by the same actor, and to interesting effect.[1] The casting out of Oliver and the seizing of his estates is echoed in the turning of the villains against Gloucester; and Oliver's recantation is a comedy version of Edmund's puzzled relenting in the face of death. Orlando sees himself as possibly be-coming an outcast in quite precisely 'Poor Tom' terms (the madness apart, II, iii, 31–3).[2] The response of the two girls in *As You Like It* to the idea of banishment is paralleled by Kent's reaction in *King Lear*, in which the same terms are used (*AYLI*, I, iii, 133–4; *Lear*, I, i, 180–1). Each speech is preluded in the same way, as the speaker, in the teeth of warnings, pleads for another who is being tyranically banished. The girls also foreshadow Edgar in their disguises, Celia browning her skin, as Edgar does, both in mean attire, and Rosalind with curtle-axe and boar-spear, as Edgar is later armed with a sword. Le Beau, the courtier who generously warns Orlando of his danger, re-appears in *King Lear*, speaking exactly the same exaggerated court language, as the Gentleman who keeps Kent informed, and who later leads the rescue of Lear. Old Adam reappears as the Old Man who, servant to Gloucester, is found leading him after he has been blinded: both men, as they promptly assure us, are four-score years or more, both are distressed at the fate of their masters and determined to risk all to stand by them in their need. Both are assured by their masters that they can do no good; and while Gloucester fears lest the Old Man come to harm for lending help, Orlando takes Old Adam with him rather to protect and care for him than to profit by his aid.

The role of the Fool in both plays is so nearly the same as to lure us into forgetting differences. Probably Armin played both parts, and, as one who himself contributed signifi-cantly to 'fool literature', possibly helped in the fashioning of the characters he played. Whatever the truth of that, the two Fools are conceived alike though differently projected – as we should expect with a change of filter. The inspiration for both was – it is commonly accepted – the *Moriae Encomium* of Erasmus, a book with which Shakespeare seems to have been very familiar. The somewhat ambiguous presentation of Touchstone is perhaps the closer of the two to Folly, as realised by Erasmus. Touchstone sometimes strikes us as being less wise than he thinks himself, and at other times a good deal wiser than those with whom he converses. He exposes the shoddiness of some qualities in others, but is in some ways shoddy himself. Ultimately, he is rather elusive. Just so is Folly in the *Moriae Encomium*: she can make asses of those she attacks, but is, in every essential save her capacity for detecting folly in others, utterly foolish herself. Never-theless, just as the force of Erasmus's presenta-tion depends upon constant shifts of response in the reader, and upon a sharp eye for the multi-layered ironies, so Shakespeare's presenta-tion of Touchstone demands a sophisticated response in the audience. Certainly, it is point-less to try to adopt a uniform response to

---

[1] Even the names may be confused, though little could be argued from what may be no more than a printer's error. The confusion – if that is what it is – is discussed by Agnes Latham in the introduction to the Arden edition (1975), pp. *xxx-xxxi*, and in her footnote at I, ii, 74.

[2] All references are to the *Complete Works*, ed. Peter Alexander (London and Glasgow, 1951).

Touchstone, to attempt to fix him in one mould, or to resent supposed inconsistencies:[1] the essence of his presentation lies in the fact that we aren't ever quite sure which way to have him; he is a thoroughly Erasmian fool. Duke Senior speaks of Touchstone (v, iv, 100ff.) as one who 'uses his folly like a stalking-horse, and under the presentation of that he shoots his wit'. Whether or not we agree with James Smith[2] that this is simply not true of Touchstone, we should have to accept that the notion of wisdom-in-folly, though much developed in the Fool of *King Lear*, is a central concept in the presentation of Touchstone. He expounds it himself (v, i, 28–31), going on to make a joke about the 'heathen philosopher' whom he has just effectively quoted, from the *Moriae Encomium*.[3]

Like Lear's Fool, Touchstone has his moments of loyalty and courage, for he is ready at a moment's notice to go with the girls into exile as their escort. Like Lear's Fool, he regrets the need for this exile, and doubts the wisdom of it in moments of understandable concern about his own predicament (II, iv, 13–15; cf. *Lear*, III, ii, 12–14). The wit of both Fools is barbed, sometimes even cruelly, yet each engages the sympathy of the audience in a surprising degree. The affinities are certainly numerous, and worth the exploring, for there can be no serious doubt that Touchstone was the source for the Fool in *King Lear*: there is no such figure in any of the generally accepted sources of that play.

Thus far, we have considered what seem to me to be the very obvious common elements of these two plays, each concerned with the consequences of the exile of a prince. The relationship, however, is very much deeper than anything we have so far considered might suggest. A long series of complex echoes and parallels suggests that Shakespeare never had the earlier play very far from his mind while writing the later. These echoes and parallels are not all of the same kind, nor do they occur in a regular pattern; but this is not something we should expect. Some scenes of *King Lear* are cluttered with material deriving from *As You Like It*; others have little or none. What is arresting is not the placing of the corresponding passages, nor even, ultimately, the corresponding passages themselves; it is rather the remarkable similarity of the ideas, thought processes, manner of expression, in two plays which, on the face, are totally dissimilar. But even more is it the way in which the thematic dispositions and development of the later play seem to be emanating directly from the earlier.

The opening scenes of the two plays have much in common: there is talk of weighing comparisons, of breeding, of what is proper, of order of merit, of management, and so on. The themes are being set, the same in both plays. In *As You Like It*, Celia swears an oath in which she vows her affection and support for Rosalind, saying that the breaking of that oath will turn her monster (I, ii, 18ff.). This is taken up in *King Lear* in the play upon the word 'monster', in which France turns the term upon Lear for failing in his 'fore-vouch'd affection' (I, i, 218ff.). The whole run of thought is the same in the two passages. So too is it at other points in the plays, as for instance in the passage in which Rosalind declares love a madness that deserves whipping, only, as all the whippers are afflicted with it, no one is fit to do the whipping (III, ii, 370ff.); and Lear arraigns the beadle for whipping the whore after whom he lusts (IV, vi, 160ff.). Each passage echoes the *Moriae Encomium* in its own way: each has the same pattern of thought, the same association

[1] As Agnes Latham, Introduction to Arden *As You Like It*, p. *liv*.
[2] James Smith, '*As You Like It*', *Scrutiny*, IX (1940), 25.
[3] See John D. Rea, 'Jaques in Praise of Folly', *Modern Philology*, XVII (1919), 465–9.

of ideas; only the sentiment has become soured, the image degraded, in the later version. We have here a striking illustration of the changing of the filter.

'Civet' is referred to in only three of the plays, two of them being those with which we are concerned. Corin speaks of courtiers' hands being sweetened with civet. Touchstone complains that civet is a filthy thing (III, ii, 56ff.). Lear asks his imaginary apothecary for civet to sweeten his imagination (IV, vi, 129ff.); Gloucester asks to kiss Lear's hand, but he says, 'Let me wipe it first; it smells of mortality.' The run of thought is the same, the same associations are made; but the 'very uncleanly flux of a cat' has been transferred to humanity.

These are interesting and instructive parallels, but they are on a very simple level, and highly localised. Before going on to look at others of a more complex and permeating kind, however, it is worth pausing over the snails and the oysters. It is not often the case that a set of related allusions in one play may best be explained by reference to another; such nevertheless may be the case at one point in *King Lear*. Snails are infrequent in Shakespeare's plays; in fact, the word occurs only eight times, and four of these are in *As You Like It*. The passage in which Rosalind reproves Orlando for his lateness, saying she would rather be wooed by a snail (IV, i, 46ff.) has a curious echo in the Fool's exchange with Lear:

Fool. I can tell why a snail has a house.
Lear. Why?
Fool. Why, to put's head in; not to give it away to his daughters, and leave his horns without a case.

(I, v, 26 ff.)

In her exchange, Rosalind warns Orlando that women often give their husbands horns, and the threatening drift of her thought is perfectly explicable in the context. But why the Fool goes on to refer to horns is not clear, and has been found a grave distraction, seeming to hint some confirmation of Lear's recurring thought

of Goneril as a bastard (cf. II, iv, 130, *et passim*). The idea of the horns coming in simply because a snail has been mentioned seems altogether too flippant for the seriousness of the moment, in which Shakespeare is trying to present the Fool – as he does elsewhere – talking with an inconsequentiality which is only apparent; underneath, there is a dense complexity of imagistic relationships. The horns may have come in accidentally along with the rest, for the two contexts are a good deal closer than they seem, each being concerned with jointures and legal settlements of property upon unworthy women. There's more than a snail involved. The first reference to *house* in the exchange between Lear and the Fool comes with the oyster and its shell. Why the Fool introduces this image is not at all clear; but if we look at *As You Like It*, we find Touchstone speaking of the pearl dwelling in 'your foul oyster' like a miser 'in a poor house' (V, iv, 58f.). The Fool, we assume, was attempting to make a quite different point, but he nevertheless uses 'oyster' as a house image, as does Touchstone; then he swops it for Rosalind's house image, the snail, taking over more of it than was appropriate to the context. It is a set of related ideas that is carried over, rather than isolated images or precise meanings. It may finally be observed that oysters, like snails, are fairly rare in Shakespeare's plays, referred to only seven times, and only in *As You Like It* and *King Lear* in connection with *house*.

The effect of changing the filter through which a situation is viewed is, inevitably, that some things which showed up clearly before show up less clearly now, while other things which before were scarcely noticed acquire new importance and greater significance. Dispositions *seem* different; the texture is seen in a new light which, perhaps, emphasises some relationships which formerly seemed less significant, while leaving others unaltered. The two pictures thus seen are, of course, in the completest sense complementary.

One of the characters who, in the alteration of filter, changes quite startlingly in significance is Phebe. Shakespeare's reasons for retaining Phebe from the Lodge story are obvious enough: she is in *As You Like It* to contrast, with her selfishness and Petrarchan affectation, the pure and generous love of Rosalind. But in many ways she foreshadows the evil sisters in *King Lear*, and especially Goneril, whose counterpart she is. Rosalind's attacks upon Phebe (in III, v and IV, iii) are conducted in *King Lear* against Goneril by the Fool, Edgar, Cordelia, and ultimately by Albany. What happens is that all the Petrarchan vocabulary used of and by Phebe is turned to utterly vicious significance in its application to Goneril and Regan. So 'tyrant', 'cruel', 'Turk', 'proud', 'pitiless', 'frowning', and even the reference to her 'glass': all are echoed directly, but with more horrific meaning, in *King Lear*. 'Pitiless' is used to describe the storm (III, iv, 29), the previous use of this rare word in Shakespeare coming in *As You Like It* to describe Phebe (III, v, 40); seven lines later Rosalind refers to Phebe's 'bugle eyeballs': bugle was a storm flower, or thunder flower. The associations are more complex than appears superficially. Phebe and Goneril even have a similar turn of phrase:

Phebe. I marvel why I answer'd not again.

(*AYLI*, III, v, 131)

Goneril.   I marvel our mild husband
Not met us on the way.   (*Lear*, IV, ii, 1–2)

In each, it is a vulgarism, insincere, mocking, self-important; and, with good irony, each is deluded in the man she is thinking of. Both women are writers of letters which are received in the wrong quarters and read either to or by the lover or husband, to the discomfiting of the sender. The last eight lines of the unfeeling letter Phebe sends to 'Ganymede' are accurately epitomised in Goneril's comment upon the relative claims of Albany and Edmund (IV, ii, 26ff.). And Rosalind's rebuke to Silvius:

'Tis such fools as you
That makes the world full of ill-favour'd children

(III, v, 52–3)

is pregnant with meaning for *King Lear*.

It is Phebe too who introduces the violent eye-imagery common to these two plays, with her reference to 'eyes, that are the frail'st and softest things' (III, v, 12), a description which emphasises their vulnerability rather than their beauty. The regular association of eyes and violence which is characteristic of *King Lear* is found running through Phebe's speeches in this scene. She speaks of them shutting 'their coward gates on atomies' (l. 13), again stressing vulnerability; scoffs at the Petrarchan hyperbole which would have them 'tyrants, butchers, murderers' (l. 14) even as her scorn is attempting to murder the love Silvius has for her; and if she denies that her eyes can 'wound' or 'kill', nevertheless concentrates her talk on *wounding* and *killing*, *swooning* and *falling*, and even on *scratching* and *scarring*. She speaks of the 'cicatrice' left upon the flesh by a rush, a unique usage, and very odd, but entirely in keeping with the exaggerated violence of her language: her mind is running on mortal wounds and scars, and effectively confuses the 'impressure' with a bloody incision. She goes on to speak of having 'darted' her eyes at Silvius, and ends with the claim that there is 'no force in eyes/ That can do hurt'. Silvius's answer is highly pertinent, but Phebe takes scant notice even when Rosalind shows the same startled response to her gaze (ll. 41, 69).

All this has a very complex set of echoes in *King Lear*, and it is with Phebe's counterpart (counterparts, if we regard Regan separately) that the violent eye-imagery is chiefly associated. Kent first makes the association in his slightly ambiguous 'true blank of thine eye' (I, i, 158), an archery image not unlike that offered by Silvius (III, v, 30–31); but it is Lear himself who makes the first unambiguous conjunction when, confronted with the undisguised hostility of Goneril, he threatens his own eyes, 'Old fond eyes,/Beweep this cause again, I'll pluck ye out' (I, iv, 301–2), where 'old' and 'fond' convey the vulnerability of the eyes. The *darting* eyes of Phebe find an inverted echo in Lear's curse upon Goneril (II, iv, 163–4). This scarifying imagery reaches its horrific climax in the physical blinding of Gloucester, who himself talks of protecting 'the poor old eyes' of Lear from the 'cruel nails' of the evil sisters (III, vii, 55–6), even as the 'vile jelly' of his own eyes is about to be ripped out. The repeated association of eyes and violence does not end here, but runs on eventually to a surprisingly complex image in Edmund's argument (V, iii, 50–2) that Lear had better be guarded carefully, since both his age and his title had 'charms':

> To pluck the common bosom on his side,
> And turn our impress'd lances in our eyes
> Which do command them.

The play ends with almost intolerably poignant efforts to see some hope, some consolation which the gods seem to deny in this life. The 'promised end' of *As You Like It* is more comforting; for though Orlando sustains the Phebe conjunction of eyes and wounding (V, ii, 23), Rosalind in her generous all-giving love promises:

> . . .to set her before your eyes tomorrow, human as she is, and without any danger. (ll. 63–4)

If Phebe stands in the picture of *As You Like It* where Goneril and Regan stand in that of *King Lear*, Jaques and Oliver stand in the place of Edmund. Oliver plays Edmund to Orlando's Edgar in most respects – the calumniating and discrediting, the seizing of revenues and management; but he offers no comparable 'philosophy': this is provided by Jaques. Jaques seems originally, as Harold Jenkins has argued, to have been one and the same with 'the mysterious middle brother':[1] Edmund combines the two with Oliver.

Two words, more than any others, place Jaques in *As You Like It*: 'foul' and 'contemplation'. *Contemplation* seems to have had a very strong coloration for Shakespeare, and he never uses the word neutrally to indicate simply 'a mental viewing'. It is discredited as an occupation in *Love's Labour's Lost*; it is used as part of a deception in both *Richard III* and *The Merchant of Venice*; it is associated with crass stupidity in *Twelfth Night*, and with smut in *Othello*. And it is used twice in *As You Like It* in reference to Jaques, in each case with some obvious irony, though clearly with much more for Shakespeare than for us. When, for instance, Jaques speaks of the 'sundry contemplation of my travels' (IV, i, 15–16), it is difficult for us to grasp the full force of the derision he calls down upon himself. Rosalind makes some of it clear; the rest we have to work out for ourselves. 'Contemplation' occurs once in *King Lear*, when Edgar, in what sounds to us like a flippantly jocose question, asks Edmund, 'What serious contemplation are you in?' (I, ii, 132–3). If it is a flippant question, it isn't flippant in the way we might suppose; for in Shakespeare's usage, there is here an implied charge of either silliness or skullduggery. All that need concern us, however, is that this curious word should be applied to both Jaques and Edmund. As is generally the case, the comic use is more light-hearted than the tragic: one of the effects of changing the filter is that tones darken.

Foulness is not something we remember very clearly being associated with Jaques: caustic and unobliging, but not specially foul, despite the associations of his name. Jaques is, nonetheless, sufficiently involved in the fair/foul paradox, which occurs in *As You Like It* in the same manner as it does in *King Lear*. We may not

[1] Harold Jenkins, 'As You Like It', *Shakespeare Survey 8* (Cambridge, 1955), p. 42.

doubt from the evidence that Phebe is fair to look upon, nor that Audrey is foul; the paradox is summed up by Celia when she and Rosalind are discussing the 'good hussif Fortune':

those that she makes fair, she scarce makes honest; and those that she makes honest she makes very ill-favouredly. (I, ii, 34–5)

The subtlety of the play, however, permits no such simple equation; nor does *King Lear*, where the Fool persistently asks, 'Dost thou know the difference...?' Most importantly, it is a case of knowing the difference between those who are wise and fair, and those who only seem so, and in fact are foul and foolish. Lear's Fool speaks of wise men grown 'foppish', their manners 'apish' (I, iv, 165ff.). Just so 'apish' does the affected Jaques appear when he declares himself 'ambitious for a motley coat' (II, vii, 43). Thus apparelled, he will, he says, 'Cleanse the foul body of th'infected world' in the manner of Lear's Fool. But Duke Senior sees clearly that it would be a case of 'most mischievous foul sin, in chiding sin':

For thou thyself hast been a libertine. (ll. 64–5)

Jaques is dismissed as both foul and foolish, as the Duke pursues the matter in terms which would seem appropriate enough in a description of Goneril herself. It is an amusing exchange: but in *King Lear*, the amusement we find in Edmund's postulation of his sham philosophy soon runs out, as its practical implications become clear to us.

We must, therefore, be very cautious in responding to anything that Jaques says. If he himself is discredited in *As You Like It*, however, the views he expresses are discredited much more thoroughly in *King Lear*. Jaques's 'Seven Ages' speech, savouring more of rhetorical elegance than of genuine conviction, is more worthy of a Goneril than of Jaques, we might think. Shakespeare is careful to off-set the view it offers with Rosalind's more humane

exchange with Orlando (III, ii), which is pointed further by her later dismissal of Jaques's humour as that of the contemplative traveller (IV, i). In *King Lear*, there is no less humanity: the vision of Jaques is almost systematically attacked, first by the kind of heightening that effectively alters implication, then by plain demonstration of its inadequacy. So, the world that is a stage becomes 'this great stage of fools' (IV, vi, 184). The rather comic picture of infancy as 'Mewling and puking' turns to pathos in Lear's insistence upon *crying* (IV, vi, 179ff.).[1] The purely satirical view of the lover, 'Sighing like furnace', finds an acrid echo in Lear's 'centaurs' in 'the sulphurous pit – burning...' (IV, vi, 124ff.). The justice 'In fair round belly, with good capon lin'd' is mildly satirical; in *King Lear* it becomes savagely so, the 'rascal beadle' (l. 160) being protected by his dress, since 'Robes and furr'd gowns hide all' (l. 165): the *lining* has become a clothes image in the translation. These are details, but taken generally, act IV scene vi of *King Lear* is a picture of two old men apparently illustrating Jaques's description of old age. The 'lean and slipper'd pantaloon' is sadly reflected in the old wasted men, the buffoons of their evil children – Gloucester with his 'corky arms' (III, vii, 28), Lear with his 'slip-shod' (slippered) wit (I, v, 11). The reference to spectacles has been taken up in I, ii, 35, *et passim*; but if Gloucester ends his days blind, and Lear must protest that his eyes are 'not o'th'best' (V, iii, 279), in fact both men see more clearly in age than they have ever done, and a good deal better than Jaques or Edmund. The childishness Jaques speaks of is what Goneril terms 'the unruly waywardness that infirm and choleric years bring with them' (I, i, 298ff.), or,

[1] In a parallel passage in the Chaloner version, *The Praise of Folie* (E.E.T.S., 1965), we find 'Iniuriis exposita' rendered 'weak and pewling'. Jaques, like Chaloner, takes the emphasis off the notion of vulnerability in order to make a joke of it.

as she prefers to think of it, 'dotage'. But Jaques is refuted along with Goneril when Old Adam is given so much tender care later in the same scene; and in act IV, scene vi of *King Lear*, the scene which particularly echoes and modifies Jaques's version of the seven ages, we find the word 'remember' occurring six times. Shakespeare insistently shows Lear coping with any temptation to let himself slip into the 'mere oblivion' to which his evil daughters (and Jaques) would cheerfully consign him. So far from ending their 'strange eventful history . . . sans everything', Lear and Gloucester may be thought to have grasped all that ultimately matters. The autumnal vision is not without hope of seeing salvation.

Nearly everything Jaques has to say is, then, pointedly modified, first in *As You Like It*, then in *King Lear*. Since so much of what he says is re-stated in cruder terms by the evil characters of the later play, the rebuttals are firmer and more of the implications worked out than in *As You Like It*.[1] But it is not simply the case that *King Lear* subtilises simple categories proposed in *As You Like It*, and darkens lighter tones. The subtlety is there in the earlier play, and it is of the same quality: indeed, it is often, by the very lightness of touch, made even more impressive than in the later play. Jaques is not all bad, and perhaps is not bad at all; Phebe is not all foul, and Oliver relents and repents most handsomely. On the other hand – though in the purest comic manner – Orlando is very rough on poor Charles, as is Rosalind with Phebe; Celia has a bawdy turn of mind and a quick temper; Amiens has a dourness which almost prevails over the cheerfulness of the Duke. And Rosalind shows scarcely any filial feeling for her unfortunate father. These are hints of a largely unexplored complexity in *As You Like It* which shows up much more clearly through the filter of tragedy in *King Lear*. A recent RSC production of *King Lear*[2] demonstrated convincingly how much sympathy can

be attracted by the evil sisters in the opening phases of the play; and Ernst Honigmann has argued powerfully for acknowledgement of the angularity of the Fool, Cordelia, and even Kent.[3] The *Schadenfreude* in *King Lear*, on the importance of which Honigmann rightly insists, is an import from the comedies in general, but especially from the Erasmian *As You Like It* and *Twelfth Night*: how different it appears in the context of tragedy is one very useful illustration of the effect of changing the filter.

The sources of *King Lear* are extremely complex; as Kenneth Muir says: '. . . he pressed into his service incidents, ideas, phrases, and even words from books and plays; and the remarkable richness of texture apparent in *King Lear* may be explained, at least, in part, by Shakespeare's use of such a method.'[4] It is no doubt difficult, in considering so rich a variety of sources, to keep the nature of the special relationship with *As You Like It* clearly in mind, no matter how many parallels and echoes might be identified. Nevertheless, what I wish to argue at this point is that Shakespeare's use of those sources was in fact very largely determined by the relationships he recognised between the play he was writing and the comedy he had written six years before.

The lessons learned in the wilderness by Duke Senior are not elaborated in *As You Like It* as Lear's are in the later play, but what we are told of them rings as true of the one play as of the other. The second act of *As You Like It* opens with a conventionally cheerful compari-

[1] James Smith (*'As You Like It'*, p. 17) takes a similar view, though I could not agree with his further speculations about the *evasions* of comedy.

[2] Directed by Trevor Nunn, 1976.

[3] E. A. J. Honigmann, *Shakespeare: Seven Tragedies: The Dramatist's Manipulation of Response* (London and Basingstoke, 1976), pp. 116ff.

[4] Introduction to the Arden edition (1952), pp. *xlii-xliii*.

son of life in the forest with the *pomp* and *peril* of life at court, terms which find bitter echoes in *King Lear*. But we find that the Duke must in fact endure 'the icy fang/And churlish chiding of the winter's wind', which 'bites and blows upon my body,/ Even till I shrink with cold'. The passage is echoed repeatedly in *King Lear*, perhaps most obviously in Edgar's determination to 'outface/The winds and persecutions of the sky' (II, iii, 11–12), and in Lear's reflection that 'the rain came to wet me once, and the wind to make me chatter' (IV, vi, 101ff.). The Duke's recourse is to the stoical observation that 'This is no flattery'; so too is Lear's – 'They flattered me like a dog' (IV, vi, 96), but the wind and the rain, and the thunder that 'would not peace at my bidding', had given the game away: 'there I found 'em, there I smelt 'em out'. The Duke's speech contains a set of related images which are to be central in *King Lear*, introduced with words like 'fang', 'bites', 'toad', 'venomous', all summed up in 'adversity', which is ascribed at the end of this act to *ingratitude*. The speech is a brief but accurate scenario, not only for the Duke's own drama, but also for Lear's. It is, of course, too brief to carry conviction: in 'Blow, blow, thou winter wind', Shakespeare elaborates further.

This song has sometimes been thought to have rather too severe a tenour for the generally light and easygoing atmosphere of *As You Like It*; even in its own day, it must have been rather surprising: 'The mixture of cynicism and jollity set forth by the lyric does not find general expression in English song until it appears in the cavalier lyrics.'[1] The songs of Lear's Fool, nevertheless, though in a different genre, are just this mixture of superficial jollity and wintry cynicism; and 'Blow, blow, thou winter wind', sentiment by sentiment, fits itself to *King Lear*. The theme is Man's ingratitude, which is stridently denounced in the later play (as at I, iv, 259 and I, v, 37). The opening lines of the song are powerfully echoed in Lear's speech to the elements, 'Blow, winds. . . all germens spill at once/That makes ingrateful man!' (III, ii, 1ff.). The opening of the second verse:

> Freeze, freeze, thou bitter sky,
> That dost not bite so nigh
>   As benefits forgot. . .

is the basis of what Lear goes on to say:

> I tax not you, you elements, with unkindness;
> I never gave you kingdom, call'd you children;
> You owe me no subscription. . .

The rude breath of the wind is echoed in Albany's just rebuke of Goneril (IV, ii, 29ff.), in which he contemns the ingratitude of those 'so benefited'. The word *warp/warped* occurs only eight times in the plays, three times in *As You Like It*, once in the song, where water is described as *warping* into ice. It is not water, however, but morals that is the issue, the warm flow of gratitude warping into the cold reserve of ingratitude. The other two occurrences of this word in *As You Like It* (both at III, iii, 77) also indicate a moral rather than a physical shrinkage. In *King Lear*, we find:

> And here's another, whose warp'd looks proclaim
> What store her heart is made on;   (III, vi, 52–3)

where Lear thinks he sees Regan. (He goes on to suggest that Regan be 'anatomised' – another rare word in Shakespeare, but shared by these plays.) For the rest, the lexical and thematic connections fall into place. 'Thy tooth is not so keen' is echoed in:

> How sharper than a serpent's tooth it is
> To have a thankless child.   (I, iv, 288–9)

And again in Edgar's reference to the 'Tooth that poisons if it bite' (III, vi, 66). The poisonous sting of being forgotten is echoed in Lear's remorse at the way he treated Cordelia (IV, iii, 45ff.). And 'sharp' is certainly echoed in

[1] John H. Long, *Shakespeare's Use of Music: A Study of the Music and its Performance in the Original Production of Seven Comedies* (Gainesville, 1955; repr. 1961), p. 148.

'Through the sharp hawthorn blows the cold wind' of Edgar's first entry as Poor Tom, where the whole tenour of the song is caught at once. The 'winter wind' is the force blowing through the last days of the two old men in *King Lear*.

Winter, which figures in *As You Like It* more prominently than we often remember, is twice referred to in speeches of the Fool in act II, scene iv of *King Lear*, and in such a way as to imply that Lear has reached the winter of his life, in which he is really too old to learn. The Fool nevertheless tries to counsel him, concluding with his perhaps most memorable song, about the fools and the knaves. Kent is moved to ask him where he learned it, but is not told; the source, however, might well be that of the sentiment of the song in *As You Like It*. Together the two songs tell us that most friendship is feigning by those who serve only to seek for gain; they will leave thee in the storm of adversity which will reveal them for the ungrateful knaves they are; only the fool will stay, for most loving is mere folly. The source could again be the *Moriae Encomium*,[1] the spirit of which imbues the whole of these two plays, not only the two songs. For so delightful a comedy, *As You Like It* is surprisingly littered with words like 'winter', 'bitter', 'foul', 'chide', 'rail', and 'tax', much more so than any other of the comedies. As Folly puts it in one of the famous passages in which she discusses the 'ages of man': '...in all thynges he fyndeth more galle than hony.'[2] What is apparent here is that these two plays have not only an *object* in common, not just *something seen*, but significantly enough even a manner of seeing, a trick of vision. We might call it 'ironic' or 'Erasmian', or 'sweet-and-bitter' (another term occurring only in these two plays), but it seems to be common to them despite the change of filter. That there are differences is obvious enough; but what are the *essential* differences introduced with the change of filter?

Are there any at all, apart from cheerful and despondent endings?

In *As You Like It*, there is a sense of winter past, of better days to come; though the sharp wind can still freeze, it is a time of looking forward, of doing. In *King Lear*, the atmosphere is autumnal, with the sharp wind promising only the bleakness of winter, and death:

> Why, this would make a man a man of salt,
> To use his eyes for garden water-pots,
> Ay, and laying autumn's dust...
> I will die bravely, like a smug bridegroom.
>
> (IV, vi, 196ff.)

So says Lear, who will die a bridegroom rather different from those gracing the conclusion of *As You Like It*. In *King Lear*, there is a different apprehension of time; it is in a consideration of the implications of this difference that we must seek our answers.

King Lear is preoccupied with the *use of time* as the determinant of our 'times'. Time is the

---

[1] Chaloner, *The Praise of Folie* p. 27: 'Now though we see, howe commenly these thinges are doen, and commenly laughed to skorne, yet such fondnesse is it that souldreth, and holdeth a pleasaunt felowship of life atwixe you.' Not only the *Moriae Encomium*, but also the *Adagia* and *Colloquiae* provide all sorts of parallel texts in which friendship is extolled (the *Amicorum communia omnia* is pointedly placed first in the *Adagiorum Chiliades*), and deception and hypocrisy condemned (*Pseudocheus and Philetymus*, *Things and Names*, and *Sympathy* – the last being the colloquy from which Shakespeare possibly borrowed the story of the snake which threatened to enter the mouth of the sleeping Oliver, reported at IV, iii, 106ff.).

[2] Erasmus has 'Nihil usquam non plurimo felle tinctum'. Betty Radice (*Praise of Folly* (Harmondsworth, 1971)) translates this more properly as, 'There's nothing without its tinge of acute bitterness' (p. 108); Chaloner succumbs to his usual temptation to adapt a currently popular proverb, derived from Cicero's 'Amor et melle et felle est fecundissimus'. Shakespeare's 'small latine' may also have known Ovid's association of 'fel' with the bites of poisonous serpents: *As You Like It* is commonly accepted as revealing both direct and indirect acquaintance with Ovid on a significant scale.

great maturer, though it may fail to bring men to the maturity it offers. Time will unfold matters which men who have failed to profit by their time have failed to see for themselves. Time is stern, but to be used, co-operated with: Man must not try to ignore it, to sleep it out, or else he will be old before his time; that is to say, he will be aged by time before he has learned to profit by time.

Time in *As You Like It* is presented without the deeply moving philosophical force of time in *King Lear*, but it is presented insistently enough to announce its philosophical importance.[1] Certainly, it is a more important issue in *As You Like It* than in any other of the comedies, even *The Comedy of Errors*, where time figures significantly enough. Learning how to use time profitably is a theme sustained throughout the play. In the first scene, Charles reports to Oliver that the 'many young gentlemen' who flock to Duke Senior every day 'fleet the time carelessly, as they did in the golden world'. Orlando takes a similar mistaken view, wanting to know who they are:

> That in this desert inaccessible...
> Lose and neglect the creeping hours of time.
>
> (II, vii, 109ff.)

The reality accords more closely than he thinks with his own concern for the proper use of time ('propriety' being another key concept in this play).

The girls, of course, show a correct response to time. Celia declares that time has taught her to value Rosalind (I, iii, 65ff.).[2] Rosalind, in her own slightly formal but amusing way, when teasing Orlando, considers Man's experience of time in terms a surprising number of which find echoes in passages of *King Lear* which are similarly concerned with the use and expenditure of time.[3] In a later scene, Rosalind will urge Orlando to promptness with an ingenuous earnestness that provokes Celia to one of her delightful indecencies. But Rosalind has the right notion, nonetheless, when she observes, in parting with her lover:

> Well, Time is the old justice that examines all such offenders, and let Time try.   (IV, i, 177–8)

In the happy aura that hangs round her love, Rosalind's comment seems almost too portentous, carrying too much weight of significance for any sentence at such a moment. It takes its place, nevertheless, in a pattern of references which the singing of 'It was a lover' brings very obviously to the surface in the final act, with its recommendation to 'take the present time'.[4] In fact, in this 'desert inaccessible', we find that 'These pretty country fools'[5] have learned to 'take the present time',

[1] Its importance is recognised by Jay L. Halio, '"No Clock in the Forest": Time in *As You Like It*', *Studies in English Literature*, II (1962), 197-207; repr. in *As You Like It: Twentieth Century Views*, ed. Jay L. Halio (Englewood Cliffs, N.J., 1968), pp. 88-97. He takes a view very different from that taken here, speaking of 'the timeless pastoral world of the Forest of Arden, where past and present merge' (p. 91).

[2] The scene ends with Celia urging the need to 'Devise the fittest time and safest way' to escape 'To liberty, and not to banishment', thereby revealing that she, like Old Adam, is 'not for the fashion of these times' (II, iii, 59).

[3] III, ii, 28off.: 'trots' is picked up by Poor Tom in a rather obscure comment upon time spent in sin (III, iv, 99); the 'se'ennight' that seems seven years is echoed a few lines later (l. 136); the reference to the incompetent priest is echoed in the Fool's chant about the time to come (III, ii, 81ff.); the reference to penury by Edgar (II, iii, 8–9); the reference to the thief hastened to the gallows by Lear (IV, vi, 151ff.). Rosalind's comment on lawyers in vacation conjoins the lexis of Sight (less obtrusive than in *King Lear*, but in fact slightly denser, in a ratio of about 24:23) with the lexis of Time, as does Kent (IV, vii, 93–4) and, most memorably, Lear (IV, i, 47).

[4] The point is reinforced in Touchstone's teasing of the Pages, and the play upon the word *time* as signifying 'time', 'tune', and 'beat' or 'measure'.

[5] This is the Morley rendering, published in his *First Book of Airs, or Little Short Songs* in 1600: 'fools' is much more appropriate than Folio's 'folks'. Folio got the song quite muddled altogether.

and not to lose it. It is, as Duke Senior says, those:

> That have endur'd shrewd days and nights with us,
> Shall share the good of our returned fortune.
>
> (v, iv, 167–8)

Jaques commends his lord for the 'patience'[1] and 'virtue' that have earned the restoration of his former honour, but will not stay 'To see pastime'. There is something churlish about this refusal to recognise that there is: 'A time to weep, and a time to laugh; a time to mourn and a time to dance.'[2] The Duke calls for music and dance, but Jaques leaves, unable to respond to the notion of time redeemed.

Much of the close of *King Lear* goes over the same ground, but in harrowing terms. If friends shall be rewarded, foes shall taste 'The cup of their deservings' (v, iii, 304). Most of the foes are already dead. Edmund has been allowed a kind of repentance, and his last request has been an urgent instruction to 'send in time'. But as one speech after another makes clear, time is running sadly out. If *As You Like It* ends with a 'time to dance', *King Lear* ends with a 'time to mourn'. Lear and Gloucester have redeemed their time, but Edgar can only feel that such redemption has been of an order that few could bear: this may not be as we like it, but how it well may be.

If the end of *As You Like It* begs one question, however, the end of *King Lear* begs another; and to leave matters here would be distorting. 'As you like it' is more usefully taken to mean 'as you like to see it' than 'how you like it to work out'; and *King Lear* offers a version of 'as you prefer not to see it'. Theoretically, the 'it' is constant: only the manner of seeing, only the filter is different. It is a theory, however, which is likely to trap us in judgments of a very facile sort. With McLuhan, we must demur.

If we leave aside the Epilogue, *As You Like It* ends with the Duke's exhortation:

> Proceed, proceed. We will begin these rites,
> As we do trust they'll end, in true delights.
>
> (v, iv, 191–2)

The emphasis seems to be upon 'rites' and 'delights', but equally upon 'trust'. There is, certainly, a clear-ringing optimism here. The parallel passage in *King Lear*, we must think, is Kent's despondent, if not despairing question, 'Is this the promis'd end?' (v, iii, 263), where the emphasis is upon 'end', and upon the frustrations of puzzlement and pain. It is not Kent's last speech, however. He still has to tell us:

> I have a journey, sir, shortly to go.

'Journey' draws our attention to what is certainly the most important word in the Duke's closing exhortation: 'Proceed, proceed.' The difference is in the sense of that journey: in Kent's case, it is to be taken 'shortly', and is clearly an end: the Duke speaks of a *beginning*. Time, in *As You Like It*, is still abundant: in *King Lear*, it has run out. It is a crucial and essential difference. The Erasmian style is the same; many of the terms employed are the same; the characters are grouped in the same ways and endowed with what are essentially the same qualities. The same themes are pursued in the cross-currents of thought in the two plays, and the same version of Christian stoicism is the philosophical basis of each. Both plays have the same things to tell us about Man in his encounter with Life and about his use of Time: these features together form the constant 'it' of 'as you like it' and 'as you like it not'. But it doesn't come out the same: the 'it' proves not to be a constant after all. If both these plays are concerned with trial, endurance – *passion* in its precise meaning – they differ in the experience of *resurrection*. And this, we may say, is the direct and inescapable effect of changing the

---

[1] 'Patience' has the same force here as in *King Lear*. (See Muir, introduction to the Arden edition, p. *lxi*.).

[2] *Ecclesiastes*, iii, 4.

filter. One may present the same argument to express the same convictions, but the conclusions reached must diverge.

As You Like It and *King Lear* demonstrate, classically, the advantages of using, respectively, the comic filter and the tragic filter; but they also demonstrate the limitations imposed by each. *Resurrection* in *As You Like It* is at once more accessible and less profound and permanent than in *King Lear*; while that in *King Lear* depends upon a massive and unquestioning faith that is not demanded in *As You Like It*. In the comedy, the resurrection is lived through, and Man is free to live in its benefits; it might hurt him as a process, it might tax and weary him, but at the end of it he is refreshed. The redemptive process, in effect, is an equipping of Man for Life: Resurrection is in Time. Such is the effect of seeing the redemptive process through the filter of comedy. The comic vision sees it as being cyclic, a process which Man may have to go through many times: Man is redeemed, but still – though the play does not stress this – free to fall again. In *King Lear*, what is fundamentally different is the sense that the redemptive process is one which lasts a lifetime, leaving Man free only for translation into some other state through death. It is not the case that Life offers redemptive processes, but that Life is itself *the* Redemptive Process. Resurrection is not in Time, but in Eternity.

Such is the conclusion compelled upon the dramatist by his choice of the tragic filter. Neither the tragic filter nor the comic filter left Shakespeare entirely free to say what, perhaps, he wanted to say: that *both* conclusions are correct.

That Shakespeare was less than satisfied with the comic and tragic filters, and with the limited complexity of the conclusions they reduced him to, is at least arguable. It was to the theme of redemption and resurrection that he turned in his last four plays; and it is significant that he abandoned both the tragic and comic filters for the infinitely more subtle – though theatrically perhaps less satisfying – filter of romance. The affinities of *Cymbeline* with *King Lear* suggest a tentative re-working; the close lexical relationship between *As You Like It* and *The Tempest* has a similar significance. And quite strikingly in *The Winter's Tale*, more subtly in *The Tempest* – two plays centrally preoccupied with trial and resurrection – Shakespeare attempts to combine the conclusions of *As You Like It* and *King Lear*. Whatever dramatic and theatrical difficulties romance imposed, its filter permitted things to be seen in a richer complexity, allowing Shakespeare a philosophical freedom that many in fact think he abused. But that is a different debate.

© FRANK McCOMBIE 1980

PLAYING KING LEAR: DONALD SINDEN TALKS TO J. W. R. MEADOWCROFT

JWRM. It's eighteen months since I first heard that you were rejoining the Royal Shakespeare Company to play Benedick and King Lear. I particularly wanted to see your Lear because I've always admired the things that you've done, and the play is a favourite of mine. Now that I've finally seen it during the Aldwych run, I find that the production poses a number of questions for me as an academic. But before we get down to specifics, perhaps you'd tell me how you go about preparing a Shakespeare role, one that you haven't previously done.

DS. Well, you mustn't take this personally, Bob, but I never read any authorities; and the first thing I do is go through my text and cross out all stage directions.

JWRM. What text do you use?

DS. For *Lear* we used – not because of its value as a text – we used the New Penguin Shakespeare, merely because of its size.

JWRM. I think it's a very good text.

DS. Is it? Well, I mean it's easy to slip into the pocket and have around. My only source books that I ever use are the facsimile of the First Folio, the Norton – you know the one that they did at the Folger – and the *Oxford English Dictionary*. They're the only two things I want to know about.

JWRM. Not the thirteen-volume *Oxford?*

DS. The thirteen-volume, yes. Robert Graves put me on to that some fifteen years ago. He

said it was the best purchase he'd ever made in his life; and he made me promise to buy a set when I got back. I was in Majorca then. And he said 'On condition you look up two words a day for the rest of your life', and I'm afraid I haven't, I haven't. But it's invaluable, you see, it's unbelievable. I resent editors getting between me and...all right, so Heminge and Condell get between us and Shakespeare in the First Folio. But we're getting back to something there, aren't we?

It's on odd theatrical readings of lines that the Folio has been most useful to me. As for instance, in 1946 when I was playing William in *As You Like It*, I noticed that the word 'ay' was spelled 'I'. I thought how fascinating, and so I changed it to an 'I' meaning the first person, whereas all the modern texts have 'ay'. Little gimmicks like that I was able to pick up, especially with doing Malvolio. The way 'M.O.A.I.' is printed in the Folio gave me a marvellous idea for Malvolio to try to pronounce it as if it were a word. So when I came to that piece, I said 'Mo'ah-ee', you see, 'Mo'ah-ee, Mo'ah-ee' before it dawned upon me that it was meant to be M-O-A-I. That sort of thing you can pick up from the facsimile that you don't get in any modern text.

JWRM. How did you go about preparing for *King Lear?* You say you don't read literary criticism.

DS. No, no, I don't read any – this may be short-sighted, but it's the only way I find I can work – I just start on the text: get to know the character I'm playing, and hammer away at it, and do what I can within my experience to theatricalise the part I'm playing. Lear, now, we are told his age near enough, 'four score years and upward'. The biggest breakthrough that I think I had was in discussing with the director, and he eventually agreed with me, thank God, on the actual meaning of the word 'madness'. To what degree is Lear mad? Because he does nothing that is certifiable in the play; he's actually more lucid when he's mad. So I hinged my entire interpretation of the second half of the play on senility, rather than on madness.

JWRM. Now there I did question your interpretation. I think that certainly there is a point in the play when senility does overcome Lear, but I would place it later than you do. I would place it at the point where he is reunited with Cordelia.

DS. Oh really, as late as that?

JWRM. Yes, because I feel that up to that time Lear has been a man of almost superhuman energy. Everything he's done he's done with tremendous vigour: the way he comes in from hunting, and the way he rushes about even in the storm, until finally when he goes to sleep, there is a temporary calm, but it's not enough to cure him. And I feel that when he comes upon Gloucester, he is still going very strongly.

DS. Ah, I don't agree with you there, you see. This is the wonderful thing about Shakespeare, isn't it? Open to so many different interpretations. John Barton dropped a line – it's difficult to say that this is Trevor Nunn's production; he takes responsibility for it, but, in fact, John Barton set most of the play himself before Trevor Nunn joined us – and I got a lot from John, I'd worked a lot with him. He said one day that he'd always felt that the first scene of *Lear* was actually the last scene of some other play. Very interesting thought, and we explored

this. You were talking at lunch just now about that electrifying moment when Volpone leaps from his couch to confront Celia. Well, *Volpone* gave us an idea for the opening of the play. We nearly set the first scene with Lear in a four-poster bed – he's dying, and this is the reading of the last will and testament. Then when Cordelia was to say 'Nothing', he was out of that bed like a shot: 'Right! That's it! Out!' – which might have been an interesting way of doing it.

But, with the total acquiescence of Trevor Nunn, I think that Lear is not far off death at the opening of the play. He himself realises that he's on his way out, he can't cope any more with running his kingdom – it's time he gave it up. He really is almost senile then, and it's only second wind that takes him to Goneril and then to Regan, and then into the storm. It's that extra burst that has exhausted him: the lack of sleep and the fact that he's determinedly living it up, in an endeavour to show himself that he was right and Cordelia was wrong. He is the cause of his own undoing, his own senility. But you're talking about the energy of Lear in the hunting scene, his second scene. I think it's a totally false energy that he's discovered; he's saying 'I'm still one of the chaps', and dying on his feet.

JWRM. You think then that Lear has divided the kingdom because he genuinely believes he's dying. He isn't trying to shed his regal obligations, but to ensure a smooth succession. And when Cordelia refuses to play his little game…

DS. He is suddenly driven into a corner, he's up against it. Because the whole thing has been pre-planned; he thinks he knows exactly where he stands. Cordelia is bound to say she loves him most. It's all worked out; he's got it drawn on the map: your third, your third, your third. But now what's going to happen? He'd already planned to go and live with Cordelia. So the one part of the scene that isn't pre-planned is when he suddenly screams at Cornwall and Albany, 'With my two daughters' dowers digest the third' [I, i, 128].[1] He gives them her third. 'Ourself', and he's thinking this up on the spur of the moment, that's why I have to get my secretary [Kent] to write it down. 'Ourself by monthly course', and then for the first time he says, 'Oh, I've got to have a few chaps around',

> With reservation of an hundred knights,
> By you to be sustained,   (I, i, 133-4)

'And you're going to pay for them.' Now the important thing is that nobody in that scene actually agrees to it. He thinks, because he's said it, that they've agreed to it. They never do. Nobody says anything. Is he right in assuming that they will agree to it, or what? After all, he is still king; except that he's not. He's just given it away.

The other thing we hinged on is the fact that it's 'With reservation of an hundred knights' – that a hundred knights are not a hundred servants, they are a hundred knights *plus* their servants. We are therefore talking of an entourage of possibly four hundred people. The only person who gives that clue away is Goneril, when she says 'Here do you keep a hundred knights and squires' [I, iv, 237]. What that constitutes, a hundred knights, is a private army. And that's what the girls are frightened of. They don't worry about a hundred people; who's worrying about that in those days? They're worried – until they manage to reduce his train – that at any moment he has it within his power to take back everything by force.

JWRM. That accounts then for the fact that the director takes literally the remarks that Goneril makes about the knights, that they are transforming her graced palace into a riotous inn, a brothel. I must say that when Lear comes in from hunting in the Mother Courage wagon,

and you're all firing off the guns, I'm quite shocked.

DS. Well it's rather a good entrance, isn't it? I mean they've all been out on horses, or running, or something. Lear's the one in the cart. And he's the one kidding himself he's enjoying himself. He's hating it. What a life! To spend a month there, and a month there, and a month there, for the rest of time. It's an awful existence, you see, when he hoped to be sitting by the fire. And so he's determined to bloody well enjoy himself, and at that age he can't. But he's putting on a good show; all the time he's trying to prove that he was right and Cordelia wrong. And doesn't one know old people who do that? Out of spite.

JWRM. Well, it certainly is an interpretation that I have never considered myself, but it is all consistent, I see, with the rationale of the production. I don't know whether I agree with it, but that doesn't spoil it for me.

DS. A lot of people disagree with the period in which our production is set.

JWRM. I don't think one should worry about that. *Lear*, after all, is set in 750 BC. What kind of costumes are you going to find for 750 BC that don't look ridiculous, or make the actors feel uncomfortable?

DS. That's right. Historically, we know that for hundreds of years Shakespeare was only produced in contemporary dress, right the way through to the early nineteenth century. Trevor Nunn wanted to do a modern dress production of this play, but realised that the last time in history when any one man was able to give away a kingdom was just before the 14–18 war, when we had the Czar and the Kaiser and Franz Joseph of Austria. After the 14–18 war that type of autocratic monarch no longer existed;

[1] Act, scene, and line references to *King Lear* are to the New Penguin edition of the play, ed. G. K. Hunter (Harmondsworth, 1972).

so that was the last period in which he could actually set the play. You see we're setting it in, what, 1914. [See Plate III.]

JWRM. Now I'd like to ask you about cutting the text.

DS. Oh, yes. In the first place, I should say that I'm a great believer in cutting. I said to Trevor Nunn as soon as he asked me if I'd do it, I said only if he cuts it. But I feel the same about Wagner; I think they both improve by cutting – by half, if possible. I'd like to see a two-hour *Lear*.

JWRM. Like Donald Wolfit's.

DS. Theatrically exciting, you see. If the uncut play is so good, well then go home and read it; don't bother about it in the theatre.

JWRM. On the other hand, I have always thought that you believe a well-trained professional actor can make any line, or any sequence of lines, in any of Shakespeare's plays intelligible to an audience, if he wants to.

DS. I do believe it, yes. Do you mean, and so why cut?

JWRM. So why cut.

DS. I think it's unforgivable to bore an audience. Although the actor may understand the line perfectly, you know the moment when you've lost an audience. There are certain lines you cannot hold the audience with. The hardest work I've ever had to do was Henry VIII's speech at the end of the trial scene [II, iv], when he goes into detail as to why he wants his divorce. It is the most boring speech in Shakespeare almost, and you've got to work like mad to make it theatrically effective.

JWRM. Prospero's speech to Miranda...

DS. Oh, Prospero's speech, yes.

JWRM. I can see why you didn't want to do Prospero.

DS. But it has the advantage, that one, of being at the beginning of the play; and you feel, well, it can only get better. But when it comes towards the end of a play, the audience are tired anyway.

JWRM. I begin to understand why there was progressively increased cutting as you got towards the end of *King Lear*. I felt sorry that Albany's line...

DS. Now, Bob, can I butt in here on something that is very important? Playing Shakespeare at Stratford-on-Avon is a daunting task. (Last year our season ran for eleven months.) Ninety-five per cent, if not more, of our audience are people who are seeing a Shakespeare play for the very first time, or that particular play for the first time: a lot of children, young people, tourists coming to Stratford – 'Better see one of his plays.' The other five per cent is made up of the aficionado and the scholar, those who know the plays backwards, inside out, like yourself, and relish every word. But the general public would much prefer the performance to run an hour and a half for their first effort; then go home and read the play; then see it again. We've got to cater for both elements of the audience, and it's a very difficult bridge to tread.

JWRM. Well, I have to do that with my students. They come from such diverse backgrounds.

DS. But you can take more than two hours. We've got to sell Shakespeare in two, what, three hours. For instance, one of the most perfect examples in the play is some of the Poor Tom material in the hovel scene. Totally incomprehensible for the first time of seeing; when you know the play, marvellous stuff. As an actor, Edgar is better off to have half the things to say; then he can work harder on hitting those home. But there's nothing worse than boring them.

JWRM. If it's not too trite a question, why particularly did you want to do King Lear?

DS. No, it's not a trite question, I suppose, but...I must be very careful here, you see. I have always maintained that of all theatrical forms the most difficult for an actor, the one that calls upon the most expertise, is farce – progressing right the way through the stages of comedy – that the easiest are the big tragedies. I once asked Edith Evans to come and see a farce I was in, and she said, 'Oh, darling, do I have to?' And I said 'No, no, but you'd be surprised how difficult I'm finding it to do.' She said, 'Of course you are, my dear, you have no play to help you.' You see, it's all on the expertise of the actor. Now people have said to me 'Ah, it's all very well for you, you've never done any of the big ones.' So having done *Lear* – and I've done some of the others, but not the tragedies – I now know that they're easier to do than farce. The idea, actually, of playing Lear came about two years ago at Chichester when I did Dr Stockmann in *An Enemy of the People.* He was a sort of monolithic chap, and I thought 'By golly, if I can do this, I'm going to have a go at Lear.' So when Trevor Nunn asked me to, well I said 'Yes!' In this country you get so little money for playing in the classics that you only want to do them if you're going to get something worth playing, don't you?

Talking to various other Lears about the play, I found all of them agreed that you've got to pace yourself, because Lear leads the play for the first half, and after that other people are leading it for him. He can then sit back and coast for the mad scenes; I mean, theatrically you can't, not as an actor. The drive of the play is taken off Lear's shoulders in the second half, which is one of the reasons why it's such a difficult part to play. Most actors want to play a part that gets more and more and more drive, until you're driving over the finishing line – which most of the great parts do. But here, it's a gradual decline.

JWRM. In fact, Lear is very passive from the moment...

DS. From the storm.

JWRM. Well really, even before that. From the end of the first scene, he is a character who is more acted upon than acting. Yes, he takes the initiative and leaves Goneril; he takes the initiative and leaves Gloucester's residence; but he is being driven to do this, rather than actively...

DS. That's right. But you can, as an actor, dominate those scenes, whereas with some of the later ones, you can't. So many productions I've seen where Lear in the first scene has swept on to the stage: '*Come on!* Let's get a move on!' And we're working against that in this production. It's a very quiet opening; it isn't until everything starts to fall to pieces that he gets any energy at all. Then, with the storm scene, a brilliant idea of the assistant director came up. He said that the first speech, 'Blow, winds, and crack your cheeks!' – that if you study those lines of text, they surely are an invocation that a storm *should* happen, rather than a comment on one that is already happening. And we worked on that, and, by golly, it's lovely to do. It means that one can begin in a whisper, '"Blow, winds"...Come on, blow!' Onomatopoeically, it is beautifully written because it's: wind, rain, lightning, thunder – he's left the thunder till last. He doesn't say, 'Let's have some lightning and thunder, and some wind and rain.' Orchestrally too, it's the right way of doing it, because you get the sound at the end. Donald Wolfit, you see, used to dominate a great storm effect the whole time. It's quite a long scene to just go on shouting for; the audience begin to lose interest.

JWRM. And the lines are so beautiful. You want to hear the words; you don't want them thrown away.

DS. Well, the director even had to stop me, because I was going too far on the lightning –

trying to make it like when you put two live wires together: psst-tt-tt-t!

> Vaunt-curriers of oak-cleaving thunderbolts,
> Singe my white head! (III, ii, 5–6)

Psst-tt-tt-t! I wanted to do it like that, you see, but the director said 'We're losing the words.' But it's nearly there: it's like a spitting of lightning. And then the thunder is superb:

> Strike flat the thick rotundity o' the world,

it's wonderful, isn't it? Thunderous lines.

I am convinced that when a number of times Lear says 'O let me not be mad', it's not mad in the psychiatric sense of the word, but 'Let me not lose my reason.' That's what I latched on to. I changed some punctuation there; and in a number of lines I devised my own punctuation, I must admit.

JWRM. One, I can think of: 'Let me wipe it first it smells. Of mortality.' [IV, vi, 134]

DS. You don't like that, Bob, do you? No, but the point is that it's suiting the action to the word, if you'll remember what I've been doing with my hand before. He's on about 'there is the sulphurous pit – burning, scalding, stench, consumption!' [IV, vi, 128–9]: he's talking about the female organs.

JWRM. I thought that wasn't a bad bit of business, actually.

DS. And so when Gloucester says 'O, let me kiss that hand!' I cut out the comma entirely, I said, 'Let me wipe it first it smells.' And then, if you're wondering why it smells: 'Of mortality', which hinges up with the female organ again. I thought; that's why I did it. Procreation, you see.

JWRM. Whatever reservations I may have about the production, I was tremendously impressed by the thought that went into your performance.

DS. As an actor, Bob, I never do anything perversely. You may say it is perverse to do, but nevertheless, I have got good rhyme and reason for everything I do. I never like to leave anything to chance to see how it comes out. I hammered away at one speech because I couldn't make it my own.

Ellen Terry said the best line that's ever been said about acting, as far as I'm concerned. Two sentences in which every word is of monumental importance. She said, 'To act, you must make the thing written your own. You must steal the words, steal the thought, and *convey* the stolen treasure to others with great art.' Every word in those two sentences is important: the use of the word 'steal', not borrow, or beg, you know; 'steal the words, steal the thought'. And I find I can judge any performance I've ever seen on whether or not the actor is doing the things in that statement. The most common fault is the last bit, 'with great art'. But then, who can do that? You've got to make the lines your own.

In this particular speech, it's rather like 'What a piece of work is a man' from *Hamlet*: 'Is man no more than this? Consider him well. Thou owest the worm no silk, . . . Here's three on's are sophisticated. Thou art the thing itself!' [III, iv, 99–103] Now I can't remember the original punctuation, but I couldn't make it my own until I said

Thou art the thing itself – unaccommodated. Man is no more but such a poor, bare, forked animal as thou art.

JWRM. You see I have a query against that line.

DS. Oh, how extraordinary! But there he is naked, or as good as theatrically he's allowed to be naked. 'Is man no more than this?' And I can use the word 'unaccommodated', I mean unencumbered, untrammelled. You may say it sounds perverse, but it was me hammering to make it my own.

JWRM. I didn't say it sounded perverse; it took me by surprise. One final question. Have you ever fancied directing a Shakespeare play yourself?

DS. No, not in so far as modern directing is concerned, because style is all, isn't it? But Trevor Nunn saying he's setting *Lear* in 1914 – I never have ideas like that. I want somebody else to say that; that's something unimportant as far as I'm concerned. A painter used to paint a picture, the picture he wanted, and then he took it to the framers to have it framed. And today it's rather like saying to a painter, 'Well there's a frame, now paint me a picture to fit it.' Do you know, it's what modern directors do.

I don't want to know about making the frames, it's not my business. But what I find I'm very good at is helping actors over problems which are totally technical. I can see an actor unable to put an idea into performance, and I'm usually frightfully good about putting my finger on the trouble spot. I can help actors fulfil, but not in the way of directing a play as from scratch. If somebody'd like to say, 'Look, would you direct a production of *Hamlet*, and you're all dressed as Martians?' O.K. I'll do that. I don't care about that; that's immaterial for me. But that's what so many directors get their reputations on – because they made it Martian.

© J. W. R. MEADOWCROFT 1980

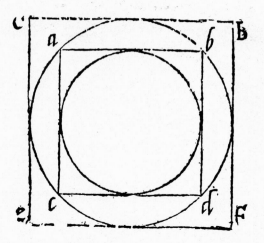

IA   An *ad quadratum* diagram, from Sebastiano Serlio,
The Book of Architecture (London, 1611) Book 1, fol. 2ᵛ

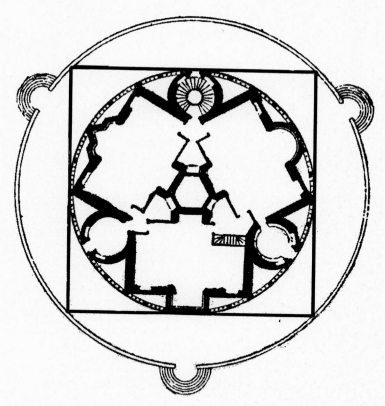

IB   John Thorpe, house on a circular terrace

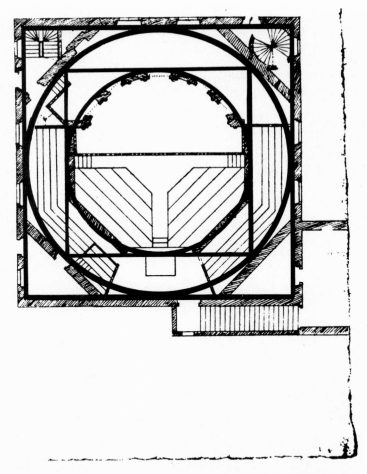

IIA *Ad quadratum* proportions of the cockpit at Whitehall. Jones/Webb drawings 1, 27

IIB Hollar, the Globe (left) and the Hope

III *King Lear*, Royal Shakespeare Theatre, 1976. Directed by John Barton, Barry Kyle and Trevor Nunn, designed by John Napier. Richard Durden as Albany, Barbara Leigh-Hunt as Goneril and Donald Sinden as King Lear

IV *Twelfth Night*, Royal Shakespeare Theatre, 1979. Directed by Terry Hands, designed by John Napier. Cherie Lunghi as Viola and Gareth Thomas as Orsino

VA *Pericles*, The Other Place, Stratford, 1979. Directed by Ron Daniels, designed by Chris Dyer. Peter McEnery as Pericles

VB *Pericles*, The Other Place, Stratford, 1979. Julie Peasgood as Marina

VI. *Pericles*. The Other Place, Stratford, 1979. The tournament at Pentapolis

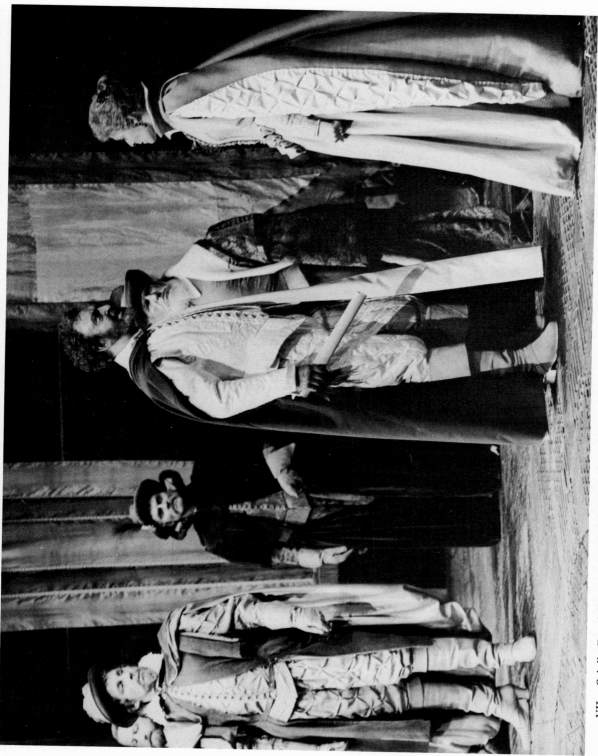

VII *Othello*, Royal Shakespeare Theatre, 1979. Directed by Ronald Eyre, designed by Pamela Howard. Bob Peck as Iago (far left); foreground: Jeffery Dench as Lodovico, Donald Sinden as Othello, Suzanne Bertish as Desdemona

VIII *As You Like It*, National Theatre, 1979. Directed by John Dexter, designed by Hayden Griffin. Ma... ... Yvonne Collis, Greg Hicks as Silvius, Sara Kestelman as Rosalind.

HAMLET'S SPECIAL PROVIDENCE

ALAN SINFIELD

We defy augury: there is a special providence in the fall of a sparrow. If it be now, 'tis not to come; if it be not to come, it will be now; if it be not now, yet it will come – the readiness is all. Since no man owes of aught he leaves, what is't to leave betimes? Let be.

(*Hamlet*, v, ii, 210–16)[1]

[God is] a Governor and Preserver, and that, not by producing a kind of general motion in the machine of the globe as well as in each of its parts, but by a special Providence sustaining, cherishing, superintending, all the things which he has made, to the very minutest, even to a sparrow.

(Calvin, *Institutes of the Christian Religion*)[2]

Fate guides us, and it was settled at the first hour of birth what length of time remains for each. Cause is linked with cause, and all public and private issues are directed by a long sequence of events. Therefore everything should be endured with fortitude, since things do not, as we suppose, simply happen – they all come.

(Seneca, 'De Providentia')[3]

The first passage quoted, where Hamlet declares that 'there is a special providence in the fall of a sparrow', is of key importance in the longstanding critical debate about *Hamlet* and Christianity. The way we relate it to the attitudes represented in the quotations from Calvin and Seneca bears crucially upon our choice between three rival interpretations of the play. Bradley recognises Hamlet's phraseology here as Christian but regards its tone and the play generally as pagan in implication: Hamlet expresses 'that kind of religious resignation which, however beautiful in one aspect, really deserves the name of fatalism rather than

that of faith in Providence, because it is not united to any determination to do what is believed to be the will of Providence.'[4] Roland Mushat Frye believes these lines show Hamlet 'relying upon an unmistakably Christian providence' and hence achieving true faith.[5] Roy W. Battenhouse agrees with Frye that the play has a Christian tendency but also with Bradley that Hamlet's own attitude is unChristian: 'A biblical echo, the sparrow reference, when found in this upside-down context, alerts us to the tragic parody in Hamlet's version of readiness.'[6] Hamlet is either a pagan in a pagan play, a good Christian in a Christian play, or a sinner in a Christian play.

A Senecan frame of reference seems appropriate in the first four acts of the play, for

[1] Plays by Shakespeare are quoted from the *Complete Works*, ed. Peter Alexander (London and Glasgow, 1951). Unattributed act, scene and line numbers are from *Hamlet*.

[2] John Calvin, *Calvin's Institutes*, [trans. Henry Beveridge], (Florida, n.d.), 1, xvi, 1.

[3] Seneca, *Moral Essays*, trans. John W. Basore, 3 vols (Loeb edition, London and Cambridge, Mass., 1958), 'De Providentia', v. 7.

[4] A. C. Bradley, *Shakespearean Tragedy* (1960), p. 116. See also H. B. Charlton, *Shakespearian Tragedy* (Cambridge, 1949), pp. 103–4.

[5] *Shakespeare and Christian Doctrine* (Princeton, 1963), p. 231. See also Ivor Morris, *Shakespeare's God* (1972), pp. 422–30.

[6] *Shakespearean Tragedy, its Art and its Christian Premises* (Bloomington, 1969), p. 250. See also Lily B. Campbell, *Shakespeare's Tragic Heroes* (New York, 1966), pp. 141–7.

Hamlet's great need is Stoic tranquillity of mind. He values Horatio because he is 'A man that Fortune's buffets and rewards/Hast ta'en with equal thanks;...not a pipe for Fortune's finger/To sound what stop she please...not passion's slave' (III, ii, 65–70). By subduing his emotions Horatio frees himself from the effects of fortune and becomes the Stoics' wise and happy man.

It is not the principle of revenge which troubles Hamlet, but the achievement of a state of mind where he can do something coherent about it. Seneca declares,

The good man will perform his duties undisturbed and unafraid; and he will in such a way do all that is worthy of a good man as to do nothing that is unworthy of a man. My father is being murdered – I will defend him; he is slain – I will avenge him, not because I grieve, but because it is my duty.

(*Moral Essays*, 'De Ira', I, xii, 2)

Hamlet cannot act so calmly; he cannot focus sufficiently coolly upon any matter to determine a policy and carry it through. His most sustained venture is the mouse-trap play but it is all brilliant improvisation. He is nervous and excited before and wildly exuberant afterwards; he vaunts, 'Now could I drink hot blood' (III, ii, 380), but spares the praying King and strikes out recklessly, killing Polonius. Though he has the evidence he sought he leaves at Claudius's command for England. The issue which oppresses Hamlet is not how or whether to be revenged, but how to do anything purposeful at all. In the face of the manifold injunctions, distractions, plots and crimes which assail him he can hardly hold himself single-mindedly to any action.

Hamlet presents himself as an unsuccessful Stoic in his first exchange with Rosencrantz and Guildenstern. They perhaps engaged in light-hearted philosophical banter as students, but here the subtext is their manoeuvring to discover each other's purposes. Rosencrantz denies that Denmark is a prison; Hamlet replies, 'Why, then, 'tis none to you; for there is nothing either good or bad, but thinking makes it so' (II, ii, 248–50). This characteristically Stoic notion usually has a contrary import – that one can be happy and free if the mind chooses. Rosencrantz should be amused but is determined to turn the discussion to ambition. Hamlet replies, more earnestly, 'O God, I could be bounded in a nutshell and count myself a king of infinite space, were it not that I have bad dreams' (II, ii, 253–55). Compare the Chorus in Seneca's *Thyestes*: 'It is the mynde that onely makes a king...A kyng hee is that feareth nought at all./Eche man him selfe this kyngdome geeves at hand.'[1]

It is of course Stoic to entertain suicide as a solution to intolerable emotional pressure. Horatio, at Hamlet's death, terms himself 'more an antique Roman than a Dane' (V, ii, 333). The secular manner in which Hamlet discusses it (III, i, 56–88) recalls the disputes between Oedipus and Antigone in Seneca's *Phoenissae* (1–319), and Deianira, the Nurse and Hyllas in *Hercules Oetaeus* (842–1030). For Seneca it is indeed a 'question' whether it is nobler to suffer or to kill oneself. Death is always the way out, yet it is base to flinch: 'The brave and wise man should not beat a hasty retreat from life.'[2] His main theme is that it is superstitious and irrational to fear death or what might follow it, but such anxieties preoccupy Hamlet, who again falls short of Stoic detachment.

For Seneca, the man who achieves Stoic self-mastery is godlike:

the wise man is next-door neighbour to the gods and like a god in all save his mortality. As he struggles and presses on towards those things that are lofty, well-ordered, undaunted, that flow on with even and harmonious current, that are untroubled, kindly,

[1] *Seneca, his Tenne Tragedies*, ed. Thomas Newton (1581), 2 vols (New York, 1967), I, 67.
[2] Seneca, *Ad Lucilium Epistulae Morales*, trans. Richard M. Gunmere, 3 vols (Loeb edition, Cambridge, Mass. and London, 1961), XXIV, 25.

adapted to the public good, beneficial both to himself and to others, the wise man will covet nothing low, will never repine.

(*Moral Essays*, 'De Constantia', viii, 2)

Hamlet is perplexed and disillusioned at the failure of this ideal in others and in himself. Man is said to be 'in apprehension, how like a god! the beauty of the world! the paragon of animals! And yet, to me, what is this quintessence of dust?' (II, ii, 303–5). He ponders:

> Sure he that made us with such large discourse,
> Looking before and after, gave us not
> That capability and godlike reason
> To fust in us unus'd. (IV, iv, 36–9)

But Hamlet is far from such cool judgement and unimpressed by the divine qualities of himself or those around him.

The plausibility of the godlike Stoic hero is questioned in similar terms by Marston in the Antonio plays, which seem strongly to have influenced *Hamlet*. In *Antonio and Mellida* Andrugio affects indifference to the loss of his kingdom but falls at once into a rage when it is mentioned: 'Name not the Genoese; that very word/Unkings me quite, makes me vile passion's slave' (IV, i, 68–9). In *Antonio's Revenge* Pandulpho remains tranquil about the murder of his son for many scenes, but suddenly declares, 'Man will break out, despite philosophy.... I spake more than a god,/Yet am less than a man' (IV, iii, 69–75).[1] In fact the inadequacy of Stoicism is implicit in Seneca's writings, where alongside the godlike, rational man is an acute awareness of the difficulty of withstanding the adversities which afflict mankind. Miriam T. Griffin terms it 'the schizophrenia endemic in Stoic philosophy, with its vision of the *sapiens* and its code of behaviour for the *imperfectus*'.[2] In Seneca's plays there are almost no successful Stoics. The eschewal of passion is in theory a stance of strength and self-sufficiency, but it can easily seem a weak, fall-back position – a retreat from the intolerable.

What is at issue in *Hamlet* is optimistic humanism – that strand in Renaissance thought which exalted man's capacity to achieve, through the exercise of rational powers, a moral stature which the incautious termed godlike. Even a man of Hamlet's intelligence and sensitivity cannot assert himself in this world and gain a workable degree of self-sufficiency, but is overwhelmed by emotional turmoil and the follies and crimes of his fellow men. When Ophelia laments his instability – 'that noble and most sovereign reason,/Like sweet bells jangled, out of time and harsh' (III, i, 157–8) – she draws attention to the collapse of a whole world view.

It is usual and proper to contrast Hamlet with the other young men in the play. But we should notice also that Laertes is no more successful (he kills Hamlet but wishes he had not), and although Fortinbras is presumably elected king of Denmark, this is by chance not design – the throne he and his father fought and schemed for is gained not through their godlike qualities but by default. Only the stolid Horatio approaches the ideal, and when his test comes at the end of the play he is hardly dissuaded from suicide. It seems impossible to act meaningfully in a universe tragically ill-adapted to human kind. The only dignified option seems to be that offered in the plays of Seneca, Webster and Ford: a heroic death.

Thus far we have placed *Hamlet* in a secular context, but Protestant thinkers anticipated the failure of Stoicism. Calvin did not expect fallen men to achieve rationality and equanimity, let alone be godlike; he termed 'absurd' the Stoic hero 'who, divested of humanity, was affected in the same way by adversity and prosperity, grief and joy; or rather, like a stone, was not affected by anything' (*Institutes*, III, viii, 9). The error of 'philosophers generally'

---

[1] Ed. G. K. Hunter (1965, 1966).
[2] *Seneca, a Philosopher in Politics* (Oxford, 1976), p. 177.

is that 'they maintain that the intellect is endued with reason, the best guide to a virtuous and happy life, provided it duly avails itself of its excellence, and exerts the power with which it is naturally endued' (*Institutes*, II, ii, 2). According to the Protestant analysis, we should not be surprised or disappointed at the collapse of the Stoic ideal in *Hamlet*.

Upon his return from England Hamlet seems to have accepted this view. He no longer expects to achieve mastery of himself or his circumstances. In the Graveyard he meditates upon a jester's skull, an emblem of the limits which confound mortal aspirations. The cause of his change seems to be the extraordinary turns events have taken – the appearance of the Ghost when Claudius seemed secure, the arrival of the players prompting the test of the king, Hamlet's felicitous discovery of the plot against his life and above all his amazing delivery through the pirates. The latter especially is so improbable, and so unnecessary to the plot, that we may suppose Shakespeare wishes the audience also to be impressed with the special interventions of providence. Hence when Hamlet describes how he discovered Claudius's letter and changed it he attributes the whole sequence to providence: 'There's a divinity that shapes our ends,/Rough-hew them how we will' (v, ii, 10–11). He was able to seal the altered instructions: 'Why, even in that was heaven ordinant' (v, ii, 48). Thus he reaches the assertion that 'there is a special providence in the fall of a sparrow' (v, ii, 212). In phraseology at least Stoic doctrine has been superseded by Christian.

The choice of Calvin to represent contemporary Protestant opinion should no longer need arguing. Amongst historians his influence upon the Elizabethan Church is scarcely disputed and several literary scholars have recently related it to plays of the period.[1] Calvin is particularly relevant here because he insisted upon the doctrine of providence in the strong

form which it takes at this point in *Hamlet*. One axis of his theology is the impotence of fallen humanity; the other is God's total power to govern the world in accord with his divine (though incomprehensible) plan.

Moreover, it is against Stoic fate or fortune that Calvin is arguing when he speaks of special providence and the fall of a sparrow – both in the quotation with which we began and again during the supporting argument:

The Christian . . . will have no doubt that a special providence is awake for his preservation, and will not suffer anything to happen that will not turn to his good and safety. . . . Hence, our Saviour, after declaring that even a sparrow falls not to the ground without the will of his Father, immediately makes the application, that being more valuable than many sparrows, we ought to consider that God provides more carefully for us.   (*Institutes*, I, xvii, 6)

In Calvin's Latin the words are usually 'singularis providentia'; his French has alternately 'la providence singulière' and 'la providence spéciale'; the translation by Thomas Norton (1561) has both 'singular providence' and 'special providence' (see I, xvi, 1, 4, 7).

Whether the allusion and phraseology shared by Calvin and Hamlet necessarily imply predestination is not entirely clear. Christ's remark about the sparrow is problematic for Christians who assert free will – Erasmus in his argument against Luther is obliged to take it as 'hyperbole'.[2] Bertram Joseph notices the term 'special providence' in several divines (though not Calvin) and thinks it consistent with free will,

---

[1] See Frye, *Shakespeare and Christian Doctrine*; William R. Elton, *King Lear and the Gods* (San Marino, 1968); Dominic Baker-Smith, 'Religion and John Webster' in Brian Morris, ed., *John Webster* (1970); Paul R. Sellin, 'The Hidden God' in *The Darker Vision of the Renaissance*, ed. Robert S. Kinsman (Berkeley and London, 1974); Robert G. Hunter, *Shakespeare and the Mystery of the Gods* (Georgia, 1976).

[2] *Luther and Erasmus: Free Will and Salvation*, ed. E. Gordon Rupp and Philip S. Watson (1969), pp. 83–4.

but he misses the dominant thrust of the phrase and the Reformation when he explains, 'Calvinists, too, could agree... that God through His special providence creates the opportunity, and the individual, if he is the right man, will take it'.[1] But Calvin and Luther alike believed that God has predetermined all events, and of the theologians Joseph mentions – William Perkins, Hugh Latimer, Joseph Hall and Lancelot Andrewes – all but the last took the same view. This is the doctrine Elizabethans generally understood in the tenth, eleventh and seventeenth of the Thirty-Nine Articles. When it was challenged at Cambridge in 1595 Archbishop Whitgift (no puritan) sponsored the Lambeth Articles to affirm it; they had no official status but indicate the position of the Church establishment.

Hamlet's words sound like predestination: 'If it be now, 'tis not to come; if it be not to come, it will be now; if it be not now, yet it will come' (v, ii, 213–15); 'ordinant' (v, ii, 48) means 'directing, controlling'. Notice also that in the 'bad' First Quarto Hamlet is made to say, 'theres a predestiuate prouidence in the fall of a sparrow'. Even if this is no more than a faulty memorial construct it shows how one well-placed contemporary understood Shakespeare's meaning. However, my argument does not require that we take Hamlet's phrase as Calvinistic in the fullest sense, only that we see Hamlet proposing a high degree of divine intervention and suggesting predestination.

We seem to have arrived at a Protestant interpretation of *Hamlet*: the prince recognises the folly of humanistic aspiration and the controlling power of providence, and the shape of the action, with purposes eventually falling on the inventors' heads, confirms it. Some readers may wonder why, if the play is governed by providence, it is manifestly composed of 'carnal, bloody, and unnatural acts' (v, ii, 373) with very little of love, mercy and forgiveness. At this point our attention to Calvin is surely

justified, for his account of earthly life is as grim as that of any tragedian:

> Various diseases ever and anon attack us: at one time pestilence rages; at another we are involved in all the calamities of war. Frost and hail, destroying the promise of the year, cause sterility, which reduces us to penury; wife, parents, children, relatives, are carried off by death; our house is destroyed by fire. These are the events which make men curse their life, detest the day of their birth, execrate the light of heaven, even censure God, and (as they are eloquent in blasphemy) charge him with cruelty and injustice.
>
> (*Institutes*, III, vii, 10)

Calvin does not repudiate this description of the human condition; nor does he throw any stress upon the consolation of an after-life. Instead he asserts through the concept of providence that all is due to the just will of God.

However dreadful and apparently unfair the affliction, 'the rule of piety is, that the hand of God is the ruler and arbiter of the fortunes of all, and, instead of rushing on with thoughtless violence, dispenses good and evil with perfect regularity' (*Institutes*, III, vii, 10). Calvin sustains this statement mainly by insisting that all men are fallen and sinful and so deserve the worst that can happen to them. Nevertheless, he distinguishes the sufferings of the wicked from those of believers. In the former case, 'God is to be understood as taking vengeance on his enemies, by displaying his anger against them, confounding, scattering, and annihilating them'; in the latter 'it is not properly punishment or vengeance, but correction and admonition' (*Institutes*, III, iv, 31). But all receive afflictions. Even theologians who denied predestination believed with Calvin that human suffering is caused by God intervening in the world to afflict and punish good and bad men. Lancelot Andrewes in his 'Sermon Preached at Chiswick in the Time of Pestilence' (1603)

[1] Bertram Joseph, *Conscience and the King* (1953), p. 139; also pp. 136–41.

refers to providence and the sparrow to show that God must be the cause of the plague. He concludes, 'So our inventions beget sin, sin provokes the wrath of God, the wrath of God sends the Plague among us.'[1]

The violent and punitive providence of Calvin and even of Andrewes could certainly be the moving force behind the diseased action of Shakespeare's play. Thus it is that Hamlet can claim, with the deaths of his father, Polonius, Ophelia and Rosencrantz and Guildenstern in mind, 'there is a special providence in the fall of a sparrow'. That is how God was believed to manage affairs.

So *Hamlet* appears to be a Christian play in the Elizabethan sense of the term. We are slow to recognise this because we have been taught a more amiable conception of the Christian God. Indeed, dwelling upon the rigours of Protestant doctrine produces an intriguing solution to the question of how Christian Elizabethans wrote and enjoyed such bleak tragedies. Perhaps it is not that they understood the plays differently from the modern reader: they too saw in *Hamlet* man's feeble attempts to act purposefully in a hostile world. But what they perceived as the working out in typical fashion of God's mysterious providential plan strikes us as bitterly tragic. We read the plays similarly but place them differently in relation to a shifting concept of Christianity.

A whole group of plays might fall within this insight. *The Jew of Malta, The Spanish Tragedy, Richard III, Antonio's Revenge, Macbeth* and *The Revenger's Tragedy* all suggest by the intricate, violent and inexorable way in which events work out that a deity of the Protestant stamp is in control, and the characters often invoke him. They call upon God to destroy the wicked and eventually he does; we need not take ironically their devout satisfaction. The sufferings of innocent by-standers are instances of the crosses we are required to bear.

Yet such an interpretation is not satisfactory for *Hamlet*, and the difficulties emanate from the very speech about providence and the sparrow. The issue is not the killing of the king, the moral status of which seems to be uncertain. Most Reformation Protestants would be pleased at the violent death of a manifest wrongdoer like Claudius, but they would question the action of the killer. Calvin was opposed to private vengeance though he believed that God works through it. However, like Aquinas, he was sympathetic to tyrannicide, at least when performed by lesser magistrates who 'by the ordinance of God' are the 'appointed guardians' of the people (*Institutes*, IV, xx, 31). Tudor propaganda, of course, saw rebellion as the worst of evils, but the Dutch and Huguenots developed from Calvin's hint a complete theory of controlled revolt. Already in the closet scene Hamlet regards himself as Heaven's 'scourge and minister' (III, iv, 175), and just before the appearance of Osric he recalls to Horatio Claudius's manifold crimes and asks,

> is't not perfect conscience
> To quit him with this arm? And is't not to be damn'd
> To let this canker of our nature come
> In further evil? (V, ii, 67–70)

Politically, ethically, theologically it can be argued either way.

The more pressing problem is Bradley's sense that the tone and implication of Hamlet's speech, however Christian its terminology, are fatalistic. Some commentators feel that, having recognised God's controlling hand, Hamlet's proper course is to do nothing. This was not Protestant doctrine. Although predestination means that individual actions can make no difference Calvinists, always afraid of antinomianism, urged that the true Christian should show his delight in God's will by co-operating as far as he is able (*Institutes*, I, xvii, 3, 4).

[1] Lancelot Andrewes, *Works*, 11 vols (Oxford, 1854), V, 224, 234.

Hamlet believes that providence wants Claudius removed and that he should do it – 'the interim is mine', he says (v, ii, 73). However, 'the readiness is all' refers not to action but to death. Hamlet plays with Osric (surely this scene is purposely desultory), competes with Laertes and makes no plans against the king. The final killing occurs in a burst of passionate inspiration and when Hamlet himself is, in effect, slain.

Consider also the context of the speech. Hamlet is not making a general statement about the rightness of God's control of the world, but sweeping aside Horatio's very reasonable suspicion about the duel. Thus he ignores Calvin's argument that 'the Lord has furnished men with the arts of deliberation and caution, that they may employ them in subservience to his providence, in the preservation of their life' (*Institutes*, I, xvii, 4). Hamlet's thought has a contrary tendency: he sees no point in troubling about what will happen. And this is implicit in the tone of the speech. Editors disagree about the last line; the Second Quarto has 'since no man of ought he leaves, knowes what ist to leave betimes, let be'. However we emend this, it sounds fatalistic.

Hamlet acknowledges divine determination of events, but without enthusiasm. Our theme turns back upon itself, for his resignation, like his earlier godlike aspiration, is Senecan. Stoic world weariness is felt despite the distinctively Protestant phraseology; the context, the tone of the speech and Hamlet's subsequent inactivity all recall the quotation from 'De Providentia' with which we began: 'it was settled at the first hour of birth what length of time remains for each. . . . Therefore everything should be endured with fortitude, since things do not, as we suppose, simply happen – they all come.' Playing upon the ambivalence in Seneca's work, Shakespeare is developing the sense of futility which often underlies the theory of rational self-sufficiency. And this is in the very teeth of Calvinist doctrine for, as I have observed, it is actually whilst repudiating Stoic fate that Calvin alludes to providence and the sparrow. The Stoics 'feign a universal providence, which does not condescend to take special care of every creature' (*Institutes*, I, xvii, 6; see also I, xvi, 8), and it is against such an impersonal force that Calvin and Hamlet maintain a 'special providence' which cares for every individual in every detail of his life.

The intricate working out of events obliges Hamlet to recognise the precise control of the Protestant God but he does not find in himself the joyful response theologians anticipated. Calvin distinguished Stoic patience, which accepts what happens because 'so it must be', and Christian, which cheerfully embraces God's will 'with calm and grateful minds' (*Institutes*, III, viii, 11). Hamlet contemplates God's intimate and pervasive direction of the universe with only Stoic patience. It makes him wonder; temporarily, when he is sending Rosencrantz and Guildenstern to their doom, it exhilarates him; but ultimately it depresses him. 'There is a special providence in the fall of a sparrow' and in the corruption and suffering of Denmark, and it inspires in Hamlet not joyful co-operation but weary acquiescence. His attitude provokes the thought that the world is unjustly governed by such a God.

Commentators have disagreed about Hamlet's attitude to providence because it is confused, but I believe purposefully. Shakespeare is exploiting the contradictions in Stoicism and the embarrassments in Calvinism. For those who assert a beneficent order in the universe there are two alternatives with the problem of evil. One is that God allows considerable freedom to his creation; the danger here is that things begin to get out of control, the sense of God's concern slips away and we might as well regard events as absurd or the work of blind fortune.

The other alternative is that God is in complete control, but then he has to assume an awkwardly immediate responsibility for evil. Seneca tries to slide between these two positions, partly by saying different things at different times, partly by proposing controlling gods who do not concern themselves with details.

The dilemma should trouble all Christians but Calvin confronts it head on: his doctrine of providence asserts defiantly that God directs everything and that he is perfectly good. All unpleasantness in the world occurs immediately and justly by God's will, and mere men should not expect to understand. Yet Calvin tries to explain, and runs repeatedly into difficulties. For instance, is it fair that God refuses to allow a man like Claudius (or Dr Faustus) to repent?

To some it seems harsh, and at variance with the divine mercy, utterly to deny forgiveness to any who betake themselves to it. This is easily disposed of. It is not said that pardon will be refused if they turn to the Lord, but it is altogether denied that they can turn to repentance, inasmuch as for their ingratitude they are struck by the just judgement of God with eternal blindness. (*Institutes*, III, iii, 24)

Calvin falls back continually upon assertion and divine inscrutability: 'The will of God is the supreme rule of righteousness, so that everything which he wills must be held to be righteous by the mere fact of his willing it' (*Institutes*, III, xxiii, 2).

Calvin argues rigorously from his first principles and with ample scriptural support, and creates a superbly self-contained system. But he cannot make it satisfy ordinary, common sense morality. It is not that one cannot easily assemble signs of the operations of such a deity in the world; what is unacceptable is the demand that we marvel at its goodness and mercy. My contention is that the paradoxes of Protestant theology provoked alarm and confusion and that it is apparent in *Hamlet* and other tragedies.

Evidence of humane objections to Protestant orthodoxy ranges from Andrewes's complaint that the Lambeth Articles make God appear unjust to the development by General Baptists from about 1600 of a doctrine of universal salvation. Robert Burton (who, it may be noted, condemns in Calvin's manner Seneca's concept of fate)[1] describes fully, among the 'Causes of Despair' in religion, how Calvin's favourite Biblical sentences

terrify the souls of many; election, predestination, reprobation, preposterously conceived, offend divers, with a deal of foolish presumption, curiosity, needless speculation, contemplation, solicitude, wherein they trouble and puzzle themselves about those questions of grace, free will, perseverance, God's secrets.

(*Anatomy of Melancholy*, III, 398–9)

Burton himself seems to hanker after a liberal theology: 'For how can he be merciful that shall condemn any creature to eternal unspeakable punishment...But these absurd paradoxes are exploded by our Church, we teach otherwise' – and he goes on to restate Calvinist orthodoxy (III, 423–4).

Surely we cannot overestimate the impact upon the Reformation mind of the Church's insistence upon attributing good and bad alike to a special providence whose justice cannot be demonstrated to the ordinary intellect. It has much to do, I believe, with the peculiar theological stance of many Elizabethan tragedies. We have observed that characters often call upon a violent deity whose controlling presence is eventually confirmed by the intricate working out of events. At the same time, the beneficence of this system is brought into question by our sympathy for the characters, by the provocative interweaving of Jove, revenge, fate and fortune with Christian divinities, by a pervasive fatalism and by the harshness of some attitudes attributed to the deity – in *Antonio's Revenge*, for instance, the ghost of Andrugio

[1] *The Anatomy of Melancholy*, ed. Holbrook Jackson, 3 vols (1968), III, 385, 387.

declares, 'Now looks down providence/T'attend the last act of my son's revenge' (v, i, 10–11). We may be able to demonstrate from the *Institutes* the broad compatibility of such plays with Protestantism but we cannot feel comforted by the world they present. Hence the appeal of Seneca to Elizabethan dramatists: Stoicism offers complex variations upon Christianity in respect of its estimate of man and its conception of divine power. All this manifests a deep unease with Christian doctrine as it was customarily preached. These writers have gone half-way with Calvin: they are convinced that men are fallen and in a fallen world but have only nominal confidence in God's redemptive goodness. They lurch back towards fatalism; it is a recipe for tragedy.

Hamlet presents this dissatisfaction with orthodox theology in an unusually coherent form. By undermining humanistic Stoicism and positing a controlling deity in words deriving from Calvin the play takes us to the brink of a Protestant affirmation, but Hamlet's fatalistic attitude encourages us to question divine justice. We understand and respect his reluctance to co-operate with a divinity whose doings are so arbitrary and overwhelming. Senecan resignation seems a reasonable response.

It will be felt that I have been teasing out strands in popular plays that only a theologian would recognise in the theatre. This is true: the disquiet of these writers with Protestant doctrine was probably scarcely formulated. Their plays do not present a coherent philosophy but a confused sense of alarm and wonderment at the mysterious ways of providence. However, Marlowe for one seems fully conscious of the distinction between pagan and Christian and how it may be used to suggest a critique of providence. *The Jew of Malta* concludes, 'So march away; and let due praise be given,/Neither to Fate nor Fortune, but to Heaven.'[1] Ferneze prefers Christian doctrine to pagan and attributes events to God's providence, but the action makes us wonder whether fate or fortune is not a more likely presiding deity. In *Hamlet* Christian statements supersede pagan ones in a theologically precise form, but the action remains ambiguous.

[1] *The Plays of Christopher Marlowe*, ed. Roma Gill (Oxford, 1971).

© ALAN SINFIELD 1980

'ANTONY AND CLEOPATRA':
'THE TIME OF UNIVERSAL PEACE'

ANDREW FICHTER

I

With his victory at Actium still hanging in the balance, Shakespeare's Octavius speaks prophetically of a new era of peace:

The time of universal peace is near:
Prove this a prosperous day, the three-nook'd world
Shall bear the olive freely.[1]   (IV, vi, 5–7)

That the 'universal peace' Octavius envisions nearly coincides with that proclaimed thirty years later at Christ's nativity (Luke, ii, 14) is, of course, beyond the capacity of Octavius to see; but a tradition of Christian historiography extending from the early Church Fathers through the Renaissance regards the proximity of these two events with a different awareness.[2] Christian historians viewing the advent of the *Pax Romana* retrospectively could see in it an adumbration of the *Pax Christiana*, and they could see in the closeness with which one event followed the other the unfolding of a providential plan. Thus Eusebius, for instance, speaks of the twin triumphs of monarchy and monotheism as emanations from a common source:

Two great powers sprang up fully as out of one stream and they gave peace to all and brought all together to a state of friendship: the Roman empire, which from that time appeared as one kingdom, and the power of the Saviour of all, whose aid was at once extended to and established with everyone.[3]

While only the pagan perspective on history is overtly dramatized in *Antony and Cleopatra*, Shakespeare gives us sufficient evidence, I think,

to conclude that we are meant to be aware of the Christian perspective as well. As Antony

[1] Quotations are taken from the Arden edition of *Antony and Cleopatra*, ed. M. R. Ridley, 9th edn. (1954; repr. Cambridge, Mass., 1956).

[2] Theodore E. Mommsen traces the earliest manifestations of this tradition from Bishop Melito of Sardis, Tertullian, and Eusebius in 'St Augustine and the Christian Idea of Progress: The Background of *The City of God*', *Journal of the History of Ideas*, XII (1951), 346–74, and 'Aponius and Orosius on the Significance of the Epiphany', *Late Classical and Medieval Studies in Honor of Albert Mathias Friend, Jr.*, ed. Kurt Weitzman (Princeton, 1955), pp. 92–111. Both articles are reprinted in Theodore E. Mommsen, *Medieval and Renaissance Studies*, ed. Eugene F. Rice, Jr (Ithaca, 1959). For medieval appearances of the inclination to see the *Pax Romana* as a prefiguration of the *Pax Christiana*, see Otto of Freising, *De duabus civitatibus*, III, 6; Dante, *Convivio*, fourth treatise, ch. 5, *Monarchia*, I, 16, and *Purgatorio*, XXXII, 102; and the story of Octavian's vision of the Ara Coeli on the day of the Nativity, recorded by Jacobus de Voragine in *The Golden Legend* and evident in iconography from the late thirteenth century on (see Millard Meiss, *French Painting in the Time of Jean de Berry: The Late Fourteenth Century and the Patronage of the Duke* (1967), 2 vols, pp. 233ff. and plates 814–20; and the 'Bladelin Altarpiece' by Roger van der Weyden in Erwin Panofsky, *Early Netherlandish Painting: Its Origins and Character* (Cambridge, Mass., 1953), 2 vols, p. 277 and plates 197–201). The legend of the Ara Coeli figures prominently in the Nativity play of the *Chester Mystery Cycle*, whose last known manuscripts date as late as the beginning of the seventeenth century. The providential coincidence of the *Pax Romana* and the *Pax Christiana* is also mentioned in the chronicles of Hardyng and Grafton.

[3] *Theophania* 3.2, translated by S. Lee, *Eusebius on the Theophania* (Cambridge, 1843), 156f.; cited by Mommsen, *Medieval and Renaissance Studies*, p. 283.

and Cleopatra paradoxically assert for themselves a love transcending death and a triumph emerging from defeat we are meant to recognize an impulse that is completed in Christian miracle; but we are also meant to realize that in the pre-Christian world of Shakespeare's play the transcendence to which the lovers aspire is tragically impossible. Seen in the light of both Plutarch and Scripture, then, the historical setting of *Antony and Cleopatra*, as J. L. Simmons has observed, establishes the play's moral and dramatic contingencies. Antony and Cleopatra claim an ideal of love that remains untenable in their pagan world. To romanticize their vision of an eternity in one another's lips (I, iii, 35) is to ignore the play's moral environment (or environments, if we may invoke both Roman and Christian morality); but to condemn the lovers is to condemn 'not only the heroic but the divine urge'.[1]

Yet it remains difficult to avoid the conclusion that as we view the play retrospectively from the vantage afforded by Christian historiography we are seeing a world in which even the most heroic aspirations are ironically delimited. While we are not called upon to dismiss Antony and Cleopatra for having failed according to standards not yet revealed to them, we are, I think, entitled to speak more broadly of the limitations of tragic vision itself. *Antony and Cleopatra* evokes a world in transition, but one ironically unaware of the magnitude of the change about to occur offstage. The action of the play is prologue to a greater action that will ultimately reverse tragedy's fundamental laws. Were the hyperbolical and paradoxical rhetoric of Antony and Cleopatra to have been set in a Christian universe it might have been heard as the language of romance rather than that of tragedy. (We have only to look at Shakespeare's other Augustan play, *Cymbeline*, to see the impact of the Incarnation reflected in drama.) As it is, paradox cannot fully sustain itself in the world of *Antony and Cleopatra*; yet this

failure is testimony to the significance of the impending miracle of grace. Through its own collapse, that is, the heroic discourse of the play announces the imminence of the Christian era.

Clearly the difference between the Roman and the Christian fulfillments of Octavius's prophecy of a 'time of universal peace' is for Shakespeare a matter of no little irony. One involves the self-deification of Octavius as Augustus Caesar while the other announces the incarnation of a deity in human form. The *Pax Romana* is the result of the manipulations of one of Shakespeare's most self-serving and irreducibly political characters; Christianity, on the other hand, offers a standard of selflessness of which the actions of Octavius are morally an inversion. In *Antony and Cleopatra*, moreover, we witness the emergence of the *Pax Romana* from the point of view of its antagonists, and if we adopt their perspective we take history to be an essentially tragic process. The progress of Roman civilization leaves a world more impoverished than it found:

> the odds is gone,
> And there is nothing left remarkable
> Beneath the visiting moon. (IV, xv, 66–8)

The Christian narrative, however, reverses the premise of tragic consciousness, and paradoxically asks that a death be taken as a means to greater enrichment.

The dramatic world of *Antony and Cleopatra* is aware of the emergence of *imperium* only in its Roman and temporal form. To the extent that its Christian and spiritual counterpart is relevant to the play, that relevance can only be stated obliquely. With this Shakespeare has reversed the paradox frequently confronted by Renaissance poets concerned with Christian myth – its historical remoteness and its spiritual immanence. In *Antony and Cleopatra* we are close to the Incarnation in time, but the meta-

[1] J. L. Simmons, *Shakespeare's Pagan World: The Roman Tragedies* (Charlottesville, 1973), pp. 113–14.

physical distance between the world of the play and the Christian cosmos is considerable.

This inversion of the relationship between history and an informing myth may help explain why *Antony and Cleopatra* is often described as somehow imperfect within its genre, an episodic, epic drama straining to conform to the norms of tragedy. Antony, we are told, is unable to act as a conventional tragic hero;[1] nor are we permitted to engage with him or Cleopatra as fully as tragedy normally requires.[2] If we accept Antony and Cleopatra as they describe themselves, immortal in spite of their deaths, 'marble-constant' and monumental in their love, we must overlook much evidence of their frailty, ambivalence, and even triviality to the contrary. The play lacks the single, compelling perspective from which tragic insight is usually communicated. Our attention is divided between the spectacle of Antony's failure to measure up to Roman heroic standards and the implication that those standards are inadequate to define his true heroism. This inability of the play and its protagonists to conform to the norms of tragic vision is an invitation to consider another kind of vision, and to go beyond the world of the play to find it.

II

The first scene of *Antony and Cleopatra* mirrors the play's thematic movement towards Christian revelation. Antony stands accused by one of his Roman followers, Philo, of a 'dotage' that 'O'erflows the measure' – words that unmistakably convey the revulsion he feels at the sight of his general's infatuation with Cleopatra. Antony speaks of his love in terms that alter the tone but retain some of the substance of Philo's remarks:

Cleopatra.
If it be love indeed, tell me how much.
Antony.
There's beggary in the love that can be reckon'd.
Cleopatra.
I'll set a bourn how far to be belov'd.
Antony.
Then must thou needs find out new heaven,
new earth.   (I, i, 14–17)

The 'dotage' which 'O'erflows the measure' becomes a love that cannot be reckoned. Against Philo's Roman sense of propriety and measure Antony asserts a romanticist's impulse to deny limit, finitude and degree, to transgress the boundaries by which a rationalist mind orders its world. He has confounded, Philo complains, the occupation of a soldier with that of a lover. Antony's banter with Cleopatra already indicates the inherently tragic disposition of his energy and will.

But Antony's words have a prophetic resonance; they refer us to a context in which the quest for 'new heaven, new earth' is no longer an expression of will tragically opposed to reality. Antony and Cleopatra are led by their syllogistic dialogue to what God speaks of to Isaiah and John sees directly in his vision of the Day of Judgement:

For lo, I will create new heavens and a new earth: and the former shall not be remembered nor come into mind.
          (From The Geneva Bible, Isaiah, lxv, 17)

And I saw a new heaven, and a new earth: for the first heaven, and the first earth were passed away, and there was no more sea. And I John saw the holy city new Jerusalem come down from God out of heaven, prepared as a bride trimmed for her husband. And I heard a great voice out of heaven, saying, 'Behold, the Tabernacle of God is with men, and he will dwell with them: and they shall be his people, and God himself shall be their God with them. And God shall wipe away all tears from their eyes: and there shall be no more death, neither sorrow, neither crying, neither

[1] Arthur H. Bell, 'Time and Convention in *Antony and Cleopatra*', *Shakespeare Quarterly*, 20 (1973), no. 3, 253–64.
[2] Janet Adelman, *The Common Liar* (New Haven, 1973), pp. 40–9.

shall there be any more pain: for the first things are passed.'   (Revelation, xxi, 1–4)

There remains an important difference between syllogism and revelation, between Antony's assertion of unbounded love and the divine love of which John speaks. Antony and Cleopatra may pursue the logic of transcendence to the point where it verges on a new perception of the universe, but the vision John records depends on divine intercession rather than heroic romanticism. Antony and Cleopatra come to associate love with eternity, and they approach death as if it were 'a lover's bed'; they speak of one another as bride and husband in their final moments, and thereby bring new significance to conventional terms; but the apocalyptic marriage of which John speaks, the final reconciliation between God and humanity, remains beyond their imagination. Antony does not have access to the vision that fully transforms tragic experience. He assumes instead a posture of heroic denial:

> Let Rome in Tiber melt, and the wide arch
> Of the rang'd empire fall!   (I, i, 33–4)

Antony is bounded on one side by the Christian visionary tradition to which he cannot attain and on the other by the Roman epic tradition he partly forsakes. His Roman followers see him making the choice that Roman history denies to its first hero, Aeneas. Antony, that is, chooses love over empire, passion over reason, a foreign 'marriage' over a Roman one, and thus aligns himself with those forces Roman civilization sees as impediments to its progress. Yet in a sense Antony does not wholly remove himself from epic tradition. He refers to love as though it were another *imperium*, 'new heaven, new earth', and he embraces Cleopatra – 'Here is my space' – in the spirit of an Aeneas arriving on Italian shores – 'hic domus, haec patria est' ['Here is our home, here our country!']. The love Antony speaks of is both an alternative to empire and an alternative empire.

Antony, as Adelman has observed, is in a sense an antitype of Aeneas.[1] Shakespeare seems to have invited the comparison by simplifying the itinerary of Antony's travels he finds in Plutarch. Shakespeare's Antony closely imitates the career of Aeneas up to a point – the play's dramatic and philosophical turning point – before finally reversing its direction. Virgil's Aeneas is required to extricate himself from his romantic entanglement with Dido for the sake of his destined marriage to Lavinia, an alliance with more political than amorous connotations. Similarly, Antony leaves 'Egypt's widow' for Rome (I, iii) and agrees to a political marriage with Octavia (II, ii); but thereafter his movements are, from a Roman point of view, retrogressive. He returns to Egypt, where his pleasure lies. Even then he continues to assume the stance of a Roman hero, though increasingly the posture becomes incongruous. And in his last moments he envisions himself as having surpassed Aeneas:

> Where souls do couch on flowers, we'll hand in hand,
> And with our sprightly port make the ghosts gaze:
> Dido, and her Aeneas, shall want troops,
> And all the haunt be ours.   (IV, xiv, 51–4)

Antony may be thought to surpass Aeneas, however, only if the *Aeneid* is read from the perspective of love rather than empire, from Dido's and Antony's point of view rather than the Roman one. Only in an imaginative arrest of history does the Dido and Aeneas tragedy suggest an amorous eternity. Still, Antony does not so much dissociate himself from Roman history as reinterpret it from his own vantage. Whether his return to Egypt is a moral regression and an act of self-betrayal, as his Roman followers see it, or a reaction aimed at transcending a limited and insufficient heroic ideal is the critical issue with which the play presents us.

[1] *Ibid.*, pp. 68–78.

Antony and Cleopatra, then, stands chrono-logically and metaphysically between the quest traditions of Roman epic and Christianity. On one hand the play looks to Augustan empire as the culmination of historical processes, and on the other hand it conveys the feeling that the energies of its principals are misdirected, that their goals are insufficient to their needs. The urgency with which the protagonists pursue their ambitions mounts in direct proportion to their disillusionment: 'Whiles we are suitors to their throne, decays/The thing we sue for' (II, i, 4–5). The voice of triumphant, purposeful action is heard together with that of com-passionate regret, as when Antony is remember-ed to have wept on finding Brutus dead at Philippi (III, ii, 55–6), or when Agrippa in turn expresses sorrow for the death of Antony:

> And strange it is,
> That nature must compel us to lament
> Our most persisted deeds.   (v, i, 28–30)

The play describes yearnings for which it en-visions no moral or aesthetic gratification. The protagonists are repeatedly brought to the point of realizing their desires only to dis-cover what Antony discovers when Fulvia is reported dead:

> The present pleasure,
> By revolution lowering, does become
> The opposite of itself....   (I, ii, 121–3)

Given the world he finds himself in, Antony's involvement with Cleopatra is perhaps logically as well as emotionally justified. She represents, if not stasis and fulfillment, the unbroken circle of appetitive nature. Hers is the art of elusive-ness which keeps desires alive:

> If you find him sad,
> Say I am dancing; if in mirth, report
> That I am sudden sick.   (I, iii, 3–5)

Enobarbus somewhat cynically but revealingly speaks of her as quasi-divine and above the laws of time:

> Age cannot wither her, nor custom stale
> Her infinite variety: other women cloy
> The appetites they feed, but she makes hungry,
> Where most she satisfies. For vilest things
> Become themselves in her, that the holy priests
> Bless her, when she is riggish.   (II, ii, 235–40)

'Appetite' is, of course, the crucial term, for while it may be morally ambiguous as Eno-barbus uses it, it is not so in Christian thought. If Cleopatra 'makes hungry,/Where most she satisfies', she inverts the promise of the Beati-tudes to fill those who hunger after righteous-ness (Matthew, v, 6). She is not the absolute eternity of Christian vision, but the time-bound *aevum* of natural processes, 'infinite' only in their variation between hunger and satiety.

The rhythms of *Antony and Cleopatra* are the natural, sexual, and political manifestations of appetite – circular, continuous, and in-conclusive. Momentum is ultimately the play's most compelling variable – a giddy inebriation at one extreme, where the rulers of the world are seen dancing the 'Egyptian Bacchanals' in a ring (II, vii, 103 ff.), and a feeling of self-strangulation at the other:

> Now all labour
> Mars what it does: yea, very force entangles
> Itself with strength....   (IV, xiv, 47–9)

This is perhaps appropriate to a play consciously imitating the to and fro, episodic structure of epic; but it is also a comment on the aimlessness of a universe lacking moral focus from the perspective of one that has achieved coherence through divine revelation.

III

The battle of Actium, a conflict, as Shakespeare presents it, as much between Antony and him-self as between Antony and Octavius, stands at what is both the structural and metaphysical center of the play. It marks the point at which

Antony reverses the Virgilian epic itinerary, turning away from Rome and Octavia towards Egypt and Cleopatra. It is also the place where Roman and Christian perspectives on the play fully intersect. On one hand we are asked to see Antony's rejection of Roman values as the sufficient cause of his tragic fall; on the other hand that fall, in which Antony and Cleopatra paradoxically envision themselves triumphant and transcendent, ironically anticipates Christian redemption. We see Antony in part as an exemplum of moral degradation offered to a Roman audience, a hero debased by his extravagant love for an exotic woman, irrationally bound on a course of self-destruction, simultaneously asserting and undermining his own heroic stature. But Antony may also be judged by the standard of divine love, in which death is, as he imagines, encompassed by an eternity. That his passion for Cleopatra falls short of Christian *caritas*, the movement of the soul towards God, places his tragedy in a different light, making it less an instance of decadent immoderation than one of misdirected love.

This dualism is felt in the widening gap between Antony and his onstage audience – Enobarbus, Canidius, Scarus, and those Octavius sends to

> Observe how Antony becomes his flaw,
> And what thou think'st his very action speaks
> In every power that moves. (III, xii, 34–6)

Antony is the object of a universal scrutiny incapable of penetrating the enigma he now becomes. Between their uncomprehending distress at what seems Antony's derangement and Antony's own assertiveness there is no middle ground. Loyalty to Antony, Enobarbus admits, is equally 'faith' and 'folly', defensible only in paradoxical terms:

> ...he that can endure
> To follow with allegiance a fall'n lord,
> Does conquer him that did his master conquer,
> And earns a place i' the story. (III, xiii, 43–6)

From the moment Antony returns to Egypt his speech and actions are clouded with discrepancies which constitute if nothing else a problem of tone. He irrationally decides to oppose Octavius's forces at sea rather than on land where his own 'absolute soldiership' lies, and issues a boisterous challenge to Octavius to meet in single combat; but these are the reflexes of a stage hero rather than an experienced soldier. In his self-aggrandizement there is a potential for burlesque, which Shakespeare does not hesitate to exploit. Enobarbus undercuts Antony's pomposity in the acerbic asides of comic convention:

> Yes, like enough! High-battled Caesar will
> Unstate his happiness, and be stag'd to the show
> Against a sworder! I see men's judgements are
> A parcel of their fortunes.... (III, xiii, 29–32)

Antony's actions are in form if not in substance the material of comedy – he flies into a jealous rage at seeing a messenger from Octavius kiss Cleopatra's hand, ironically mistaking Cleopatra's gesture of compliance with Octavius (to which he might more justifiably object) for flirtation with the messenger; he follows Cleopatra's retreat from battle 'like a doting mallard', then vacillates between self-pity and heroic rant. He becomes, as Adelman has observed,[1] the comic, effeminate Hercules of the Omphale myth rather than the 'Herculean Roman' of heroic tradition:

> so our leader's led,
> And we are women's men. (III, vii, 69–70)

Even his last attempt to salvage a Roman dignity, his suicide, is almost farcically mishandled.

To the extent that the play provides no critical consensus where Antony and Cleopatra are concerned, it has been read as the product of an irreducibly ironic vision, a reflection of the intractability of life to moral evaluation. The play does not finally decide between the

---

[1] *Ibid.*, p. 91.

Antony his Roman critics see, 'a fall'n lord' whose judgement is subdued by his fortunes, and the 'Lord of lords' Cleopatra imagines – between a didactic and a mythic vision of Antony. That Shakespeare erects such an ambiguity, however, does not mean that no standard exists against which Antony may be measured. Where his behavior seems most disjointed we are referred to Christian myth. Antony's outburst of jealousy when he encounters Thidias kissing Cleopatra's hand, for instance, may be both an overreaction and a potentially comic misdirection of anger –

> O that I were
> Upon the hill of Basan, to outroar
> The horned herd, for I have savage cause –
>
> (III, xiii, 126–8)

but the discrepancy disappears when the words are heard in their original context:

> Be not far from me, because trouble is near: for there is none to help me.
> Many young bulls have compassed me: mighty bulls of Bashan have closed me about. (Psalms xxii, 11–12)

This Old Testament outcry against injustice and betrayal in turn provides the material for the moment Christianity holds to be the ultimate reversal of tragic consciousness, the Crucifixion. It is the psalm from whose beginning Christ quotes as he dies, 'My God, my God, why hast thou forsaken me?' transforming despair into hopefulness as he speaks by using these words to confirm himself as the fulfillment of Old Testament messianic prophecies.

In contrast to Christ's deliberate and ultimately redemptive reference to the psalm, Antony's unconscious and contorted allusion confirms him in his tragic posture, outroaring the surrounding herds. Jealousy and grace work radically dissimilar transformations. But at the same time Antony's allusion suggests the frame of reference from which we may finally arrive at more than a morally ambiguous perception of the play.

Two scenes later Antony proposes a final 'gaudy night', his Last Supper, as J. Middleton Murry suggests,[1] echoes of which may be found both in Plutarch and in the Passion narrative, as the interplay between the Roman and the Christian senses of an ending continues. As in Plutarch Antony asks his followers to fill his cups and make as much of him as they can, but then disheartens them with his gloom:

> Tend me to-night;
> May be it is the period of your duty,
> Haply you shall not see me more, or if,
> A mangled shadow. Perchance to-morrow
> You'll serve another master. I look on you,
> As one that takes his leave.   (IV, ii, 24–9)

The words can be found in North's translation of Plutarch, but the tone suggests another reference: Antony's strangely prescient mood and his wavering resolve to accept death are also reminiscent of Christ's agony in the garden at Gethsemane. Like Christ, Antony asks three times that his followers tend him in what he senses are his last hours. The appeal for loyalty subtly draws attention to Enobarbus, who, Judas-like,[2] has by now decided to betray his master. The scene requires of the reader a double vision in which the Christian future is superimposed over the Roman narrative.

Plutarch is again Shakespeare's source when Antony tries to reassure his soldiers:

> I hope well of to-morrow, and will lead you
> Where rather I'll expect victorious life,
> Than death, and honor.   (ll. 42–4)

But Shakespeare's Antony contributes another version of this speech in which the distinction between life and death becomes blurred:

> To-morrow, soldier,
> By sea and land I'll fight: or I will live,
> Or bathe my dying honour in the blood
> Shall make it live again.   (ll. 4–7)

[1] John Middleton Murry, *Shakespeare* (New York, 1936), p. 303.
[2] The parallel between Judas and Enobarbus is suggested by Murry, *ibid.*, p. 307.

The language is susceptible equally to Stoic and Eucharistic interpretations. Though it is his own blood, not Christ's, and the resurrection of his honor, not his body, that Antony has in mind, this is Plutarch rewritten in anticipation of Christian ritual.

It becomes evident that we lack a single standard by which to measure the relative failure or success of Antony's rhetoric. Throughout this scene we are given the disconcerting spectacle of Rome's master orator alienating his audience and evoking tears where he intends to give comfort. He inadvertently distresses his attendants by speaking of a reversal of roles they find unimaginable, but which again touches on the meaning of the Eucharist:

> I wish I could be made so many men,
> And all of you clapp'd up together in
> An Antony; that I might do you service,
> So good as you have done.   (ll. 16–19)

This seems to Enobarbus further proof of Antony's distraction, 'one of those odd tricks which sorrow shoots/ Out of the mind'; but at this point Antony's rhetorical failures and Christian thought are in a sense logically continuous. ('So might an unknown – or maybe a known – disciple', Murry suggests, 'have said that the Last Supper itself was "one of those odd tricks which sorrow shoots out of the mind".')[1] Shakespeare's Antony here begins the imaginative revision of Plutarch's narrative that Christianity will eventually complete. Antony's language, that is, contains logical and visual discrepancies that cannot be resolved in the terms accessible to the world of the play, but which become meaningful in the context of a future discourse. The hermeneutic method *Antony and Cleopatra* asks us to adopt is one that implies the inadequacy of the knowledge available in the dramatic present to unlock the enigmas of the text.

Antony's speech is charged with meanings neither he nor his hearers can comprehend.

Even his rather awkward attempt to explain himself reinforces our awareness of the central irony:

> Ho, ho, ho!
> Now the witch take me, if I meant it thus!
> Grace grow where those drops fall....
> > (ll. 36–8)

'Grace' is the crux, for were he conscious of the eventual significance of the term Antony's attempts to console his followers by speaking of 'another master', a revival of 'dying honor' in a mysterious 'To-morrow' would not seem so disjointed. It is precisely because he lacks the concept of grace that he can only communicate fatalism to his audience. In the end he returns to a literal and Roman feast rather than a symbolic and Christian one, ironically distorting the meaning of that which he prefigures:

> Let's to supper, come,
> And drown consideration.   (ll. 44–5)

We can account for the awkwardness of the scene, I think, by seeing in it an implicit juxtaposition of Roman and biblical texts. The co-existence of Christian and Roman perspectives is necessarily unharmonious: Christ's propitiatory self-sacrifice will reverse the fatalistic, Stoic self-conquest Antony envisions. Antony's unmodulated ambivalence is a parody of Christ's agony, a failing show of courage in the face of despair, just as his jealousy of Thidias was a parody of Christ's moment of cupidity on the cross. We see darkly through the surface of the dramatic present to the Christian future because we are seeing the reflection of an essentially comic myth in a tragic medium.

The greatest loss Antony suffers at Actium is the one he speaks of, perhaps somewhat hypocritically, when he frames his excuse to Octavia for breaking with Octavius:

> if I lose mine honour,
> I lose myself....   (III, iv, 22–3)

---

[1] *Ibid.*, p. 303.

As it happens he loses both honor and self in the course of the battle that follows. Those who eventually desert him do so in the conviction that he has already betrayed himself, by fighting at sea ('you therein throw away/ The absolute soldiership you have by land' III, vii, 41–2) and by not gearing his actions to his strengths ('his whole action grows/ Not in the power on't' III, vii, 68–9). Antony, that is, forgets himself: 'Had our general/ Been what he knew himself, it had gone well' (III, x, 26–7). Enobarbus describes what becomes an internal war among the elements of Antony's character:

> and I see still,
> A diminution in our captain's brain
> Restores his heart; when valour preys on reason,
> It eats the sword it fights with....
>
> (III, xiii, 197–200)

Antony is not unaware of his 'diminution'; he perceives authority melting from him (III, xiii, 90), knows he has 'lost command' (xi, 23), and even justifies the desertion of his followers on the grounds that he has set the example: 'Let that be left/ Which leaves itself' (xi, 19–20). But when he is brought 'to the very heart of loss' (IV, xii, 29) after his second defeat at sea, he begins to experience tragedy's expression of the law of diminishing returns: self-destruction can be a means of self-recovery. Ironically Antony is led to this discovery by the example of his follower, Eros, and by that which Antony supposes Cleopatra has set in killing herself. We find Eros, of course, in Plutarch; but Shakespeare seems to have seen in the name a significance that the rationalist Plutarch did not. Shakespeare's Eros teaches the way to a death that is more than mere loss: 'Thy master dies thy scholar.' Cleopatra, whom moments before Antony had thought the cause of his undoing, the 'Triple-turn'd whore', becomes with Eros the model of nobility and the agent of his redemption:

> Thrice-nobler than myself,
> Thou teachest me, O valiant Eros, what
> I should, and thou couldst not; my queen and Eros
> Have by their brave instruction got upon me
> A nobleness in record. (IV, xiv, 95–9)

As previously, the Roman leader is led by Cleopatra; but in this moment of vertiginous climax Antony finds honor in the direction of his downfall, a potential for self-affirmation in self-destruction, and triumph in defeat. Antony expresses it in its Stoic formulation: 'With a wound I must be cur'd' (l. 78); but in this rush of reversals we may also recognize one of Christianity's most fundamental precepts: one must first lose oneself in order to find oneself.

We are on the verge of more than one Christian mystery as Antony envisions a romantic afterlife with Cleopatra (ll. 51–4), and then metaphorically construes his death as an act of love:

> But I will be
> A bridegroom in my death, and run into't
> As to a lover's bed. (ll. 99–101)

As in its other manifestations throughout the play this conceit has both sexual and spiritual overtones. It is Cleopatra's lover speaking, but the words are also reminiscent of John's vision of the New Jerusalem, coming down out of heaven from God, 'prepared as a bride trimmed for her husband'. Echoes from Revelation continue to be heard as Antony, having thrown himself on his sword without managing to kill himself, pleads with the guardsmen to dispatch him. But once again the allusion underscores Antony's separation from the promise of Christian redemption, as he is compared to 'those men which have not the seal of God in their foreheads' when the Apocalypse comes:

Therefore in those days men shall seek death, and shall not find it, and shall desire to die, and death shall flee from them. (Revelation, ix, 6)[1]

[1] The allusions to Revelation in this scene are specified by Ethel Seaton, '*Antony and Cleopatra* and

Antony's death returns us to the beginning of the play where in another mood he unknowingly alluded to John's vision of 'a new heaven and a new earth', and where he first spoke of finding 'the nobleness of life' in Cleopatra rather than Rome. That the completion of these gestures confirms the tragic nature of Antony's experience is a measure of the metaphysical distance between his world and the Christian one. If we need a reminder of the sharp discrepancy between Christian apocalypse and Antony's suicide it is provided in the element of mistiming involved in Antony's death. He is at first impatient to die, to 'o'ertake' Cleopatra, whom he erroneously believes to be dead: 'for now/ All length is torture' (ll. 45–6). When it is already too late he finds that Cleopatra is still alive. His death is then protracted through a disconcertingly awkward interval, and yet still seems premature when the stage time remaining to the play is considered. Antony's death is a travesty of apocalyptic finality, the end toward which human history is thought to ripen.

Where Christian apocalypse opens toward a transcendent reality, a revelation of cosmic purpose, Antony's vision is totally reflexive and personal. He is left to console himself with images from the interior space of tragic consciousness – an amorous eternity with Cleopatra, the dignity of self-conquest, the memory of his 'former fortunes':

> The miserable change now at my end
> Lament nor sorrow at: but please your thoughts
> In feeding them with those my former fortunes
> Wherein I liv'd: the greatest prince o' the world,
> The noblest; and do now not basely die,
> Not cowardly put off my helmet to
> My countryman: a Roman, by a Roman
> Valiantly vanquish'd.   (IV, xv, 51–8)

His claim to have regained nobility in death comes from the core of the play's tragic sensibility; but *Antony and Cleopatra* asks that we compare this sensibility to one that reverses its fundamental premise and denies its ultimate reality.

IV

The last scene of the play is in tone both an ending and a beginning, a denouement and an overture to greater actions to follow. On a simple narrative level it is hard to be certain whether Cleopatra is angling for her own preservation or deceiving Octavius by acting so in order to be free to kill herself. The ambiguity extends to her language with deeper implications: 'My desolation does begin to make/ A better life'; 'I hourly learn/ A doctrine of obedience'; 'I have/ Immortal longings in me'. Like Antony, Cleopatra presents her audience with a problem of perspective – whether to see in tragedy a diminishment or an aggrandizement of human stature, whether to take death as final and defeating or as a step towards liberation, 'that thing that ends all other deeds,/ Which shackles accidents, and bolts up change' (V, ii, 5–6).

Cleopatra defiantly imagines Antony in terms of the choice he did not make in life, but paradoxically asserted with his death. She envisions him in an imperial and heroic posture; and she asks, moreover, that this 'dream' be taken literally. Such a demand on credulity might not be out of place in either a Christian or a romance context, but Cleopatra confronts a politely sceptical audience:

Cleopatra.
  I dreamt there was an Emperor Antony.
  O such another sleep, that I might see
  But such another man!
Dolabella.   If it might please ye, –
Cleopatra.
  His face was as the heavens, and therein stuck
  A sun and moon, which kept their course, and lighted
  The little O, the earth.

The Book of Revelation', Review of English Studies, 22 (1946), no. 87, 219–24. See also Kenneth Muir, *Shakespeare's Sources* (1957; repr. 1965), I, 217–19.

Dolabella.　　　　Most sovereign creature, –
Cleopatra.
　His legs bestrid the ocean, his rear'd arm
　Crested the world: his voice was propertied
　As all the tuned spheres, and that to friends:
　But when he meant to quail, and shake the orb,
　He was as rattling thunder. For his bounty,
　There was no winter in't: an autumn 'twas
　That grew the more by reaping: his delights
　Were dolphin-like, they show'd his back above
　The element they lived in: in his livery
　Walk'd crowns and crownets: realms and islands
　　were
　As plates dropp'd from his pocket.
Dolabella.　　　　Cleopatra!
Cleopatra.
　Think you there was, or might be such a man
　As this I dreamt of?　　　　(v, ii, 76–94)

Dolabella's answer is justifiably 'no'; but the provocatively subjunctive mood of Cleopatra's speech and the intensity of her yearning, 'that I might see/ But such another man', invites another response. In fact a figure like the one Cleopatra envisions does exist in John's vision of the Apocalypse: it is a 'mighty Angel', bestriding the sea, lifting his hand to heaven, announcing in a thunderous voice 'that time should be no more' (Revelation, ix, 1–6).[1] Christian revelation affirms what Cleopatra hypothesizes, a mystery 'past the size of dreaming'.

We are aware of an analogy between what Cleopatra and Christianity respectively ask of their believers, that a death may paradoxically lead to fulfillment and that endings may ultimately be joined with beginnings: 'I am again for Cydnus,/ To meet Mark Antony' (ll. 227–8). It is not a great step from here to see in Cleopatra a foreshadowing of the New Eve, simultaneously accepting and transforming the curse of enmity between herself and the serpent (Genesis, iii, 15):

Cleopatra.　　　　Come, thou mortal wretch,
[*To an asp, which she applies to her breast.*]
　With thy sharp teeth this knot intrinsicate
　Of life at once untie: poor venomous fool,

　Be angry, and despatch. O, couldst thou speak,
　That I might hear thee call great Caesar ass,
　Unpolicied!
Charmian.　　　　O eastern star!
Cleopatra.　　　　Peace, peace!
　Dost thou not see my baby at my breast,
　That sucks the nurse asleep?　　　(ll. 302–9)

Cleopatra at once fulfills the curse of Genesis and prefigures its reversal by speaking of her death as a moment of love, 'a lover's pinch,/ Which hurts, and is desir'd' (ll. 294–5). Hers are only the reflexes of the flesh, inadequate to convey spiritual insight; but, as Elizabeth Holmes has suggested, we are invited to see beyond the tableau of her death, the grotesque image of Cleopatra nursing the serpent like a baby, to another 'eastern star' and another nativity.[2]

The juxtaposition of these two images – Cleopatra's death and Christ's nativity – is both visually and morally incongruous; but as elsewhere in the play such incongruity is calculated to move us beyond the scope of the tragic universe for a vision of greater substantive reality. From this vantage Cleopatra's death is an inversion of the moment it prefigures.

In a similarly prophetic vein the serpent-bearing clown unconsciously mingles phallic humor with Christian ideology, nonsense with spiritual truth. The serpent's 'biting', he claims, 'is immortal'; and his mislocutions invest dying with both sexual and Christian connotations:

Cleopatra. Remember'st thou any that have died on't?
Clown. Very many, men and women too. I heard of
　one of them no longer than yesterday, a very honest
　woman, but something given to lie, as a woman
　should not do, but in the way of honesty, how she
　died of the biting of it, what pain she felt: truly, she
　makes a very good report o' the worm: but he that
　will believe all that they say, shall never be saved by
　half that they do....

[1] Seaton, '*Antony and Cleopatra* and *The Book of Revelation*', pp. 220–21.
[2] Elizabeth Holmes, *Aspects of Elizabethan Imagery* (Oxford, 1929), p. 50.

Cleopatra. Will it eat me?

Clown. You must not think I am so simple but I know the devil himself will not eat a woman: I know, that a woman is a dish for the gods, if the devil dress her not. But truly, these same whoreson devils do the gods great harm in their women: for in every ten that they make, the devils mar five. (ll. 248–76)

The last phrase curiously echoes Christ's analogy between the kingdom of heaven and ten virgins – five wise and five foolish (Matt., xxv, 1–12) – preparing (as Cleopatra is doing on another level) to meet the bridegroom. It is an extension of the play's central irony that the burlesque, disjointed language of the clown foreshadows the later use of veiled discourse in Christian parable.

We sense in Antony and Cleopatra desires their language is incapable of expressing except as its surface is distorted and its normal logic is inverted. They aspire to a reconciliation of opposites they can only imperfectly articulate. Antony seeks a death which would both elevate him to the status of a Roman hero and reject the premise of that ideal; Cleopatra paradoxically invests her death with the sexual energies that impelled her in life, and she claims for herself – strangely – a Romanness in her dying. Antony and Cleopatra remain constrained by a dialectic of equally delimiting choices – empire and romantic love, world and flesh, Roman morality and Alexandrian amorality; but by confounding their alternatives, by insisting on both love *and* empire, death *and* immortality, they approach Christian paradox as closely as is possible without divine intercession.

Their tragedy, however, is circumscribed by an irony that threatens them with insubstantiality, the imminence of a vision as paradoxical as theirs that will nevertheless repeal tragedy's laws. As Cleopatra is aware of the parody she would become were she to live and be displayed in Octavius's triumphal pageants (ll. 213–20), so the reader is continually made aware of the

parody the play will become in the light of Christian revelation. The indictment against drama goes beyond Cleopatra's dread of being staged in Rome and finally applies to the play itself. If *Antony and Cleopatra* seems a formally imperfect tragedy, ambiguous in perspective and problematic in tone, it is because from the point of view of Christian thought tragedy itself is an imperfect perception of experience, shadowy, solipsistic, and ultimately self-negating. Christian vision bears a relation to reality to which tragic imagination cannot attain; it is the fulfillment of Cleopatra's dream of Antony, 'nature's piece, 'gainst fancy,/ Condemning shadows quite'. In a sense Christian vision denies the substance of all tragic consciousness, but there is a particular urgency to this irony in *Antony and Cleopatra*, whose discord so strenuously anticipates its own inversion in the resolving concord of Christian paradox.

Shakespeare approaches Augustan Rome from another angle in *Cymbeline* some two or three years later, but preserves something of *Antony and Cleopatra's* dialectic between Christian and non-Christian perspectives. Here again the dramatic world of the play is ironically unaware of the proximity of the Christian era, though by now the 'time of universal peace' has arrived in both its Roman and its Christian senses. Octavius has become Augustus, the sole ruler of the Roman empire, and Christ has been born 'in fleshly slime', as Spenser tells us, 'To purge away the guilt of sinfull crime' (*Faerie Queene*, II, x, 50). With the transition into a Christian universe comes a concomitant transformation of dramatic form, a change from tragedy to romance, whose central themes – recovery, revival, reconciliation – everywhere imply the presence of grace. That Christian myth exerts a determinative influence on both plays but remains in both cases offstage and inaccessible to direct dramatic representation leads to an awareness of the constraints inherent in mimetic art conceived within a Christian framework. Shakespearian romance imaginatively recapitulates the miracle of grace; but romance, too, finally acknowledges the baselessness of its fabric and the insubstantiality of its pageant. Shakespeare's drama is fully conscious of itself as artifice, and thus as a medium in which Christian vision can only be invoked obliquely. In *Antony and Cleopatra*, and later in *Cymbeline*, Shakespeare explores settings in which such obliqueness is determined by history itself.

© ANDREW FICHTER 1980

PATTERNS OF MOTION IN 'ANTONY AND CLEOPATRA'

SUSAN SNYDER

More than twenty-five years ago, R. A. Foakes spoke out persuasively for a new approach to Shakespeare's imagery that would go beyond the lines laid down by Caroline Spurgeon. Specifically, he appealed for attention to dramatic as well as poetic imagery, including props and stage effects; and for analysis and classification of images on bases other than subject-matter.[1] By and large, critics have heeded the first call more than the second. Recent times have witnessed a new concentration on the direct imagery of stage production, and a corollary withdrawal from verbal imagery – for fear of committing the new cardinal sin, reading the play as a poem. Other critics remain faithful to 'the poetry', assuming that *Hamlet* can be apprehended in the same way as, say, *Paradise Lost*. Yet drama is a temporal art, much more so than poetry, and its essence is action. Perhaps one reason that image-critics of the traditional sort and theatre-oriented critics have little to say to each other is that the former are, for the most part, still attending only to image patterns created by static subject-matter, recurring objects like jewels or qualities like darkness. But verbs have their effect in Shakespeare's language as well as nouns and adjectives. Images create other patterns through repeated *motion*, and it is this dynamic aspect of imagery that connects most naturally with stage movements and groupings.

Not that the dynamics of images have been completely ignored. Few critics will discuss poison or disease references in *Hamlet* without pointing out their characteristic common movement – spreading unseen, mining all within, and at last breaking forth to betray the inner corruption that can no longer be contained. Yet it is not sufficiently recognized that a recurrent motion connects these images with others in the play whose 'subject' is not poison or sickness: for example, with Hamlet's early prediction that 'foul deeds will rise,/ Though all the earth o'erwhelm them, to men's eyes', (I, ii, 256–7) and with his later one that the hidden, decaying body of Polonius will eventually give away its whereabouts by smell (IV, iii, 35–7).[2]

In one play, *Richard II*, a very pronounced pattern of iterated motion has attracted critical comment. First Paul A. Jorgensen and later Arthur Suzman pointed out the persistent up-and-down action that informs not only verbal images as diverse as buckets, scales, plants, and the sun, but gesture and stage movement as well – gages thrown down and taken up, kneeling and rising, and most tellingly of all, in the scene at Flint Castle that marks the real end of his temporal power, Richard's descent from the upper stage to the level where his challenger awaits him:

Down, down I come, like glist'ring Phaethon,
Wanting the manage of unruly jades.

[1] Foakes, 'Suggestions for a New Approach to Shakespeare's Imagery', *Shakespeare Survey 5* (Cambridge, 1952), pp. 81–92.
[2] All Shakespeare references are to the *Complete Works*, ed. Peter Alexander (London and Glasgow, 1951).

In the base court? Base court, where kings grow base,
To come at traitors' calls . . .
            Down, court! down, king!
For night-owls shriek where mounting larks should
    sing.   [*Exeunt from above.*][1]   (III, iii, 178–83)

It is possible to go further than Jorgensen or Suzman have in relating this imagery to dramatic structure. *Richard II* has a built-in structural ambivalence: politically, Richard's course is downward and Bolingbroke's is upward, but in audience sympathies Bolingbroke is the one who falls while Richard rises. Many of the up-down images convey versions of this ambivalence, either in themselves or as qualified one by another. The equation of Richard with the setting sun, for instance, suggests a natural, right transition 'from Richard's night to Bolingbroke's fair day'. But this image is associated with a less natural, more awesome phenomenon when Salisbury imagines Richard not only as the sun setting but as a shooting star, plummeting suddenly to the base earth and presaging 'storms to come, woe, and unrest' (II, iv, 19–22). Richard's own choice of Phaeton rather than Apollo in the Flint Castle speech reminds us that his night is an abrupt, violent thing, a violation of natural process rather than the timely closing of day. Night owls forcibly displace the larks of day that *should* be singing. When in III, iv the Gardener speaks in his own idiom of Richard's flourishing and fall – 'He that hath suffer'd this disorder'd spring/ Hath now himself met with the fall of leaf' (ll. 48–9) – the abrupt passage from spring to fall of leaf carries the same implication that Richard's decline, while inevitable, is unnatural. So, too, the later image of the scales (84–89) is more ambivalent than it seems. Bolingbroke prevails because his side is heavy with allies, while Richard's contains only himself and his 'light' vanities. Straightforward enough, except that in changing his metaphor the Gardener has also changed, in fact reversed, the values that he and other speakers have established for up and

down. Up has been the desirable position, yet this vision of Bolingbroke solid in power and popularity and Richard dangling vainly in the air suggests that up can be bad as well as good. The suggestion carries over into the deposition scene that follows, when Richard applies the opposition of up and down to himself and his rival, and reverses the values back again – or does he? In his simile of the two buckets (IV, i, 184–9), the King is once again on the down side, freighted with tears, while Bolingbroke dances in the air. But this lightness of Bolingbroke's recalls the implication of 'light' in the Gardener's scale conceit, especially when Richard calls his successor 'empty'. The ambiguity may well be conscious on the speaker's part as well as the playwright's. Bolingbroke is empty in being free of Richard's griefs, the weight of tears, but also in lacking proper sanction as a king; without the weight of tradition and inheritance his position is shaky.

It is clear from the examples of *Hamlet* and *Richard II* that a pattern of kinetically linked images can support, even embody, a major movement of the dramatic action. Up-and-down, with all its ambiguities, is the shaping movement of *Richard II*. In *Hamlet*, corruption spreads to infect all the characters while they seek, and mistake, the cause of the sickness until it is finally exposed: 'The King, the King's to blame'. All this suggests that, when their common motions are isolated, images in other plays may connect similarly to reinforce movements that are apparent and perhaps to indicate less obvious ones. *Antony and Cleopatra* offers a good example: here Shakespeare has set images of solid fixity or speedy directness against images of flux and of motion unpurposive but beautiful to express kinetically

[1] See Paul A. Jorgensen, 'Vertical Patterns in *Richard II*', *Shakespeare Association Bulletin*, 23 (1948), 119–34, and Arthur Suzman, 'Imagery and Symbolism in *Richard II*', *Shakespeare Quarterly*, 7 (1956), 255–70.

the opposition of Rome and Egypt and, through their incompatibility, the nature of Antony's tragic dilemma.

The play's first scene presents without delay the opposed forces that are working and will continue to work on Antony – Egypt in Cleopatra's changeable, demanding charm and Rome in the harsh judgements of Philo and Demetrius. Philo's opening lines set up the contrast between what he stands for and what he sees in the Alexandrian court:

Nay, but this dotage of our general's
O'erflows the measure. Those his goodly eyes,
That o'er the files and musters of the war
Have glow'd like plated Mars, now bend, now turn,
The office and devotion of their view
Upon a tawny front. His captain's heart,
Which in the scuffles of great fights hath burst
The buckles of his breast, reneges all temper,
And is become the bellows and the fan
To cool a gypsy's lust.
Flourish. Enter Antony, Cleopatra, *her* Ladies,
the Train, *with* Eunuchs *fanning her.*

Look where they come!
Take but good note, and you shall see in him
The triple pillar of the world transform'd
Into a strumpet's fool.   (I, i, 1–13)

Uniting the images of speech and action are two opposed ideas: one of steadfast, rigid immobility – a fixed *measure* and *temper*, the orderly *files* of ranked soldiers, the hard solidity of *plated Mars*, the unmoving *pillar of the world* – and the other of fluid, shifting movement, of overflowing, bending, turning, fanning. This last is reinforced by stage action when Cleopatra enters with eunuchs fanning her.

Philo's disapproving stand is simple enough, but the scene goes on to explore and complicate the values of fixity and flux. *Measure*, a positive notion in Philo's speech, is undercut in Antony's 'There's beggary in the love that can be reckon'd' (l. 15). Roman measure has no room for a new heaven or a new earth.[1] Similarly,

Antony makes Rome's solidity yield to his larger vision of human fulfillment:

Let Rome in Tiber melt, and the wide arch
Of the rang'd empire fall! Here is my space.
Kingdoms are clay; our dungy earth alike
Feeds beast as man. The nobleness of life
Is to do thus [*embracing*], when such a mutual pair
And such a twain can do't, in which I bind,
On pain of punishment, the world to weet
We stand up peerless.   (ll. 33–9)

The stable pillars and arches of Rome dissolve into fluidity, a fluidity however that is seen as expanding and completing rather than destroying. In what sense can Antony find positive value in dissolution? Against the Roman message, with its implications of purposive action and thinking for the future, he sets up the ideal of the immediate moment perfectly fulfilled: 'There's not a minute of our lives should stretch/ Without some pleasure *now*' (ll. 46–7, my italics). This is Cleopatra's gift, the full realization of all moments and moods.

Fie, wrangling queen!
Whom everything becomes – to chide, to laugh,
To weep; whose every passion fully strives
To make itself in thee fair and admir'd.
                              (ll. 48–51)

Antony celebrates a mode of life like the fanning motion which is the visual background to his words, directed to no end except motion itself and the beautifying of the moment. His word *becomes* is an important one. Cleopatra's moods serve no consistent purpose except to realize themselves, and her, perfectly. Later uses of the word will bring out the link between gracing the moment and expanding into fuller being. For now, Philo and Demetrius sway the balance back again, posing against this hint of identity expanding infinitely a contrary notion

[1] In *The Common Liar: An Essay on 'Antony and Cleopatra'* (New Haven and London, 1973), Janet Adelman discusses the play's images, including many that I cite below, in terms of measure and overflow (pp. 122–31).

of identity as defined by Roman duties. Philo uses *become* negatively, for *degenerated into*: Antony's martial heart 'is become the bellows and the fan . . . ' In his eyes, Antony by seeking escape from Roman measure has simply fallen below it, diminished and negated the self that is based on his Roman achievements. 'He comes too short of that great property/ Which still should go with Antony' (58–9).

On this note the scene ends. Its very structure carries out the opposition of fixity and flux, framing Antony's hyperboles and Cleopatra's quicksilver shifts with the unyielding judgement of the two Roman onlookers who open and close the scene.[1] An equally intractable, though silent, presence is the Roman message itself. The lovers can describe arabesques of constant motion around it, but they cannot blow it away. Antony's tragedy will be played out between these two imagistic poles, of solid stillness (or direct, purposive motion) and continual shifting activity, with their ambiguous implications for the self.

The images that follow continue and fill out the pattern set in the first scene. Cleopatra's Nile journey, as later described by Enobarbus (II, ii, 195–222), is all beautiful, self-fulfilling, self-justifying motion. The barge will eventually land somewhere, but there is no sense of direction toward an end in the action of sails and oars. On the contrary, the sails are there to dally with the 'love-sick' winds and the oars to keep time with flutes while playing similar games with the water, which is 'amorous of their strokes'. The point is in the process – as it is also with the fans plied by pretty boys 'whose wind did seem/ To glow the delicate cheeks which they did cool,/And what they undid did'. So, too, Cleopatra's waiting women make 'their bends adornings', achieving nothing beyond the graceful movements themselves.

Antony calls Cleopatra his serpent of old Nile, and water with its unending shift and flow is clearly her element as solid earth is natural to the Roman soldier Antony. While Shakespeare is not so eager as Plutarch to blame Antony's decision to fight Caesar by sea rather than by land on his passion for Cleopatra,[2] she certainly gives instant support to the choice – 'By sea! What else?' (III, vii, 28) – and her only forces mentioned in the play are naval ones. The Cleopatra who first caught Antony's heart on the river of Cydnus dreams in terms of their favorite river-sport of catching him again and again with her angle and bended hook (II, v, 10–15). Enobarbus, who first identified her with winds and waters (I, ii, 143), at Actium defines the slippery changeability of her element in relation to stable land when he warns Antony not to 'give up yourself merely to chance and hazard,/From firm security' (III, vii, 47–8).[3] Cleopatra's actions have the ebb and flow of water: laughing Antony out of patience and then laughing him back in (II, v, 19–20), meeting his sadness with dancing and his mirth with sudden sickness (I, iii, 3–5). Her verbs, so to speak, are intransitive, objectless like the movements of winds and waves and fans. Hopping forty paces in the street, as Enobarbus recalls her doing (II, ii, 232–3), has no object beyond

---

[1] The contrast between hard Roman efficiency and the lush prodigality of Egypt comes out in Antony's own speech patterns. Compare the leisured, expansive quality of his 'Let Rome in Tiber melt' speech with the brusque economy of this interchange with the Roman messenger:

> *Messenger.* News, my good lord, from Rome.
> *Antony.*   Grates me, the sum.

(I, i, 18; I follow the Folio punctuation, a comma between Antony's terse phrases. Alexander omits the comma, but the phrases make better sense separated.)

[2] 'Now Antonius was made so subject to a womans will, that though he was a great deale the stronger by land, yet for Cleopatraes sake, he would needes have this battell tryed by sea.' North's Plutarch (1579), cited in the New Arden edition, ed. M. R. Ridley (Cambridge, Mass., 1954), p. 274.

[3] Compare in this same scene the Roman soldier: 'Let th'Egyptians/ And the Phoenicians go a-ducking; we/ Have us'd to conquer standing on the earth/ And fighting foot to foot' (ll. 63–6).

spirited activity. It is surely no way to *arrive* anywhere. Even when Cleopatra is being apparently purposeful, sending messages to the absent Antony (I, v, 61–78), what counts is not the message but the act of sending. It hardly needed the 'twenty several messengers' already dispatched to make Antony understand her love and longing for him, yet she goes on from there to vow extravagantly, 'He shall have every day a several greeting,/Or I'll unpeople Egypt.'

Roman movement, when there is any at all, is direct, efficient, transitive. The best example is Caesar's incredibly rapid passage with his troops from Italy to Epirus, which so impresses Antony and Canidius (III, vii, 20–5; 54–7; 74–5). Antony's first bemused image is of Caesar, supposed so far away, *cutting* the sea like a sword to conquer Toryne near Antony's own camp. For the most part, though, Rome evokes images of stationary firmness. Opposed to Cleopatra's constant movement is Octavia, who is 'holy, cold, and still' in her behavior (II, vi, 119), 'still' too in her judgement (IV, xv, 28), who seems 'a body rather than a life,/A statue than a breather' (III, iii, 20–1). Antony's marriage to her is a *binding* (II, v, 58), Maecenas hopes she will *settle* his heart (II, ii, 245–7), and he himself vows his reform to her in terms of fixed, straight lines: 'I have not kept my *square*, but that to come/Shall all be done by th'*rule*' (II, iii, 6–7, my italics).

From this Roman perspective, Egyptian movement looks stupid and degrading in its lack of purpose. Caesar's verbs to describe Antony's 'pleasure now' – tumbling on the bed of Ptolemy, keeping the turn of tippling, reeling, standing the buffet – have no beauty in them (I, iv, 16–21). Jostling with knaves 'that smell of sweat', no longer commander of himself or his situation, Antony in Caesar's eyes is at the mercy of the moment, like the vulgar populace whose loyalties shift with every tide. Caesar might say of him, as he does of the despised public,

> This common body,
> Like to a vagabond flag upon the stream,
> Goes to, and back, lackeying the varying tide,
> To rot itself with motion.   (I, iv, 44–7)

In the Roman's contemptuous image, watery instability is simply servitude – 'lackeying the tide' – and unpurposive motion leads only to helpless decay. Pompey even finds a kind of stasis in Antony's pleasures of the moment: for him Antony is a tame animal tethered in a field of feasts (II, i, 23). Indeed, Antony in his Roman mood can also see the restless motions of pleasure as imprisoning. In the expansive sentiment of 'Let Rome in Tiber melt', it was the world he would 'bind' to admire in the activities of Cleopatra and himself the full nobleness of life. When struck by Roman thoughts, however, he sees *himself* as immobilized, 'bound...up/From mine own knowledge' (II, ii, 94–5), pinned down by strong Egyptian fetters (I, ii, 113). He can even share Caesar's disdain for the undirected flux of public opinion, now flowing for no good reason toward Pompey – 'our slippery people' (I, ii, 179). Later, after he has failed to stand firm at Actium, Antony harks back to that Roman norm of fixed, straight lines to image his disgrace: 'I have offended reputation – /A most unnoble *swerving*' (III, xi, 49–50, my italics). And, as if in response to his own lack of fixity, others now fall away from him – kings, captains, Enobarbus, Fortune, the god Hercules – in a pattern of repeated desertions that shapes most of act IV.

Nowhere after the first scene does the opposition between Roman fixity and Egyptian fluidity come into sharper focus than in II, vii, the feast aboard Pompey's galley. The setting itself is suggestive. But only a film version could give us as direct dramatic image the solid ship on ever-shifting water, secured in place by a single cable. In this play written for the bare Shakespearian stage, it is words and gestures that must keep us aware of the chancy, changeable element that surrounds this gathering of Romans. Drink is the main reminder, of course. The characters reel and stagger in varying degrees, Lepidus most and Caesar and Menas least, and finally join in the dance whose dizzying motion is indicated in its refrain – 'Cup us till the world go round'. Verbal imagery reinforces the effect of Roman *terra firma* threatened and undermined by other, alien elements or perversions of its own. The Romans are ill-rooted plants at the mercy of the wind, Lepidus is sinking in quicksands, cares drown in Bacchus's vats, Menas wishes the whole world could 'go on wheels' (II, vii, 1–3; 58–9; 113; 90–1). In answering Lepidus's drunken catechism Antony invokes Egyptian undulation directly, the swell and ebb of the Nile and the serpentine crocodile it breeds, which like Cleopatra lives by no other law than itself. Caesar is inevitably ill at ease amid all this living for the moment. He cannot, as Antony counsels, 'be a child o' the time'. That is Antony's way, the way he learned in Egypt, but not Caesar's.

If Caesar has misgivings about flux undermining firmness, they are justified. While Antony is being a child of the time, Menas urgently reminds Pompey that he need only cut one cable to set the whole Roman government adrift and manipulate it at his own pleasure. Order and stability are worth something, after all, and in a play not notably sympathetic to Rome Shakespeare makes us feel here, at least, how vulnerable and how necessary Roman order is. Where Caesar offers in his bearing a dramatic image of fixity at the reeling feast, Menas is the other image of Rome – direct, purposive action. He dogs Pompey's steps relentlessly about the stage to prod him to the decisive act. 'Wilt thou be lord of all the world? ... Wilt thou be lord of the whole world? ... Let me cut the cable.' Menas's urgent movements and speech-rhythms are another kind of Roman counterpoint to these self-fulfilling Egyptian Bacchanals. The plot to cut the cable

comes to nothing, because of Pompey's ambiguous but nevertheless inhibiting honor. Caesar, the real man of the future, who will later cut the sea, has no such inhibitions.

The galley scene is typical of *Antony and Cleopatra* as a whole in its ambivalence about the values of fixity/direct-drive and flux. Menas's plan of action, which involves cutting throats as well as cables, makes the boasting talk of Egyptian tourist attractions seem trivial; but Antony, the child of the time, is more alive than cautious, calculating Caesar. When the Nile's flow quickens Egypt, Antony tells Lepidus, it brings forth grain and also crocodiles. So it is with Antony's Egyptian excess, as Janet Adelman observes: 'it too will breed serpents as well as crops. But the man of measure – the man who never overflows – will not breed at all.'[1]

Both aspects of breeding, positive and negative, come through in the play's persistent references to melting, merging, and 'becoming'. As in Antony's speech in the first scene Rome's hard outlines melt to allow a new heaven and a new earth, so later we learn that Egyptian life breaks down normal divisions between day and night (II, ii, 181–2), between land and water again (II, v, 78), even between male and female. Cleopatra recalls how she and Antony expanded into each other's roles, he wearing her tires and mantles and she his sword Philippan (II, v, 22–3). What was play then becomes a more profound merging later, in Antony's startling invitation to her:

> Leap thou, attire and all,
> Through proof of harness to my heart, and there
> Ride on the pants triumphing. (IV, viii, 14–16)

Hard-and-fast limits ('proof of harness') give way, in his imagination at least, before the leaping, pulsing motion that fuses separate selves. Antony has also said that every passion becomes Cleopatra, gracing her by its full realization;

[1] *The Common Liar*, p. 130.

later she will likewise expect him to 'become/ The carriage of his chafe' (I, iii, 84–5), make his anger an ennobling thing. 'Be'st thou sad or merry', she says of him in his absence, 'The violence of either thee becomes,/So does it no man else' (I, v, 59–61). The Roman notion of 'becoming' is conversely narrow: soldierly dress becomes Romans, reveling does not (Caesar's 'say this becomes him' after that unattractive list of Antony's activities in Egypt is obviously ironic). *Becoming* means 'fitting for a Roman', and any other kind of becoming is degeneration – as in Philo's image Antony has degenerated into a mere appliance catering to Cleopatra's lust. Egypt finds even negative passions 'becomings', ways to fuller being. When Enobarbus claims that 'vilest things become themselves' in Cleopatra, it is impossible to disentangle in the knotted sense 'vilest things are graces' from 'vilest things are fully realized'. In this paradoxical merging of meanings divisions between good and bad also give way to the expansiveness of endless process.[1]

Rome, in contrast, finds true being only in sharp outlines and distinctions. Caesar is aware in his own way of the melting of sex distinctions between Antony and Cleopatra – as adulterating Antony's soldier-self, not enlarging it: '[Antony] is not more manlike/Than Cleopatra, nor the queen of Ptolemy/More womanly than he' (I, iv, 5–7). For Caesar that self of Antony's was defined by hardship and his unyielding sameness in the face of it, the retreat from Modena when, in spite of eating strange flesh and drinking horses' urine, his cheek 'so much as lank'd not' (I, iv, 56–71). Later events bear out to a certain extent Caesar's view of identity as persisting in one's own ways, observing one's own boundaries. After Antony has yielded at Actium to Cleopatra and her fluid element instead of standing fast on his own, images of wayward movement express disintegration rather than fuller being. Antony is 'unqualited';

he has left himself, lost his way forever, lost command (III, xi, 44; 19–20; 3–4; 23). Melting is not completion but loss, as authority melts *from* him (III, xiii, 90). Like Caesar, he seeks 'Antony' in past exploits of war:

> He [Caesar] at Philippi kept
> His sword e'en like a dancer, while I struck
> The lean and wrinkled Cassius; and 'twas I
> That the mad Brutus ended; he alone
> Dealt on lieutenantry, and no practice had
> In the brave squares of war. Yet now...
>
> (III, xi, 35–40)

Antony is very Roman here. He defines his past self by opposition, between himself and Cassius, himself and Brutus, himself and Caesar. And his typically Roman images combine direct, efficient action ('struck', 'ended') with the right-angled solidity of 'squares'.

But the Egyptian notion of identity has not been dropped. I have been looking at the two scenes that follow the defeat at Actium, III, xi and xiii. While both of them give full expression to Antony's Roman mood, both also swing up eventually from despair to an affirmation of self that includes Cleopatra. Indeed, the first seems to discard Roman values entirely for Egyptian ones: 'Fall not a tear, I say; one of them rates/All that is won and lost. Give me a kiss;/Even this repays me' (III, xi, 69–71). The second affirmation is more comprehensive. When Antony exclaims, 'Where hast thou been, my heart?' (III, xiii, 172) he is recovering both his own essence and the Cleopatra he had earlier thought lost to him ('what's her name/ Since she was Cleopatra?' ll. 98–9). Thus restored, Antony can in the same speech proclaim himself tripled in strength and valor, and call for one other gaudy night of feasting (III, xiii, 178–85). In the final movement of act IV, Antony again feels his outline dissolving like the dragonish cloud (IV, xiv, 2–14), melting

---

[1] On the dual meaning of 'becoming', cf. Adelman, *The Common Liar*, p. 144: 'process – infinite variety – is her decorum.'

into indistinctness like water in water. It is important here that this newly endangered identity is not simply the Roman soldier but the fused self of warrior and lover. His earlier promise, on leaving Cleopatra for Rome, to make peace or war according to her wishes (I, iii, 69–71) was only words: the peace he concluded with Caesar was pure Roman policy and its seal, his marriage to Octavia, could not have been less to Cleopatra's liking. In the last battle it is finally true that he has 'made these wars for Egypt and the queen' (IV, xiv, 15). Again the pendulum swings to affirmation. Antony dies affirming both sides of that greater self – a Roman by a Roman valiantly vanquished, still relishing wine and Cleopatra's kiss.

Still, Antony can bring together incompatible modes of life only when he has no more life to live. Images of fixity and flux have acted out kinetically the terms of his dilemma, the fixity necessary to define the self and the fluidity necessary to transcend the self's limitations. However much Antony wants to encompass both, he cannot be fixed and constantly moving at the same time, calculate and seize just the right moment for action while living every moment for its own sake. *Antony and Cleopatra* is distinctive among Shakespeare's tragedies not only in its relative lack of high-drama scenes, which Bradley noted,[1] but in a corollary lack of dramatic build-up. Actium is a turning-point, to be sure, but there is no long sequence building toward it as the early scenes of *Macbeth* build toward the murder of Duncan or the early scenes of *King Lear* toward Lear's self-exile and madness on the heath. In *Antony and Cleopatra*, although we are reminded in various ways that the triumph of Caesarism is inevitably coming,[2] scenes tend to be complete in themselves. Each fulfills the potential of the immediate situation, and if it links with what follows it is by ironic juxtaposition rather than as part of a sustained dramatic crescendo. Pleasure is a term in Antony's tragedy, and its

quality of immediacy ('pleasure *now*') is bound to create a different kind of structure than such motives as power and revenge. Bradley also observed, with some regret, that Shakespeare had passed up the opportunity to make intense drama of inner conflict out of the contrary pulls of Rome and Cleopatra on Antony.[3] Such a conflict, though, would necessarily undercut Antony's capacity – which is both his weakness and his greatness – to fulfill each moment wholeheartedly. He cannot, as Ernest Schanzer remarks, be shown like Brutus or Macbeth, 'with himself at war'; rather, 'he is like a chronic deserter, forever changing sides'.[4]

In the end both Antony and Cleopatra opt for stillness over constant flux. Once Cleopatra challenged the hard pillars and arches of the Eternal City with something softer, more alive, more mobile: 'Eternity was in our lips and eyes,/Bliss in our brows' bent' (I, iii, 35–6). But that claim was undercut by its situation (Antony is leaving her) and even by its form. 'Eternity *was*' is a contradiction. Ultimately she must be something less malleable, 'marble-constant' (V, ii, 238), and commit her volatile self to the act 'which shackles accidents, and bolts up change' (l. 6). Yet her death is not, any

---

[1] 'Shakespeare's *Antony and Cleopatra*', *Oxford Lectures on Poetry* (1909), pp. 283–4.

[2] Direct reminders are the soothsayer's warning to Antony that Caesar's daemon will defeat his in any contest (II, iii, 18–31) and Caesar's own prophecy of the *pax romana*, 'The time of universal peace is near' (IV, vi, 4). Awareness comes more indirectly from the stress on Antony's age and Caesar's youth, and from the overplot movement in which Caesar eliminates as a 'world-sharer' first Pompey and then Lepidus, creating the expectation that Antony will be eliminated in his turn. The conflict between Antony and Caesar, 'half to half the world oppos'd' (III, xiii, 9) is imaged by Enobarbus as two jaws inevitably grinding against each other (III, v, 13–15), a picture which combines Roman stillness and directness in its slow but inexorable motion.

[3] *Oxford Lectures*, pp. 285–7.

[4] *The Problem Plays of Shakespeare* (1963), p. 135.

more than Antony's, a simple submission to Roman fixity. It is not just that her mode of dying combines Egyptian means with Roman end. Beyond that, image and reference project the sense that in dying both lovers rise to the moment one last time and do it so perfectly as to arrest time. Each strains toward death as to a lover's embrace (IV, xiv, 99–101; V, ii, 292–4). Cleopatra prepares again for Cydnus (V, ii, 227–8), catching up that perfect moment out of the flux of time. Even Caesar sees in the dead queen not so much cessation as eternal attraction, 'as she would catch another Antony...' At Antony's suicide what the onlookers sense is time itself frozen:

> The star is fall'n.
> And time is at his period.   (IV, xiv, 106–7)

This effect of rising *through* constant motion to timelessness is what distinguishes the resting point of Antony and Cleopatra from the hard immobility of Rome. The paradox comes across most compactly in the climax of Cleopatra's rhapsody on the dead Antony, the last of the fish images.

> His delights
> Were dolphin-like: they show'd his back above
> The element they liv'd in.   (V, ii, 88–90)

What meanings attach to flux and superior solidity in this vision of the dolphin's firm back gleaming above the dancing, shifting sea? For Kittredge, who was later followed by Dover Wilson, Cleopatra means that 'as the dolphin shows his back above the water, so Antony always rose superior to the pleasures in which he lived'. This separates Antony's superiority from his pleasures, opposes them in fact. But 'delights' are the agents of his rising: it is they who show his back above the sea. Another gloss, this one from the *Riverside Shakespeare*, says that Antony 'in his pleasures... rose above the common as a dolphin rises out of its element, the sea'.[1] Now the pleasures have been dissoci-

ated from the sea, which is simply 'the common'. But the sea with its unceasing flux is the element in which those uncommon pleasures lived. Antony's delights are both flux, the succession of moments, and that which ultimately lifts him above flux – because the moment is fully realized. Finally, then, the motion patterns convey not only the essential, tragic incompatibility between stillness and flux but also a hint of transcendence.

Image-patterns created by actions may shape other plays as well. Indeed, the whole question of motion in Shakespeare's verse invites further study. Years ago, F. C. Prescott pronounced that Portia's 'the quality of mercy is not strain'd' was not poetry, because it presented an abstraction rather than the concretes that characterize true poetry.[2] Prescott would doubtless grant more pictorial respectability to Portia's following words, 'It droppeth as the gentle rain from heaven/Upon the place beneath' (*Merchant of Venice*, IV, i, 179–81). But in fact the whole passage has a poetic force, which is more kinetic than visual: the tightness of 'strain'd' easing into the free release of 'droppeth', heaven's benign gesture refusing even the constraint of a single line to spill over into the next. Even critics who would reject Prescott's dogmatism have not paid enough attention to the peculiarly kinaesthetic qualities of Shakespeare's word-painting. His descriptive passages typically depend more on verbs than on adjectives. Consider Perdita's 'daffodils,/That come before the swallow dares, and take/The winds of March with beauty' (*Winter's Tale*, IV, iv, 118–20); or Romeo's warning, 'Night's candles are burnt out, and jocund day/Stands tiptoe on the misty mountain tops' (*Romeo and Juliet*, III, v, 9–10); or even the Shakespeare of the sonnets.

---

[1] Kittredge ed. (Boston, 1941); New Cambridge ed. (Cambridge, 1950); *Riverside Shakespeare* (Boston, 1974).

[2] *The Poetic Mind* (New York, 1922), p. 44.

Full many a glorious morning have I seen
Flatter the mountain-tops with sovereign eye,
Kissing with golden face the meadows green,
Gilding pale streams with heavenly alchemy.

(Sonnet 33)

It is *kissing* and *gilding*, not *golden*, that makes us feel the sun lighting up a landscape, just as outdaring the swallow and taking the March winds express the daffodils' brave yellow better than any color-adjective could. To return to our beginning: drama's essence is action, and Shakespeare – in his lyric verse as well as his plays – is preeminently a dramatic artist.

© SUSAN SNYDER 1980

THEME AND STRUCTURE IN
'THE WINTER'S TALE'

ROY BATTENHOUSE

Theme in *The Winter's Tale* is both one and many-sided. It can be stated symbolically as the victory of spring over winter. But inherent in this, as in a seed, are flowerings of implication and amplification. Emotionally, joy comes to supersede sorrow, though to do so it must first wade in tears. Morally, a virtuous innocence succeeds over vice and tyranny. Metaphysically, order surmounts disorder, and harmony replaces discord. Theologically, grace is victorious over sin, and faith over doubt and suspicion. In religious terms, the hopes of a palace and a garden, the court and the country, find their fulfilment in a chapel, where art achieves a breathtaking holiness and nature an immortal art. Socially, a broken marriage is mended and regenerated in a more glorious form, with two new marriages added for a triple epiphany. The disbranched have been regrafted into an enlarged family tree. Alienations between parents and children and servants end in a household communion that spans the generations.

History's continuity is thus affirmed despite interim disasters. Nature's creative purpose is shown overcoming contingencies of tempest and human bellowing and a greedy growly bear, which typify the forces let loose when reason is obscured or a bawdy planet obsesses the human imagination. For the faithful such misfortunes pose a trial, as they did for ancient Job, testing patience and in the process brightening virtue while also putting to shame false friends. Mysteries of providence, which in

Shakespeare's play are associated with Apollo, a god of light and oracle, outlast the vagaries of fortune and of human benightedness. We see the better instincts of mankind, divine in their orientation, rewarded providentially with an unveiling of secret tokens and then, to the sound of chapel music, the further disclosure of a life of love returned from its grave. This is indeed an 'old tale' – one that has analogy not only to motifs in Greek romance but also to those of Bible story. Its wonder is such that, 'Were it but told you, it should be hooted at', as Paulina remarks at its ending. But when imaginatively experienced by Paulina's auditors, and by us in the theatre, its trans-sensible truth is accepted with awesome joy.

In summarizing I have touched on both theme and structure since these share a common logic. In the play they are interdependent aspects of the action, theme being articulated through structure. That is true, likewise, of Robert Greene's *Pandosto, or the Triumph of Time*, an Elizabethan prose romance which Shakespeare took as his immediate source but reminted. If we compare the two, a significant difference of logic, and hence of shape, becomes evident. Shakespeare's version is the more satisfying because more comprehensive in its vision of what constitutes romance.

Greene's concern was to cater to contemporary fashion by painting a contrast between the vice of jealousy and the courtesy of chaste love. Unlike Shakespeare, however, he uses only once the word 'grace' and then for describing the pretty 'blush' of Fawnia which dyed her crystal cheeks a 'vermillion red' when she spoke to Dorastus. The grace of Shakespeare's Perdita is less colorful, more intrinsic. Greene exploits a rhetoric of Euphuistic elegance, decorated at every turn. Yet in his story there is no winter and spring symbolism. The closest we get is a reference to Fawnia's 'defending herself from the heat of the sun' with a garland of flowers that made her seem like the goddess Flora. But that is all: the flowers are unnamed and serve merely as a head dress.

Greene has organized his narrative in terms of the turnings of Fortune's wheel, through round after round of prosperity and misery until finally Fawnia's shepherd-father produces the tokens which identify her. Leading up to this, Pandosto has cycled into a renewed villainy by rejecting conscience, broiling in lust for Fawnia, and then flip-flopping into a rage which she defies by declaring: 'I will alwaies preferre fame before life; and rather choose death than dishonor.' This statement epitomizes Greene's sense of moral polarities. The tokens serve simply as lucky evidence of Fawnia's parentage, whereas for Shakespeare their disclosure is preceded by an awareness in Leontes of something 'gracious' and 'precious' in the girl that makes him think of Hermione and offer to act as Florizel's advocate. For Pandosto the sudden turn of fortune brings only a temporary joy. It lasts long enough for him to voyage with the young couple to Dorastus's homeland and there re-establish friendship with Egistus over bonfires celebrating the royal wedding, after which he falls into melancholy and commits suicide on calling to mind his prior acts of shameful behavior. Since he has caused his wife's actual death years earlier when his false charges caused her to expire despairingly in bitter tears, Greene apparently thinks Pandosto's compensating suicide an exemplum of divine justice. The story as a whole he terms in his preface a

'pleasant Historie' for encouraging age to avoid drowsy thoughts, and youth to eschew wanton pastimes. We may discover in it, he says, how Time reveals Truth, which sinister Fortune has concealed. He apparently means that Time triumphs over Fortune by exposing virtue's reward and vice's punishment.

How does this theme differ from Shakespeare's? In Shakespeare's story, I would say, what triumphs is not Time but Grace, or more precisely, engraced human nature in the course of time. Time enters the drama personified as a chorus and a witness, but not as the effective cause of romance fulfilment. Shakespeare's Time identifies himself simply as a tester of good and bad and a power that can plant or overwhelm custom. As a reporter of the 'freshest things now reigning', Time says his argument is the wonder that will ensue from and adhere to a Perdita 'now grown in grace'.[1]

The Perdita we encounter at the sheep-shearing festival has a grace that is natural and human but also a heavenly gift. Florizel says he blesses the time he met her. In Greene's story it was not quite so. Dorastus on first seeing Fawnia *after* a country feast felt himself 'bewitched' by her beauty and departed 'cursing Love' for having like a siren enslaved him. His inflamed fancy then led him to a second meeting, during which Fawnia held out for a chaste love, promised on condition that he woo as a shepherd. Dorastus after recalling that the god Apollo thus 'shamed' himself for love's sake was constrained to adopt this garb, and at a third meeting he found himself drawn to offer

[1] Inga-Stina Ewbank, in 'The Triumph of Time in *The Winter's Tale*', *Review of English Literature*, v (1964), 83–100, has discussed Greene's failure to work out his story's motto. She also notes Shakespeare's concept of time as a ripening process of 'branching' in which the heavens 'continue their loves'. Perdita's restoration *defeats* time in that the lifelines of Leontes are stretching into the future; and Hermione's return is another victory over time in that she is living proof that love is not 'time's fool' (Sonnet 116).

and swear a trothplight. Shakespeare has omitted any suggestion of shame on Florizel's part and of inveigling on Perdita's. His scene begins with Florizel's speaking of a nuptial the lovers 'have sworn shall come', and for which the festival is to be used as an anticipatory celebration. Let it be like a meeting of 'the petty gods', he suggests, but then adds that his desires are more chaste and honorably faithful than those of the deities whose example he is borrowing. And Perdita, on her part, regards her garb of Flora as 'borrowed flaunts' put on for custom's sake. Shakespeare is indicating a motivation that transcends pagan connotations, and this becomes the more evident when we hear Perdita speak of her disposition to play as in 'Whitsun pastorals' – that is, folk rites dedicated to the holiday of Pentecost. As Douglas Peterson has noted, she resists on the one hand a 'goddess' identity and on the other hand a careless 'jollity'. She adopts neither Florizel's suggestion to 'be red with mirth' nor her foster-father's ideal of his wife's hostessing.[1] Rather, she qualifies and transforms these options through a graciousness of her own that is natural but not naturalistic, 'lowly' but queenly.

At no time does she resolve, as in Greene's story, to 'sigh out love' on a hillside while making a garland, or blushingly tell her wooer that the homely thoughts of shepherds delight to 'talke of Pan and his cuntry prankes'. Instead, we see Perdita using flowers to welcome the feast's guests, and first of all giving rosemary and rue to the 'reverend sirs', the disguised Camillo and Polixenes. Those flowers are for 'grace and remembrance', she says. For Shakespeare rue is a herb of grace connoting repentance; and remembrance would have the mystical connotation of recalling the soul's inner garden within and above the everyday world. After this beginning, Perdita turns to her 'fair'st friend' Florizel and on him invokes Proserpina's 'virgin' flowers as a garland –

indeed, she would strew these on him, she says, as a bank for love to lie on 'in mine arms'.

This confession of love, may I suggest, is like the shepherd-maiden's in the Song of Solomon who pictured her lover amid lilies (vi, 2) and spoke of his left hand under her head and his right hand embracing her (ii, 6). And Florizel's comment that 'all your acts are queens' provides us a further echo of that ancient paradigm since in Canticles, vi, 8 Solomon's beloved is termed the most perfect of queens, her mother's chosen one, 'my dove'. The turtledove image is used archetypally by Florizel when he invites Perdita to a dance unlike that of the satyrs:

> ...come, our dance, I pray.
> Your hand, my Perdita: so turtles pair
> That never mean to part.   (IV, iv, 153–5)

Here the invitation to 'come' may be compared with the Song's invitation (ii, 10–12): 'Rise up, my love, my fair one, and come away. For, lo, the winter is over and gone; the flowers appear on the earth...and the voice of the turtle is heard in our land.' In obedience to this love-call, Florizel and Perdita come away even from Bohemia. We see them undertake a voyage of faith whose theme is that of Canticles, viii, 7:

> Many waters cannot quench love,
> neither can the floods drown it.
>   (King James Version)

And the preceding verse (viii, 6) says: 'Love is as strong as death.' This truth may be said to be the unifying faith of Shakespeare's play as a whole, its climactic proof being the figurative resurrection of Hermione. Her triumph over death overarches and completes the love quest of Florizel and Perdita.

What could have prompted Shakespeare to invent this crowning episode? Many factors, no doubt. I would suggest, however, that among them may have been an idea provided by

[1] Douglas Peterson, *Time, Tide and Tempest* (San Marino, 1973), pp. 174–6.

Christian interpreters of the Song of Solomon who viewed its love-quest as a foreshadowing of the greater pastoral love of Christ in re-espousing mankind through dying and returning. The dramatist needed only to analogize this pattern by adapting it to the cultural circumstances of his fictionalized Sicily, a country associated with Persephone legend. In this setting, comedy could be given a religious aura. The conventional ending in wedding takes on aspects of miracle in Shakespeare's story and is ascribed, appropriately, to 'heavens directing' and human faith in oracle. Moreover, Hermione offers in blessing a final prayer to the gods to pour down sacred 'graces' on Perdita's head. And this is in keeping with the many references to grace that Shakespeare has attached to Hermione throughout the play,[1] and with Time's reference to 'grace' in Perdita.

In Shakespeare's day, as now, grace had the general meaning of a glow of excellence and favor. Its more particular sense depended on context. It could refer simply to a socially given title of rank or name, or more intrinsically to a divinely given quality of soul. Perception might equate it with a beauty of manners, or more basically with a moral goodness dependent on heavenly aid. When Hermione on being sentenced to prison declares that the action she is going on is 'for my better grace' the second of these meanings is evidently uppermost. The context is her comment that she must be patient 'till the heavens look/With an aspect more favorable'. And of further significance is her counsel to her attending women not to weep for her; this counsel, as Shakespearian auditors might know, resembles Christ's words to the foolish weepers of Luke, xxiii, 28. Moreover, we hear Hermione declare during her trial a confident faith that 'powers divine' are overseeing human actions and will vindicate ultimately her patience and her integrity.

The vindication emerges in act v. 'She was as tender/As infancy and grace', says Leontes as he looks on Hermione's statue, which a moment later inspires in him feelings 'no settled senses of the world' can match. A scene earlier, we have heard a court gentleman who has witnessed the wonder of Perdita's recovery predict: 'Every wink of an eye, some new grace will be born.' The biblical idea of being led from grace to grace is here being echoed, and in particular St Paul's phrase describing Resurrection: 'In the twinkling of an eye we shall all be changed' (1 Cor., xv, 52). The grace 'born' in the palace-yard experience is seen as promising still more to come. But the colloquy of the Gentlemen itself has overtones of Bible story. 'I heard the shepherd say – he found the child', First Gentleman tells us, and goes on to remark that the kings 'looked as they had heard of a world ransomed'. Why are the speakers in this scene three in number? It is Shakespeare's structural arrangement, I would guess, for suggesting an analogy to the three wise men of the Christmas story who, alongside shepherds, experienced the finding of a redemptive royal child. Readers may recall (from *Richard III*) Christianity's idea of 'the world's ransom, blessed Mary's Son'. The ransom in the present situation, by analogy, is the engraced daughter of a Hermione whose sacral quality in the chapel scene requires of us, in C. L. Barber's judgement,[2] 'the discovery of the Holy Mother within the wife'.

In the contexts I have so far mentioned, grace has connotations of a divine gift. But in other contexts Shakespeare sets up in contrast a superficial notion of grace as something resid-

---

[1] S. L. Bethell, *The Winter's Tale: A Study* (1947), pp. 38–9, called attention to several of Hermione's references to grace. His feeling that they along with other religious language in the play were reflecting a Christian understanding on Shakespeare's part seems to me on a right track although too loosely stated. It predictably has met with disapproval by critics unaccustomed to typological interpretation.

[2] *Shakespeare Survey* 22 (Cambridge, 1969), p. 66.

ing simply in high station.[1] Autolycus in act IV mimics a worldly courtier's understanding of grace when he predicts curses and tortures for the old shepherd who is journeying to the court. He says to him disdainfully:

An old sheep-whistling rogue, a ram-tender, to offer to have his daughter *come into grace*! Some say he shall be stoned; but that death is too soft for him, say I. Draw our throne into a sheepcote! All deaths are too few, the sharpest too easy. (IV, iv, 777–82, emphasis added)

Autolycus is here reflecting accurately, although with comic exaggeration, the attitude of King Polixenes. Polixenes at the sheepshearing festival could not but admire Perdita, terming her 'the prettiest lowborn lass that ever/Ran on the greensward', but he utterly rejected her suitability for the grace of courtly station. He denounced her as 'thou fresh piece/Of excellent witchcraft' when Prince Florizel asked to be contracted to her. Shakespeare's point is that an intrinsically gracious nature is something different from the courtly manners which royal custom equates with grace. An Autolycus dressed in Florizel's garments while at heart still roguish is an emblem of the court's superficial concept. 'See'st thou not the air of the court in these enfoldings?' he asks. 'Hath not my gait in it the measure of the court? Receives not thy nose court-odor from me?' This is Shakespeare's satire of fashions mistaken for grace.

We begin now to see how Shakespeare has doubled the jealousy theme in the symphonic structure of his story. The early jealousy of Leontes took the form of a crude sexual jealousy, but a reprise of this motif is the jealousy of Polixenes which takes the form of a self-centered concern for family eminence. Whereas Leontes was jealous of his private rights, Polixenes is jealous of his social prerogatives. We notice at the festival that his ideal of nobility is not fidelity in love but simply a display of fashionable bounty. Thus he chides

Florizel by saying: 'When I was young...I was wont/To load my she with knacks: I would have ransack'd/The pedlar's silken treasury, and have pour'd it/To her acceptance.' Silken values (which Autolycus has called 'toys for your head') are this king's chief ones, whereas Florizel considers them 'trifles' and says: 'The gifts she looks from me are pack'd and lock'd/Up in my heart.' For Florizel, love is an inner life to be *breathed* forth and witnessed by handclasp (IV, iv, 361).

The concern of Polixenes for external ornament can prompt us to ask whether in act I his appreciation of Hermione was not grounded more in an admiration for her courtesies than a recognition of the grace of heart inspiriting her style of courtesy. Its aspect of social dexterity and playful wit on that occasion was what thawed his willful stand on his dignity. But did he really appreciate her motive of good deeds for the sake of love of husband? Probably not, for we see no attempt at a reciprocal good deed by Polixenes when faced by the report of Leontes's jealousy. Polixenes makes no move to protect Hermione and is unconcerned for the husband's future welfare – concerns that motivate Camillo. Polixenes simply protests his innocence to Camillo and accepts Camillo's help in escaping.

Bearing in mind this imperception of the deeper meaning of grace (as something under-

---

[1] Duty to station looms large in Greene's story. Dorastus when wooing Fawnia has lengthy debate with himself over the 'folly' of loving beneath his station, but he finds himself 'forced' by love 'in despight of honor' to follow fancy. Then when the lovers after eloping are cast ashore in another country where Dorastus is imprisoned, he interprets his imprisonment as a punishment: 'Art thou not worthie for thy base minde to have bad fortune?...Wil not the Gods plague him with despight that payneth his father with disobedience?' Only the good luck of having Fawnia turn out to be a king's daughter resolves this dilemma. See Geoffrey Bullough, ed., *Narrative and Dramatic Sources of Shakespeare*, VIII (1975), esp. pp. 183 and 195.

neath and besides mannerly charm), let us examine closely the beginning of the play. We learn in the opening scene that Archidamus, a lord in Polixenes's company, is tremendously impressed by the 'magnificence' of the hospitality they have received and seems eager to outdo it when a return visit is paid in Bohemia. 'We will give you sleepy drinks', he says, 'that your senses (unintelligent of our insufficience) may, though they cannot praise us, as little accuse us.' This is a Euphuistic language of prettified boast and concessive self-depreciation in a balanced elegance. It sounds very much like the gamesmanship in artifice that opens *Much Ado About Nothing*, an earlier comedy set in supersophisticated Sicily.[1] The result in that play was a maligning of Hero, an innocent bride, whose marriage ultimately was saved by the intervention of a holy Friar. The Friar's counsel of pretending a death so that the groom will be brought to repentance and then be regiven his bride through her resurrection from the dead is similar to Paulina's more secret remedy in *The Winter's Tale*. Of Paulina's more complex role I shall speak later. For the moment I am focusing on the elaborate formality of Archidamus. It serves to prepare us for the formality of the farewell speech by Polixenes which opens the next scene.

'Nine changes of the watery star hath been/ The shepherd's note', etcetera, launches a very pretty piece of rhetoric, but its nine lines are more elegant in their watery sentiment than based on concern for shepherding. The reply of Leontes is a conventional parry, as in a duel of etiquette: 'Stay your thanks awhile,/And pay them when you part.' If his words here and in his subsequent parries seem laconic, it is perhaps because he lacks the social fluency of his friend and is therefore resorting to the gruff manner of a magisterial host. Some critics have argued that Leontes begins the scene already suspicious of an affair between Polixenes and Hermione, and that the brevity of his speeches hides an intention to set a trap to test his suspicions. I doubt this interpretation. Leontes could simply be less socially adept, and therefore using a blunt banter as his way of moving toward striking a bargain for a longer stay that will redound to his self-esteem. Besides, he has a trump card up his sleeve, his wife's gifts of speech, and he soon calls on this aid.

We notice when she speaks how much more than flexible her contrasting manners are. Her courtesy has a spontaneity in place of the studied flourishes of the two men. It carries a warm interest in family well-being, and it includes cheerful banter about thwacking Polixenes homeward with distaffs if he will but say that a longing to see his son is his motive. She asks only to 'borrow' a week of his royal presence, and offers in return to give her husband permission to add a month when he visits even though her eagerness for his return will be second to none. It is now Polixenes who retreats into laconic reply: 'No, madam', and 'I may not, verily'. Very likely her generosity has abashed him, and yet he feels he would lose dignity by changing his mind. Alert to this, Hermione chides his 'limber' or weak answer and offers him a mock-choice between being her prisoner or her guest, thereby making it possible for him to abandon stubbornness without losing face, since he can handsomely reply that to be her prisoner would demean his own courtesy.

As 'kind hostess' she then questions him regarding the boyhood behavior of 'pretty lordings'. Were they not waggish tricksters? Her intent seems to be to get him to examine his motives and perhaps to suggest that the present gamesmanship of the two friends is an understandable extension of boyish sparring. His reply that their boyhood was all guiltless

[1] As instances of courtly Euphuism in *Much Ado*, note especially the Messenger's report (I, i, 12–17) and the initial interchange between Don Pedro and his host Leonato.

until experiencing a later (adolescent) 'stronger blood' prompts her indirect query about the lapse. To this he offers the flattering excuse that sight of a sacred lady such as 'your precious self' gave birth to temptations. Hermione's rejoinder, 'Grace to boot!', has puzzled some readers, but surely its meaning is that 'grace as well' was given with such sight, else he is doubting the 'sacred' and implying a devilishness in women. The wives can properly answer, she suggests, by doubting whether the men's first sin was a wife-made offense. If my reading is accurate Hermione may be questioning whether the behavior as boys had been as completely clear of hereditary sin as Polixenes supposes, and in reply she is saying that to trace sin's beginning to wives as its cause is to overlook the 'grace' a 'sacred' lady offers for overcoming temptation. This infers in him a neglect of grace (the flaw which Christian theory identifies as original sin). Am I elaborating unduly? Hermione of course is no trained theologian; but simply in reacting intuitively to her guest's equivocal self-justification she does in fact come up with a reply that is more insightful than his. She is enabled to do so, I think we may say, because of her basic belief (stated later) that 'Grace' is the 'elder sister' of any good deed done by a loving woman for her husband.

Leontes, when informed she has won Polixenes to prolong his visit, is at first well pleased: 'Hermione, my dearest, thou never spok'st/ To better purpose' is the compliment he gives her. Up to this point no jealousy as I read the text – except that there lurks his egoistic bent for enhancing himself by winning the duel as host. But from this preoccupation it is easy to lapse next into jealousy. For it is one thing to value Hermione as his stand-in in a contest and quite another thing to accept her view that in the name of Grace the earning of a friend is a good deed equal to that of earning a husband. This view strikes Leontes as a threat to his own

importance. Did he not endure three 'crabbed' months to gain her in marriage? And now, behold, she is giving her hand to Polixenes, as if that hand were not the exclusive and sole possession of Leontes! Greene had provided circumstantial grounds for jealousy by depicting a wife who was attracted by the 'bountifull minde' of Egistus and often visited his bedchamber for 'honest' inquiry as to his welfare; but Shakespeare has radically changed this, allowing no basis for the husband's jealousy other than his own blind premises.

Let us notice that the reference by Leontes to his courtship months as crabbed and sour implies no awareness of adversity's sweet uses in testing love. He seems to view the wooing as a time, not of 'sweet and bitter fancy' as in Orlando's case (*AYLI*, IV, iii, 101), but simply of disliked delay in achieving his blood's erotic desire. And as he looks back on Hermione's promise, 'I am yours forever', he overlooks this vow's quality of love as friendship, permanent in that commitment. So although she has mentioned Grace three times before her statement linking husband and friend, his imagination reads her motive as a satisfying of hot blood and plunges immediately into sensual interpretation. What Hermione will refer to in act III as 'the level of your dreams' has been in Leontes an initially inadequate level, thus making him vulnerable to downfall. So now the only grace he can see in his wife is that of cunning artifice ('practised smiles') and of erotic favor ('paddling palms') – a tragic misreading.

His self-centered heart generates a world of farmyard imaginings. He slurs his wife by terming his son a calf and he likens her to a pond being fished by a thievish neighbor, though in fact he himself is the one now angling to thieve – may we say, like the Nero of *King Lear* in a lake of darkness (III, vi, 7). With his own lack of trust causing a false seeing, he insists Camillo agree that 'My wife's a hobby horse' – else, he says, Camillo has no 'eyes nor ears nor thought'. And later, when Antigonus protests against this judgement, the king retorts: 'Cease; no more./You smell this business with a sense as cold/As is a dead man's nose: but I do see't and feel't.' Thus all the evidence of his senses is being distorted to support false opinion. Yet his confidence in its rightness is so great that he himself (Shakespeare here differing from Greene) proposes an embassy to Apollo's oracle 'for a greater confirmation'. And when the messengers bring back the oracle's contrary judgement, Leontes exposes a height of pride not in Greene's story by declaring: 'There is no truth at all i' th' oracle.' Only the death of his son Mamillius (for which Shakespeare, unlike Greene, assigns also a proximate cause, the boy's grief over his mother's shaming) collapses the impiety of Leontes and convinces him he is being punished by the Heavens. He then realizes he has defrauded not only others but himself when transported by jealousy. The dimensions of sin are larger than Greene imagined.

I have already described how Autolycus is used by Shakespeare to cast a comic light on the courtly code of Polixenes. Is it possible that Shakespeare, elsewhere, uses Autolycus to provide a comic version of the code of Leontes? I think there is evidence this is indeed so, even though Autolycus enters the play only in act IV. Autolycus is important thematically to the play as a whole. He represents the scapegrace enterprise and moonshine values which the mainplot shows us in Leontes and Polixenes prior to conversion. Let me turn therefore to a pointing up of this subplot function of Autolycus.[1]

His first trick is to defraud an old shepherd's clownish son. Pretending to be a gentleman beaten and robbed, Autolycus falls down in front of the guileless young man and cries out, 'O, help me, help me'. Then when the good-hearted fellow stoops to lend a hand he gets his pocket picked. This episode, we know, was adapted by Shakespeare from one of Robert Greene's pamphlets about the wily arts of London's underworld, but its significance in the drama has been aptly recognized by G. Wilson Knight's naming it a parody of the parable of the Good Samaritan. And I would add that it provides an analogy to the behavior of Leontes in act I when he called on Hermione to help him and then robbed her of her good name when she lent him aid. Indeed, Leontes took away her baby too. The difference that Leontes thieves when mad with a deadly jealousy whereas Autolycus makes thievery his gay delight does not cancel the analogy.

A comparable structural analogy can be found in *The Tempest*. In that play Antonio and Sebastian treacherously seek to rob their king of his life, while in an adjacent scene Trinculo and Stephano are prompted merely by a carefree greed to steal trumpery from Prospero's clothesline. Shakespeare likes to use low comedy characters in this way to parallel in a contrasting mode a theme treated seriously in his mainplot. And in *The Winter's Tale* it enables him to desentimentalize Robert Greene's pastoral by putting some of Greene's London underworld within what is aptly named Bohemia. At the same time the name Autolycus is that of the grandfather of ancient Odysseus, thus universalizing him as an old-tale type of

[1] One benefit of this focus is that it can help remove the puzzlement some critics have felt regarding the role Shakespeare intended for Autolycus. Dover Wilson, for instance, was driven to surmise that 'Possibly Shakespeare meant to make a good deal of him, carefully elaborated him to take a prominent and amusing part in the recognition scene, tired of it all, and suddenly resolving to scalp the Leontes–Perdita recognition scene, smothered him up along with it' (Cambridge edition, 1931, p. xxi). This supposition recurs in Kenneth Muir's *Shakespeare's Sources*, I (1957), 251, but Muir withdraws it in his revised *The Sources of Shakespeare's Plays* (1977), p. 276. It seems to me misdirected speculation. It overlooks the possibility that Shakespeare approached the task of plot construction with an analogical imagination.

thief. In etymology his name means 'very wolf', and who can doubt that Leontes the lion falls into an unroyal wolfishness – until providentially the heavens restore him to a better love?

Autolycus the wanderer by moonlight and 'snapper-up of unconsidered trifles' has obvious points of analogy with a Leontes who wanders into communicating with dreams, makes a pack of scandal of his nothings, and hawks them for public approval. In the one case, of course, there is a carefree delight in unhallowed trumperies such as gloves and pins and poking sticks that bring no benediction to the buyer, while in the other case there is a diseased obsession with paddling palms and pinching fingers and horsing foot on foot. Autolycus has a heart that pulses to the thought of 'doxy' love, whereas the heart of Leontes dances, but not for joy, at the thought of a 'hobby horse' wife. But both have an imagination limited to a world of the senses as interpreted by self-love. The boast of Leontes that he has eyes and nose for understanding dishonest business may be compared with that of Autolycus: 'I understand the business, I hear it. To have an open ear, a quick eye, and a nimble hand, is necessary for a cutpurse; a good nose is requisite also, to smell out work for the other senses' (IV, iv, 670). Both these men feel sure they have the gods on their side, Leontes appealing to Apollo and Autolycus saying: 'Sure the gods do this year connive at us.' Each comes to find his prideful belief controverted. Then the king and the rascal turn to the play's shepherding persons to help them to a better future. Thus from opposite levels of the social spectrum, madness and mischief undergo analogous experiences. The play's theme is being manifested symphonically.

In the scene where Autolycus plays wounded man to the Good Samaritan clown, he attributes his wounds to a *cowardly* rogue and then elaborates on the rogue's history as follows:

'He hath been...an ape-bearer, then a process-server,...then he compassed a motion of the Prodigal Son...Some call him Autolycus.' The fiction here of having taken a beating from an outsider, who in fact is the victim's undivulged self, is ironically the real truth about Autolycus. It is also the real truth about Leontes in act I, since Leontes was there self-victimized. Added to that, the roles of ape-bearer and Prodigal Son fit Autolycus and Leontes better than either of them knows. Each (if I may borrow a motif from *Measure for Measure*) is an instance of proud man ignorant of his essence, who 'like an angry ape,/Plays such fantastic tricks before high Heaven/As makes the angels weep' – or would make angels laugh if they had mortal spleens. And each is a prodigal who wastes himself. The remark of Autolycus that as regards 'the life to come, I sleep out the thought of it' is metaphorically true of Leontes in his spiritual drowsiness of jealousy. The life to come, whether in the sense of a heavenly future or in the sense of a future earthly welfare, is so sleepily apprehended by Leontes that he prefers his wanton dreams and thus wastes his family inheritance in riotous living, just as the other prodigal Autolycus wastes his cleverness in a scheme that brings him no 'preferment'. Indeed, the treachery of Autolycus in diverting the shepherds onto a ship for foreign shores is analogous to what Leontes did to Perdita. Both cases remind me of a truism stated in *Romeo and Juliet*: 'Virtue itself turns vice, being misapplied', a misapplication traceable to cowardice – 'Thy noble shape is but a form of wax,/Digressing from the valor of a man.' Recovery of the valor of a man is possible only when scapegrace Autolycus and scapegrace Leontes (and in a different way scapegrace Polixenes) repent and like the Prodigal of Bible story turn homeward to serve grace and family reunion.

It may seem esoteric if I suggest a symbolism in the ballads Autolycus peddles in Bohemia.

The usual editorial comment is merely that they allow Jacobean auditors to laugh at a popular taste of their time for ballads almost equally absurd. So was not Shakespeare inventing them simply for incidental satire and to give variety and range to his pastoral scene? Still, I'm willing to risk guessing at implications of an emblematic kind, provided my readers will tolerate suggestions that are marginal and not essential to my argument. One of the ballads is about a fish that beached itself high out of water and then sang against hard hearts. Could this be figurative, on Shakespeare's part, not of any woman in his play but of Leontes and Polixenes? Through a hardness of heart in rejecting one who loves them, do not these kings strand themselves in a prideful isolation? A ballad even more monstrous is the one about the usurer's wife who gave birth to money-bags and longed to eat adders' heads and toads. If adders' heads perhaps signify venomous thoughts and toads an ugly jealousy, might this ballad be figurative of the play's kings, who are like usurers in trying to profit themselves with a fool's gold of jealousy? 'Bless me from marrying a usurer', says the country maid Dorcas on being told the ballad. I would think any sensible woman in Shakespeare's audience would react similarly to some of the monstrous business the play's kings engage in. It is notable that the two girls at the fair are willing to lay aside the ghoulish ballads in favour of a third, a merry one. This one has the theme of 'Two maids wooing a man' and it consists of dialogue between an evasive man and the maids who persist in asking him where he is going. If this ballad has figurative significance it could be in the parallel attempt of Leontes as a vagabond lover to brush off Paulina and Hermione, who nevertheless pursue him with undeterred love. Notice, in any case, that Autolycus himself sings the man's lines in the ballad, for he is the play's emblematic vagabond, as I have been arguing.

Just as Leontes failed to perceive the mystery of grace in Hermione in act I, Autolycus in act IV fails to look into the fardel the shepherds carry. Belatedly and to his chagrin he learns from three lords the secret he missed investigating. Their awesome story dumbfounds the usually talkative Autolycus for 120 lines. When then he revaluates his chosen 'profession' of thievery, we see him turning to the very shepherds he had deceived as their advocate and asking them to be *his* advocate. He is now ready to profess a new outlook:

Autolycus. I humbly beseech you, sir, to pardon me all the faults I have committed to your Worship, and to give me your good report to the Prince my master.
Shepherd. Prithee, son, do; for we must be gentle, now we are gentlemen.
Clown. Thou wilt amend thy life?
Autolycus. Ay, an it like your good Worship.
Clown. Give me thy hand. I will swear to the Prince thou art as honest a true fellow as any is in Bohemia. (v, ii, 149–57)

Critics have differed in evaluating this conversion. Some think it a further nimble pretense on the part of Autolycus. But Shakespeare has placed the proffered amendment of life in a scene immediately between the enlightenment of the kings on opening the fardel and the resurrection of Hermione in the chapel. I believe, along with the critic Lee Cox,[1] that the conversion is genuine although open-ended as to its lastingness. It seems to me as credible as the conversion of Caliban in the final scene of *The Tempest*. For in Caliban's case, too, we are presented the surprise of 'I'll be wise hereafter,/And seek for grace' – a miracle which, were it but told you, would be hooted at. Each of these seemingly unredeemable 'naturals' has come to recognize the unprofitability of his former life, and that discovery when set beside

[1] See 'The Role of Autolycus in *The Winter's Tale'*, *Studies in English Literature*, IX (1969), 283–301.

the happy one of neighbors becomes the basis for a humble turnabout. When Autolycus discovers that 'Here [in the shepherds' elevation to a status of gentlemen] come those I have done good to against my will, and already appearing in the blossoms of their fortune' (v, ii, 124–6), his own desire for such a blossoming leads him to become a suppliant – not with courtier-like smoothtalk but with sober speech, like a candidate at a Confirmation service answering to catechetical questions. So the shepherd's son admits him to the status of 'friend' and seals this with a promise to swear to it; for although realistic enough to know Autolycus will sometimes get drunk, yet he hopes and has faith in the man's potential goodness. In short, this is a case of faith responding to faith, even while witty byplay salts it. In the play's structure it prepares us for the emphasis on faith which comes next, at a contrastingly awesome level, in the chapel scene. Thus as the play's score rises to a finale, the theme of conversion is given a triple resonance.

The happy ending depends on a grace of forgiveness Hermione has maintained while a growth in grace by Perdita has come to include Florizel. But also it depends, in support of these three, on the good deeds of four guardian figures. Thus we may say that the structure of the play emerges as a sevenfold manifestation of faith in balance against the threefold manifestation of faithlessness in prodigal Leontes, Polixenes, and Autolycus. Of the four guardians, the old Shepherd and his son are rustics while Camillo and Paulina are courtiers. But all four have shepherding roles which develop progressively in the drama's action. Let me therefore now comment on the individual realism Shakespeare gives each of these guardians in making them servitors of the play's redemptive theme.

Shakespeare's old Shepherd, unlike Greene's, is not a 'mercenary' who has a dilemma of conscience on finding a child. Greene's

shepherd Porrus felt he ought to carry the child to the king for a rearing in accord with its birth. But on seeing the gold coins a 'covetousness' overcame him, says Greene; 'for what will not the greedy desire of Golde cause a man to do?' So Porrus salved his conscience by reasoning that a secret keeping of the gold would be justified if he reared the child as his heir. Years later he has another dilemma when neighbors report Fawnia is meeting secretly with the king's son. Fearing that her honesty will soon not be worth 'a halfpenny', he decides to prevent the mischief of a pregnancy by taking the tokens to the king and hoping he will take Fawnia into his service and thus relieve the shepherd of blame for 'whatsoever chanceth'. Greene's portrait implies a crudely lower-class utilitarianism with no depth of faith. Porrus when kidnapped by Capnio has a scene with Dorastus in which he swears to keep the whole matter secret if only released to go home. At Pandosto's court he tells his story only to disburden his conscience when sentenced to die.

In Shakespeare's revised portrait the Shepherd is more like a rustic from the *Second Shepherds' Play* in that he has a natural piety beneath some social comment on the vexations of tempest and pillage which are his lot. A hunting party of youths (presumably gentry) has frightened off two of his sheep, and it is while longing for relief from stealing and fighting that he comes across the lucky find of a 'pretty barne' and cries out 'Mercy on's'. Since he infers some transgression at court here in evidence, his pity for the child includes no sense of duty to have it reared at court. Instead, he summons his son to behold 'a thing to talk on when thou art dead and rotten' – that is, the finding of this child, a wonder more significant than the disasters the clownish boy is entering to report. To the boy's graphic tale of the 'piteous cry' of shipwrecked souls and in particular that of Antigonus, the father responds with compassion, invoking 'mercy' and lamenting: 'Would I had been by, to have helped the old man.' But as between the competing 'sights', he admonishes the boy to look *here* and 'Now bless thy self', since 'things dying' are less to be thought on than 'things new-born'. Pointing then to the baby's bearing-cloth (baptismal robe), he urges the boy to look inside it while recalling an old prediction of being made rich by fairies. In this context, the gold that is espied is immediately named a 'fairy gold' that signalizes a secret to be kept, a supernatural fulfillment of promise, the beginning of a lucky day which calls for 'good deeds' in celebration of it. I have summarized carefully because, although this scene is not a Bible-story nativity, it does seem to me analogous to such a pattern from within the limits of a rustic natural piety.

At the sheepshearing festival the Shepherd and his son are hosts to a natural hospitality. We notice their concern to encourage song and courtship within the bounds of wholesome manners. The Shepherd, moreover, has intuitive good judgement: not knowing the rank of Perdita's swain, he thinks the couple well matched for betrothal. Then comes the shock revelation of Florizel's royalty, to which he reacts with a stunned sense of being 'undone' by the king's rebuke and by Perdita's having ventured a faith beyond her station. Shamed by this turn of events, he shows his piety in dreading more than a hanging the prospect of a burial deprived of priestly rites.

When next we see this guardian he is on his way to the palace to prove his honesty by telling his story. But his sense of mission differs from that of Greene's shepherd. He has a half-prophetic insight that the fardel's secrets will make the king 'scratch his beard'. And Shakespeare adds the clown's confident 'comfort' that once they show the fardel's 'strange sights' the law can simply 'go whistle'. What I find interesting in these phrases is a comic parallel to St Paul's idea that freedom from the law is possible by sights that transcend human custom. These shepherds of course have only a cloudy notion of what the higher mystery is, but they travel with a faith that the tokens will reveal it and they are willing to offer Autolycus their gold, and even put the clown in pawn, in pursuit of this hope. Naively they view Autolycus as 'provided to do us good', and ironically they are right, since providentially he *does* do them good despite his wicked intention. They are, so to speak, pilgrims who see only as in a glass darkly yet with this foolish half-sight risk their goods and lives to safeguard a hope of justification. Hence providence rewards them. For by their service of patient good will they prove their own inner gentility and qualify to become, by adoption, genuine brothers of the gracious Perdita. Shakespeare's version is reflecting by analogy, it seems to me, motifs as ancient as the biblical ones of justification by faith and adoption into grace.

Camillo exhibits a comparable questing within a court environment. His counterpart in Greene's story, however, was merely a household menial. When offered by his king a bribe of a thousand crowns to poison the visiting king, Franion replied (whether because of conscience or to save face, says Greene) with conventional truisms: that murder was an offense against the gods, that a causeless cruelty would be dishonorable and politically dangerous, and other such persuasions (but none with a focus on defending the queen and countering diseased aspersions). When this moralizing merely enraged Pandosto to offer Franion a choice of preferment or death, Franion agreed to do the murder. But a debate of conscience within him intervened and led to his decision to inform the visiting Egistus and (in order to prove himself honest and no sly trapper) to offer to fly with Egistus. The grateful visitor thereupon promised Franion to make him a duke if he would arrange for a boat and be its navigator. Franion complied and we hear no more of him in Greene's story. We assume the reward of a dukedom amply satisfied Franion's aspirations.

In Shakespeare's revision, Camillo is introduced as a royal cupbearer honored by Leontes for his 'priestlike' counsel. And he is also, as we soon see, a diplomat of real courage. When questioned about Hermione he names her 'good' and 'gracious' and rejects vigorously the 'hobby horse' epithet of Leontes. 'You never spoke what did become you less/Than this', he says; 'Good my Lord, be cured/Of this diseased opinion.' When Leontes makes it a test of loyalty to 'bespice a cup', Camillo dodges with the reply that he 'could' do this but cannot believe any crack in Hermione's honor. Only under further pressure does he promise to 'fetch off' Bohemia, on condition that the king reaccept the queen for his son's sake. But the phrase 'fetch off' is ambiguous, as is also the promise that 'If from me he have wholesome beverage,/Account me not your servant.' And soon Camillo turns these promises into a giving of unwholesome news to Polixenes and fetching him off from the danger. Camillo has not lied but only reinterpreted his words. He remains a loyal servant of Leontes by preventing the murder. A grateful Polixenes begs, 'Be pilot to me' – and here 'pilot' means moral guide.

Camillo has, of course, let Leontes be deceived by an equivocal promise. But Leontes will later call him 'most humane' and pious. What Camillo has done, I suggest, is to act like a gardener who uses art to mend nature, this art being itself nature's. He does so again sixteen years later in Bohemia. He goes to the sheep-shearing in disguise, but not as a sharer of Polixenes's selfish purpose. And when this king denounces Perdita as an 'enchantment' too base for 'a scepter's heir', Camillo lets him stomp off while he himself lingers to give guidance to the lovers. Perhaps he has been

impressed in particular by the spunk of Perdita, who says of the king:

I was not much afeard, for once or twice
I was about to speak and tell him plainly
The selfsame sun that shines upon his Court
Hides not his visage from our cottage but
Looks on alike.   (IV, iv, 443–7)

Echoed here is a verse in Matthew (v, 45) about a Father in heaven who makes his sun rise equally on all persons. The context of that verse, an injunction to 'do good to them that hate you', aptly describes the direction Camillo now gives the lovers.

The situation is precarious. Florizel is determined not to violate his faith to Perdita but is talking of reckoning themselves 'slaves of chance' and putting to sea for who knows where. At this point Camillo asks that they 'embrace but my direction' and take 'A course more promising/Than a wild dedication' to unpathed waters. Camillo's proposal is that Florizel visit Leontes in an assumed role of ambassador from Polixenes and disguise Perdita as his 'fair princess' – 'For so I see she must be', says Camillo with the half-sight of prophetic insight. And he promises, without saying how, that he will 'qualify' Florizel's father and 'bring him up to liking'. Is Camillo perpetrating falsehoods? Rather, he is using art to mend nature by grafting into the wild purpose of the lovers a nobler role which he sees their natures fit them to play, and by playing which they will become indeed what they play.

Camillo's strategy turns flight into mission, to the delight of Florizel who hails Camillo as the 'medicine of our house'. The strategy accords, moreover, with Camillo's love for Polixenes and Leontes alike. True, Polixenes is in no mood for friendship with Leontes, having in IV, ii pushed aside Camillo's wish to return to Sicily to 'allay' the penitent king's sorrow. His stated reason, however, was his own need to retain Camillo's 'goodness' for the sake of 'my profit therein, the heaping friendships' Camillo provides him. This very profit of friendship, but in a surprising mode, Camillo now hopes to heap on Polixenes. Florizel, likewise guided by hope, terms what he hears of the plan a 'miracle', and then later thinks it a betrayal when he finds Camillo has sent Polixenes chasing after him to Sicily. But the double deception turns into miracle when, by providential accident, Camillo and Polixenes encounter in Sicily the old shepherd. While Polixenes is threatening the shepherd, Camillo reacts by looking into the fardel. This alertness to hidden possibility is typical of his faith. It becomes the means by which nature is mended.

Paulina is a character wholly invented by Shakespeare. He shows her growing in wisdom and skill in the process of suffering adversity. After learning patience she is able to tutor Leontes. Her initial good will is evident in her indignation on hearing of Hermione's imprisonment, but she is naively over-confident of her ability to soften the king's heart through verbal protest. Disdaining to be 'honey-mouthed', she forgets to apply to herself her own adage that 'The *silence* often of pure innocence/ Persuades when speaking fails'. With blunt audacity like that of Kent in *King Lear*, she names herself the king's physician on behalf of the 'Good queen'. When Leontes mockingly retorts, 'Good queen', she tosses the phrase back at him three times and adds she would make her good by combat if she were a man. Inevitably this approach exasperates Leontes. With a rising anger he denounces her as a witch, a crone, and a Dame Partlet, ordering her out and giving command for both the baby and the queen to be burnt. One recent critic has commented that Shakespeare is inviting our sympathy for Leontes by the shrewishness of Paulina, thus holding in tension comedy and pathos.[1]

But is Paulina really a shrew? Is not the tag unfairly seized on by Leontes to distort the repute of this Pertelote and intimidate her Chanticleer husband? True, a woman of conscience becomes comic when she scolds; but at the same time the very rigor of her faith protects her from falling victim to worldly values. Antigonus, on the other hand, in seeking to maintain a conventional social dignity, gets foxed into a compromise with the tyrant, a consenting to take up the babe and discard it on foreign soil, even though he feels a present death would have been more merciful. Shakespeare is undoubtedly implying here a deficiency in this courtier's faith. We hear Paulina warn: 'For ever/Unvenerable be thy hands, if thou/Tak'st up the princess' so long as the bastardy charge is on her. Yet Antigonus does so, and even relapses into believing this charge himself. Symbolically that is why he gets eaten by a bear – the fate which in the Bible came on the foolish ones who mocked the prophet Elisha (2 Kings, ii, 24). Antigonus has in effect mocked his wife's vision and, more than that, his own vision of a Hermione in 'pure white robes/Like very sanctity'. So he and his crew simply get swallowed up, as in old allegories of moral shipwreck.[2]

Shakespeare has depicted in Paulina, nevertheless, an initial immaturity. Her indignation's half-sight climaxes in the tongue-lashing she gives Leontes even after he has acknowledged heaven's judgement and has requested 'remedies for life' for Hermione. Paulina by going offstage to attend the queen has not heard his further repentance in asking Apollo to pardon his profaneness. She returns in high dudgeon to announce the queen dead and cry woe on the tyrant. Does she know the death to be more apparent than real? Is she dissimulating

[1] Joan Hartwig, 'The Tragicomic Perspective in *The Winter's Tale*', *English Literary History*, 37 (1970), 12–36, notably pp. 13–19.
[2] See Dennis Biggins, 'Exit pursued by a Beare', *Shakespeare Quarterly*, XIII (1962), 3–14.

a fury in order to drive home by rhetoric the moral judgement Leontes deserves? More likely, a hasty belief that Hermione has died, overwhelmed at the very moment of her vindication, so shocks Paulina's moral sensibilities as to release a bitter anger (comparable to the old Shepherd's moment of despair on finding his feast wrecked and his hopes 'undone'). And for the drama's emotional effect on us as auditors in the theatre it is important that we experience with her the full weight of the king's sin and ruin. The disaster must *seem* to us irreparable. At the same time, however, the contriteness of Leontes is proved and consolidated by his welcoming of Paulina's chastisement: 'Go on, go on', he says; 'Thou canst not speak too much; I have deserv'd/All tongues to talk their bitt'rest.' Yet Paulina's diatribe is intemperate in mocking him not to repent but betake himself to 'nothing but despair'. It is wildly negative.

But with this emotion exhausted, Paulina is able to notice the humility of Leontes and hearken to a bystander's rebuke of her fault of boldness. She repents her too much 'rashness' and begs Leontes to forgive 'a foolish woman'. The scene then ends with a request by Leontes that she lead him to the chapel graves of wife and son that he may henceforth visit these daily to sorrow for his shame. In act V we learn that he has achieved a saint-like sorrow and that he has come to esteem Paulina's counsel. But now her concern is to prevent a premature conclusion of his penance. And for this purpose she focuses on a twofold remembering – of the peerlessness of Hermione and of the oracle's promise, using these to stimulate a more than mortal love, faith and hope.

Shakespeare's intent, we may infer, is to depict in Paulina a spiritual progress from an initially moralistic rigidity to a more gracious shepherding, analogous perhaps to the growth of the biblical Saul of Tarsus into a St Paul. Occasional scholars have speculated that Shakespeare's naming her Paulina carries an analogy to the Apostle.[1] For other scholars, who may demur at that suggestion, the play provides as an index of Paulina's growth her leaving behind associations with Pertelote and naming herself at the end an 'old turtle' (the dove of the Song of Solomon). Her second marriage, to a diplomat of more faith and courage than Antigonus, holds promise of being more rewarding than her first. The play when viewed linearly has, as readers easily recognize, a 'diptych' structure – and may we not add that so likewise does the Bible with its two-phased story of the logic of grace within history and time.

In any case, it seems evident that once Paulina's sense of mission shifts from denunciation to an aiding of Leontes to 'New woo my queen' (his resolve at III, ii, 156), she manifests arts characteristic of a mature pastor. The pastoral care she then exercises may be compared with a model Shakespeare may have read about in a well-known treatise by Gregory the Great. Gregory (in his *Pastoral Care* III, iv) urges that 'the deeds of superiors are not to be smitten by the sword of the mouth, even when they are rightly judged to be worthy of blame'. Rather, says Gregory, the example to be followed is that of pious David who took care not to smite Saul but only to cut, as it were silently, the border of his robe. For does not Proverbs, xxix, 11 say: 'A fool uttereth all his mind, but a wise man putteth it off, and reserves it till afterwards'? If we remember these precepts of Gregory, surely Paulina's crowning glory is what she reserves till afterwards. Its distinctive quality then fits Gregory's model of a Good Samaritan. Let me quote:

Whosoever superintends the healing of wounds must needs administer in wine the smart of pain, and in oil the softness of loving-kindness, to the end that

[1] For instance, J. A. Bryant, *Hippolyta's View: Some Christian Aspects of Shakespeare's Plays* (Lexington, 1961), p. 216.

through wine what is festering may be purged, and through oil what is curable may be soothed. Gentleness, then, is to be made of both; so that subjects be neither exulcerated by too much asperity, nor relaxed by too great kindness. (II, vi)

Compare with this the procedure of Paulina in act v. Against the court's urging of Leontes to remarry, she sternly admonishes: 'Care not for issue,/The crown will find an heir.' Yet also she soothes with a mysterious promise that Leontes will marry when his 'first queen's again in breath'. That breath is later revealed, but preceded by Paulina's requirement that 'You do awake your faith'. Only thus can 'dear life' redeem Leontes. Paulina's sacred magic, 'an art/ Lawful as eating', relies on nature's own best potentialities to mend nature. As in Christian traditional theology, nature is understood as in need of grace and available for the use of grace.

I regard Paulina and Autolycus, the two major additions to Greene's cast of characters, as being of polar importance to the distinctively new dimensions of Shakespeare's story. For in the revised romance world of Shakespeare's vision the horizons of action move between, on the one hand, human nature's vagabond proclivity epitomized in an Autolycus who enters as a merrygreeke mocker of a gullible Good Samaritan, and on the other hand, Paulina's eventual attaining of a maturely Good Samaritan skill for assisting a wounded neighbor. Paulina's initially naive good will is comparable to the initial foolishness of the clownish shepherd's son, while her final more artful benevolence is analogous to this clown's catechizing of a repentant Autolycus. That analogy pertains to parallel levels of social comedy. But other innovations by Shakespeare pertain to levels of religious tone – for instance, the analogy between the reported 'solemn and unearthly' atmosphere of the Delphos temple and the more amazing atmosphere of Paulina's chapel in which a transformation of 'stone' into speaking life is enacted. A relation of foreshadowing 'type' to its surpassing antitype is here evident, and by this structuring of the story Shakespeare replaces Greene's limited moral outlook with horizons more profoundly revelatory.

I have tried to show how richly symbolic Shakespeare's structure is by probing its complex patternings. The balancings are far more subtle and variegated than Robert Greene's, and more fully comprehensive of 'old tale' wonders. Shakespeare offers us a grandly architectonic network of integrated symbol, but along with this an observant realism that is as ingrained as the streaks of a tulip. Since his *Winter's Tale* concludes, as does his earlier *Pericles*, with incremental stages of revelation and joy, we can aptly apply to it the words of Gower in recommending *Pericles*: here is a 'restorative' appropriate for 'ember eves and holy ales'. Shakespeare was at his full maturity when writing this restorative. It remains a classic for all time.

© ROY BATTENHOUSE 1980

PETER STREET AT THE FORTUNE
AND THE GLOBE

JOHN ORRELL

Of all the documents on which our knowledge of the Elizabethan stage is founded, none is more tantalizing than the Fortune contract. It is unique in giving precise dimensions for a public theatre, but it is in just these specifications that it is most likely to differ from its models, the other theatres of the age and especially the first Globe. Four times it mentions 'the late erected Plaiehowse On the Banck in the saide pishe of Ste Savio^rs Called the Globe',[1] and on three of these occasions it is to avoid having to go into unnecessary detail when the model is so readily available and its building of such recent memory. It is hard to escape the conclusion that the contract goes into most detail when the proposals for the Fortune differ most from the example of the Globe, and in nothing is this truer than in the very dimensions which give the document its dangerous fascination. Some scholars, anxious to seize on any evidence that will lead towards an understanding of Shakespeare's playhouse, have too hastily assumed that the stage at the Globe was 43 feet (13·11 m) across, simply because that is the figure given for the Fortune. Yet on this point the language of the contract is ambiguous, to say the least. It calls for a stage and tiring house to be set up:

...wch Stadge shall conteine in length ffortie and Three foote of lawfull assize and in breadth to extende to the middle of the yarde.... And the saide Stadge to be in all other proporcōns Contryved and fashioned like vnto the Stadge of the saide Plaiehowse Called the Globe...

'All other proporcōns' may perhaps mean 'in all other respects *as well as*' the specified width and forward extension, but it more naturally reads 'in all other respects *except*' the specifications just given. That this is the intention of the clause is suggested by the near-certainty that the remaining dimensions of the Fortune plan were not those of the Globe; the 80-foot (24·38 m) square with its 55-foot (16·76 m) courtyard within were measures more appropriate to a square building than a round or polygonal one. Such a plan, inscribed within the 80-foot dimensions, would be much too small to contain the large audiences described by contemporaries. If particular figures were given for the frame because it differed from its model, so too for the stage. Any comparative study of the plans of the Fortune and the Globe must begin, then, by laying an old ghost to rest, appropriately enough in the cellarage: the one thing we can be reasonably sure of about the Globe's stage is that it was *not* 43 feet across. But where, in that case, does the figure in the Fortune contract come from? And where also its companions, 55 feet and 80 feet? I propose in this paper to offer a rationale for the plan of the Fortune, and then to enquire what relevance our findings have for an understanding of the plan of Shakespeare's Globe.

We must begin with a very practical problem. How is the plan of the Fortune actually to be

---

[1] The quotations from the Fortune contract are from R. A. Foakes and R. T. Rickert (eds.), *Henslowe's Diary* (Cambridge, 1961), pp. 306–15.

laid out on the ground? This is a task for a craftsman, not for an owner like Henslowe or an actor like Alleyn. The general idea of the playhouse will doubtless be theirs, but the specific design solution, the particular dimensions and proportions, will be the product of a technical interpretation of their brief. And since their contract is with Peter Street the carpenter it is to him that we must turn for enlightenment. Nobody here is an 'architect' – the term has hardly entered the English language by 1600 –[1] but Street is an experienced theatre builder and a man used to working in timber. In a few years' time he will be renting his specialized equipment to the King's Works for 'boringe the greate Collumbes in the Banquettinge house' at Whitehall.[2] But however accomplished and experienced, he is an illiterate man who can only set his mark to his contract with Henslowe and Alleyn. His skill is more likely to be traditional than newfangled and book-fed. It may be that he has heard of Vitruvius, but it is extremely unlikely that he has read the *De Architectura*, or that he would design and build a Vitruvian theatre on the antique model.[3] What he knows of design geometry will be what the generations have known, and if we are to seek for his intellectual methods we shall do better to look for them among the medieval and Tudor craftsmen than to search out the kind of Italian sophistication that would appeal to an Inigo Jones.

Elizabethan builders often went by the name of surveyors. Thus Fale's *Horologiographia* (1593), an account of dialling, was intended 'not onely for Students of the Arts Mathematicall, but also for diuers Artificers, Architects, Surueyours of buildings, free-Masons and others'. Leonard Digges's *Tectonicon* (1556) was addressed to 'Surueyers, Landmeaters, Ioyners, Carpenters, and Masons'. In his *English Art 1557–1625*[4] Eric Mercer gives a well-documented account of the relation between the Elizabethan builder and the owner

for whom he worked, illustrating by the way how often the term 'surveyor' occurred where now we might be tempted to use the anachronistic 'architect'. These examples show that two senses of the word tended to merge: the overseer (as in Surveyor of Taxes) and the measurer of land (as in Ordnance Survey). The building contractor included something of both skills in his repertoire, but it is the latter that is of interest to us in the present enquiry. The science of surveying was comparatively new in Street's day, but it was developing rapidly while borrowing much of its technical apparatus from the traditions of the builder. Thus although we know comparatively little about the techniques used by craftsmen in the sixteenth century to set out a building, something may be deduced from the nature of their tools and much more from the related skills of the surveyors, which are extensively documented. Here, if anywhere, we shall find Peter Street's intellectual milieu.

The chief measuring instruments of a carpenter were his square and his rod. By the middle of the seventeenth century the carpenter's rod was customarily 10 feet (3·05 m) long, a *decempeda* marked off in feet and inches, and used for laying out work.[5] Street may have had a 10-foot rod, but if so it would have hung next to a rather longer one in his tool-room. This rod, like those of the surveyors, was 16 feet 6 inches (5·03 m) long, a statute rod or

[1] See the discussion of 'Designers and Craftsmen' in John Summerson, *Architecture in Britain 1530 to 1830* (Harmondsworth, 1970), pp. 56–9.
[2] PRO E351/3242, account for 1606–7.
[3] For an account of the Globe along Vitruvian lines see Frances Yates, *Theatre of the World* (Chicago, 1969); Richard Kohler has offered an analysis of 'The Fortune Contract and Vitruvian Symmetry' in *Shakespeare Studies VI* (1970), pp. 311–26. See also Ernest L. Rhodes, *Henslowe's Rose* (Lexington, 1976).
[4] (Oxford, 1962), pp. 53–9. Compare 2 *Henry IV*, I, iii, 42 and 53.
[5] Joseph Moxon, *Mechanick Exercises* (1677), p. 129, describes the carpenter's 10-foot rod.

perch. It gave the prime unit of land measurement, used by all Tudor surveyors and interchangeably interpreted as a linear or area quantity, the latter being 16 feet 6 inches square. Simply as a carpenter, Street doubtless thought in feet; but as a measurer of land – a necessary if subordinate part of his craft – he would more naturally have thought in rods. Such a unit was used of the timberwork set up in the tiltyard in 1619–20 at Whitehall, and by custom to measure the amount of brickwork used in foundation walls.[1] But even a 16 feet 6 inches measuring stick is not a very handy instrument for accurately laying out such distances as 80 feet (24·38 m), and for that Street would have been equipped with a line marked off, like the surveyors' lines, in rod lengths. Valentine Leigh had put the matter succinctly in his *Science of Surveyinge* (1578):

To aunswere by Rodde or by Line, it is at your pleasure, but of them bothe, the line is the spedier, and most commodious, and also of moste antiquitie. Your Line beyng fower Perches of length, and at euery Perche ende a knot, would bee well seared with hoate Waxe and Rosen, to auoide stretching thereof in the wete, and shrinkyng in the drought.[2]

It is with instruments such as these that we must imagine Peter Street setting out the Fortune site, not with chains or measuring tapes. They would give him a specialized idea of what he was doing, quite unlike the assumptions we should bring to the task ourselves.

Street will also have had his specialized way of thinking about the frame of the theatre. The contract specifies overall dimensions 'of lawfull assize', measured from surface to surface to ensure that there should be no ambiguity about the area to be covered by the building or the quantity of materials to be used. But Street built in timber bays, and he was used to thinking also in terms of distances between post centres, since that is the way structural bays must be measured. An 11-foot (3·35 m) bay is defined by the distance, not between timbers,

but between the centres of the timbers. Thus for him the frame of the Fortune, while 80 feet (24·38 m) across measured overall, was actually some 79 feet 2 inches (24·13 m) between the centres, assuming that the posts of the ground storey were 10 inches by 10 inches (254 × 254 mm), as they are in the specifications handily provided by the contract for the Hope in 1613. This outer wall of the theatre would be 'beam-filled' with lath and plaster, and the timbers left showing:[3] thus the 80-foot measure refers to the outer surfaces of the posts. The courtyard within was to be paled 'wᵗʰ good stronge and sufficyent newe oken bourdes', and although the scantlings of the boards are not given we may assume that they were 1½ inches (38 mm) thick, so that the post centres of the yard were 56 feet 1 inch (17·09 m) apart. The construction of the stage was quite different from that of the massive frame, and would have been known to Street simply by its overall dimensions as a piece of ambitious joinery. Thinking in Street's terms, then, rather than the legal specifications of the contract, we see a 43-foot stage surrounded by a timber frame made square, 56 feet 1 inch centre-to-centre for the yard, and 79 feet 2 inches centre-to-centre for the outer walls.

Our next task is to marry these two sorts of traditional thought as they might have been married in Street's mind. The surveyor's line with its rod measurements must somehow be hitched to the very irregular-looking dimensions of the Fortune plan considered centre-to-centre. Of course Peter Street left no record of his

[1] For the tiltyard, PRO E351/3253; for brickwork at Whitehall and Royston PRO E351/3242 and 3244.
[2] Valentine Leigh, *The Moste Profitable and Commendable Science, of Surueiyng of Landes, Tenementes, and Hereditamentes* (1578), o2ᵇ.
[3] The contract calls for the frame to be 'sufficyently enclosed withoute with lathe, lyme & haire', materials that would be used between the timbers rather than over them. See L. F. Salzman, *Building in England down to 1540: a Documentary History* (Oxford, 1967), p. 192.

theories of design, but we can perhaps come close to them in the sketchy memoranda on architecture drawn up in November 1597 by Robert Stickells, a clerk in the Queen's Works.[1] Stickells appears to have been hardly more literate than Street, but his papers show that he had considered Vitruvius and was acutely conscious of the fundamental difference between Roman and medieval architecture, though he seems not to have been able to make up his mind which he preferred. In one document he condemns Vitruvian modular regularity, with its proportions based on the commensurable repetition of a single unit of measure, as lifeless or 'insencable':

...fore that I see all Buildenges, grownded upon the emperfect sence, the bookes of, Architecktur, victriuces & all thoos Authers have, taken the wronge sense; ther in wardes woorkes are dead when theay shewe no lif in ther owtward Doweinges.[2]

In a second paper he defends the antique against the modern, using the word 'sence' in a quite different way, to mean the technical rationality of numbers. Vitruvian proportions are usually multiples of a single unit, and so are commensurable; Gothic proportions derive from geometrical figures formed with the dividers (and so called 'cirkler' by Stickells) which involve incommensurable and irrational values such as $\sqrt{2}$, $\sqrt{3}$, and $\sqrt{5}$. This time Stickells is an emphatic Vitruvian:

Thear ar too sortes of byldenges, the on in sence; the other withowt sence; The antikes in sence; the moddarn witheout sence; Because it is from cirkler demonstraction, witheowt sence; for that no cirkell Riseth in evenness of nomber, the antikes allwayes in evennes of nombre be cauese the ar derived from an Ichnographicall ground; it the unevn may be broght into proporctions, as well as the even, &c.

There is no mor but Right & wrong in all thinges whatsoever, The sqear Right the cirkell wronge, &c.[3]

It would be unwise to conclude from this that Street was a Vitruvian too; what matters is that Stickells characterizes the architecture of his own day as unVitruvian and irrational in its proportions, and in that tradition we may assume stood the builders of the Elizabethan theatres.

The builder and the surveyor shared a common interest in constructive geometry. In his dialogue on the faults of inexpert surveyors, published in 1582, Edward Worsop regretted that there were no civic geometers appointed in English cities, as there were in Europe:

Masons, Carpenters, Joyners, Paynters, clockmakers, Inginors, and such others vnto whose faculties most needefully appertaine the knowledges of making squares, roundes, triangles, and many other figures, with their transformations according to any proportion assigned resort vnto these professors and Geometers, to learne certaine grounds, & chiefe mechanicall rules.[4]

To judge from the tone of his book Worsop was a crusty and opinionated soul, and there is no need to take his account of the shortcomings of English technicians at face value. But in this passage we have an insight into the methods of Elizabethan craftsmen, including carpenters. They needed to know the sort of geometry the skilled land surveyor could teach them, and indeed we have seen that builders often actually were surveyors as well, capable of 'making squares, roundes, triangles, and many other figures, with their transformations...'. In describing Street's methods at the Fortune we may therefore begin with an observation that will take some of the mystery from that remarkable figure of the stage width, 43 feet. 43 feet is the altitude (to within about $1\frac{1}{2}$ inches) of an equilateral triangle whose sides

[1] See John Summerson, 'Three Elizabethan Architects', *Bulletin of the John Rylands Library*, 40 (1957), pp. 202–28.

[2] B. L. Lansdowne MS 84, no. 10, i, cited by Summerson, 'Three Elizabethan Architects', p. 227.

[3] B. L. Lansdowne MS 84, no. 10, ii, cited by Summerson, 'Three Elizabethan Architects', p. 228.

[4] Edward Worsop, *A Discoverie of Sundrie Errours and Faults Daily Committed by Landemeaters* (1582), 01b.

are three rods (or 49 feet 6 inches/15·09 m). Such triangles were used in two ways that Street could be expected to know about. They were employed by the land surveyors as a standard technique for measuring area, and they had been used since time immemorial by masons and carpenters in the layout of buildings according to the method called *ad triangulum*.[1] For the surveyor the equilateral triangle was important as one of the simple shapes to which complex tracts of land might be reduced for quantification.[2] Most of the surveyors' textbooks dealt with it, and its proportions were well known to anyone engaged in the measurement of land, since the area of the triangle is calculated from the product of its altitude and half its base. For his part the builder was less concerned with the area covered than with the trueness of the measures he could make by the simple deployment of his waxed lines in triangles. Of course the mathematical geometry was not always very precise, and Street's notion of the altitude of a 49 feet 6 inches equilateral triangle may well have been that it was exactly 43 feet, even though in fact it was not. But since I shall show that he proceeded in the traditional way by staking out his measurements on the ground according to the proportions reached by the use of his line, his interpretation of the exact height of the triangle is irrelevant, except for its translation into the specification given in the contract; what matters is that he used the triangle, and that he appears to have used it well.

We have to imagine Peter Street and perhaps Gilbert East, Henslowe's bailiff, standing on the site near Golden Lane in the early part of 1600. Of the nearby buildings, it may be that one is to abut on the proposed theatre, offering complications to the process I am about to describe.[3] Dealing with them would involve fiddly calculations too confusing to enter into now, but perfectly manageable even so. We safely ignore them. What Street and East first lay out on the ground is a square whose sides

are three rods long. Every Elizabethan surveyor knew how to do that, judging its corners by sighting along the arms of a carpenter's square, and testing its trueness by checking that the diagonals were equal. The line our men use is the traditional surveyor's line, marked with knots for every perch or rod. When the corners of the square have been pegged they use this line with a similar one to erect two equilateral triangles within the three-rod square, thus:

Through the apexes thus formed they run lines parallel to those of the square, so forming a smaller square within the original:

Now with the three-rod line they drop perpendiculars from the apexes and at their extremes set new pegs, through which they pass new lines parallel to the remaining sides of

[1] The *ad triangulum* method is much documented, but see especially Paul Frankl, 'The Secret of the Mediaeval Masons', *Art Bulletin*, 27 (1945), 46–60 and François Bucher, 'Design in Gothic Architecture: a Preliminary Assessment', *Journal of the Society of Architectural Historians*, 27 (1968), 49–71, particularly the comments on the survival of triangulation techniques into the seventeenth century on p. 54.

[2] For the equilateral triangle see Richard Benese, ...*the Maner of Measurynge of all Manner of Lande* ...(1537), Bii[b]; for triangulation in general see Leonard Digges, *A Booke Named Tectonicon* (1556), A3[b]—A4[b]; Leigh, Oiv[a–b]; and Worsop, *A Discoverie of Sundrie Errours*, 12[b]. A critical introduction to these texts is given in A. W. Richeson, *English Land Measuring to 1800: Instruments and Practices* (Cambridge, Mass., 1966), pp. 29–89.

[3] W. W. Greg, *Henslowe Papers* (1907), I, 15 and II, 57.

the square, this time making a larger square within which the others are contained:

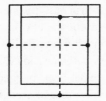

The dimensions of this diagram are as follows: the original square is 49 feet 6 inches (15·09 m) each way; the smaller one is 49 feet 6 inches × $\frac{\sqrt{3}}{2}$ or 42 feet 10½ inches (13·07 m); and the largest one is the difference between these two plus three rods (49 feet 6 inches — 42 feet 10½ inches = 6 feet 7½ inches + 49 feet 6 inches), or 56 feet 1½ inches (17·11 m). The smallest defines the width of the stage, while the largest defines the size of the yard, measured between centres. The plan on the ground comes to within 1½ inches (38 mm) of what the surface dimensions specified in the contract led us to expect, and yet it has been arrived at entirely by the deployment of the one traditional surveyor's tool, the three-rod line, and by means of only the most traditional of methods.

At one time there was a 'plott' or drawing attached to the Fortune contract, giving details of the layout. It is now lost, but we may be sure that the proportions we have discovered could be checked on it by the manipulation of a pair of compasses set to the equivalent of the three-rod measure. The proportions of the courtyard and the stage could be established and checked on the paper just as they were set out by the line on the ground. Any student of architecture knows how drawings of buildings, especially of centrally-planned buildings, will yield information about their proportions to the wielder of a pair of dividers. We have to make something of an imaginative leap to recognize that these patterns are not there merely to please, but to allow the plan to be set out on the ground with a line, and to ensure

that once the building is under way its trueness may be readily checkable by the same method.

Having established the central part of their plan, Street and East are now ready to set out the foundations of the outer wall. They run diagonals across their 56-foot (17·07 m) square to find its centre, and then describe a circle round it, touching its corners. It is simply a matter of one man taking a line in a ring about the site like a pony on a lunge. As he reaches each of the quadrants of the circle he drives in a peg, and through these four pegs a new square is set out, tangential to the circle:

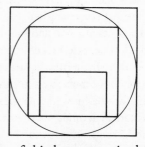

The trueness of this last square is checked by the diagonal test, and also by ensuring that its sides equal the diagonal of the courtyard square, both operations that can easily be performed by the deployment of a line. This square has been arrived at by the venerable *ad quadratum* method, and its sides are those of the yard times $\sqrt{2}$: 56 feet 1½ inches × $\sqrt{2}$ = 79 feet 4½ inches (24·19 m), or within 2½ inches (63 mm) of what the contract led us to expect. No further specific measure has been employed beyond the original three-rod line; the greater dimensions of the outside wall are derived from those contained within the court-yard plan.

The *ad quadratum* method is often met in sixteenth- and early seventeenth-century architectural design, especially in centrally planned buildings. Sebastiano Serlio included it among the basic geometrical figures of his *Book of Architecture* (plate IA). Its roots are very old, and it was much used by medieval craftsmen, but Inigo Jones employed it too, for example in his scheme for an anatomy theatre for the Barber-Surgeons' Company in 1636.[1] Its chief merit was its practicality, although it may also have appealed from time to time because it suggested the mystery of the squaring of the circle. We may be sure that Street used it for pragmatic reasons, but John Thorpe in his fanciful design for a triangular house inscribed within a four-rod circle may have thought of it as a symbol. Here the house is related to the surrounding terrace *ad quadratum* [plate IB].[2] The method was employed in the design of the cockpit at Whitehall in the 1530s [plate IIA],[3] in Stephan von Hoschenperg's coastal forts for Henry VIII in the next decade,[4] by Robert Stickells in his unexecuted drawing for a lantern at Lyveden New Bield,[5] and in quite another vein by Jones in his project for a Stuart mausoleum, presumably of 1625.[6] How could we ever have missed seeing that it would be the Elizabethan builder's preferred way of laying out a centrally-planned theatre? Nothing could be more traditional, more practical, or more secure.

The methods and the measure used to establish the proportions of the Fortune plan have their implications for the Globe, too. The Fortune imitated the Globe and it is probable that Peter Street built them both. Certainly it was he who supervised the dismantling of the timbers of the Theatre out of which the Globe was constructed,[7] and it is a reasonable assumption that he also supervised their re-erection. And here we must try again for a moment to enter into Peter Street's adroit and technically accomplished mind. We must imagine him standing in the old empty Theatre in Shoreditch, thinking already of how he will put its pieces together again on the south bank. He knows the site there, but the first thing he has to

[1] On the *ad quadratum* method see Frankl, 'The Secret of the Mediaeval Masons'; James S. Ackerman, '"Ars sine scientia nihil est": Gothic Theory of

Architecture at the Cathedral of Milan', *Art Bulletin*, 31 (1949), pp. 84–111; and Howard Saalman, 'Early Renaissance Architectural Theory and Practice in Antonio Filarete's *Trattato di Architettura*', *Art Bulletin*, 41 (1959), pp. 89–106. That the courtyard plan of the Fortune could be constructed without adjusting the dividers was in accord with the habits, aesthetic as well as practical, of late medieval builders. See for example Mathes Roriczer's demonstration of how 'to draw a pentagon with unchanged dividers' in *Geometria deutsch* in Lon R. Shelby, *Gothic Design Techniques* (Carbondale and Edwardsville, 1977), p. 116. The scheme for the Barber-Surgeons' anatomy theatre is at Worcester College, Jones/Webb, I, 7, and is reproduced in John Harris, Stephen Orgel and Roy Strong, *The King's Arcadia: Inigo Jones and the Stuart Court* (1973), p. 186. It shows an oval building whose dimensions derive from the $\sqrt{2}$ series beginning with 3 feet (0·91 m) (the width of the central anatomy table): 4 feet 3 inches (1·29 m), 8 feet 6 inches (2·59 m), 17 feet (5·18 m) (the spacing of the windows) and 34 feet (10·36 m) (overall width). Here the method is doubtless more ideal and symbolic than practical, but the building shows interesting general affinities with the Elizabethan public theatres.

[2] Sir John Soane's Museum, T 145–6 (iii-v), reproduced in John Summerson (ed.), *The Book of Architecture of John Thorpe* (Walpole Society, 1966), plate 67. The plan reproduced here as plate IB is a redrawn version with the four-rod *ad quadratum* square superimposed.

[3] Worcester College, Jones/Webb, I, 27. John Webb's plan shows the central octagon of the original cockpit surrounded by more recent galleries. The square-planned outer wall was built higher to accommodate the theatre of 1629–30, but appears to have used at least the foundations of an original battlemented wall shown in earlier drawings. The inner surfaces of the octagon posts are located on a circle derived *ad quadratum* (to within a few inches) from the inner surface of the boundary wall.

[4] Both Deal and Walmer castles are centrally-planned forts constructed in 1539–40. Many of their proportions are developed *ad quadratum*, including the relation between inner and outer surfaces of the massive keep walls, and the relation between the keep and the curtain. See the plans in A. D. Saunders, *Deal and Walmer Castles* (1963), pp. 25 and 33.

[5] B.L. Add. MS 39831, reproduced in Summerson, *Architecture in Britain*, p. 29.

[6] Worcester College, Jones/Webb, I, 33, reproduced in *The King's Arcadia*, p. 137.

[7] C. W. Wallace, *The First London Theatre: Materials for a History* (New York, 1969[1913]), pp. 164–80, 218, 222 and 278–9.

do is to prepare it, sink piles and have foundation walls brought up ready to take the ground-sills of the frame of the building. One of his most important tasks, therefore, will be to measure the plan of the Theatre with great exactness, so that he can set out the foundation walls at Bankside. The building he is looking at is a many-sided polygon, and he will measure it most naturally by taking the diameter from one outer post to its opposite, centre-to-centre. Presumably he will do a good deal of detailed checking, but the controlling idea of the plan will be a circle, or rather two circles, in which the inner and outer walls of the frame will be inscribed as polygons. This is the information he will take to the new site, and will use to set out the new polygonal foundation walls there. For we must notice that the re-use of the Theatre timbers at the Globe leaves no room for compromise; the Globe plan must have been the same as that of the Theatre, otherwise the timbers might just as well have been a job lot of used material, not needing Street's supervision at all.[1] Elizabethan timber structures were not made with entirely standardized pieces. Each joint was individually cut, and although the pieces might fit to perfection they could not be interchanged at will. A many-sided polygonal frame is a fairly complicated structure, and it could not readily be adapted or modified. Once there, there it was. The Globe was the Theatre transpontine, but not transformed. What Peter Street saw as he measured the Theatre was the plan of what was to become the Globe.

And what did he see? If we are to judge by what he did the following year at the Fortune, we may suppose that he found a building whose layout could be established by the simple deployment of a single measure, possibly the three-rod line. Our evidence suggests that it would be designed *ad quadratum*. It is a characteristic of the *ad quadratum* method that each successive square or circle doubles the area of the one within. Thus the whole area of the

Fortune (measured between centres) doubles the area of its yard (similarly measured); or, to put it another way, the area of the ground-floor gallery equals that of the yard. Such considerations were well-known to Elizabethan surveyors and, one surmises, to the owners of theatre galleries. If the Fortune was mostly to be based on the Globe, doubtless it was also in this financially-pregnant consideration.

We have reason to believe that the Globe stage was not 43 feet wide. Now, however, our analysis of the Fortune has given us a new figure to conjure with in the three-rod basis of the whole design. Let us suppose that the stage at the Globe was 49 feet 6 inches wide and that the frame was developed from it *ad quadratum*. The result would be a yard precisely 70 feet (21·34 m) across and an overall diameter of just 99 feet (30·17 m) (that is, six rods), centre-to-centre:

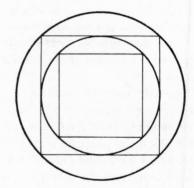

Of course as yet this plan is the merest conjecture, based only on the methods Street went on to apply at the Fortune. Yet it can be tested against such evidence as we have about the Globe, and the test will lead to some remarkable conclusions.

An admirable summary of all that we know

[1] The notion that the Globe used the timbers of the Theatre 'in an other forme' (Andrew Gurr, *The Shakespearean Stage 1574-1642* (Cambridge, 1970), p. 92) stems from a misreading of Henry Johnson's deposition in a Court of Requests suit. See Wallace, *The First London Theatre*, p. 222.

about the characteristics of the first Globe is given by the ever-fastidious Richard Hosley in *The Revels History of English Drama*.[1] Knowledge of its size derives solely from a drawing and etching by Hollar of the second Globe which however was built on the foundations of the first after the fire of 1613. Because my argument will depend on this identity of plan between the two Globe theatres, I must take a moment to establish it. In 1634 at the behest of the Earl Marshal a draft was made for a return of new and divided buildings in the parish of Saint Saviour's, and among them the Globe was mentioned:

The Globe playhouse nere Maid lane built by the company of players, with the dwelling house thereto adjoyninge, built w^t timber, about 20 yeares past, upon an old foundation....[2]

The context of this draft is the series of proclamations issued by James I against new building in and about London. Rendle, who first printed it, remarked that it was drawn up 'at a time when the authorities were insanely jealous of allowing new building' in the London region.[3] I have argued in connection with the Cockpit in Drury Lane that the building proclamations should be taken seriously by theatre historians;[4] offending buildings were often pulled down, and although the great number of recorded violations shows the comparative ineffectiveness of the proclamations, it likewise indicates with what vigour they were followed up. The draft of the return to the Earl Marshal in which the Globe is mentioned is but one mark of this attempt to enforce a building code; there are many more, in the Acts of the Privy Council, in what remains of the Star Chamber records,[5] in the *Index to Repertories* at the Guildhall and of course in the series of proclamations themselves.

When the draft return reads 'upon an old foundation', that is precisely what it means. The new building was legal, within the terms of the proclamations, because it did not involve the building of new foundations or even the extension of old ones. The restriction of new developments, and hence of overcrowding, by this doubtless self-defeating means was one of the leading purposes of James's regulations. Certainly the second Globe was 'far fairer' than the first, but equally certainly it was the same size in plan. It would not, incidentally, have had the juttying galleries of the Fortune; such overhangings were specifically forbidden by two proclamations issued in 1611[6] and in any case cannot have improved the sightlines from the upper galleries. Therefore the upper parts of the walls of the yard directly reflected the proportions of the lowermost parts.

Our best information, then, about the plan of the first Globe is to be deduced from Hollar's depictions of its successor. Here much of our work has been done for us by Walter Hodges, who in his *Shakespeare's Second Globe*[7] enquires carefully into Hollar's reliability as a topographical witness, and concludes that '...his evidence for the appearance of particular buildings shown in the Long View of London may be accepted as generally correct', and further that the preparatory sketch of the Globe [plate 11B] is more reliable than the etch-

---

[1] *Volume III: 1576-1613*, ed. Clifford Leech and T. W. Craik (1975), pp. 176–81.

[2] William Rendle, 'The Bankside, Southwark, and the Globe Playhouse', in Frederick J. Furnivall (ed.), *Harrison's Description of England*, Part II, Book 3 (1877–78), Appendix, p. xvii.

[3] *Ibid.*

[4] 'Inigo Jones at the Cockpit', *Shakespeare Survey 30* (Cambridge, 1977), pp. 161–2.

[5] John Hawarde, *Les Reportes del Cases in Camera Stellata 1593 to 1609*, ed. W. P. Baildon (1894), pp. 318–19 and 328–9. See also E. P. Cheyney, 'The Court of Star Chamber', *American Historical Review*, 18 (1912–13), pp. 735–6.

[6] James F. Larkin and Paul L. Hughes (eds), *Stuart Royal Proclamations* (Oxford, 1973–), I, nos. 120 and 121, dated 3 August and 10 September 1611. Such juttying was therefore not called for in the Hope contract of 1613.

[7] (Oxford, 1973). The quotation is from p. 32.

ing derived from it.[1] That is, I think, a fair conclusion, precisely stated. One must take exaggerated claims for Hollar's accuracy with a pinch of salt: he makes numerous errors of omission and not a few of commission too, as for example in his plate depicting St Paul's Covent Garden.[2] But on one point we must surely follow Hollar or give him up altogether, and that is the overall proportion of his depiction of the Globe. It is by this proportion – the ratio of height to width – that he would judge the 'rightness' of the drawing as he made it. Other topographers such as Visscher or Merian habitually exaggerated the height of the major buildings they represented. Hollar seems consciously to have rejected this mannerism. Whatever the truth of his detailed reporting, or of his relative sitings of buildings, he must surely have got the *look* of the Globe right, and especially its most prominent feature as seen from the artist's viewpoint, its arresting and nicely-drawn roofline. The sketch has the freely-handled authority of direct observation and to the right of it we can still see, beneath the superimposed ink outlines, the adjustments Hollar's pencil made as it sought the precise rendering of the pitch and the ridge of the roof. This, we may agree with Hodges, is good evidence. Although it is not strictly accountable as an exact survey I shall, faute de mieux, treat it as if it were and so perhaps misrepresent the value of its testimony. But a close look at the sketch reveals consistencies that should not go unstated, and the risk seems worth taking.

It shows that the Globe was designed *ad quadratum*. Again Hodges has done our work for us by extrapolating a plan from the information contained in the perspective sketch. Allowing again, as we did in the analysis of the Fortune, that the conceptual lines of the plan pass through the post centres rather than the wall surfaces, we find that Hodges' plan fits the *ad quadratum* scheme. As he presents it on p. 39 of his book it shows a circular outer wall 90·5 mm across with a yard diameter of 62·5 mm. 1% of the overall width is the estimated thickness of a post, and this must be subtracted from the larger figure and added to the smaller in order to find the centre-to-centre proportion, which may then be expressed as 63·405:89·595, or 1:1·413. Thus the diameter of the yard measured between centres is related to the diameter of the round in a very close approximation to the proportion of $1 : \sqrt{2}$ (that is, 1:1·414).

The exactness of this demonstration is, I confess, a little embarrassing. It is inconceivable that measures which have gone through so many processes of presentation, extrapolation and deduction should retain their precise ratio so unswervingly. The exactness must be an accident of one error cancelling out another. One may however check Hodges on this point quite easily without going to the error-prone trouble of attempting to reconstruct his admirable diagram. We may deduce the width of the yard from the drawing by subtracting the ridge-to-ridge width of the roof from the overall width of the round, doubling the difference and subtracting that from the overall width. In the enlargement of the drawing that Hodges publishes on p. 46 the overall width is 68 mm. The ridge-to-ridge distance is difficult to measure because of the uncertainty on the right-hand side, compounded by some clumsy inking-in, but a fair estimate is 57·75 mm, from which we deduce that the yard must be 47·5 mm wide. Allowing 1% of the overall width for each measurement to represent the thickness of

[1] The sketch, along with three other associated drawings, was first published by Iolo Williams, 'Hollar: a Discovery', *The Connoisseur*, 92 (1933), pp. 318–21.

[2] Hollar shows the church with Ionic instead of Tuscan columns and square-topped instead of arched windows, and his rendering of the piazza is inaccurate. See A. C. Downs Jr., 'Inigo Jones's Covent Garden: the First Seventy-Five Years', *Journal of the Society of Architectural Historians*, 26 (1967), p. 8.

a post, we have a centre-to-centre ratio of 1·397:1. This is not as close to the *ad quadratum* proportion as Hodges' diagram, but quite close enough to carry conviction. The etching is less satisfactory as evidence than the drawing because its presentation of the roofline lacks symmetry, implying a wider frame to the left than to the right. Hodges draws his plan from this (p. 38) as a compromise between the two frame widths, and the result is close to the $\sqrt{2}$ proportion, again assuming measurement between the post centres: 1·447:1. The ridge-to-ridge test, carried out on the detail on p. 36, produces the ratio of 1·394:1. Plainly these figures are all approximations to the *ad quadratum* ratio of 1·414:1, and all are very close. The conclusion seems unavoidable that the second Globe, and like it the first, was built *ad quadratum*. If that was indeed the case, then Peter Street was not merely applying a familiar principle when he evolved the Fortune design; he was faithfully following his model, as his contract with Henslowe and Alleyn generally enjoined him to do.

There remains the question of the three-rod measure which Street used at the Fortune and may have carried over from his work at the Globe. While we have concluded that the *proportions* of the Globe derive from the *ad quadratum* method, we still have to discover what the actual measurements were. There are two suggestive pieces of evidence to consider: the known height of the galleries at the Fortune, and the proportion of width to height at the second Globe as shown in Hollar's sketch, and restated with some variation in his etching. Walter Hodges and Richard Hosley have both considered this evidence, and have arrived at different conclusions. Both begin with the premise that the height of the Fortune was 'standard' or 'traditional', and therefore to be used as a control in an examination of the Globe. Hodges differs somewhat from Hosley in his assessment of this figure, but the gap between

the two accounts is slight and we may safely ignore it, Hodges giving 33 feet (10·06 m) and Hosley 34 feet (10·36 m).[1] (Doubtless it is merely a charming coincidence that 33-foot walls would be just two rods high: there is no evidence that rods or perches were used to measure elevations.) It is in their treatment of this 'standard' that the two master investigators part company. Hodges abandons his 33 feet measure for the lower one of 31 feet (9·45 m) at the second Globe without giving any adequate reason for doing so. It would also seem that he abandons the preferred sketch for the more remote etching, for he deduces from the evidence before him that the overall width of the Globe was 92 feet (28·04 m), a figure that can only be sustained – and then at a pinch – by accepting the more upright proportions of the etching instead of the eye-witness sketch.[2] If the Globe had the proportions Hodges claims – 31 feet to the wall-plates and 92 feet across – its ground line in the sketch would have to appear well below the bushes that obscure it, clearly an impossibility. But for once Richard Hosley, though in reviewing Hodges' book he sees the mistake, fails to follow his insight through. If the sketch really is to be preferred to the etching either the theatre was much wider than Hodges says it was (and wider than Hosley's own figure of 100 feet/30·48 m) or it was lower than Hosley says it was (possibly as low as 31 feet from ground to plate) or both.

There is no decisive reason why the galleries at the second Globe should have been the same height as those at the Fortune. Like the other dimensions given in the contract these may well have been specified simply because they differed from those at the first Globe, and in any case it is not known whether the second Globe

[1] Hodges, *Shakespeare's Second Globe*, p. 47; Hosley, 'The Second Globe', *Theatre Notebook*, 29 (1975), p. 142.

[2] Hodges, *Shakespeare's Second Globe*, p. 49.

imitated the first in this respect. Appeals to later builders' handbooks such as Moxon's *Mechanick Exercises* (London, 1679)[1] are of little avail, since the *Act for Rebuilding the City of London*, passed in 1667, defined regulation storey-heights according to quite new standards, and any correspondence between these domestic specifications and the figures given in a public theatre contract of 1600 is mere coincidence. There is, however, yet another pertinent fact offered by Hollar. He shows the Hope as well as the Globe, and we do know from the Hope contract that like the Fortune it had a first gallery 12 feet (3·66 m) high. Specifications for the upper galleries are not given, but it is a fair assumption that they too followed the Fortune since the first one did, and that the Hope measured 34 feet (10·36 m) to the plates. Hollar's depiction of this theatre-cum-beargarden shows it further off than the Globe, and much narrower, partly no doubt because it had different proportions, but partly also because of perspective foreshortening. And yet its height, taken at the picture plane, is just the same as that of the Globe, if we judge both from the bottoms of the bushes by the wall up to the level of the eaves. Clearly the building further off must be taller than the one closer in, and while we have no exact way of checking Hodges' figure of 31 feet for the Globe we should accept it as preferable to Hosley's 34 feet. Relying still on the sketch rather than the derivative etching we may now calculate the width of the Globe, very roughly, as about 100 feet. Its width in the photograph on Hodges' p. 46 is 68 mm; the height to the plates as nearly as one may judge it is 21 mm. If we accept 31 feet as the height to the plates the width of the round will be 31 feet × 68/21 = 100 feet, to the nearest foot. Here we are relieved to find ourselves once more in the company of Richard Hosley, who by a sensible compromise has already arrived at this same conclusion that the first Globe was 'about 100

feet in diameter'.[2] A theatre of that size will measure 99 feet (30·17 m) centre-to-centre; its yard, according to the *ad quadratum* proportions of Hollar's sketch, will be just 70 feet (21·34 m) between centres, or 69 feet (21·03 m) wide surface-to-surface. And it is a fair deduction that the stage, again proportioned *ad quadratum*, will be 49 feet 6 inches (15·09 m) across.

Peter Street, standing in the empty Theatre in 1599 and wondering how to go about setting out his new foundations at Bankside, will soon see that the controlling measure of his plan must be a three-rod line, the same line that Burbage used when he set the building out in the first place. At Bankside he will probably begin by pegging out a 49 feet 6 inches square. Around this he will describe the 70-foot circle which will define the placing of the gallery posts. There will be no need to describe a further square around this circle, since he can move directly to the line of the outer wall by using the three-rod measure as a radius centred in the midst of his original square. The circles thus produced will enable him to construct the necessary polygons to take the straight groundsills of the timber walls. We do not know how many sides those polygons had, but the *ad quadratum* method suggests that the figure would be a multiple of four, since then the sides of the stage would meet the principal posts in a direct and satisfactory way. Once again we may follow Hosley in guessing at twenty-four sides, so that the outer wall of each bay might be kept to a manageable length, in this case about 13 feet (3·96 m) between centres.[3]

---

[1] Cited by Hosley, *Revels History*, III, 150.
[2] *Ibid.*, p. 176.
[3] Hosley's conclusion for the Globe, *ibid.*, p. 177, is based on the discussion of the Swan, *ibid.*, pp. 145–8. But if Neil Carson is correct in his attractive argument that a drawing among the Henslowe papers represents a view of one of the frame bays of the Globe seen from the yard ('New Light on the Structure of the Globe', *Shakespeare Survey 29* (Cambridge, 1976), pp. 127–32),

We notice that the gallery depth at the Globe is 15 feet 6 inches (4·72 m) overall, or 14 feet 6 inches (4·42 m) between centres. This figure is somewhat larger than the 12 feet 6 inches (3·81 m) overall of the Fortune galleries at ground-floor level, and allows a row or two more of spectators, but these are crowded into a smaller headroom, at least at the second Globe (we have been able to discover nothing about the heights of the galleries at the first Globe). The great width of the theatre softens the effect somewhat, but doubtless the sightlines leave something to be desired, as they do in most London theatres to this day.

In breaking with the 12 feet 6 inches gallery depth we have abandoned the last of the 'controlling' dimensions of the Fortune contract. Yet in departing from the figures themselves we have looked beyond them to the reasons for their being. Once Street had measured the Theatre and set out the foundations for the Globe, all with the single three-rod line, what more natural than that he should have used the same technique for the smaller, square-planned Fortune? There he reduced the width of the stage *ad triangulum*, then by quite logical and economical means established the width of the yard, from which, as at the Globe, he constructed the plan of the outer wall *ad quadratum*. In doing so he produced figures that had to be stated one way to himself as a carpenter and another way to his contractual partners as 'lawfull assize', with the result that we have all been confused. Yet Street himself could hardly have been more direct or more economical of means. His design methods had the simple grace of their origins, in the traditions of the surveyor and the builder in oak.

and assuming that the upper gallery floor is 12 feet (3·66 m) above the ground, the aspect ratio of the bay shown is consistent with that produced by a twelve-sided polygon inscribed within the courtyard diameter of 70 feet (21·34 m) between centres. But if the Globe were so constructed, its inner bressumers would be 18 feet (5·49 m) long, probably an unmanageable length.

Since finishing this article, the author has developed a new way of measuring from Hollar's sketch. To describe it would unfortunately require another longish article, so the present account of Hollar's evidence has been allowed to stand. It is hoped that the new method will be published in the proceedings of the Symposium for the Reconstruction of the Globe Playhouse, held at Wayne State University in Detroit, May 1979.

© JOHN ORRELL 1980

ENGLISH ACTORS AT THE COURTS OF WOLFENBÜTTEL, BRUSSELS AND GRAZ DURING THE LIFETIME OF SHAKESPEARE

WILLEM SCHRICKX

Sir Edmund K. Chambers and Walter Wilson Greg devoted their best efforts to disentangling the complicated threads of the theatrical history of the early nineties in Elizabethan England and very few voices have been raised in dissent from the interpretations they proposed. It is nevertheless hoped that new light can be shed on a period of disorganisation in the theatre world around 1590 by examining the careers of certain English actors who seem to have spent the best part of their lives wandering about the continent. As everyone knows, numerous acting companies had sprung into existence at this time and to list and discuss them all is certainly not my aim. As to the actors, those who are of central importance in the following pages are Robert Browne and Thomas Sackville, who are mentioned together with John Bradstreet and Richard Jones in a passport granting permission for a continental journey, issued on 10 February 1592, by the Lord High Admiral. Since this passport is used in many scholarly works in the incomplete and inaccurate version printed in Albert Cohn's *Shakespeare in Germany in the Sixteenth and Seventeenth Centuries* (1865), pp. xxviii–xxix (no fewer than ten words are missing), we had better begin by giving a fresh transcript of the original.[1]

Messieurs, Com*m*e les presentz porteurs, Robert Browne, Jehan Bradstriet, Thomas Saxfield, Richard Jones, auec leurs consortz estantz mes Joueurs et seruiteurs ont deliberé de faire vng voyage en Allemagne, auec Intention de passer par les païs de Zelande, Hollande et Frise. Et allantz en leur d*i*ct voyage

d'exercer leurs qualitez en faict de musicque, agilitez et joeuz de com*m*edies, Tragedies et histoires, pour s'entretenir et fournir à leurs despenses en leur d*i*ct voyage. Cestes sont p*a*rtant pour vous requerir leur monstrer et prester toute faueur en voz païs et Jurisdictions, et leur octroyer en ma faueur vo*st*re ample passeport soubz le seel des Estatz, à fin que les Bourg*mestre*s des villes estantz soubz voz Jurisdictions, ne les empeschent en passant d'exercer leur d*i*ctes qualitez par tout. Enquoy faisant, je vous en demeureray à tous obligé, et me trouuerez très appareillé à me reuencher de vo*st*re courtoisie en plus grand cas. De ma chambre, à la court d'Ang*le*ter*re* ce x*me* jour de Febvrier 1591.

Vostre tres affecsionné à vous fayre plaisir et sarvis
C. Howard

The man who signed this passport was Charles Howard (1536–1624), the Lord High Admiral from 1585 to 1619, well known in the annals of Elizabethan drama as the patron of the Admiral's men. But Sir Edmund Chambers, *The Elizabethan Stage* (1923), II, 138, 274,

---

[1] General Archives, The Hague, *Lias* England of 1591 (Staten-Generaal 5882 1). To facilitate reading a few punctuation marks have been supplied in this and in all documents subsequently to be cited. I wish to thank Beatrijs De Groote, who has helped me in my fairly thorough search of Belgian archives, for drawing my attention to the Brussels passport to be printed here. Thanks are also due to the staffs of the Archives in The Hague, Brussels, Hanover and Frankfort on the Main and to Annemarie Deegen (Wolfenbüttel) and Peter Brand, who sent me a copy of his typescript study *Der englische Komödiant Robert Browne, (1563-ca. 1621/39)* (Heidelberg, 1978), which contains new and valuable material concerning Browne.

believes that in 1592 the actors were not under the Admiral's patronage and that Howard had granted the passport in his capacity as warden of the seas rather than in that of their lord. I agree with Dr J. G. Riewald,[1] however, that the reference in the safe conduct to 'estantz mes Joueurs et seruiteurs' is convincing evidence that the actors were servants of the Lord Admiral. In fact, Chambers relied for his interpretation on the version of the passport printed in Cohn where this reference is simply omitted. Furthermore, the original document bears the date 'ce xme jour de Febvrier, 1591', which has led many to the erroneous view that the voyage was made in the year 1591. The confusion arises of course from the practice in England of keeping to the old style of dating even after the introduction on the Continent of the Gregorian calendar in 1582. In spite of its being largely a Protestant country Holland had for the most part gone along with this innovation of Pope Gregory so that if the passport had been drafted there it would have borne the date 20 February 1592, a difference of ten days with an added change of one in the year date.[2] The text of the passport, then, establishes beyond doubt that Robert Browne, John Bradstreet, Thomas Sackville and Richard Jones (they are all obviously mentioned in order of their status), as well as *leurs consortz*, were all members of the Admiral's company in February 1592. This interpretation will be confirmed later in my article.

Robert Browne and Richard Jones begin to emerge from the records as members of Worcester's troupe in the abstract of the licence of 14 January 1583 in the Leicester records (*Elizabethan Stage*, II, 222). We next hear of them on 3 January 1589 when they were concerned in a transference to Edward Alleyn of their shares in a stock of theatrical goods held jointly with Edward and John Alleyn. Edwin Nungezer[3] writes that 'this conveyance seems to mark either a break-up of Worcester's

men or an internal change in the organization of the Admiral's men', and thus there is some uncertainty as to whether Browne and Jones were with the Worcester or the Admiral troupe in January 1589. It is clear from what Chambers writes (*William Shakespeare*, I, 38), however, that they were with the Admiral's men. About November 1587 an accident happened at their London theatre, which was related by Philip Gawdy to his father in a surviving letter. A woman and a child were killed during a shooting scene, which must have been the execution of the Governor of Babylon in 2 *Tamburlaine*, V, i. As a result of this tragedy the company may well have gone into retirement for not much is heard of them until there is evidence in 1590–1 of there being a kind of amalgamation between the Admiral's and Lord Strange's men. Marlowe's *Tamburlaine* was still published in 1590, however, as 'shewed upon stages in the City of London' by the Admiral's men. There may have been more than an occasional collaboration between the two companies but I believe, with W. W. Greg,[4] that between the autumn of 1590 and the summer of 1594 the Admiral's men were more or less dispersed, some going to the continent, some touring in the provinces. In point of fact, Browne was already on the continent in 1590 where he is traceable at Leyden in October, and he was

[1] 'New Light on the English Actors in the Netherlands, c. 1590–c.1660', *English Studies*, 41 (Amsterdam, 1960), 65–92, esp. p. 71.

[2] There is bound to be some occasional confusion. If the date does not bear significantly on the argument the dates of the documents themselves will be used, but it is well to bear in mind that Frankfort-on-the-Main and Strassburg followed the Old Style. When discussing the presence of English actors in Strassburg it has been found useful occasionally to mention the two dates divided by a diagonal.

[3] *A Dictionary of Actors and of Other Persons Associated with the Public Representation of Plays in England before 1642* (Cornell Studies in English, XIII, 1929), pp. 60, 208.

[4] *Two Elizabethan Stage Abridgements: The Battle of Alcazar & Orlando Furioso* (1923), p. 18.

accompanied, as we know, by several other actors on a second foreign journey in February 1592.

The first continental stopping-place where the Browne company can be shown to have acted was Arnhem, the capital of the county of Gelderland, where they secured an acting licence from Maurice of Orange. The entry in the Arnhem account-books for 1592 is unfortunately not datable with precision but, besides containing the names of Browne, Bradstreet, Sackville and Jones, it also includes that of a hitherto unidentified Everhart Sauss or Sanss.[1] Browne's presence in Arnhem had doubtless something to do also, as we will see later, with the fact that Ernest Casimir, Count of Nassau, had his residence there. But what about the next recorded stopping-place of the strolling actors? It is highly likely that the ultimate goal of their wanderings had from the very beginning been Wolfenbüttel for that is where we have evidence that they were feasted by Duke Henry Julius of Brunswick-Wolfenbüttel (1564–1613) about 20 June 1592, as appears clearly from an entry in the preserved account-books. The notion that the actors did not deliberately visit Wolfenbüttel in 1592 derives from a long passage in Chambers (*Elizabethan Stage*, II, 275), where he dismisses the idea of such an intended visit as a mere conjecture and then goes on to say that 'unfortunately the Brunswick household accounts for 1590–1601 are missing, and with them all direct evidence of the first formation of his English company by the Duke has probably gone'. Chambers's treatment of the Duke's achievement in the field of drama was obviously based on Albert Cohn's *Shakespeare in Germany*. Cohn himself had mentioned a further gap in the Wolfenbüttel records pointing out that 'from 1603 to 1607, the accounts are missing'. It is in fact only recently that it has come to be realised that Cohn is not always reliable and he can definitely be proved wrong

in the present instance. The household accounts have been preserved over a forty-year period from 1585 to 1625. Of the forty account-books that should have survived only eight are missing,[2] those relating to 1587–8, 1590–1, 1591–2, 1600–1, 1601–2, 1609–10, 1620–1 and 1621–2. In spite of these gaps the presence of Browne and his men at Wolfenbüttel can still be deduced from an entry in the account-book for 1592–3, alluding to Browne's second continental visit. An *Ausgabe extraordinarie* dated *anno 1592. 20 Junij* orders the payment of 30 Taler to actors and of 40 Taler to vaulters, who spent their earnings in a local inn. The entry relating to the actors runs: 'desgleichen etzlichen andern aus Engeland so Musicirt und eine Comediam agirt', which, because of the date, must refer to Browne's troupe for he appeared in Frankfort-on-the-Main soon afterwards. Reassuringly, as we will see later, the name of Browne himself emerges from the Wolfenbüttel records in 1595, when the actor was no longer in the service of Henry Julius. The critical orthodoxy of Chambers, always ready to dismiss conjectures and scornful of special pleading, deserves high praise indeed

[1] See G. van Hasselt, *Arnhemsche Oudheden* (Arnhem, 1803), I, 244 and Riewald, 'New Light on the English Actors', p. 71.

[2] See the excerpts from the accounts in H. Niedecken-Gebhart's article 'Neues Aktenmaterial über die Englischen Komödianten in Deutschland', *Euphorion*, 21 (1914), 72–85. This article – of which the transcripts are not always reliable – has remained unknown because of its not having been noticed by Chambers, nor is it included in the bibliography at the end of Nungezer's *Dictionary*. See also P. Zimmermann, 'Englische Komödianten am Hofe zu Wolfenbüttel', *Braunschweigisches Magazin* (April 1902), pp. 37–45, 53–57. The original *Kammerrechnungen* of the Wolfenbüttel court are now preserved in the *Niedersächsisches Hauptstaatsarchiv* in Hanover (Ms. Hann. 76 c A) and special thanks are due to its staff for providing photostat copies of all the entries quoted. The mention of two year-dates per account-book arises from the fact that dating was from 'Trinitatis' to 'Trinitatis', from Trinity Sunday, the Sunday following Pentecost.

but here the facts of the case are against his conclusions.

In the light of H. Niedecken-Gebhart's article of 1914, the date of which might explain why it was overlooked by Chambers and others, a different picture emerges so that a fresh examination of the careers of the actors connected with the Wolfenbüttel court suggests itself. It seems reasonable to think that the *Ausgabe extra-ordinarie* was occasioned by a feast which was organised by Henry Julius for the actors as a kind of leave-taking ceremony, for soon after June 1592 we find them in Frankfort-on-the-Main where they appeared at the autumn fair in August and gave *Gammer Gurton's Needle* and some of Marlowe's plays. The Frankfort fairs, held twice yearly in spring and autumn, attracted large numbers of people from all over Europe. On account of the favourable geographical situation of the city it had become a central mart for Western Europe for the sale of cloth, wine and a wide range of other articles but once it had become the regular rendezvous of the book trade, the number of foreign visitors greatly increased and many of these could be expected to understand English. Many Elizabethan printers visited the fairs regularly to establish contacts with book dealers and printers from foreign parts and the actors could therefore rely on sympathetic audiences.

Two contemporary accounts of the wandering actors in Frankfort have come down to us. The first occurs in Fynes Moryson's *Itinerary* (first printed in 1903) and the second is by a German, Balthasar Baumgartner the Younger, a citizen of Nuremberg, who wrote to his wife on 13 September 1592 that the English comedians 'habenn so ein herliche, guette musicha, unnd sinnd sie so perfect mitt springen, tantzen, deren gleichen ich noch nye gehörtt noch gesehen hab'. The company numbered from ten to twelve players and were 'khöstlich herrlich wol geklayded'.[1] The

archives frequently fail to record individual names and such anonymous entries as there are will be mostly passed over in silence, but there is one puzzling entry in the minutes of the Nuremberg city council dated 20 August 1593, which refers to 'Ruberto Gruen vnd seinen gesellen'.[2] As 'Robert Braun, Thomas Sacksweil und Johan Bradenstreit' appeared shortly afterwards at the Frankfort autumn fair, it is only natural to suppose that the Nuremberg actors were the Browne company, while continental archives, as we will see, do not contain any reference to an actor called Green until 1603, when Browne appears at Lille together with John Green. When in Frankfort in 1593 the company gave a performance of *Abraham and Loth* and *The Destruction of Sodom and Gomorrah*. We may note in passing that an *Abraham and Lot* play was performed by Sussex's men at Henslowe's theatre on 7, 17 and 31 January 1593/4.

When Browne was making his mark as an actors' leader in Frankfort in August–September 1593 the plague, which had been raging in London throughout the year, attacked with special ferocity in the month of August. Philip Henslowe, writing from London about August 1593 to his son-in-law Edward Alleyn, the celebrated actor, told him that his family had been 'flytted wth ffeare of the sycknes', and then mentioned that 'Robart brownes wife in shordech & all her chelldren & howshowld be dead'.[3] It was this sad news which must have called the actor back to England for, as the researches of Peter Brand have shown, Browne's

[1] G. Steinhausen, ed. *Briefwechsel Balthasar Baumgartners des Jüngern mit seiner Gattin Magdalena* (Tübingen, 1895), p. 176. Quoted by Brand, *Der englische Komödiant Robert Browne*, p. 27.
[2] K. Trautmann, 'Englische Komödianten in Nürnberg, bis zum Schlusse des dreissigjährigen Krieges (1593–1648)', *Archiv für Litteraturgeschichte*, 14 (1886), 115.
[3] See R. A. Foakes and R. T. Rickert (eds.), *Henslowe's Diary* (Cambridge, 1961), p. 277.

wife was buried on 17 September 1593, while her former husband remarried in Shoreditch, taking to wife Cicely Sands on 7 March 1593/4.[1] The actor who may have accompanied Browne on his journey home was Richard Jones, who is traceable in Henslowe's *Diary* from 2 September 1594. But what about the other actors mentioned in the Howard passport? Both Sackville and Bradstreet were apparently never to return to England, with the result that there is a great deal of evidence of their presence in Germany, mostly either in Wolfenbüttel or in Frankfort (see Nungezer, *Dictionary*, p. 56 and pp. 308-9). At a later stage of this article we will devote attention to those entries in the Wolfenbüttel records which modify the accounts of actors' lives presented by Nungezer. As regards those mentioned in the Howard passport as *leurs consortz* it seems likely that some stayed behind in Wolfenbüttel, while others were attracted to the court of Maurice the Learned, Landgrave of Hesse-Cassel. Browne, for example, was certainly a Landgrave's man by 16 April 1595.

That some members of the Browne company did actually stay behind at Wolfenbüttel is revealed by two further entries which contain very surprising information indeed. The first entry mentions the actors' leader explicitly and suggests clearly that the English actors had, as it were, become members of the Duke's household.

[Ausgab Extraordinarie anno 1595] 18. [augusti] Anthoniussen Jeffes, einem Engelischen Jungen, wilchen Meister Braun alhir gelassenn, geben 12 Taler zu Leinengezeug, thun 21 Gulden 12 Mgr.
[Ausgab auff die Hofbesoldung. anno 1596] 20 hujus [Decembris] Demnach mein gnediger Fürst und Herr fünff Engelendische Comoedianten neben einem Jungen bestalt und Jedem vermüge Ihrer Bestallung 250 Taler, und dem Jungen 50 Taler vermacht thuet von Trinitatis anno 95 bis Trinitatis 96.[2]

We are left in no doubt, of course, that 'Master' Browne had left a young boy behind, probably from the time of his last visit to the Brunswick

court in 1592: Anthoniussen Jeffes (dative form) is of course to be identified with the boy actor Anthony Jeffes of whom we find traces in Elizabethan theatrical records. It is practically certain that the entry for court expenses under 20 December 1596 with its special reference to a payment to an (English) youth also bears on Anthony Jeffes. Edwin Nungezer (*Dictionary*, pp. 203-4) writes that this actor may have been a Chamberlain's or a Pembroke's man before he became associated with the Admiral's company in 1597 (see also *Elizabethan Stage*, II, 133, 200), the same early theatrical connection also being suggested for Humphrey Jeffes, who, critics say, may or may not have been Anthony's brother. But an examination of a parish register of St Saviour's, Southwark, catalogued under the reference R 278/1 and preserved in County Hall, London, has revealed that Humphrey and Anthony *were* brothers. This register records the baptism at St Saviour's of the following children of Richard Jeffes: Richard, 8 August 1574; Humphrey, 23 December 1576; William, 11 January 1577/8; Anthony, 14 December 1578; Elizabeth, 12 March 1579/80; Agnes, 10 July 1581 and John, 17 October 1582. Considering the close family ties between Humphrey and Anthony the Wolfenbüttel records have now made it clear that the early theatrical connection of these two actors was practically certainly with the Admiral's men, as was the case for Anthony who made his first cross-channel journey in the company of Browne's men and, for some reason or other, had to stay behind at Wolfenbüttel and, consequently, may almost be said never really to have left the Admiral's.

Anthony Jeffes actually becomes known as an Admiral's man in the accounts of Philip Henslowe, the celebrated theatre manager of

[1] Brand, *Der englische Komödiant Robert Browne*, p. 34, quoting Guildhall Library Ms. 7493, marriages fol. 17r. Possibly Cicely Sands was related to the 'Sanss' mentioned in Arnhem in 1592.
[2] See *Euphorion*, 21 (1914), 74, where the actor's name is mistranscribed as 'Umphoniussen Jaffes'.

the time. The latter's *Diary* contains an account with the date 11 October 1597 which gives us a list of Admiral's men: 'A Juste a cownt of All suche money as I haue layd owt for my admeralles [men] players begynyng the xi of octob3, whose names ar as foloweth borne gabrell shaw Jonnes dowten Jube towne synger & the ij geffes 1597'.[1] As deciphered the actors first mentioned here are William Bird, Gabriel Spenser, Robert Shaa, Richard Jones, Thomas Downton, Edward Juby, Thomas Towne and John Singer. In the known records Anthony very often appears in the company of Humphrey and here we have them together as the 'ij geffes'. In view of the fact that neither Humphrey nor Anthony have been traced with certainty in Elizabethan theatrical records between February 1592 and October 1597 it looks as though the brothers, instead of touring the provinces with the Admiral's men in 1592–4 as many scholars have been inclined to believe (at least as far as Humphrey is concerned), had in fact joined Browne on his second continental trip. This opens up a very interesting line of inquiry.

It is well known that in the stage directions of the Folio edition of *3 Henry VI* appear the actors' names of Gabriel, Sinclo and Humphrey. Stage directions read 'Enter Gabriel' at I, ii, 48 and 'Enter Sinklo, and Humfrey, with Crossebowes in their hands' at III, i, 1, all three names also being used as speech-prefixes throughout their parts. Are these speech-prefixes attributable to Shakespeare or are they of playhouse origin and therefore those of the prompter? Since the articles of Allison Gaw[2] scholarly opinion has favoured the idea that they stem from Shakespeare. 'Gabriel', 'Sinklo' and 'Humfrey' must stand for Gabriel Spenser, John Sinkler and Humphrey Jeffes, for Henslowe in his *Diary* frequently calls Spenser Gabriel, while Jeffes is the only actor of the time bearing the first name of Humphrey and, besides, he was associated, as we have just seen,

with Gabriel Spenser in the Lord Admiral's company of 1597. But the investigations of W. W. Greg in his *Alcazar & Orlando* (1923) and *Dramatic Documents from the Elizabethan Playhouses* (1931) showed that the names of Humphrey and Anthony Jeffes also occur in two playhouse documents called 'plots', which were skeleton outlines of plays scene by scene, written on large boards for the actors' convenience. A dating different from that usually accepted for the Plot of *The Battle of Alcazar* can perhaps be suggested on the basis of the absence from home of Anthony Jeffes. The play itself has always been ascribed to George Peele and its quarto edition appeared in 1594. According to the title page the drama was 'sundrie times playd by the Lord high Admirall his seruants'. The printed play is clearly an abridged version so that 'it is generally supposed that *Alcazar* was originally performed before the Admiral's men left London in 1591, and that the text was cut to accommodate a small company on the road'.[3]

The date of the Plot of *Alcazar* has been much debated. W. W. Greg holds that 'the cast it reveals proves that it must in any case have been drawn up between October 1597 and February 1602'.[4] But is this view correct? What Greg writes is of course based exclusively on the actors' lists which appear after the reconstruction of the Admiral's company in 1597. I think it much more likely that the Plot dates from before February 1592, for not only does it list the names of Anthony and Humphrey Jeffes but also that of Richard Jones, another Admiral's

[1] Foakes and Rickert (eds.), *Henslowe's Diary*, p. 84.
[2] 'Actors' Names in Basic Shakespearean Texts', *Publications of the Modern Language Association of America*, 40 (1925), 530–50. See also *Anglia*, 37 (1926), 289–303.
[3] John Yoklavich, ed. *The Battle of Alcazar* in *The Dramatic Works of George Peele* (1961), p. 221.
[4] *The Battle of Alcazar & Orlando Furioso* (1923), p. 14.

man who certainly went to Wolfenbüttel in 1592.

It has been pointed out earlier that the two Jeffes do not emerge from the pages of Henslowe's *Diary* or from any contract until 11 October 1597. The fact that these two actors very probably left England in February 1592 also renders it extremely unlikely that they were ever connected with Pembroke's men, as Chambers (*Elizabethan Stage*, II, 200) and others have suggested. It is precisely from this point in time that the so-called fusion or amalgamation between the English branch of the Admiral's company and Strange's servants became operative during their tenancy of the Rose Theatre, for Strange's men produced *A Knack to Know a Knave* on 10 June 1592, the quarto edition of 1594 stating on its title page that it had been 'sundrie tymes played by Ed. Allen and his Company'. The career of the Admiral's men is uneventful until February 1597 when two of their principal members, Richard Jones and Thomas Downton, broke away to join with several servants of the Earl of Pembroke, entering into contract to play at the Swan. It was during the months prior to October 1597 that the two Jeffes and a number of other actors must have returned to the London theatrical scene, for it will be recalled that Anthony Jeffes was certainly still in Wolfenbüttel at Christmas 1596.[1]

It is reassuring and pleasing to recall here that the Young Mahamet whom Anthony represented about 1588–90 was about ten at the time of the battle of Alcazar so that the young actor may well have been the same age as the character he had to portray on the stage. 'Muly Mahamet Seth, played by Humphrey, was also a youthful character', Greg tells us in his notes on the cast of the Plot, while we know already that Humphrey was the elder of the two. The main objection to a dating after 1597 is that there is no evidence that the famous actor Edward Alleyn, who also appears in the cast of the Plot

of *Alcazar*, acted between his retirement late in 1597 and 1600. It can now be recognised that the objection is a fundamental and crucial one: the Plot may not relate to a late revival at all but is perhaps connected with very early productions which can be situated before either the first or the second of Browne's continental trips. Of course, an early dating of the Plot also involves a reassessment of the careers of all the other actors named in it. However, we must return to the fortunes of the Browne company.

Lack of space forbids me to deal in detail with the vicissitudes of the foreign branch of the Admiral's company between 1595 and 1599 and so I have thought it best to take up the thread of the narrative at the end of 1599 when Robert Browne is to be found at Strassburg.

To begin with, it should be pointed out that in Strassburg, unlike in the rest of Alsace, the Old Style calendar was still in use at this time since the transition to New Style dating was not made until 5/16 February 1692, a fact which all those who have dealt with the references to actors in the Strassburg accounts have failed to mention. They were all printed by Johannes Crüger.[2]

In the winter of 1599–1600 there are two entries in the city accounts, the first carrying the date 'Samstag, den 22. December 1599', the second carrying the date 'Freitag, den 11. Januar 1600'. The first entry records that 'Robertus Braun der Englische Commoediant sambt noch 12 personen' offers to play twelve 'Commoedien', the magistrates allowing them to play for a fortnight as from Thursday, but the second entry makes no mention of a master actor's name and declares that 'Engellandische Commoedianten' offer to play comedies and tragedies for another fortnight. Since we know

---

[1] W. W. Greg, *Dramatic Documents from the Elizabethan Playhouses* (1931), pp. 56–7.
[2] 'Englische Komoedianten in Strassburg im Elsass', *Archiv für Litteraturgeschichte*, 15 (1887), 113–25.

that during the winters of 1599–1600 and 1600–1 Browne appeared as payee for the Earl of Derby's men when they performed at court, the two accounts just referred to also make it clear that very soon after arriving in Strassburg the actor must have left and in doing so must have turned over the conduct of affairs to another actor, for the entry of 11/21 January 1600 does not include Browne's name. The following Christmas the Browne company was again in Strassburg without its leader, because the man who had taken over from him opened his request dated '13. December 1600' with 'Engellandische Commoedianten, die vor einem Jar auch hie gewessen...'. But Browne did not abandon his men completely for he was to join them in Frankfort at Easter 1601; in other words the company resumed contact with its leader. One of the purposes of Browne's visits to England in the winters of 1600 and 1601 may well have been to supply his continental company with fresh playscripts precisely at a time when the great Shakespearian masterpieces such as *Romeo and Juliet*, *Julius Caesar*, *Twelfth Night* and *Hamlet* were being staged, though we should never lose sight of the fact that Browne belonged to a company, the Admiral's men, who were the rivals of the Chamberlain's men, Shakespeare's company, which explains the comparative paucity of Shakespearian plays in the repertoires that have survived in continental archives. One thing should be noted, though: Browne, when in England, revived in some way the earlier amalgamation between the Admiral's and the Lord Strange's men by temporarily becoming one of Derby's men. Chambers (*Elizabethan Stage*, II, 127) writes that 'four performances were given, on 3 and 5 February 1600 and 1 and 6 January 1601' and that 'to this company are doubtless to be assigned *Edward IV*, perhaps by Heywood (1600, S.R. 28 August 1599), and the anonymous *Trial of Chivalry* (1605, S.R. 4 December 1604), both of which are credited to Derby's

men on their title-pages'. Significantly, as we will have occasion to point out later, a play on the same subject as *Edward IV* was performed at Graz about 19 November 1607 by English actors under the leadership of John Green, a former associate of Browne, the strolling actor.

In March 1601 Browne emerges again in Frankfort in a petition to the city councillors signed with two others, Robert Kingsman and Robert Ledbetter, these two having made their first appearance in Heidelberg in 1598.[1] But the petition itself included a significant reference to the participation of 'Johannes Buscheten', the nickname of Thomas Sackville in the character of the clown. In other words it seems that Sackville had temporarily joined his old leader to appear as a sort of guest actor. It should also be noted that Ledbetter was a former Admiral's man, because we know that he was in the cast of *Frederick and Basilea* in which he acted the part of Pedro at the Rose, Henslowe's playhouse, probably in 1597.

At this point in the wanderings of Robert Browne we have to introduce another theatre man of the same name, who died in London during one of the worst visits of the plague which hit the city in 1603 while his namesake was gaining significant theatrical successes in Germany. On 21 October 1603 Joan Alleyn reported to her husband Edward Alleyn that 'All the Companyes be Come hoame & well for ought we knowe, but that Browne of the Boares head is dead & dyed very pore, he went not into the Countrye at all'.[2] The Boar's Head Inn was an inn-yard theatre just outside the city-bounds in Stepney, which about 1599 was subleased to an actor called Robert Browne whom Chambers prudently refused to identify

[1] For all this see E. Mentzel, *Geschichte der Schauspielkunst in Frankfurt am Main* (Frankfort, 1882), p. 47 and A. Duncker, 'Landgraf Moritz von Hessen und die englischen Komödianten', *Deutsche Rundschau*, 48 (1886), 266.

[2] Quoted in *Henslowe's Diary* in the edition cited, p. 297.

with our continental Browne. However, both C. J. Sisson and Herbert Berry have argued that, on the contrary, the Browne of the Boar's Head is identifiable with both the Derby's man who led an actors' company at court in the winters of 1600 and 1601 and the continental Browne.[1] It seems to me that their views rest on a misinterpretation of the records. Apart from that contained in legal documents, where an actor called Robert Browne is clearly involved, the only evidence we have of the actual use made of the Boar's Head for acting purposes appears, in the first place, in a Privy Council order on 31 March 1602 whereby Oxford's and Worcester's men, 'beinge ioyned by agrement togeather in on companie', were to be allowed to play there and nowhere else (see Chambers, *Elizabethan Stage*, II, 225); and, secondly, in a draft patent for a royal licence to the Queen's men, which may be assigned to March 1603/4 and from which we learn that the actors were allowed to use the Curtain, along with the Boar's Head, as their regular houses (see *Elizabethan Stage*, II, 230). Of course, the 'German' Browne had originally been a Worcester's man, but he had become an Admiral's man and on his return to England in 1600 and again in 1601 he became a payee for Derby's actors. The words used by Joan Alleyn make it abundantly clear that she is not thinking of the former fellow-actor of her husband, but of an entirely different man whom she differentiates by characterising him as the Browne of the Boar's Head. The confusion arises from the fact that both Brownes were at one time under the patronage of the Earl of Worcester, the Browne of German fame from 1583 to 1589 whilst the theatre-manager and actor-lessee still occupied the Boar's Head Inn theatre in 1602, a circumstance from which his involvement with Worcester's men has been inferred. After his death the latter's widow Susan married the actor Thomas Greene and the company 'made a fresh and promising start at

the new Red Bull Theatre, under the high patronage of Queen Anne since 1603'.[2]

But we have dwelt long enough on the English theatrical scene around 1600 and must return to the European scene. Passing over in silence a number of (mostly) anonymous entries relating to actors in German records in 1601 and 1602, we had best take up the thread of the narrative in August 1602, a year which seems to have marked the full expansion of Browne's activity. His troupe, it is highly probable, paid a return visit to Wolfenbüttel in August 1602. The account relating to this performance runs as follows:

[Gnadengelt. 30 Augusti 1602] Uff Meiner Gnedigen Fürstin und Frawen mündtlichen bevelig den Engelischen Comedianten so Tohmas [sic] Sacheviell bekommen auss gnaden 200 Thaler.

Following Cohn and others, this is usually interpreted as referring to a payment for a farewell performance by Sackville, quitting the actor's profession, while Chambers (*Elizabethan Stage*, II, 276) writes that 'on 30 August 1602 he took a payment for the English comedians'. But there is sufficient reason to infer from the very peculiar wording of this account that Sackville acted as payee for somebody else, and who could that possibly be but Browne who no doubt felt the need to visit his former patron to revive old memories and to meet old friends while at the same time reciprocating the Frankfort guest performance?[3] Nor should it be forgotten that the *gnädige Fürstin*, Elizabeth,

[1] C. J. Sisson, *The Boar's Head Theatre*, ed. S. Wells (1972), p. 42 and H. Berry, 'The Playhouse in the Boar's Head Inn, Whitechapel', *The Elizabethan Theatre*, ed. D. Galloway (Toronto, 1969), p. 53 and 'The Boar's Head Again', *ibid.*, III (1971), 33–65.

[2] See C. J. Sisson, 'The Red Bull Company and the Importunate Widow', *Shakespeare Survey 7* (Cambridge, 1954), p. 61.

[3] Zimmermann, 'Englische Komödianten am Hofe zu Wolfenbüttel', p. 39 advances a similar suggestion pointing out that the peculiar wording of the entry could not possibly refer to regular members of the Duchess's household.

Duchess of Brunswick was the sister of Anne, the wife of King James of Scotland, who was soon to ascend the throne of England.

In April 1603, as we will see, the Browne company merged temporarily with another troupe which was passing through Frankfort. From a petition submitted to the city council (dated 11 March 1603), which was discovered by Peter Brand, it appears that Browne and his company must have acted in Regensburg during the period that the Diet was convening there. The Diet was officially opened on 11/21 March by the Archduke Matthias, who deputised for his brother, the Emperor Rudolf II. A second petition for performing in Frankfort, submitted probably between 8 and 15 April, shows that Robert Browne had decided on a temporary amalgamation of his troupe with another led by Ralph Reeve and Richard Machin, the petition itself mentioning two companies.

Robert Browne, however, seems to have struck out on his own again and perhaps travelling via Cologne, where an English company is traceable in May,[1] and Brussels, he finally arrived in Lille where the city accounts for 1603 contain an entry revealing his presence there.

A Robert broen Jehan griyen Robert le better et consors la somme de vingt quattre livres parisis pour avoir joué d'Instrumens et faict exhibition de quelques commédies en la présence de messieurs à ceste cause icy lesdits... ... 24£.[2]

Léon Lefebvre, the author of a valuable theatre history of Lille, also cited this entry but transcribed the names wrongly as Brame, Gruson and Le Batteur, thus transforming the actors into Frenchmen. Even so this valiant attempt at naturalisation has failed to prevent them from being unmasked by J. G. Riewald as Robert Browne, John Green and Robert Ledbetter.[3] To add to the mystery Lefebvre failed to mention where 'l'argentier de la ville' had entered the account in the massive volume of the comptes de la ville for 1603. As to dating,

an entry on the verso side of folio 469 carrying the date 4 July makes it clear that the actors were in Lille at about that time.

Lille has never yet been known to have been included in strolling actors' circuits. It was one of the most important cities in the territories ruled by the Archduke Albert, brother of the Emperor Rudolf II and of the Archduke Matthias. It is important to stress that the city was not within French territory until 1667, a fact often forgotten by those who had to deal with aspects of Lille's theatrical history. Albert's court, situated in Brussels in the heart of the Spanish Netherlands, had recently achieved a certain degree of independence from the court of Madrid, in spite of the fact that Philip III, brother to Albert's wife, Isabella, had tried to curb its recently acquired freedom, mostly by limiting the supply of money. In England likewise, the year 1603 had seen an important change in the political scene, for the death of Queen Elizabeth on 24 March and the consequent resolution of a six-year period of theatrical crisis following upon the performance of *The Isle of Dogs* in 1597 had resulted in the setting up of three actors' companies, all under the patronage of members of the royal family. The Lord Chamberlain's company became the King's men, the Earl of Worcester surrendered his company to Queen Anne, and the Lord Admiral's passed to Prince Henry.[4] The Earl of Worcester's men had had dealings with Henslowe from 17 August 1602 and of the actors' names entered in the 'diary' those of

[1] See Carl Niessen, *Dramatische Darstellungen in Köln von 1526–1700* (Cologne, 1917), p. 72.

[2] Lille city accounts 1603, fol. 473.

[3] L. Lefebvre, *Histoire du théâtre de Lille de ses origines à nos jours* (Lille, 1907), I, 135 and Riewald, 'New Light on the English Actors', p. 73. Incidentally, I may be permitted to mention here that I had myself 'unmasked' the actors in the first *thèse annexe* appended to a study presented at the University of Ghent in 1956.

[4] See Glynne Wickham, *Early English Stages*, vol. II, part 2 (1972), p. 26.

John Thare (Thayer) and Robert Blackwood were soon to turn up at the Frankfort autumn fair of 1603, Thare's name appearing subsequently in the minutes of the Augsburg city council in December. Chambers assumes that these actors were also at the Easter fair but this is mistaken, because this view derives from the incorrect information provided by Mentzel's theatre history of Frankfort. The name of Blackwood appears, for that matter, in Henslowe's *Diary* in an entry with the date 7 March 1602/3, which shows unmistakably that he could hardly have been at Frankfort at Easter that year. It is reasonable, therefore, to assume that the first emergence on the Continent of John Green, Blackwood and Thare after July 1603 was a consequence of the fact that Elizabeth's death had temporarily closed the London theatres.

It would lengthen this article unduly to describe in detail the further wanderings of Browne and his men. A brief mention of places visited and relevant dates will suffice: Ghent (March 1604), Paris (August 1604), Lille where 'Robert o bron' is named in the city accounts for 1605 (fol. 440 v°, date 31 October 1605), Lille (8 June 1606: the entry is anonymous, but the reference is probably to Browne's men) and Strassburg (21/31 June 1606).[1] The minutes of the Strassburg city council have the peculiarity that the first account, dated 21 June, mentions 'Robertus Braun der Englischen Commedianten einer', whereas the second, dated 14 July, records that the actors' spokesman was 'Joann Grien' who thanked the city councillors on behalf of the company. The influence of Green in the management of affairs seems to have been growing while at the same time the Browne company had by slow degrees been drifting into the orbit of the Hapsburg family, first in Regensburg and then in the territories of the Archduke Albert. This is confirmed by the fact that – to quote the words of the Belgian historian and art-critic Charles Ruelens in an

article published in 1864 – 'on trouve, aux Archives de Bruxelles, la preuve qu'en 1605, une compagnie royale anglaise obtint l'autorisation de donner à Bruxelles des représentations'.[2] Although I have failed to discover the document here referred to, Ruelens's reference to a royal company must be authentic, since royal patronage was an aspect of theatrical conditions in England that was otherwise totally unknown to nineteenth-century Belgian historians. What could the terms imply unless an allusion to the fact that the company formed, as it were, the foreign branch of a group of actors whom Queen Anne had taken under her patronage?

The first important contacts of the Brussels court with Whitehall and the actors of Queen Anne were made through an embassy of ceremony occasioned by the preparations for the signing of the peace treaty of London in 1604, a treaty concluded to end the long-protracted hostilities between Spain and England. The Spanish delegation to the peace treaty was headed by Juan de Velasco, Duke of Frias and Constable of Castile, while the Brussels court was represented by Charles, Prince-Count of Arenberg (1550–1616). Arenberg and his retinue were accommodated at Durham House and were attended on by the Queen's men, as appears from the extracts printed by Chambers (*Elizabethan Stage*, IV, 169–170) from the Accounts of the Treasurer. At the time the Queen's men were led by Thomas Greene and included the following players: Christopher Beeston, Robert Lee, John Duke, Robert

[1] See H. R. Hoppe, 'English actors at Ghent in the Seventeenth Century', *Review of English Studies*, 25 (1949), 305–321; L. Lefebvre, *Histoire*, I, 137 who mistranscribes the name as 'Obron'; F. A. Yates, 'English Actors in Paris during the Lifetime of Shakespeare', *Review of English Studies*, I (1925), 392–403, and Crüger, 'Englische Komoedianten in Strassburg', pp. 117–18.

[2] C. Ruelens, 'Notes pour l'histoire du théâtre à Anvers', *Revue d'histoire et d'archéologie*, 4 (1864), 405. The piece of information itself came from the Brussels archivist, Charles Duvivier.

Pallant, Richard Perkins, Thomas Heywood, James Holt, Thomas Swinnerton and Robert Beeston. As we learn from Chambers (*Elizabethan Stage*, I, 312) the Queen's men were described in the Chamber Accounts as being 'Groomes of the Chamber and the Queen's Players'. Arenberg, whose residence was in Stepney, left his temporary home on 9/19 August 1604 to welcome the Spanish embassy which had arrived in Gravesend on that day. In Arenberg's unpublished correspondence with the Brussels court preserved in the General Archives (*Audience*, dossier 364, fol. 333) we find a letter in which, in the course of an interesting description of the ceremonial occasion organised by Whitehall for the reception of the Constable of Castile, Arenberg mentioned that his retinue was looked after by Queen Anne's actors. The Earl of Northampton had to conduct the Constable to Somerset House. The letter is dated from London 12/22 August 1604 and describes the ceremony which occurred on 9 August. An extract now follows.

Et au*d*ict Grauesande vint le Conte de Northampton pour le [the Constable] conduire jusques à son logis à Londres com*m*e il fist, accompagné du*d*ict Baron [Lord Edward Wotton, Treasurer of the household] et y auoient appresté vne vingtaine de barges fort bien accom*m*odées quy sont batteaux à vj et viij Reymes de quoy ces *Seigneur*s d'Angleterre vont par la Riuière et arriuant vers Grunwitz vindrent force barguettes com*m*e gandoles sur la riuière pour veoir l'entrée. Et passant le pont, vismes en vne grande barge, le grand Admiral, le Grand Chamberlain, et Milord Ciscel, auecq des dames masquées et la barge couuerte, où se recognut la Royne, arriuée à la maison laquelle estoit fort brauement accom*m*odée pour le Conestable. Ces *Seigneur*s quy l'auoient accompaigné le y laissarente, com*m*e nous fismes aussy, et allasmes en vne aultre maison quy estoit accomodé pour nous, où le Roy d'Angleterre faict vne grande despence, nous traictant à l'esgal du*d*ict Conestable, tant de ses gardes de corps, com*m*e traictement de tables, synon qu'il n'y en a pas tant, tousiours au moins de ceulx qu'il y at quy seruente, sont plus de cent personnes./ Entre lesquelz y a pluisieurs gentilzhom*m*es seruans de

ma*ístr*e d'hostel et de controleur, com*m*e aussy de toutte sorte d'office, de manière que au Président et Audiencier, comme aussy à moy, il samble qu'il ne s'en pourat sortir auecq moins de deux mille ph*ilippe*s.

Though Arenberg mentions those who served him in their capacity as grooms and no doubt exaggerates their number, he seems to have been unaware of their being actors as well. In connection with their leader Thomas Greene it deserves to be pointed out that it has been suspected that John Green, the strolling actor, was his brother. Thomas mentioned a John as his brother in the will he made on 25 July 1612. The will was witnessed, among others, by his brother Jeffrey Greene and Thomas Heywood, but not by his brother John, which suggests that the latter was not available because of his absence on the Continent.[1]

But to come back to the fortunes of the Browne–Green concern, which we left in Strassburg on 21/31 June 1606. From there, together with Ledbetter, they again turned to Frankfort where they appeared on 26 August styling themselves 'Fürstlich Hessische Commoedianten',[2] the three signatories of the petition appearing in the order of the Lille account of 1603. When the 'Hessian comedians' returned to Frankfort on 17/27 March 1607 the petition carried the names of Browne and Green, but not that of Ledbetter. Scholars have

[1] The will was printed by F. G. Fleay, *A Chronicle History of the London Stage* (1890), pp. 192–4.

[2] J. Meissner, *Die englischen Comoedianten zur Zeit Shakespeares in Oesterreich* (Vienna, 1884), p. 70. Incidentally, it is of interest that the *tota societas vonn Strassburg* (mentioned earlier) appeared at Nördlingen in early January 1604 and also at the end of that month. See K. Trautmann, *Archiv für Litteraturgeschichte*, 11 (1882), 625–6; *ibid.*, 13(1885), 70 and *Zeitschrift für vergleichende Litteraturgeschichte*, 7(1894), 62. Meisner, p. 33 calls this company 'eine Abzweigung der herzoglich braunschweigischen Comödianten'. Significantly, for E. Herz, *Englische Schauspieler und englisches Schauspiel zur Zeit Shakespeares in Deutschland* (Hamburg, 1903), p. 43, this is the troupe of Blackwood and Thare and I could not agree more on this matter with both Meissner and Herz.

always maintained that the 'Hessian comedians' spent the whole winter of 1606–7 in Cassel and they have found evidence for this in the letter of a court official telling Maurice of Hesse that he had paid the 'Englender'. But, in the first place, the letter, dated from Cassel 1 March 1607, does not say anything about the Englishmen's identity, and, secondly, scholars have never taken into account the fact that the English comedians often travelled in the Spanish Netherlands. It is precisely in the period we are here concerned with that we can fall back on an important English testimony from no less a person than Thomas Heywood, actor and playwright, who had no doubt met the Prince-Count of Arenberg in 1604, and thus knew more about the Archduke Albert ('Cardinal of Brussels') and Queen Anne's men than most people. In his *Apology for Actors* (1612), written about 1607, Heywood says that 'the Cardinall of *Bruxels*, hath at this time in pay a company of our *English* comedians'.[1] No one has ever identified these comedians but I believe that there can be little question that they constituted substantially a foreign branch of Queen Anne's men led in 1607 by Browne and/or Green. A newly discovered passport,[2] containing the date 13 February 1607 but unfortunately not disclosing any actors' names, is nevertheless explicit in indirectly calling attention to the fact that the actors enjoyed the Archduke's patronage (*nous donnons...congé*), and who else could they be but the *compagnie royale anglaise* of 1605? The company numbered seventeen actors.

Les Archiducqs & c.

A touts Lieutenants Gouuerneurs Chefs Coronels maîtres de Camp Capitaines et gens de guerre tant de pied que de cheual gardes des ponds portz et passages et à touts autres nos Justiciers, officiers et subjets cui ces regardera et ces présentes seront monstrées salut. Comme nous auons donné et donnons congé et licence aux Comédiens Angloys estans en nombre de dix sept personnes de se pouuoir transporter par voye de Hollande vers le Pays et duché de Bruynswyck,

nous vous ordonnons de les laisser par tout librement et franchement passer tant par eau que par terre, auecq leurs hardes et bagages sans leur fayre ou donner ny souffrir estre fait ou donné aulcun trouble destourbier ou empechement, ains au contrayre toute l'ayde, faueur et asistence [sic] requise pourueu qu'ils ne fassent aulcune chose préjudiciable a nostre seruice noz pays ou bons subjets, et que à leur partement ils seront tenus se présenter à Don Inigo de Borja[3] Gouuerneur de nostre Citadelle d'Anvers ou son Lieutenant ensemble ceux du siège de l'admirauté illecq pour y estre tenu note à durer ceste dicte licence le terme de troys sepmaynes prochaynement venants. Fait en nostre ville de Bruxelles soubz nostre nom et cachet secret le tresiesme Jour du moys de febvrier l'an mille six cent et sept. Rich.v.[4] Signé Albert et vn peu plus bas estoit escrit par ordonnance de Leurs Altezes, Prats,[5] seellé du Cachet secret en cire rouge.

Enregistré le 2.ᵉᵐ de Mars 1607.

The wording of this passport, of which the original bore the signature of the Archduke Albert himself, Governor-General of the Spanish Netherlands from 1598 to his death in 1621, makes clear that the actors were patronised by the Archduke, but the accounts of his court for the year 1607 have not survived, the only records preserved being those covering the years 1612 to 1618. However that may be, at this moment the actors were on their way to Brunswick and the Wolfenbüttel court and, as in the past, their wanderings were probably

[1] See Chambers, *Elizabethan Stage*, IV, 250, 253 for date and passage. See also G. E. Bentley, ed. *The Seventeenth-Century Stage* (1968), p. 21.

[2] General Archives Brussels, *Audience*, dossier 1048 (Passeports), fol. 169v°. There are two underlinings in the original: *Comédiens Angloys...personnes* and *le terme de troys sepmaynes* and opposite the first phrase a scribe has added in a different hand *Comédiens angloys 17* in the left-hand margin.

[3] Inigo de Borja was a *maître de camp espagnol* at the siege of Ostend in 1604 and later *châtelain* of the Citadel of Antwerp.

[4] This is the characteristic paraph which President Jean Richardot (1540–1609), the president of the Archduke Albert's Privy Council, appended to all the documents which had to pass through his hands (Richardot *vidit*).

[5] Philippe Prats was Secretary to the Privy Council.

occasioned by a princely wedding, this time in Duke Henry Julius's own household.

In the early months of 1607 festivities were in preparation for the wedding of the Duke's daughter, Sophia Hedwig, to Ernest Casimir, Count of Orange-Nassau (1573–1632), one of the most important army commanders of his day. In a letter written from The Hague on 21 January 1606 (O.S.) Ralph Winwood wrote to Salisbury that 'The Count Ernest of Nassau, going shortly to solemnise his marriage with the daughter of Brunswick, the States intend to honour him with the dignity of Marshal of their army', and Sir John Ogle reported from the Hague on 7 February 1606 (O.S., i.e. 17 February 1607, N.S.), also to Salisbury, that 'Count Ernest is now setting forward upon his journey towards Brunswick, and means this summer to bring his lady to Arnhem, where he will remain', Ogle reporting to him again from The Hague on 2 November 1607: 'If being at Arnhem (whither I went to present my service to Count Ernesto and his Lady, lately come hither from Brunswick) had not hindered me, my letters had come with the formost.'[1] It is clear from the date in the Brussels passport, 13 February 1607, and that of Ogle's letter of 17 February that Count Ernest Casimir and the actors were setting out for Brunswick at about the same time and for a related purpose, but probably taking very different routes.

The marriage of Ernest Casimir and Sophia Hedwig of Brunswick was celebrated at the castle of Gröningen on 8 June 1607. The account-books for the period record a number of expenses occasioned by the marriage, but they remain silent with respect to visiting actors. In fact, the only real evidence of the actors' probable journey to Brunswick is the allusion to the 'duché de Bruynswyck' in the Brussels passport and perhaps the fact that Green's (inferred) presence there would come soon after his certain appearance at Frankfort

in the latter half of March 1607 and so would fit the chronological sequence of his wanderings. That Green had become a prominent actors' leader in the Spanish Netherlands will, however, be borne out by references in contemporary correspondence, to be discussed later.

About the middle of 1607 John Green had apparently taken charge of the management of the troupe and he struck out for himself, separating from Browne. Scholars have traced him subsequently in Elbing where he was refused permission to play on 16 July 1607; and he then moved to Danzig.[2] The further stages of his wanderings were marked by performances before the highest Austrian nobility, Green appearing in Graz and Passau in November 1607, and again in Graz, where the company acted from 6 to 20 February 1608. Concerning these performances the Archduchess Maria Magdalena of Austria wrote a letter to her brother, the later Emperor Ferdinand II, which provides 'one of the few first-hand accounts of Elizabethan actors on the Continent'.[3] Their repertoire included Marlowe's *Doctor Faustus*, a play by Dekker, a play 'about the Jew' which could, according to Irene Morris, well be *The Merchant of Venice*, but which I believe refers to *The Jew of Malta*, because of the fact that the company originated from the Admiral's men. Perhaps there was also a play, she writes, 'having similarities with *Twelfth Night*'. I may well add here that I also believe that at an earlier

[1] See *Salisbury (Cecil) Manuscripts, A.D. 1607*, XIX (H.M.S.O., 1965), ed. M. S. Giuseppi and D. McN. Lockie, pp. 18, 40, 294.

[2] J. Bolte, *Das Danziger Theater im 16. und 17. Jahrhundert* (Hamburg, 1895), p. 35. The mention at Elbing is anonymous and the visit to Danzig is inferred from a statement Green made in 1615. See Bolte, p. 45.

[3] The letter has recently been admirably edited with an excellent translation by Irene Morris in her article 'A Hapsburg Letter', *Modern Language Review*, 69(1974), 12–22. Letter datable 20 Feb. 1608.

stage of its existence, at a time when the company called itself *tota societas vonn Strassburg* (see above p. 164, n. 2), it had a repertoire which included a play on *Romeo and Juliet* and one on *Pyramus and Thisbe*. That was in early January 1604.

It remains to point out passages in the correspondence of the time which, combined with the evidence hitherto discussed, show unmistakably that Green was in the Spanish Netherlands to offer his services to the court and to the nobility generally, although it should be pointed out that this does not necessarily mean that he attached himself exclusively to that particular court. In a letter written from London, 16 November 1609, by J. Beaulieu to William Trumbull, English envoy accredited at the Brussels court, to which H. R. Hoppe[1] has already drawn attention, we find the following sentence: 'I send you a note of my Lord Deny for the finding of a certain youth of his, who hath been debauched from him by certain players and is now with them at Brussels.'[2] What has not yet been noted is that two further letters between the same correspondents disclose the respective identities of the youth and of the actors' leader. On 31 January 1610 Beaulieu tells Trumbull that 'My Lord Deny, affecting the recovery of a boy of his called William Lee, hath solicited my Lord that this matter be referred to you, fearing that Greene, the player, with whom the boy was, is come back to Antwerp, and the boy being unwilling to come back for fear of punishment, you may assure him that he may safely return'; and, again on 8 March 1610: 'I hope to hear what you had done with Green the player and about W. Lee.'[3] Alongside these extracts we can place a letter written by a local nobleman which, being so nearly contemporaneous with the Beaulieu references, almost certainly bears on the Green troupe. The letter has been mistakenly ascribed by the Ghent theatre historian P. Claeys, and subsequently by Hoppe, to Arenberg, the envoy who was in touch with Queen Anne's men in 1604, while it was in fact signed by his brother-in-law, Charles, Duke of Croy and Aarschot (1560–1612), a wellknown bibliophile, numismatist, patron of the arts and one of the richest *grands seigneurs* in the land.[4] The letter, addressed to the Ghent city councillors and preserved in the Municipal Archives in Ghent among the *Ingekomen Brieven*, recommended the players to the Council, praised their good morals and indicated that they had just finished playing both in the Duke's château at Heverlee and in Louvain itself.

Messieurs, Après que ces *présents* comédiens Englois ont hier jouez en ce mien *cha*steau de Hevrelé du loing ces derniers caresmeaux douze à treize comédies, ilz m'ont à leur partement suplié et requis vous en faire ce mot. Ce que ie ne leur ay volu dényer ains par iceluy vous tesmoigner qu'à celles qu'ay esté *présent* et suiuant le rapport quy m'a esté faict des aultres où je ne suis esté *présent*, je n'y ay veu ny recogneu quelque scandal ny choses illicites, pour y auoir occasion de le [sic] refuser la permission qu'ilz vont vous demander de pouuoir faire le mesme en *vo*stre ville com*me* ilz ont heu de mesme en celle de Louuain. Et ne seruant à aultre fin je demeure Messieurs, de Hevrelé le 18e féb*vrier* 1611,

> Vo*stre* bien affectionné amy à vous complayre,
> Charles, Sire et duc de Croy et d'Arscot

Finally, there are two entries concerning

[1] 'English Acting Companies at the Court of Brussels in the Seventeenth Century', *Review of English Studies*, n.s. 6(1955), 26–33, esp. p. 27.

[2] Hist. Ms. Commission, *Report on the Mss. of the Marquess of Downshire*, II: Papers of William Trumbull the Elder (1936), pp. 186–7.

[3] *Ibid.*, pp. 227–61. Note for what it is worth that Robert Lee (possibly a brother of William) was a prominent actor who is 'found in Queen Anne's company, which was a continuation of the Worcester troupe after the change of patronage late in 1603' (Nungezer, *Dictionary*, p. 235).

[4] P. Claeys, *Histoire du théâtre à Gand* (Ghent, 1892), II, 8. Arenberg's wife, Anne de Croy (1564–1635), was the sister of Charles, Duke of Croy. The latter's second wife, whom he married in 1605, was Dorothée de Croy (1575–1662), who was a minor poetess.

English actors which Hoppe has unearthed from the two huge volumes containing the accounts of the Archduke Albert's court. The accounts are kept in Spanish and are preserved in the General Archives in Brussels. They cover the years 1612 to 1618. The first entry is dated 19 February 1614 and speaks of *los Represent-antes yngleses*, while the second is dated 3 September 1617 and mentions *unos comediantes yngleses*.[1] It is the style of the entry that is significant here. The specifying article *los* in the first entry refers to Green's company, which was 'certainly in the Low Countries about this time, being recorded a few months earlier at Utrecht in the city-council minutes for 15 November 1613' (Hoppe), but *unos* clearly suggests a troupe unknown to the scribe and of course the actors concerned were not Green's men but John Waters, Henry Griffin, and Robert Archer, as Hoppe points out.

As to Green's repertoire of February 1608, this was discussed in detail by Irene Morris. As has been pointed out, it included two plays by Marlowe, *Doctor Faustus* and *The Jew of Malta*, as well as Dekker's *Old Fortunatus*. If we bear in mind that in November 1607 when the troupe was also in Graz, they performed 'von ein khinig auss engelandt, der ist in eins goltschmitt weib verliebt gewest',[2] which is clearly identifiable as Heywood's *Edward IV*, then it appears that Green relied for his basic stock on the plays inherited from the Admiral's and, at a later stage, from Worcester's men during their association with Henslowe.

Although Green also visited areas in Protestant Germany it can hardly be doubted that he relied heavily on the patronage of both the Spanish and the Austrian Hapsburgs, Catholic princes whose administrative machinery was very active in promoting the Counter-Reformation. Queen Anne, whose rather half-hearted Catholicism was occasionally a source of embarrassment to King James, can be looked upon as the English counterpart of her sterner 'cousins' in Brussels and Graz. Queen Anne's love of gaiety, music and dancing can be said to be reflected in the plays of English actors on the continent whose main attraction consisted in staging plays with musical and dancing interludes and 'feats of activity'. The Howard passport of 1592 had set the tone: the actors were to exercise their 'qualitez en faict de musicque, agilitez et joeuz de commedies'; and in 1603 a second group of actors, for the most part patronised by Queen Anne and soon to be dominated by Green, set sail for the continent. After the Graz visit John Green continued to provide entertainment for the Austrian Hapsburgs, but in May 1615 he again went to Wolfenbüttel.[3] In 1616 the troupe spent several months in Warsaw at the court of Sigismund III, whose wife was the sister of the Archduchess Maria Magdalena, and in 1617 they were in Prague on the occasion of Ferdinand of Styria's coronation as King of Bohemia.

In 1624 Green is again found in Ghent, but his professional career was to culminate in Dresden in 1626. The play-list that has survived here signalised the breakthrough of Shakespeare on the continent, the list comprising the titles of *Romeo and Juliet*, *Julius Caesar*, *Hamlet* and *King Lear*.

[1] *Chambre des Comptes*, reg. 1837 fol. 211 r° and reg. 1838 fol. 284 r°.

[2] Meissner, *Die englischen Comoedianten*, p. 74.

[3] See *Euphorion*, 21 (1914), 85 and Bolte, *Das Danziger Theater*, p. 47.

© WILLEM SCHRICKX 1980

SHAKESPEARE AT STRATFORD AND THE NATIONAL THEATRE, 1979

ROGER WARREN

The two outstanding Shakespeare productions of 1979 were the RSC *Pericles* at the Other Place in Stratford and the National Theatre's *As You Like It*: both broke new ground. But the main Stratford season was exceptionally uneven, and no neat summary is possible for so very disparate a group of plays and productions as those covered by this article, including the 1978 *Antony and Cleopatra* which opened too late for review last year.

I

Even in what he called a 'year of consolidation', Trevor Nunn's ostensibly 'new' *Merry Wives of Windsor* amounted to little more than a refining and paring down of the previous RSC production by Terry Hands. Production ideas were carried over: children played conkers between scenes; there was a strong contrast between the rural accents of the Windsor citizens and the aristocrats Fenton and Falstaff; the finale in Windsor Forest was a Hallowe'en revel. The autumnal colours of John Napier's costumes and his delightful set, a detailedly realistic Elizabethan town square with only a few last brown leaves on its solid trees, into which slid cosy domestic interiors, were very similar in principle and in feel to Timothy O'Brien's for the earlier version: both strongly evoked an Elizabethan country town community of the 1590s.

The country town feel was even stronger this time, especially in Patrick Godfrey's sharply pointed Shallow; Geoffrey Hutchings's admirably restrained Caius; David Threlfall's unusually vigorous, even aggressive Slender, emitting howls of sadistic glee as Shallow dangerously demonstrated his military prowess with Caius's sword, or rolling on the ground in orgasmic ecstasy at the thought of 'sweet Anne Page'; and Bob Peck's Page, the gruffly genial embodiment of the Windsor community, pipe constantly in mouth, going a-birding or warding prodigals off his hard-won cash. By contrast Ben Kingsley's Ford was clearly attempting to climb a little higher up the social ladder. Beneath his green velvet doublet he wore a yellow check waistcoat and riding boots, obviously out to join the county set – a social aspiration set at risk by his pinched, shifty manner; his receding hair, pencil moustache and (as Brook) bowler hat all suggested the stereotype of a shady commercial traveller. Ford's jealousy was not the only mocking anticipation of *Othello* here; for John Woodvine delivered Falstaff's 'now let me die, for I have liv'd long enough; this is the period of my ambition' with an expansive grandeur which suggested that it might continue

> Here is my journey's end, here is my butt,
> And very sea-mark of my utmost sail.

But the steel in Mr Woodvine's voice ('the *peaking cornuto* her husband' packed with derision) suggested rather the crafty Falstaff of *Henry IV*; he seemed too intelligent to be gulled so easily, and it was more incredible than ever that this Falstaff should be afraid of 'fairies'.

II

John Napier's set was also the most striking feature of the new *Twelfth Night*, this time a sloping platform with bare trees in large square tubs and snow on the ground; the sun came out in time for Malvolio to practise behaviour in it, and Maria's grey winter shawl was decked out with green leaves and suspended from one of the trees to provide extra 'cover' for the eaves-droppers in the letter scene; from III, i daffodils blossomed in the tubs, and green leaves had sprouted on some (but by no means all) of the bare trees, so that the stage picture for the second half was a mixture of winter and spring: but if this matched the mixture of harshness and happiness in the play, it also, less happily, reflected a certain confusion in Terry Hands's production.

Through the trees, characters were often seen upstage, preparing for the next episode: Sir Toby meeting Cesario at the gate; Viola and Olivia in conversation before coming down-stage centre for their exchange in III, iv as Sir Toby moved upstage to meditate upon some horrid message for a challenge; Viola even loosening her hair upstage and draping a shawl around her male breeches to give some sem-blance of being Orsino's mistress while the others listened to Malvolio's letter downstage. During Feste's final song, the lovers in a happy group centre were isolated from those who felt the imminence of the wind and the rain, sitting underneath the trees at the shadowed edges of the platform: the wounded Aguecheek, head in hands, the isolated Antonio, and the sobered Maria and Toby, separated and facing away from each other.

If Mr Hands gave us contrast here, he gave us contradiction elsewhere, especially in his presentation of Feste and Malvolio. Feste was on stage virtually throughout, an ill-licensed Twelfth Night Lord of Misrule, even cueing characters' entries in the finale; but since he had seen both Cesario and Sebastian, 'your name is not Master Cesario; nor this is not my nose neither' had to be made to mean the reverse of what it in fact does mean, to the extent of Feste actually removing a *false* nose to emphasise knowingly that 'nothing that is so is so'. This was the most blatant example of Mr Hands's typical habit of sacrificing the plain meaning of the text to the interests of some imposed 'concept'; but text and performance tend to resist such concepts, and Geoffrey Hutchings's quietly rustic Feste was among the *least* dominating I have seen.

John Woodvine (Malvolio) seemed at first to be carefully building a consistent character-isation of a humourless puritanical steward, self-conscious about social gaffes, having immense difficulty with the pronunciation of 'slough', speaking with a nasal twang specific-ally mocked in Feste's line 'Malvolio's nose is no whipstock', and grimly resolving 'I – will – smile' as if his life depended upon it. The result-ing physical contortion was legitimately very funny, but the antics with the cross-garters seemed to come from a more farcical character, equipped with a huge yellow codpiece for gross phallic humour at 'greatness thrust upon them'. 'I'll be revenged on the whole pack of you' was charged with deadly menace; but as he turned away upstage, the long cord which had tied his feet snaked along the floor after him out of the trapdoor from which he had emerged. What we were finally to think about Malvolio was not clear.

The most original interpretation was of the lovers, who expressed what they were feeling with unusual direct emphasis, without either lyricism or affectation. Gareth Thomas tore in-to Orsino's lines rapidly, roughly, even aggres-sively, as if he was basically a man of action who felt obliged to use conventional wooing styles and disliked them; at the end he wore a flowing white Saracen-style robe with a scimitar at his belt (looking rather like Byron in oriental costume), turning the knife violently on both Olivia and Viola, thus wringing from Viola the passionately emphatic declaration 'after him I LOVE'. This interpretation had the merit of bringing real weight to his imaging of his fierce desires as 'fell and cruel hounds' at the cost of gabbling more reflective passages ('longing, wavering, sooner lost and worn'), but its vigour was refreshing.

So, too, was that of Olivia. Interpreting a figure of speech as a statement of fact, Mr Hands did not merely 'veil' her *like* a cloistress', but dressed her in flowing black and white nun's robes; when Viola asked to see her face, Olivia removed not just the nun's veil but her entire head-dress, revealing long red tresses which made her look an odd mixture of Mary Magdalen and Salome; but at least it emphasised Olivia's vigorous coming alive, as did the force with which she virtually *assaulted* fate on the line 'Fate, show thy force'. But the actress lacked the experience to vary her subsequent delivery, and her very emphatic style ultimately became tiring.

It was Cherie Lunghi's Viola that really gained from this approach. At the start a scared waif, she gradually worked out her disguise ('an eunuch!' was a sudden inspiration), and also thought her way through the 'willow cabin' speech, which began as a genuine, thoughtful attempt to answer Olivia's question, and gradually acquired great power as she built up the plan bit by bit. In the central scene with Orsino, their passionate, almost violent exchanges ('Sooth, but you *must*!', 'Ay, but *I know*—', 'What dost *thou know*?'), flung backwards and forwards, built up to a tingling 'She never told her love', which was charged with real emotional frustration. During 'Come away death', she draped her cloak caringly around Orsino's shoulders, and their mutual absorption was so great that they virtually forgot about Feste; Orsino broke the spell with the next instruction about Olivia, thus increasing her

frustration, but at the end of the scene he returned to her to give back her cloak, and this held moment between them underlined their development during the scene and prepared for their final union. Miss Lunghi also played the humour with impish lightness, and she alone brought distinction of style and personality to a production generally lacking in the subtle undertones and detailed humanity achieved in previous Stratford productions of this play.[1]

III

Directors have usually sought to distract from the textual corruptions of *Pericles* by presenting the play within some elaborate framework – as a negro boatswain's sea-shanty to his fellow-sailors (Stratford 1958), as a neo-Platonic allegory using Renaissance iconography (Stratford 1969), even as a floor-show in a male brothel (Prospect 1973) – with the unfortunate result, in each case, that the frame not only distracted from the play's corruptions but from its positive merits too. By contrast, Ron Daniels realised that, if those merits are to have any chance to emerge, the first prerequisite is to tell the story as directly as possible, and to play each individual episode for all it is worth. The result was the only *Pericles* I have seen which succeeded almost throughout.

At the Other Place there was no set, only a circle on the floor marking out the acting area, into which such props as the heads of the suitors on poles were carried, and a wooden post to which the fishermen's nets could be

[1] It is pleasant to record here Bernard Levin's impression of Cherie Lunghi's similar achievement as Celia in the London revival of the RSC's 1977 *As You Like It*, which I reviewed in *Shakespeare Survey 31* before Miss Lunghi joined the cast: 'She speaks beautifully, musically, romantically, delicately; she moves gracefully; she conveys the mock-cynical mischief in the role as well as the genuine feeling; and she is almost alone among the players in never failing to listen, and react, to others on the stage' (*Sunday Times*, 1 October 1978). That could be a description of her Viola too.

attached, or from which a single rope stretched across the acting area was enough to suggest

the ship, upon whose deck
The sea-toss'd Pericles appears to speak.

Gower sat sleeping against this wooden post before starting his story; Pericles joined him there and told him, not Helicanus, about the events in Antioch. (Gower also spoke Helicanus's lines in act v; the other Helicanus episodes – with the flattering lords, with Thaliard, and with Escanes – were cut entirely, the only major omissions.) The focal point in the centre of the circle was emphasised by powerful overhead lighting at crucial moments: Antiochus's first entry ('yon grim looks' were his, not the suitors'); Pericles bidding farewell to the 'dead' Thaisa and her revival by Cerimon; Marina's conversion by Lysimachus.

The chief effect of the bare stage and simple costumes (robes and slippers, Sheik-like headdresses, a minimal black shift for Antiochus's daughter, an identical white one when she reappeared as Marina) was to reinforce the general critical view that, however you account for it, some scenes seem merely feeble, others to shine with what Philip Edwards in his New Penguin edition calls 'ruined greatness'. The harder Mr Daniels worked at the Pentapolis court scenes, the feebler they seemed; the elaborately dangerous quarter-staff tournament, the interpolated, unnecessarily difficult song for Pericles, the feast whose thimble-size glasses crossed the thin boundary between the symbolic and the affected – these contrivances merely underlined the weakness of these scenes, and the Simonides was too colourless to exploit the humour of the king's abrupt switches between public severity and approving asides which have sometimes carried these scenes in the past.

On the other hand, once Peter McEnery's powerful, eloquent Pericles reached the great speeches of III, i he made the very most of them, proving fully equal to their wide range from violence against the storm to tenderness for the baby Marina and haunting grief for Thaisa. And once Mr Daniels reached Cerimon's house at Ephesus, he abandoned the rather empty miming of Pentapolis in favour of practical medical detail as the text itself becomes more detailed and interesting: Cerimon and Philemon showed real concern as they carefully applied their medicines to recover Thaisa; there was a strong sense that, if Thaisa's return to life is a kind of miracle, it nonetheless happens through the agency of *human* wisdom and learning.

From the interval, after act III, the production, like the play, went from strength to strength. The brothel scenes were not only very funny (Jeffery Dench's Pandar lamenting ruefully that his profession is 'no calling', Heather Canning an effectively unexaggerated Bawd) but sinister too: an interpolated scene showed Boult advertising Marina to potential customers circling round her by singing a strident version of 'Away with these self-loving lads' in sinister half-light. Such effects helped Julie Peasgood to be a quite exceptional Marina, especially in the outstandingly successful treatment of one of the cruces of the play, Marina's conversion of Lysimachus. A double mattress was placed centre stage, upon which they both knelt; Marina seemed very vulnerable, both because of her fragile slightness and because of her close proximity to Lysimachus on a bed. She seemed to win him over, not only by her pleading (strengthened with additions from Wilkins's version of the scene), but also by her enchanting tenderness and unaffected innocence; you felt that their love was born in the process. It was a quite remarkably moving interpretation of a notoriously tricky scene; and when Peter Clough came to that awkward crux about having come to the brothel 'with no ill intent', its obvious untruth didn't *seem* awkward because of the naturalness of both performances up to this point; it was as if he was fabricating an explanation in order to excuse himself to her. Still on the mattress, she was even more vulnerable to Boult, who threw himself upon her to rape her; but he too gradually began to communicate with her; the 'What would you have me do?' speech was *his* attempt to excuse himself; and he was finally won over to a genuine human response: 'I'll do for thee what I can.'

In the reunion scene, Mr Daniels used the Twine/Wilkins 'Amongst the harlots foul I walk' for Marina's song, sung with touching directness by Miss Peasgood; and though the cloth wrappings representing Pericles's 'un-scissored' hair and beard, and his long false nails, seemed risky and unhelpful, there was a marvellous sense of an unbelievable, actually *painful* 'great sea of joys rushing upon' Pericles. Here and in the equally moving re-union with Thaisa the simple staging threw all the emphasis where it rightly belongs – on the intense but simple feelings of human love and joy and restoration of the lost which it is the achievement of this text, however 'ruined', to communicate.

IV

When *Cymbeline* in the main theatre began in the same way as this *Pericles*, with Griffith Jones walking on to a bare stage and sitting down beside the only prop (the post in *Pericles*, a plain black box in *Cymbeline*) to 'dream' the action, it seemed as if they were to be treated consciously as companion-pieces; but the re-semblance was superficial, and hopes of a similar triumph were soon cruelly dashed.

Christopher Morley's bold, clean set for *Cymbeline*, a white floor and black surround, was a huge empty space into which everything necessary for telling the story could be carried or flown: props, furniture, emblems (gold for Britain, silver for Rome), and two large rocks for Belarius's cave. Visually this strongly re-called the most successful treatment of *Cymbeline* I have seen, William Gaskill's at Stratford in 1962; but such admirably un-cluttered design invites, indeed demands, strong performances decisively directed (as in 1962), and David Jones appeared to have no consistent approach to the play.

Sometimes Mr Jones seemed to be attempting to reassess characters and avoid stereotypes, without much success: the Queen, for instance, with her excessively plain blue robe and crown-less, straggling hair was neither malevolent nor convincingly hypocritical: 'here comes a flattering rascal' was spoken with an uncon-spiratorial, glowing sincerity that was merely baffling. At other times, he appeared to be sending scenes up: it is one thing for *Cloten* to mock 'Hark, hark, the lark', quite another for the musical setting to anticipate him with mind-less roulades which distracted completely from the significance of the exquisite language, thus encouraging the audience to take the whole scene as so much nonsense; but they had already begun to chatter in derisive bewilderment at the extraordinary performance of Iachimo.

Iachimo came across as a posturing, de-mented puppet who shouted out the lines a word at a time with gross distortion and over-emphasis, thereby depriving the speeches even of their basic sense, let alone their variety, subtlety and beauty. It is true that Imogen her-self loses Iachimo's drift during the speech beginning 'It cannot be i' th' eye', but part of his intention is to confuse her, and the difficulty, even obscurity, of the expression should seem to express Iachimo's devious cunning, his *intelligence*; here it suggested not intelligence but nonsense. In Imogen's bedroom, his defective delivery threw away the gorgeous language, so that there was no hope of com-municating the complex quality of a scene where the tense expectations of rape are combined with Iachimo's lyrically expressed appreciation of Imogen's beauty and worth. This Iachimo had a ruinous effect on the play as a whole: neither subtle ironist nor Italian fiend, he was simply nothing at all, and since Iachimo is the mainspring of the first plot, neither Posthumus nor Imogen had anything to play against: it was as if they were acting in isolation. This was cruelly unfair to Roger Rees, who later showed remarkable confidence and authority in handling Posthumus's very difficult repentance and battle speeches of act v. Judi Dench's Imogen was irresistible even in its tiniest details: 'Blest be/You bees that make these locks of counsel!' on receiving Posthumus's letter was Imogen's enchantingly light-hearted, even light-headed, recognition of the silly things people say when in love; her icy courtesy in response to Iachimo's recantation of his slanders, 'but not away tomorrow', coolly maintained civility without concealing intense dislike, but it lost some of its beautifully sharp-witted effect because even a great actress perfectly cast needs something to play to.

Just at the point when the damage seemed irreparable, the production suddenly began to work with the arrival of Belarius and the princes: their ritual salute to the heavens outside their rock carried immediate conviction; and Patrick Godfrey's outstanding Belarius, sturdy, persuasive, full of rough warmth, had a human solidity which provided Judi Dench with just that context she needed for her performance at last to get under way; and as Fidele she caught exactly that Viola-like blend of impish humour ('Two beggars told me/I could not miss my way', as people always do when you ask them for directions) and grief at the thought of her lost brothers ('Would it had been so that they/Had been my father's sons' very moving, with that characteristic crack in the voice).

Even Bob Peck's Cloten, earlier a crude green giant incongruously speaking with a mock-genteel North Country accent like Thora Hird, improved when he arrived in Wales and clashed with Guiderius: he had clearly never before met anyone quite unimpressed by being told he was the Queen's son Cloten. What was missing was

the dark undertone of sadism in the role; but that darkening was in fact provided by Tim Brierley's Guiderius in his violently callous treatment of Cloten's head – the other side of the royal nature. This prepared the way for the mock-burial, and Judi Dench played Imogen's awakening by the headless corpse with a passionate commitment that quite rightly made no concessions to the currently fashionable critical view that we are meant to stay mockingly detached from her. The audience clearly felt no such detachment; for after that nervous laughter which always greets severed bloody necks and the like on stage, Imogen's speech stilled the theatre and was followed by a well-deserved burst of applause.

But this level was not sustained. Since the court characters had not been established earlier on, they could not hold interest when they reappeared, and the direction again lost its grip. Although much emphasis appeared to be given to heavenly guidance by characters looking hopefully upwards, the feebly tedious apparitions scene was given in full – only to be robbed of its climax: instead of descending, Jupiter mumbled incoherently over the tannoy, while a crystal ball, shimmering cloth and floating sunbeams had to do inadequate duty for the eagle. The production's imbalance meant that the reunion of husband and wife had less impact than that of brothers and sister, which could build on the strength of the Welsh scenes; but those scenes are after all only half the play; and that the same company which had finally proved *Pericles* stage-worthy should rob *Cymbeline* of much of its customary impact was a piece of bitter irony worthy of Jupiter himself.

V

If Ronald Eyre's straightforward *Othello* outwardly resembled the *Cymbeline* in that it was played on a bare, uncluttered stage without much sense of place or atmosphere, there the resemblance ended, since this time the director and a strong cast presented a properly thought-out view of the play, based firmly on the interdependence of Othello and Iago. As Mr Eyre put it in an interview for the RSC newspaper, it is 'significant that the Venetians always had a mercenary army... where a man like Othello, of unsettled background,... could find a sort of security... – then you find out who your friend is; he's the fellow who doesn't leave you when you are wounded'. This military society wore grey uniforms, contrasting with the civilians; Cassio was brisk and aloof, carrying his staff of office under his arm like a swagger-stick – after his fall it passed to Iago; Othello in Cyprus wore a white version of the sober Jacobean style used for the whole production, reverting to his military grey to 'execute' Desdemona. Large pieces of furniture hinted at locale or function: desks, map-cupboards, a huge mirror for the Willow scene, the bed. There was no excess business: the drinking scene was typical of the approach, tightly controlled and not elaborated a moment longer than was necessary for Iago to achieve his ends.

From his first appearance, Donald Sinden's Othello showed a laughing confidence: the authority of 'Keep up your bright swords' even turned into mocking irony at 'for the dew will rust them'. The narration to the Senate had maximum impact, delivered dead centre stage, with a real relish for the language. The first hint of another, more volcanic Othello came at the start of the crucial III, iii, in the harsh emphasis he gave to 'when I love thee not/ Chaos is come again.' He and Iago were sitting at separate desks, dealing with military documents; Iago's technique was to drop his insinuations and let long silences follow Othello's replies before his next pin-prick, what Othello calls 'these stops of thine'; then, just when Othello thought that the discussion was closed ('Certain, men should be what they seem'), Iago allowed an apparently concluding silence before adding, 'Why then, I think Cassio's an

honest man'. Othello threw down his pen and rose in exasperation: 'Nay, yet there's more in this.' The trap sprung, Iago continued his double technique of switching from pin-pricks to greater overtness: 'O, beware, my lord, of jealousy.' Othello varied with him; he laughed his way into 'Why, why is this?' and his earlier confidence returned for that characteristic statement,

> I'll see before I doubt; when I doubt, prove;
> And, on the proof, there is no more but this—
> Away at once with love or jealousy!

But then of course Iago comes out into the open with his crucial suggestion that he knows Venetian infidelity as Othello doesn't: Mr Sinden's 'Dost thou say so?' made it clear that such a thought had never occurred to him; but once the poison is injected, there is no getting rid of it: 'not much mov'd' told its own tale; and when Othello said 'Set on thy wife to observe', shamefacedly but extremely definitely, he had taken the decisive step into Iago's sphere and so into his power.

As in the Aldwych revival of the previous RSC *Othello*, the interval came halfway through III, iii, just before Emilia picks up the handkerchief. This might seem a dangerous idea, potentially disrupting the play's inexorable progress to disaster, but in practice it works: it makes the temptation more plausible because it seems to happen less quickly than if the scene is played unbroken, and so helps to avoid irrelevant novelistic questions about the speed of Othello's collapse. In any case the hints have already done their insidious damage by the time Othello leaves with Desdemona, and when he reappeared after the interval, 'Farewell the tranquil mind' seemed the logical consequence of what had happened before it. Othello raised his hands to 'yond marble heaven' to make his 'sacred vow'; Iago clasped his left hand, and they held this position, locked together, until the end of the scene, image of Mr Eyre's view of the two of them as 'almost symbiotic'.

Bob Peck traced Iago's development from the careful, hopeful laying of plots to a relishing exploitation of the situation, as his confidence grew in response to the volcanic reaction he aroused in Othello. It was as if he realised he could achieve even more than he had hoped at first; and with this came a brutish obscenity, both in him and in Othello. It began with 'Lie ...with her, on her', which directly caused Othello's prolonged and convincing epileptic fit; it was reinforced by the cutting edge of Iago's 'strangle her in her bed'; and it reached a climax when Othello gave Desdemona a brutally shattering blow with the scroll he had been reading. 'Cassio shall have my place', shouted after her as she left, was packed with double meaning.

The brutishness of the 'brothel' scene was emphasised when Othello obsessively searched a washing-basket full of sheets for some sign or smell of Cassio (a fleetingly dangerous whiff of Master Ford!), and he threw her down on to the sheets and tore at her skirts as if she were some particularly 'impudent strumpet'; but Mr Sinden also registered the survival of Othello's former feelings in the midst of his violence, and this double feeling persisted into the final scene: on the one hand, Othello was unshakably certain of his course – 'she MUST die'; but once he had killed her, he seemed to lose all sense of direction ('What's best to do?') as he rather helplessly straightened out and arranged the body, adding pathos to 'My wife! What wife? I have no wife.'

Some criticised this production as rather old-fashioned in concept and execution; but if so, it was also full of old-fashioned virtues, like trusting the text and giving it full, audible value, and (especially) recognising the need to support a strong central partnership with major actors in lesser but important roles, notably John McEnery (a richly detailed Roderigo, ever responsive to Iago), James Laurenson (who made Cassio a potential governor without underplaying any of his weaknesses), and the ever-reliable Jeffery Dench (who doubled an unforgiving Brabantio with an eloquently authoritative Lodovico, thus adding valuable weight both to the beginning and end of the play).

VI

Barry Kyle's *Julius Caesar* took place on an octagonal platform surrounded by low barriers and two massive banks of lamps, a combination of sports stadium (with Antony's race actually beginning on stage), bull-ring (especially at the assassination) and boxing-ring: after the mob literally broke down the barriers at the end of the forum scene, the wooden floor was removed to become a sand-pit for the battles, which included all-in wrestling and gladiatorial combat. The idea seemed to be that once the strong central authority of Caesar was removed, the puny, trivial survivors reduced political issues to the level of games; but this impression was given more clearly by Christopher Morley's evocative set than by the performances, where it was hard to tell (especially with an understudy as Cassius) how much was deliberate interpretation, how much accidents of casting.

While John Woodvine's Caesar was outstanding and not especially tyrannical ('this ear is deaf' was genially self-mocking), Ben Kingsley's Brutus was completely removed in manner and speech from anything remotely resembling any familiar concept of nobility: Ligarius's resolve 'to do I know not what; but it sufficeth/ That Brutus leads me on' was received with nervous deprecation, as a gigantic thunderclap offstage seemed to contrast with the puny humanity of Brutus. The trouble is that this actor is now such a prisoner to quirky, eccentric vocal mannerisms (ranting lines syllable by syllable, wrenching and distorting individual words – anything rather than speaking clearly and directly) that it is impossible to tell what the *character* is thinking and feeling.

I *thought* that his first soliloquy was suggesting that it is dangerous to kill a man for what he 'may' do; and that his disastrous military decisions before Philippi were partly a kind of death-wish in response to Portia's death (Messala later gave great emphasis to the fact that 'error' is 'melancholy's child'). But I couldn't really be sure.

Since Brutus's vocal mannerisms had spread to the understudy Cassius and to Casca, the director seemed deliberately to be cutting the noble Romans down to size; but whereas it is one thing to investigate what the 'nobility' of these Romans amounts to in practice, it is quite another to under- (or mis-) cast to the point where Antony could snarl through the part without either intelligence or guile so that it seemed inconceivable that the mob should take any notice of him at all: 'I am no orator' should sound like cunning rhetoric, not a statement of sober truth. Where the incongruity between what is said and how it is said is so great, 'interpretation' becomes irrelevant, since the actual events of the play fail to carry conviction.

VII

On another level of competence and achievement altogether (emphasising the sheer inconsistency of the current RSC) was Peter Brook's 1978 *Antony and Cleopatra*, revived at the Aldwych, though this account is of the Stratford version. Characteristically Mr Brook refused to accept traditional views of either the play itself or the main characters. As he put it in an interview in *The Times* after the play had opened: 'One of my aims...was to correct a few misunderstandings, and the chief of these is that it is a spectacular play....What Shakespeare wrote consists of 45 or so short scenes of intimate behaviour. There is no pageantry. Everything concerns personal relationships.... The Empire may be tottering but he keeps it out of sight.'[1] So the stage became an intimate area enclosed by a semi-circle of glass panels providing a number of exits to the outside world; at a stroke Sally Jacobs had solved the problem of switching rapidly from one part of the Empire to another. The sea battle was conveyed merely by silhouetting the watching Enobarbus on the far side of the glass; during the later battles the soldiers threw clots of blood on to the outside of the glass panels, which remained thus disfigured until the end; for the monument, a square red curtain was lowered behind Cleopatra, and then lowered further to become the floor of the monument: as there were no levels, the dying Antony was simply dragged to her along the floor, wrapped in her women's scarves. Perhaps this lost the point of *hauling him up* to the monument, surely a *deliberately* cumbersome proceeding, like the messy, deliberately unheroic suicide before it.

On the one hand, this neat avoidance of the awkward was surprising, since Mr Brook had so fully emphasised the unheroic aspect of the play until then; but on the other hand, this carefully, formally controlled mime fitted in with a production whose tone and style were primarily analytic, clear but rather chilly, like that glass set. It is of course true that the play itself is very analytic, and that, as Emrys Jones finely puts it, in the 'ceaseless clash of views, the descriptions and counter-descriptions, the conflicting analyses', 'everyone judges everyone else, and is himself judged'.[2] But this isn't quite the same thing as asking the actors to stand outside the characters and demonstrate (expose?) them from there.

Take, for instance, the way that Alan Howard's Antony reacted to Fulvia's death. 'There's a great spirit gone' was spoken with reverberant, hollow irony, one caustic eye on the audience, as if to suggest how little Antony *really* meant by the tribute 'What our contempts doth often hurl from us/We wish it ours again.'

[1] *The Times*, 18 October 1978.
[2] *Antony and Cleopatra*, New Penguin Shakespeare (1977), pp. 11–12.

'She's good, being *gone*' was played as a piece of crude truth, and robbed of its bitter-sweet ambiguity, so that Antony lost even a vestige of genuine human regret. The clipped economy of

> Fulvia is dead.
> Sir?
> Fulvia is dead.
> Fulvia?
> Dead

was played with neat comic timing and more hollow over-statement from Mr Howard, followed by an outburst of wild embraces and laughter, which quite spoilt the wry implication of Enobarbus's 'Why, sir, give the gods a thankful sacrifice.' Otherwise Patrick Stewart was an impeccably detailed, warmly sympathetic Enobarbus, by far the fullest, most human character on stage. In comparison, although Mr Howard had the scale and vocal range for Antony, he seemed to be demonstrating rather than embodying the character. Glenda Jackson, too, gave a coolly accurate, objective demonstration of Cleopatra's infinite variety, one mood meticulously established before giving place to the next. Her curt, astringent delivery was especially effective in clipped passages like

> See where he is, who's with him, what he does.
> I did not send you. If you find him sad,
> Say I am dancing; if in mirth, report
> That I am sudden sick. Quick, and return

or in those spare lines which are compressed to the point of secrecy:

> Then, Antony – but now. Well, on.

Her performance certainly emphasised Mr Brook's point that Shakespeare 'makes her speak in the most direct way'.

But in the last act, Mr Brook took Cleopatra on to 'a higher level of existence', as he put it: 'The death of Antony transforms Cleopatra', and from capricious variety 'she becomes simpler and simpler'. The process began with the clown, played as a red-nosed comedian by Richard Griffiths, the RSC's superb Bottom, Trinculo and Pompey. Tentatively approaching Cleopatra's glass-bound sanctuary, he removed his slippers, which he then wore on his hands; he even conjured the asps out of the air rather than from the basket, which proved to be empty; and he responded to her various 'farewells' by leaving through one exit in the glass only to reappear at another to add a further afterthought. This treatment was perhaps the ultimate example of Mr Brook's keeping the play down-to-earth; and it was the one which most fully vindicated his approach. It was a complete success, not only because it was so expertly played, but because of the effect it had on Cleopatra. Perhaps paradoxically, she seemed to establish a relationship with him as she hadn't with anyone else, including Antony; she seemed genuinely interested in what he had to say. And far from imperilling the death scene, playing up the humour intensified it by contrast: Miss Jackson went on to achieve a stunning transformation-in-death, as Mr Brook required, by becoming 'simpler and simpler'. Not for the first time in a production of this play, the last fifteen minutes or so existed on a higher, more moving, level than anything before them; what was unusual this time was Mr Brook's deliberately cool handling of the first four acts so as to make the play's change of direction for Cleopatra's transformation absolutely clear.

VIII

More interesting than any of these productions except *Pericles* was the National Theatre's *As You Like It*. We hear a great deal about the simplicity and directness of the Elizabethan theatre, but much less about another Elizabethan style, a formal, mannered elaboration, which John Dexter seized upon in an interpretation which was searching, weighty, and, often, literal: Orlando complains that he is kept 'rustically at home' among Oliver's 'hinds';

so the play began with homespun servants, including an unkempt Orlando, laboriously gathering up bundles of hay from the rough slatted boards which formed Hayden Griffin's set. In total contrast, Oliver was a strutting Elizabethan gallant dressed in stiffly elaborate court splendour, complete with starched ruff and single ear-ring; and Rosalind and (especially) Celia were almost embodiments of Elizabeth I with their jewelled brocades and curled court wigs. Some reviewers found Peter J. Hall's costumes mere ostentatious display and even a throw-back to old-fashioned production styles, thereby completely missing the point, that under Frederick's regime people were trapped within an unnatural, restricting formality: when Orlando named his father, the puppet court froze into attitudes of obsequious horror. Such formality was an appropriate framework for the rather formal, even stilted, artifice of Rosalind and Celia's discussion about Fortune and Nature as they paced gravely backwards and forwards, as if this was all the movement their imprisoning dresses and (especially) constricting ruffs allowed them.

Mr Dexter's concern seemed less to make the dialogue easily or superficially 'effective' than to explore and account for every detail of the text. There was, for instance, an interesting interpretation of one of the textual cruces: in his line 'One that old Frederick, your father, loves' Touchstone stressed 'old' as if *both* Dukes were called Frederick, but distinguished by their ages (the Banished Duke and his court were much older than Frederick and his), so that Rosalind (as in the Folio, and not Celia) could reply, 'My father's love is enough to honour him. Enough, speak no more of him; you'll be whipt for taxation one of these days.' For Rosalind to warn Touchstone that he might be whipped for mentioning *her* father in this particular court was effective – at the expense of a forced interpretation of 'old Frederick'. The deliberate, slow, weighty delivery risked monotony, but also allowed due emphasis to passages like Adam's

> He that doth the ravens feed,
> Yea, providently caters for the sparrow,
> Be comfort to my age,

which are usually scurried past in the haste to get to Arden. And this unusually serious first half ended with Oliver and Duke Frederick stopped in their tracks by Amiens's 'Come hither, come hither, come hither' sounding softly and mysteriously from offstage, foreshadowing not only Oliver's but also Duke Frederick's ultimate conversion by the values of Arden.

Those values were also seriously and thoughtfully presented, by replacing the court ritual with the age-old festivals and rites of the countryside. After the interval, a slender tree with white blossoms rose up centre stage between the timbered slats, and later expanded into an umbrella of cascading leaves, the focus for country rituals, garlanded with flowers, hung with eggs, and in the finale becoming a Maypole. The quartet of lovers formally touched hands against this tree as they made their tryst, and such formality helped the audience to accept the 'And so am I for Phebe...Ganymede...Rosalind' repetitions which usually nowadays provoke mocking laughter – though the quietly sympathetic, unsatirical treatment of Silvius also helped a great deal here too.

William was no farcical simpleton but a local country boy who had killed the deer, who was clearly employed both by the Duke as a page (and so sang 'It was a lover and his lass') and by Rosalind to play Hymen, and who was at the heart of the full-scale country rites upon which Mr Dexter based the final scenes. As in animal sacrifices, the innards of the slaughtered deer of IV, ii, formalised as a red garland, were entwined in the branches of the sacred tree, and the victorious William was smeared on his chest and back with the deer's blood and crowned with its antlers, as other actors gathered round him wearing beautifully expressive deer masks. In the finale, the stage was completely surrounded by these 'deer', with William as an antlered Hymen, naked except for fronds of leaves – a rustic god with whom Rosalind had joined forces to provide the 'rites' for her formal wedding.

Sara Kestelman's Rosalind was exceptionally persuasive in her androgynous eroticism: with her dark curls, single ear-ring, and stylish doublet, she was the very image of Hilliard's Unknown Youth Among Roses, leaning against that tree among those white flowers and fixing her dark, piercing eyes upon Orlando as she filled 'I will satisfy you if ever I satisfied man' with fierce, urgent desire. Simon Callow's Orlando shared the same dark curls, but otherwise contrasted with her sophistication, catching up on the education which Oliver had denied him by constant reading, where he no

doubt picked up the conceits for his love poems. Miss Kestelman's commanding Rosalind delivered her tart wit with formal deliberation rather than revealing the varied undertones, such as tenderness, which that wit can suggest; and in so doing she exactly matched the strengths and limitations of Mr Dexter's approach.

This production did not court easy popularity, but I found it compulsive and absorbing, thoroughly thought through, and persuasively communicated, with Marjorie Yates's Celia and Dermot Crowley's incisive Oliver only the most striking of an almost uniformly strong ensemble, in which almost everyone from Rosalind down to William/Hymen contributed fully towards realising Mr Dexter's probing interpretation. In achievement and sureness of purpose, it contrasted sharply with the main Stratford season.

© ROGER WARREN 1980

THE YEAR'S CONTRIBUTIONS TO SHAKESPEARIAN STUDY

1. CRITICAL STUDIES

reviewed by HARRIETT HAWKINS

I. *Trends in Recent Criticism*

There is nothing like enough space here to do justice to the best – or the worst – critical studies of Shakespeare available for review this year. The first part of this survey concentrates on publications which seem to indicate the way that things are going nowadays, while discussions of specific genres, texts, and topics will be cited later on.

Of obvious importance is a collection of some of the best papers presented to the first Congress of the International Shakespeare Association.[1] Their titles will indicate the range of essays by (among others) Alistair Cooke ('Shakespeare in America'); Joel Hurstfield ('The Search for the Good Society in Shakespeare's Day and Our Own'); Helen Gardner ('Tragic Mysteries'); Alvin Kernan ('Shakespeare and the Abstraction of History'); L. C. Knights ('Shakespeare: The Man in the Work – Reflections on a Reflection'); T. J. B. Spencer ('When Homer Nods: Shakespeare's Artistic Lapses'); Robert Speaight ('Truth and Relevance in Shakespeare Production'); Michael Goldman ('Acting Values and Shakespearian Meaning'); J. L. Styan ('Sight and Space: The Perception of Shakespeare on Stage and Screen'); and Inga-Stina Ewbank ('Shakespeare's Portrayal of Women: A 1970s View'). There are also short reports from the seminars on Structuralist, Marxist and Christian approaches, on stage history, on bibliography, on the text, on Shakespeare's audience, his con-

temporaries, his language, his sources, and on the validity of certain modern critical assumptions. This volume, then, is exceptionally helpful as an abstract and brief chronicle of the central concerns in Shakespeare studies at the present time.

In the first Plenary Lecture delivered at the Congress, Alistair Cooke hailed Shakespeare as 'king of the foxes'. Cooke was, of course, citing the famous distinction between two kinds of genius which Isaiah Berlin derived from an observation of Archilochus – 'The fox knows many things, but the hedgehog knows one big thing.' 'Taken figuratively', Berlin concluded, this proverb marks 'one of the deepest differences which divide writers and thinkers and, it may be, human beings in general.' So far as artists of the first rank are concerned, Berlin's distinction in kind does not imply a judgment of merit. Cooke finds it specially valuable because it does not praise Shakespeare at the expense of Dostoevski: it simply says, 'Here are two types of genius, two fundamentally distinct, if not opposed, views of life'.[2]

Given the nature of the subject there is, however, no question which category the best recent critics of Shakespeare belong in. Without exception, the most interesting books and essays are by writers who know 'many things'.

[1] *Shakespeare: Pattern of Excelling Nature*, ed. David Bevington and J. L. Halio (University of Delaware Press and Associated University Presses, 1978). Hereafter cited as *Pattern of Excelling Nature*.

[2] See Cooke, 'Shakespeare in America', *ibid.*, pp. 23–5.

Drawing on any kind of experience or information deemed appropriate – from stage history to historical statistics – they have available a wide choice of vantage points from whence to observe the behaviour of the widest-ranging, wisest fox of all. Not one is an ideological 'hedgehog'. This may be inevitable. For no matter how big it may be, the 'one big thing' known to critics who adhere to a single methodology cannot but prove irrelevant whenever the fox, Shakespeare, leaves the terrain visible through their sets of fixed binoculars to go off investigating some altogether different part of the forest.

At the beginning of his collection of essays on Shakespeare and Elizabethan drama, G. K. Hunter apologizes for its Protean range,[1] but since the tutelary deity of Elizabethan drama appears to have been Proteus himself, Hunter's own shifts in subject and frames of reference are more than justified by his results. His discussions of 'Othello and Colour Prejudice', 'The Heroism of Hamlet', 'Shakespeare's Last Tragic Heroes', 'A. C. Bradley's *Shakespearean Tragedy*', 'T. S. Eliot and the Creation of a Symbolist Shakespeare', '*Henry IV* and the Elizabethan Two-part Play', and 'Shakespeare's Earliest Tragedies' (to say nothing of the insights in his essays on other dramatists) combine to create a learned, lively, re-readable book. Likewise, Kenneth Muir's collection of lectures and essays written over a number of years is far richer than any single-topic study could possibly be.[2] Reading over his essay on 'Shakespeare and the Tragic Pattern' I was aghast to realize for how many years I have been parroting its insights without acknowledgment. '*Timon of Athens* and the Cash-Nexus' reverses the usual procedures whereby Shakespeare is pronounced a Marxist, and demonstrates that Marx was a card-carrying Shakespearian. Theatrical history illuminates 'The Conclusion of *The Winter's Tale*', even as playwrights and poets of different kinds are summoned as witnesses to 'The Singularity of Shakespeare'. There is a fascinating essay on 'The Uncomic Pun', and an objective analysis of 'Some Freudian Interpretations of Shakespeare', whilst generalizations about 'The Pursuit of Relevance', and 'Poetry as a Criticism of Life' point to the mystery of Shakespeare's art and its multifarious relationships to human experience:

> [The major characters] carry a penumbra of uncertainty.... As Morgann pointed out, the greatest dramatists introduce an apparent incongruity of character, and Shakespeare was able to give life to his characters, partly because he lived in them, and partly because 'his mimic creation agrees in general so perfectly with that of nature'. (p. 211)

> The temptation to enrol Shakespeare in one's own party is almost irresistible. It is only possible to do this, without falling into manifest absurdity, by ignoring much of the evidence.... His mind, as Keats said of his own, was a thoroughfare for all thoughts – not a select party. (p. 57)

Far from advocating any one 'approach' to Shakespeare's art, the best scholars share a profound scepticism concerning the validity of critical endeavours to pluck out the heart of his mystery. Concluding her discussion of Shakespeare's 'Tragic Mysteries' in words that should be engraved over the entrance to every English department, Helen Gardner cites Lafeu's warning to 'philosophical persons' who 'make modern and familiar, things supernatural and causeless', lest we 'make trifles of terrors, ensconcing ourselves into seeming knowledge when we should submit ourselves to an unknown fear'. 'Of all great writers', she observes, 'Shakespeare has the greatest power to show us how men act and suffer and to convince us of the truth of what we hear and

---

[1] G. K. Hunter, *Dramatic Identities and Cultural Tradition: Studies in Shakespeare and his Contemporaries* (Liverpool University Press, 1978).

[2] Kenneth Muir, *The Singularity of Shakespeare and Other Essays* (Liverpool University Press, 1977).

see, but to the question "why" his tragedies return no clear answer.'[1] Likewise, Madeleine Doran acknowledges that the questions raised in her fine study of the language in Shakespeare's tragedies 'probably have no certain answers. If they do, I do not know them.'[2]

This season of professional discontent (see J. A. Bryant, Jr, 'Shakespeare, the Lean Years')[3] has proved an opportune time for the opening up of questions, for a critical stock-taking, for a frank account of the liabilities, as well as the assets, accrued in scholarly discussions of Shakespeare over the past decades. In the first Occasional Lecture delivered to the International Shakespeare Association in 1978, Maynard Mack begins a (characteristically) seminal paper about the social and historical context of Shakespeare's plays with a review of what is past, and passing, and to come in Shakespeare studies. 'During a bare half-century', he observes, we have seen the 'School of Character Analysis' ousted by the 'School of Imagery and New Criticism' and both of these 'giving ground steadily to what I will call the School of Performance'. Meantime, 'ever more visible in the wings, though perhaps not yet quite ready to seize centre-stage, the School of Psychoanalysis, with Tarquin's ravishing strides, comes on apace'. We do, he concludes, 'learn something from each vogue as it passes', if only 'that it is not the direct "hot line" to the white radiance of eternity that it claims to be, but only a more or less cloudy prism that, if properly angled, may refract some shadow of it'.[4]

It is, by the way, dismaying to notice the paucity of references to Professor Mack's earlier work in recent indexes to *Shakespeare Survey*. One reason why insights of such validity often go unacknowledged is, I believe, that they are unconsciously appropriated by the reader. For much of the very best criticism so deepens, confirms, and enriches a natural response to the plays that it *seems* like an articulation of one's own best thoughts which strikes with the force, not of revelation, but of remembrance. Another reason why the best criticism frequently goes unacknowledged is that it tends to be characterized by common sense and, therefore, is essentially at odds with those critical vogues which, by their super-subtle nature, will have nothing to do with anything so 'common' as that.

As Scott Fitzgerald observed, 'the cleverly expressed opposite of any generally accepted idea is worth a fortune to somebody', and many a critical fortune has been amassed through asserting that nothing in Shakespeare's plays is what, for nigh on four centuries, most folks have naively believed it to be. In a devastating criticism of ironic, thematic, occasionalist, pseudo-historical, and Fluellenist 'readings' of Elizabethan plays, Richard Levin unearths whole treasure troves of nonsense recently stashed away in scholarly publications.[5] Some of them have already begun to tarnish, others to fade, but one can only be grateful to Professor Levin for accelerating the natural processes of decomposition by exposing their speciousness to the sunshine of sense. Will anyone who has read his book want to write yet another article entitled 'A New Reading of X' (name your play) or 'Hitherto Undiscovered Ironies in Y' or 'Z and the Ideas of the Time'? Will anyone again feel obliged to insist, with such misplaced (if not altogether spurious) indignation, that Juliet's

love for Romeo is rooted in passion.... She hungers ...violently for Romeo's body (and in the stridency of her imagination comes very close to panting like

[1] See *Pattern of Excelling Nature*, p. 94.
[2] Madeleine Doran, *Shakespeare's Dramatic Language* (University of Wisconsin Press, 1976), p. 32.
[3] *The Sewanee Review*, LXXXVI (1978), 405–14.
[4] Maynard Mack, *Rescuing Shakespeare* (Oxford University Press, 1979).
[5] Richard Levin, *New Readings vs. Old Plays: Recent Trends in the Reinterpretation of English Renaissance Drama* (University of Chicago Press, 1979).

an animal)....The ugliness which to an Elizabethan audience would have been implicit in the rawness of her sexual hunger is the ugliness which arises from the perversion of her natural capacity to love.

or that

Sadly enough, most spectators have also taken at face value...the play's tragic sentimentality....They fail to see that as a hero Romeo lies midway between the surrealist horror of the homicidal Richard III, and the bathos of Pyramus....Like Richard, also, Romeo is a catalyst of disaster, and something close to a mass murderer.

and that

Hamlet is a soul lost in damnable error...a serpent-like scourge...a profane fool.... At the play's ending he becomes himself the minister, and in that sense a fellow celebrant with Claudius in a Black Mass.

(pp. 80–1)

Were it not for his lethally serious (yet always witty) attack on the methodological assumptions that lie behind such preposterous statements, one could read the quotations in Levin's book for laughs. Even so, they would instruct – by negative example. The three different critics quoted above are representative of dozens quoted by Levin in that they sound exactly alike. And who, after reading only these three, would wish to sound like that? Not only do Levin's targets sound alike, their formulaic diatribes make the characters discussed all sound alike. Worse still, the clichés they insist are the messages to be derived from them end up making the various plays sound just alike:

The message...brought to us by the playwright is, then...that man's destiny is not wholly in his own hands.

The lesson taught by the play is that men are not the masters of their own fates.... What we intend, and what we actually accomplish, are often very different.

Both plays preach a moral commonplace: the natural order provided by a benevolent Providence cannot be violated with impunity. (p. 58)

Want to know which plays these critics are talking about? They are: *Antony and Cleopatra*, *Julius Caesar*, *Volpone*, and *The Alchemist*.

One can disagree with some of Levin's strictures. It is arguable that in certain plays, as in his masques, Ben Jonson does deal, dramatically, in concepts or themes, and that certain 'thematic' discussions of Elizabethan plays (like the essays on Jonson by E. B. Partridge and Ian Donaldson) genuinely illuminate them. Levin's methodological objections to the various formulas demand, however, to be answered. The 'burden of proof' *should* rest 'upon those who reject the most obvious and most reasonable' hypothesis in interpreting a given play, and 'who ask us to substitute for it...special assumptions which deny that a play can be what it appears to be'. Thus the critic advocating a 'new reading' would have to confront the 'old reading' fairly and squarely, and 'show that it is less probable than his own'. 'This does not mean, of course, that an informed and sensitive spectator will not see more in the play than a groundling... but we would still expect these further insights to represent a refinement or enrichment of the common experience of the play – not something quite different from that experience and certainly not its opposite' (pp. 203–4). Amen.

Since Levin is attacking specific methodologies, not specific critics, he does not name his targets. Moreover, the anonymity afforded to the assertions quoted demonstrates, as nothing else could, the formulaic nature, predictability of argument, and overblown rhetoric characteristic of the 'New Readings' he challenges. Still, one occasionally longs to know who wrote what. Levin, of course, gives chapter-and-verse references to the work of critics whose views he considers valid, but readers who wish to consult (whether with scorn or approval) the sources of specific statements criticized here will not find them without checking out scores of the books and articles listed at the end. Yet those arguments were not *published* anonymously. And why shouldn't the principle of personal accountability apply in our profession, as in others?

If Maynard Mack is correct in prophesying that the School of Psychoanalysis, 'with Tarquin's ravishing strides', is moving towards the centre of Shakespeare studies, then Levin had better be summoned to the rescue, posthaste, with a criticism of that methodology. So far as I am concerned, an 'Astrological Approach' would give a less reductive account of the passions which agitate, adorn, or disgrace human nature in Shakespeare's plays than the Freudian interpretations of *Coriolanus* quoted below. Resolutely making 'trifles of terrors', effortlessly explaining why human beings act and suffer as they do, denying any 'tragic mysteries' to his plays, any 'penumbra of uncertainty' to his characterization, this is, by all odds, the most facile approach to Shakespeare yet devised. There could be no easier way of 'ensconcing ourselves in seeming knowledge' than by publishing psychoanalytical articles about his works. To write one, you need only a handful of Freudian terms, any of which can, conveniently, be equated with, or 'transformed' into any of the others. Thus,

It is characteristic of Coriolanus's transformation of hunger into phallic aggression that the feared castration is imagined predominantly in oral terms: to be castrated here *is* to be a mouth.[1]   (p. 114)

You will, of course, have to repress any inclination to laugh out loud when citing the views of other psychoanalytic critics:

Wilson suggests that Corioli represents defloration; specifically, that it expresses the equation of coitus with damaging assault and the resultant dread of retaliatory castration.   (p. 122)

Otherwise, it might prove difficult to maintain due solemnity when you propound your own theories:

[His fear of castration] may help to account for the enthusiasm with which [Coriolanus] characterizes Valeria, in strikingly phallic terms, as the icicle on Dian's temple...the phallic woman may ultimately be less frightening to him than the woman who demonstrates the possibility of castration by her lack of a penis.   (p. 123)

You need not, *in any sense*, concern yourself with the literal meaning of Shakespeare's texts. For just as a Freudian interpretation of it is deemed, in Freudian circles, to be of more validity and significance than the dream which occasioned it, any psychoanalytic interpretations of them (however far-fetched or downright looney they might seem) are regarded as ultimate in authority. Thus, whatever any psychoanalytic critic says is so, 'is' so:

Otto Fenichel discusses the derivation of acting from exhibitionism: like all such derivatives, it is ultimately designed to protect against the fear of castration.   (p. 123)

As Levin's book demonstrated, critical 'approaches' that began, rather modestly, as incentives to thought, or as criteria for analysis only tentatively proposed, have a tendency to become substitutes for thought, criteria of merit. This is certainly true of the tenets of psychoanalysis as they are applied to *Coriolanus*. Yet those tenets are valid only within the closed circle of psychoanalysis itself. Their proponents thus seem like so many hedgehogs, showing off their one trick in the safety of their suburban garden – miles afield from the fox. For even if we assume (for the purposes of argument) the absolute validity of Freudian theory, and also assume that the assertions quoted above are statements of fact, some still small voice would yet be obliged to raise the overwhelming question, 'What of it?', since not one of those assertions has anything to do

---

[1] Quotations are from the text and footnotes to '"Anger's My Meat": Feeding, Dependency, and Aggression in *Coriolanus*', by Janet Adelman, in *Pattern of Excelling Nature*, pp. 108–24.

with the actual deeds of men and women as they are portrayed, by Shakespeare, in *Coriolanus*. Or in any other play.

Psychoanalytic criticism of his comedies, likewise, results in the infantilization of Shakespeare. Basing an interpretation of *Much Ado About Nothing* on the insights of Melanie Klein and other post-Freudian analysts, Simon Stuart concludes that Beatrice and Benedick, in renouncing their 'superiority to the rest of Adam's kindred' make 'just those renunciations which originate in the infant relinquishing the breast...and which, when successfully renounced, provide substitutes and sublimations which enrich the personality'. Moreover, 'in following the destinies' of these characters, 'we share also in Shakespeare's triumph over his own anxiety and depression'.[1] But it is hard to see why Stuart's conclusions about them have any more portentous (or less puerile) relevance to Beatrice and Benedick than to, say, Berowne, Richard II, King Lear, or any other characters who renounce their superiority to others. Nor is it clear why the 'remaking' of Shakespeare's 'own moral and artistic self-hood' should manifest itself in *Much Ado About Nothing* more than in any other play. His own titles happily call attention to the fundamental incongruity of those interpretations which, by investing them with some over-the-counter profundity, have resulted in what Levin calls the 'decomicalization' of Shakespeare's merriest plays.

The fact that no system of psychoanalysis, no outside body of theory, no one approach, comes anywhere close to explaining the account of our strange estate left us by our recording angel should be cause for celebration, not despair. For in its manifest variety, Shakespeare's work remains our own best weapon, shield, defense, witness, evidence, proof *against* those ideological and critical malignancies that every age is heir to.

II. *Specific Problems: Genres, Topics, Books, Journals, Monographs*

It is often said that criticism of reigning methodologies threatens to put us 'out of business'. But of course the opposite is true. As the long history of Shakespeare criticism demonstrates, there can be no action without reaction. Moreover, since Shakespeare is forever confronting the best possible case for something with the best possible arguments against it (and vice-versa), our individual responses are bound to shift, conflict, change. Thus, quite a number of one-sided interpretations that, in past decades, have oversimplified the plays are now being challenged, sometimes by counter-arguments that tend to overcomplicate them. How to avoid doing either is now – as it always has been and probably always will be – the most difficult problem that a critic of Shakespeare has to face.

Eleanor Prosser's rigidly orthodox view of Shakespeare's revengers[2] is under direct, as well as indirect, attack from several quarters. Levin makes telling arguments against it; and, in 'Hamlet: Revenge and the Critical Mirror',[3] Michael Cameron Andrews concludes that, like Macduff, Hamlet 'is no impersonal minister, but what he is doing is just'. In his discussion of 'Rape and Revenge in *Titus Andronicus*',[4] David Willbern argues that 'In the primitive logic of the unconscious, and in the primary strategies of the revenge play, *lex talionis* is the inexorable rule', while Karl P. Wentersdorf shows how, 'in an eminently natural and dramatically satisfying manner', the player episodes show Hamlet moving toward the

---

[1] Simon Stuart, *New Phoenix Wings: Reparation in Literature* (Routledge & Kegan Paul, 1979), p. 167.

[2] *Hamlet and Revenge* (Stanford University Press, 1967).

[3] *English Literary Renaissance*, VIII (1978), 9–23.

[4] *English Literary Renaissance*, VIII (1978), 159–82.

certainty that the spirit he saw on the parapet is 'an honest ghost'.[1]

Several articles focus on the way Shakespeare forces us to see both sides of a case. Discussing 'Ceremony and Civilization in Shakespeare',[2] John P. Sisk challenges both an 'anticeremonial' view of the plays – whereby ceremony and honesty are incompatible – and the view which accepts as absolute Elizabethan celebrations of ceremony itself. In a fascinating probing essay on 'The Murder of Falstaff, David Jones and "The Disciplines of War"', John Barnard explains how his own account of the problems in *Henry V* was altered by a re-reading of *In Parenthesis*.[3] Discussing 'The Structure of Exchange in *Measure for Measure*', Jan Kott gives an illuminating, provocative, account of the dramatic problems posed by its parallels and oppositions,[4] and in a superb discussion of the contradictory responses elicited by *Timon of Athens*, Leslie W. Brill points to the various contradictions that seem built into that text.[5] As these articles demonstrate, there can be no 'definitive' reading (any more than a definitive production) of any given play. Yet this does not mean that there are no limits to the spectrum of interpretation. Thus Bernard Beckerman reminds us that 'Feeling at liberty to interpret a role or scene in unlimited ways is not truly being free imaginatively. It is far more thrilling and emancipating to discover the limits within which a given work allows legitimate interpretation.'[6]

Shakespeare's vision of the historical process is the subject of continuing debate. In 'Shakespeare's Histories and The New Bardolaters', Robert P. Merrix gives a lively account of the major points of contention.[7] Discussing 'Shakespeare and History', L. C. Knights concludes that Shakespeare is 'innocent of theory: he does not so much impose as observe and explore'.[8] In *The Lost Garden*, a deeply-felt and moving book about the histories and Roman plays,[9] John Wilders explicitly chal-

lenges orthodox interpretations of Shakespeare's historiography:

The causes of national unity or division, of prosperity or decline are, in Shakespeare's view, to be found not, as some of the fifteenth-century chroniclers had believed, in the providential power of God...but in the temperaments of national leaders and in their reactions towards one another. (p. 2)

As Bacon put it, history 'propoundeth the success and issues of actions, not so agreeable to the merits of vertue and vice'. Virtue is very seldom rewarded in the world of Lancastrian and Yorkist England, and the man who survives the contest of Roman politics is Octavius Caesar, a man not morally impeccable.(p. 9)

By the way, the survivor whom Shakespeare's 'lass unparallel'd' finally labelled an 'ass, Unpolicied' was, in Elizabethan times, himself the subject of interesting discussions. In 'Shakespeare's Octavius and Elizabethan Roman History', Robert P. Kalmey quotes Renaissance accounts of that strange man who 'happened wisely and uprightly to governe that, which by force and cunning he had gotten'.[10]

Like John Wilders, Cedric Watts challenges those 'providential' interpretations of the plays which (it seems to me) could as easily rationalize the histories of Hitler and Stalin as those of *Richard III* and *Tamburlaine*. As Watts

---

[1] 'Hamlet and the Players: The "Magnificent Irrelevancies"', *Deutsche Shakespeare-Gesellschaft West, Jahrbuch* (1978–9), 73–88.

[2] *The Sewanee Review*, LXXXVI (1978), 396–405.

[3] In *Evidence in Literary Scholarship: Essays in Memory of James Marshall Osborn*, ed. René Wellek and Alvaro Ribeiro (Oxford, Clarendon Press, 1979), pp. 13–27.

[4] *Theatre Quarterly*, VIII (1978), 18–24.

[5] 'Truth and *Timon of Athens*', *Modern Language Quarterly*, XL (1979), 17–36.

[6] 'Explorations in Shakespeare's Drama', *Shakespeare Quarterly*, XXIX (1978), 133–45.

[7] *Studies in English Literature*, 19 (1979), 179–96.

[8] *The Sewanee Review*, LXXXVI (1978), 380–96.

[9] Macmillan, 1978.

[10] *Studies in English Literature*, XVIII (1978), 275–87.

observes, all such interpretations run aground against blindingly obvious instances of sheer injustice: if death is the punishment for his wicked characters, then why did Shakespeare insist that Cordelia die along with them? Watts cites G. I. Duthie, who answers that 'God moves in a mysterious way – he deals strangely with the Cordelias of this world. His methods are inscrutable.' It is, Watts concludes, 'traditional for Christian apologists to use this heads-we-win-and-tails-you-lose procedure; but the logic...remains self-contradictory. One premise is that God's goodness can clearly be inferred from events on earth, and the other is that it cannot. The antitheist could employ equivalent logic to opposite effect by letting the death of Cordelia be evidence of a malevolent deity and the punishment of evil-doers be evidence of his inscrutability.'[1]

Where there is contention about Shakespeare's historiography, there is a kind of consensus about his Romances. This poses its own problems, since recent discussions of the last plays tend to suffer, even more than most, from repetitiveness. (Does anyone still need to be reminded of their overt theatricality? Might not the worst of plays, as well as the best, call attention to its own artificiality?). Here, too, there is a straining for originality that finally becomes ludicrous. For instance, at the end of a discussion of 'The Tempest and the Concept of the Machiavellian Playwright',[2] Richard Abrams alleges that 'a complementary relationship obtains between Prospero's moral and aesthetic crimes, the one regarded as a presumption to the divine right of judgment or vengeance, the other – the playwright's crime – regarded, curiously, as the usurpation of a divine right of mercy' (italics mine). 'Curiously' indeed. And the second charge against Prospero becomes curiouser and curiouser the more one thinks about it. Apart from Abrams himself, and, of course, Fielding's Thwackum (he, too, was all for 'leaving mercy to Heaven'),

who has 'regarded' mercy as a criminal 'usurpation' of 'a divine right'? In this particular context, anyway, Shakespeare, like Prospero (and like Portia and Isabella elsewhere), explicitly echoes the judgement propounded, in His Sermon on the Mount, by the highest authority on that particular subject: 'Blessed are the merciful, for they shall obtain mercy'; 'Forgive us our trespasses, as we forgive those who trespass against us'; 'As you from crimes would pardoned be/Let your indulgence set me free'; 'We do pray for mercy,/And that same prayer, doth teach us all to render/The deeds of mercy.' Case dismissed with costs against Abrams for ignoring the obvious.

Shakespeare's Romances Reconsidered[3] is an attractive anthology of recent interpretations of the last plays, although some of them are by now too familiar to be termed 'reconsiderations'. What the book contains is a useful 'Overview of Critical Approaches to the Romances' by Norman Sanders, and interesting reflections by Northrop Frye ('Romance as Masque'), Clifford Leech ('Masking and Unmasking in the Last Plays'), Howard Felperin ('Romance and Romanticism') and Cyrus Hoy ('Fathers and Daughters in Shakespeare's Romances'), as well as essays on 'Cloten, Autolycus, and Caliban: Bearers of Parodic Burdens' (by Joan Hartwig), 'Cymbeline's Debt to Holinshed' (by Joan Warchol Rossi), 'Tragic Structure in The Winter's Tale' (by Charles Frey), 'The Restoration of Hermione' (by David Bergeron), 'Immediacy and

[1] C. T. Watts, 'Shakespearian Themes: The Dying God and the Universal Wolf' in Mario Curreli and Alberto Martino (eds.) Critical Dimensions: English, German and Comparative Literature Essays in Honour of Aurelio Zanco (Saste, Cuneo, 1978), pp. 129–30. Hereafter cited as Critical Dimensions.

[2] English Literary Renaissance, VIII (1978), 43–66.

[3] Ed. Carol McGinnis Kay and Henry E. Jacobs (University of Nebraska Press, Lincoln and London, 1978).

Remoteness in *The Taming of the Shrew* and *The Winter's Tale*' (by Charles R. Forker), and 'A Triangular Study of *Doctor Faustus*, *The Alchemist*, and *The Tempest*' (by David Young).

Discussions of pastoral elements in the comedies and romances seemed too grim to credit. Using 'Social Rank and the Pastoral Ideals of *As You Like It*' as clubs to clobber the various characters, Judy Z. Kronenfeld argues that the Duke 'enters into an exploitative relation to the forest . . . by engaging in the specifically noble leisure-time sport of hunting'.[1] Shakespeare, likewise, 'underlines the discrepancy between the pastoral virtues of the low and high' when Rosalind and Celia take 'the gifts of the world' with them to Arden whereas Adam gives up his purse before he goes. On the other hand, the 'idealistic view of the mean and sure estate is qualified by Audrey's status-seeking and corruptibility'. In 'Labour, Ease, and *The Tempest* as Pastoral Romance,'[2] Ronald B. Bond sternly insists that Shakespeare 'tempers the facile sentimentalism of ancient pastoral with the puritanical conviction that sloth is sinful, and exults not in the pleasures accruing to *otium*, but in the satisfaction of tasks well done'.

A book on Shakespeare's comic matrix by Susan Snyder (Princeton University Press, 1980) did not reach here in time for review, but the section I read before publication seemed first-rate – watch for it. Maurice Charney's general introduction to comedy is very lively, and has some acute observations about Shakespeare in particular.[3] To his credit, Charney accomplishes the increasingly difficult feat of writing about comedy without solemnity and without obeisance to the theories of Sigmund Freud. It was also good to read Charles Haines's reminder that even if merriment 'is not held to be a fully dignified endeavour, and laughter is not felt to lie as deep within as tears', it remains true that 'the general world of theatre-goers

appreciate probably more than any other the privilege of being made to laugh'.[4]

'There are few greater delights', wrote Virginia Woolf, 'than to go back three or four hundred years and become in fancy at least an Elizabethan.' This is just what T. Walter Herbert does in *Oberon's Mazéd World* – wherein 'A Judicious Young Elizabethan Contemplates *A Midsummer Night's Dream* with a Mind Shaped by the Learning of Christendom, Modified by the New Naturalist Philosophy and Excited by the Vision of a Rich, Powerful England'.[5] This book was clearly written with delight. But the governing conceit (whereby the author is an Elizabethan, yet has read Eliade, Eiseley, and any number of modern critics) soon wears thin. Herbert is best when he brings his reading in classical sources to bear upon the play. Then he occasionally hits target: the great question posed by Ovid, 'Why on earth would any man prefer Hermia to Helena?' ('*scilicet Hermionen Helenae praeponere posses?*' – quoted p. 19) receives as good an answer in *A Midsummer Night's Dream* as it is ever likely to get.

Another book devoted to one play, *Immortal Longings*, by B. Miyauchi,[6] has some good things to say about *Antony and Cleopatra*, but only when the author straightforwardly says what he thinks and feels. His attempts to impose a Thesis-Antithesis-Synthesis (TAS)

[1] *Shakespeare Quarterly*, XXIX (1978), 333–48.
[2] *Journal of English and Germanic Philology*, LXXVII (1978), 330–43.
[3] *Comedy High and Low: An Introduction to the Experience of Comedy* (Oxford University Press, New York, 1978).
[4] See Haines, 'Some Notes on Love and Money in *The Comedy of Errors*', in *Critical Dimensions*, p. 116.
[5] See T. Walter Herbert, *Oberon's Mazéd World* (Louisiana State University Press, Baton Rouge and London, 1977).
[6] *Immortal Longings: The Structure of Shakespeare's 'Antony and Cleopatra'* (Shinozaki Shorin, Tokyo, 1978).

structure on Shakespeare's poetry seems an exercise in futility.

Phyllis Rackin's introduction to *Shakespeare's Tragedies*,[1] which is intended to help 'amateurs' make 'contact' with the plays through 'a personal encounter' is flawed by sweeping overstatements. 'The good are loyal', Rackin proclaims at the beginning of the essay on *King Lear*, while 'the wicked are disloyal'. This necessitates much hemming and hawing later on: 'A servant of Cornwall's stands up and kills his master.... Thus, it seems that loyalty is not enough to justify or disloyalty enough to condemn an action in the universe of this play.' Compared to George Becker's elegant introduction to the history plays (recently published in the same series), Rackin's book needed far more work. Stanley Wells's handsome little handbook introducing *Shakespeare: The Writer and his Work* would seem of more practical use to 'amateurs' in need of one.[2] S. C. Sen Gupta's discussion of *Aspects of Shakespearian Tragedy*[3] (re-issued to include new essays on *Julius Caesar* and *Coriolanus*) is richer than Rackin's though I (for one) am tired of arguments about whether or not the various heroes of Shakespeare's tragedies are, in fact, tragic heroes. Coriolanus, according to Sen Gupta, is not one. Keith Alayre Anderson's *Essay on the Meaning of Hamlet: A Director's Approach*[4] concludes that Hamlet's main problem is his recognition of the 'mingled good and evil in all men'. But where does Hamlet recognize any good in Claudius?

For outstanding discussions of individual tragedies, see Madeleine Doran's book, *Shakespeare's Dramatic Language*, Philip Drew's 'Drama and Melodrama in King Lear'[5] and James Calderwood's '*Hamlet*: The Name of Action'.[6] In 'Othello and the Democrats,'[7] David L. Frost argues persuasively that, by reasserting Othello's heroic stature, the ending rescues the action from the 'depressing and debilitating decline of the outstanding to-

ward the commonplace'. This essay is complemented by E. A. M. Colman's argument in the same volume[8] that, although his logic falters in the exchange with Lodovico, the fault is not Othello's: it was Shakespeare who gave him those lines that seem to beg so many questions.

The fifth volume of *Shakespeare: The Critical Heritage* (1765–1774)[9] is necessarily dominated, first, by Dr Johnson's edition, and then by Garrick's *Hamlet*. In his Introduction, Brian Vickers seems too hard on the great Leviathan, finding Dr Johnson's attack on the unities less original, his criticism less acute, than they have generally been supposed to be. Yet the Preface (to my mind, anyway) still provides the best possible example of the use of a governing theory to show precisely what an individual artist does *not* do. James Black's 'Johnson, Shakespeare, and the Dyer's Hand',[10] which argues that Johnson derived some of his best insights from Shakespeare himself, is an interesting counter to Vickers.

'Shakespeare and the Classical World' is the chief subject of *Shakespeare Survey 31*.[11] The issue begins with a retrospective discussion of 'The Ancient World in Shakespeare: Authenticity or Anachronism?' by John W. Velz. This is a learned essay marred by occasional lapses

[1] Phyllis Rackin, *Shakespeare's Tragedies* (Frederick Ungar, New York, 1978).

[2] *Shakespeare: The Writer and his Work* (Longman, 1978).

[3] *Aspects of Shakespearian Tragedy* (Oxford University Press, Calcutta, 1977).

[4] Keith Alayre Anderson, *An Essay on the Meaning of Hamlet: A Director's Approach* (Saylorville Printing, Des Moines, Iowa, 1978).

[5] *English*, XXVIII (1979), 109–15.

[6] *Modern Language Quarterly*, XXXIX (1978), 331–62.

[7] *Sydney Studies in English*, IV (1978–9), 3–17.

[8] *Ibid.*, '*Othello* and the Sense of an Ending', 31–7.

[9] Routledge & Kegan Paul, 1979.

[10] In *Pattern of Excelling Nature*, 152–63.

[11] Cambridge University Press (1979).

into academese: '[In *Timon of Athens*] the failure of the *polis* to manifest its ontological essence, the reciprocities of human intercourse, leads to an atavistic collapse.' Ann Thompson's discussion of 'Philomel in *Titus Andronicus* and *Cymbeline*' (pp. 23–32) takes issue with Velz's theory that *polis* is of central concern in *Titus Andronicus*: '*Titus* is much more of a family drama, less of a political one. There are really remarkably few images of Rome as a "body politic".' Thompson is, surely, right in concluding that, in *The Rape of Lucrece*, 'the assault on the heroine's integrity' is 'defied or nullified, symbolically at least, by her suicide: she asserts her integrity by a complete and willed destruction of her body'. This seems more true to the text than arguments by S. Clark Hulse ('"A Piece of Skillful Painting" in Shakespeare's "Lucrece"', pp. 13–43) whereby the suicide 'returns us to Shakespeare's misogyny, for while Lucrece is not to blame she is clearly guilty'. Having survived rape, Lucrece does consider herself defiled, polluted, shamed, but Shakespeare *himself* surely absolves her of any guilt. The Augustinian question posed by Hulse and others, 'if she was chaste, why did she kill herself, and if guilty, why worthy of praise?' seems, in this context at least, a non-problem.

In 'Apuleius and the Bradleian Tragedies' (pp. 33–43), John J. M. Tobin cites numerous verbal parallels that illuminate obscure allusions. Discussing the 'Choice of Hercules in *Antony and Cleopatra*' (pp. 45–52), John Coates argues against the moralistic view that Shakespeare is out to debunk his greatest lovers. In 'Structure, Inversion and Game in Shakespeare's Classical World' (pp. 53–63), Bruce Erlich gives a structuralist account of the contradictions and dissonances in the various plays that sometimes seems to overcomplicate the issues involved. At the end of an outstanding, thought-provoking essay on 'Shakespeare and the Healing Power of Deceit' (pp. 115–25), Philip Edwards

notes that Shakespeare, as an artist, 'must have questioned the honesty and value of his own illusions'. I think so, too, but not *necessarily* in a pejorative or moralistic way. Coming from the greatest of poets, those reminders that the best in this kind are but shadows, that the truest poetry is most feigning, that all poets lie, seem brilliant poetic corollaries to the conundrums posed by the classical Paradox of the Liar. In 'Truth and Utterance in *The Winter's Tale*' (pp. 65–75), A. F. Bellette insists that the play's 'unity of conception, and its diversity within that unity, is the reflection of its nature as a scrupulously constructed verbal artefact' – a conclusion which, given the emotional impact of that beautiful play, seems, to say the least, a let-down. Here as elsewhere, purely literary – or systematically 'metadramatic' – accounts of his plays seem determined to deny Shakespeare's mysterious capacity to provide an experience that goes beyond the literary and is indeed extra-dramatic.

In '*Henry V*, the Chorus and the Audience' (pp. 93–104), G. P. Jones concludes that the Chorus is 'symptomatic of court performance' rather than public performance. Discussing 'The Old Honour and the New Courtesy: *1 Henry IV*' (pp. 85–91), G. M. Pinciss argues that Renaissance guides to courtly behaviour prove Hal to be 'a young man of more promise and Hotspur of less' than 'we today might appreciate' without them. In 'Adumbrations of *The Tempest* in *A Midsummer Night's Dream*', G. R. Hibbard reminds us of the major affinities between those plays (pp. 77–83). The late J. C. Maxwell once remarked that the worst article published in any given year was likely to be on *Measure for Measure*. Readers can decide for themselves whether my own entry into this list ('"The Devil's Party": Virtues and Vices in *Measure for Measure*', pp. 105–13) merits that bad eminence. Discussing the Dark Lady sequence in 'Shakespeare's Man Descending a Staircase' (pp. 127–38), Michael J. B. Allen concludes that 'No one need blame the ordering on Thorpe or Eld and restructure it in the interests of conventional causality.' The sequence 'constitutes a painting in its own right and no justification exists for making it either more naturalistic or more abstract'.

Compared to Allen's, or to John D. Bernard's account of the strange mixture 'of bitter disillusionment and ecstatic praise' in the sonnets to the Young Man, '"To Constancie Confin'de": The Poetics of Shakespeare's Sonnets',[1] recent work on the poems seemed purely perfunctory: see, for instance, David K. Weiser's comments about the 'Theme and Structure in Shakespeare's Sonnet 121'.[2] Discussing 'The Contrarieties of Venus and Adonis' in the same volume,[3] Donald G. Watson argues that 'what causes the opposition' are 'contrary aspects of the sensible soul: concupiscence and irascibility.. The passions of the concupiscible *appetitus* are love, pleasure and desire; those of the irascible are courage, hope, and anger. Venus is forward, sensual, and aggressive in her pursuit of pleasure. Adonis is peevish, ill-natured' – and so on. In her discussion of 'Shakespeare's View of Language: An Historical Perspective',[4] Margreta de Grazia informs us that 'the breakdowns of language' in the Sonnets, as in *Coriolanus* and *King Lear* 'might all have been avoided or resolved' by the 'traditional antidote' of Christian charity.

The proliferation of theses and monographs, reproduced without any discernible selectivity or editorial supervision, raises serious questions about the assembly-line approach to Shakespeare. *Landmarks of Shakespeare Criticism*, by Robert F. Willson, Jr, reprints, to no evident purpose, those extracts 'in their own voices' (in a few hundred words) from critical essays by Rymer, Pope, Johnson, Goethe, Freud and others that have already been published in *The Shakespeare Newsletter*.[5] In *Shakespeare and Alcohol*,[6] Buckner B. Trawick charts the Bard's numerous references to booze, indicating precisely who drank what, where, when, and what was said about them. At the end, Trawick endears himself to the reader by raising the question 'So what?'. 'It seems', he admits, 'a thumping let-down to examine all the plays and poems, merely to discover that Shakespeare's attitude is that alcoholic drinks are good things when used in moderation, but bad things when used to excess' (p. 56). It certainly does.

In his monograph on the Sonnets, *Of Comfort and Despair*,[7] Robert W. Witt argues that, if they are just reordered properly, those Sonnets *will* reflect the neo-Platonic progression of love described by Cardinal Bembo in *The Courtier*. This argument could have been condensed to article length since Witt's commentary amounts to paraphrase at its feeblest:

The poet has two loves, a man and a woman. The man is a 'better angel' and his love represents comfort; the woman is a 'worser spirit' and her love represents despair. Both of these loves, though, the poet says, 'work on my soul continuously'. (p. 212)

Likewise, the couplet, 'All this the world well knows; yet none knows well/To shun the heaven that leads men to this hell' conclusively demonstrates that 'The poet knew what lust was before he became ensnared by it. Yet he, like all men, became so allured by the proposed joy that he could not shun it even though he knew that it leads to torment, grief, and destruction' (p. 211). Query: Should John Carey's *Wording and Rewording: Paraphrase in Literary Criticism* (Oxford, 1977) be required reading in every English course so as to discourage this sort of thing?

[1] *Publications of the Modern Language Association*, 94 (1979), 77–90.
[2] *Studies in Philology*, LXXV (1978), 142–62.
[3] *Ibid.*, 32–63.
[4] *Shakespeare Quarterly*, XXIX (1978), 374–88.
[5] Editions Rodopi, Amsterdam, 1979.
[6] Editions Rodopi, Amsterdam, 1978.
[7] Institut für Anglistik und Amerikanistik, Universität Salzburg (1979).

In her monograph on *The Slandered Woman in Shakespeare*,[1] Joyce H. Sexton discusses 'Slander's Venom'd Spear' as it strikes in the classics, in medieval literature, in Spenser, in Garter's play about Susanna and the Elders, and, likewise, in *Much Ado About Nothing*, *Othello*, *Cymbeline*, and *The Winter's Tale*. She finds these plays 'remarkably similar in basic design': in *The Winter's Tale* Shakespeare triumphantly succeeds in transforming 'Greene's heroine into a true Susanna'. Given Sexton's tunnel-vision, there *is* no significant difference between the plays. Here we have *Much Ado* without Beatrice and Benedick, *The Winter's Tale* without Perdita and Autolycus, since these characters are only peripheral to Shakespeare's 'lasting absorption with the theme of false accusation'. So narrow is the focus of this study, one finishes it with the comic, tragic, tragicomic outlines of the plays all blurred.

It could go without saying that Shakespeare treats his slandered heroines with great sympathy. But why is his 'lasting absorption' with their plight any more noteworthy than his absorption with murdered children, usurping brothers, motherless daughters, girls-threatened-with-marriage-to-men-they-do-not-love – or what you will? Is the academic division of labour which impels individuals to scorn delights and live laborious days to produce the first systematic study of 'Shakespeare and Alcohol', 'The Slandered Woman in Shakespeare', or some such subject, really conducive to the advancement of learning, truly the best way to 'approach' the least specialized of poets? Is our twentieth-century compartmentalization *in terms of* specialized 'approaches' conducive to good criticism? Be that as it may. The monographs submitted for review this year suggest that their thesis-topics virtually force students to do what the best critics have never done: that is, to harp on similarities between the various works at the expense of that individuality which makes all the difference in the world. The obvious alternative is to ask how Shakespeare himself avoids boring us when he so frequently returns to the same subjects, same situations. At his best, surely, he recycles his materials to altogether different effects. This explains why one can read the plays for years without noticing that (say) the gulling of Malvolio and the enlightenment of Benedick are accomplished by the identical trick whereby X is persuaded that Y is in love with him. It also explains why a critical consideration of the two scenes which takes into account the dramatic differences that virtually conceal their similarity is bound to be better than one which does not. There are other alternatives as well.

'I am now, therefore, to speak of hope.' A new journal, *Signal*, which has just been produced by the students and faculty of foreign languages at the Universidade Federal de Paraíba, clearly demonstrates that anyone – from the beginning student to the greatest living critic – who reads Shakespeare for personal delight and instruction will find a myriad of topics for fruitful speculation. As one contributor puts it, there really are only two reasons to study these works: because they sharpen 'our knowledge and appreciation of beauty' and because they increase our 'understanding of human nature in breadth and depth'. These reasons for studying *Antony and Cleopatra* here manifest themselves in essays on 'Revelry and Carousing' in the most 'festive' of tragedies; on 'Defeats'; on 'Dualities'; on 'Last Farewells'; on Octavius, 'The Man of Ice'; on 'Cleopatra and the Moon'; and on Enobarbus and Eros and the way each earns his place in the story. Pondering these subjects, one cannot but conclude that this 'isolated region of Brazil' (where even 'textbooks are hard to get' and 'critical tools are practically non-existent')

[1] *English Literary Studies Monograph Series*, no. 12 (University of Victoria, 1978).

must be an absolutely fabulous place to learn *from* Shakespeare. Certainly his students there, like the very best critics (and the best of our kind are but his students), have chosen issues that anyone would delight in discussing. One puts down their journal wondering precisely which of our marble, stone, or gilded monuments could be more pleasing, to Shakespeare himself, than this sparkling little tribute from Brazil.

© HARRIETT HAWKINS 1980

2. SHAKESPEARE'S LIFE, TIMES, AND STAGE

reviewed by GĀMINI SALGĀDO

In a recent interview[1] on trends in Shakespeare studies (among many other things) Kenneth Muir, who ought to know, answered Gareth Lloyd Evans's question 'Is the file on Shakespeare's sources closed now?' with an emphatic negative. Professor Muir appears to have changed his mind since he wrote fifteen years ago in 'The Future of Source-Hunting'[2] that with the completion of Geoffrey Bullough's work there was little more to be discovered of plot sources, but that our knowledge of Shakespeare's reading is still fragmentary. Little shards and slivers are hopefully breathed, shined and blown up in *Notes and Queries* and elsewhere, but John Erskine Hankins's new book[3] is a veritable museum of exhibits, systematically catalogued and, for the most part, elegantly presented. Professor Hankins, who in *Shakespeare's Derived Imagery* provided a serviceable set of criteria for evaluating the validity of hypothetical sources, concentrates mainly on Shakespeare's use of science and philosophy. The strategy is to survey general intellectual sources and then focus on Shakespearian examples. Sometimes the survey, while interesting in itself, does not illuminate Shakespeare very much and in general it is fair to say that the author is more concerned to note the occurrence of a particular idea or image in Shakespeare than to examine his use of it; that is, he has virtually no interest in context or criticism. Even those who are habitually suspicious of source-hunting will not quarrel with the modest claim that 'There is some advantage in knowing that an image is not original but derivative, even if one mistakes the particular source from which it is derived.' The more ambitious claims about source-hunting providing a key to the author's mind remain merely hopeful gestures. On the whole, the cosmological lore is more interesting and helpful than the psychological, and Professor Hankins has many new (to me at least) things to say about the world's diameter, 'the square of sense' and hell pains. The section on psychology merely serves to illustrate how coarse an analytic tool the theory of humours is when applied to Shakespeare (or Jonson, for that matter). My understanding is not enriched by being told that Audrey and William are phlegmatic, or by the pointless antithesis between Longaville (choleric) and Dumaine (well-balanced, a characteristic he evidently shares with Brutus). Nor is my appreciation of 'the special relationship of music

[1] Interview with Gareth Lloyd Evans, *Shakespeare Quarterly*, XXX, 1 (1979), 7–14.
[2] *Shakespeare Newsletter*, 14 (1964), 35.
[3] *Backgrounds of Shakespeare's Thought* (Harvester Press, Brighton, 1978).

to love' intensified by the knowledge that 'Lucretius uses *pabula amoris* in a general reference to all things that excite the passion of love, but with no mention of music.' But for all that, the book is genuinely useful, especially to those who go on to ask the questions Professor Hankins doesn't concern himself with. At the very least it continually reminds us of the extreme physicality of Shakespearian language which we too often take to be vaguely metaphysical. It also provides an interesting counterpart to T. Walter Herbert's *Oberon's Mazéd World* discussed elsewhere in this volume.

The second most wide-ranging study of 'Shakespeare's Life, Times, and Stage' to have come my way recently is, unsurprisingly enough, by Professor Bradbrook.[1] In some ways it is a companion volume to *The Living Monument* though each work has its own freestanding strength. The earlier volume dwelt mainly on theatrical and social life in Elizabethan and Jacobean England. The new one covers the same ground but with Shakespeare's own career and corpus firmly at the centre most of the time. Professor Bradbrook's gift for the unexpected juxtaposition of facts and events is as dazzling as ever, sometimes even blinding for the reader without her range of knowledge (that is, for nearly all readers). Marlowe and Southampton are firmly accepted as the rival poet and the friend respectively, and the candidacy of Winifred Burbage for the role of Dark Lady has much to commend it, judging by recent rival claims, on the score of interest and plausibility. More seriously, the author argues with erudition and eloquence that of the three shaping forces of Shakespeare's life, Stratford and the family, London and the Court, and the theatre, the last was undeniably the strongest. Though the discussion of the plays does sometimes blur into the merely illustrative there is much that is stimulating here, notably the view of Shakespeare's comedies as his riposte to the

railing of the Wars of the Theatres and of *King Lear* as holding in tension the pieties of *Leir* and Harsnett's vindictive savagery.

Even wider in scope than *Shakespeare: The Poet in his World* is Professor G. K. Hunter's collection of essays spanning two decades.[2] There are always formal problems of revision and arrangement involved in bringing together in a single volume essays originally produced for a variety of occasions and audiences. Professor Hunter has wisely decided not to go for an impossible coherence, comprehensiveness and continuity. Instead he has divided the essays into three loose and slightly overlapping sections: Identities, Traditions and Structures. The first attempts to get at what the author calls 'the Elizabethan audience's English identity' by setting it against alternatives that help to throw it into relief. Here is the seminal essay 'On English Folly and Italian Vice' as well as the 1967 British Academy Shakespeare Lecture on 'Othello and Colour Prejudice' and three others. The second section concerns itself with the way traditions are modified by the audience and shows 'conversely, how Shakespeare has to be re-invented to suit the interests of later and different traditions'. Here are two notable essays on the Senecan influence and a splendid one on Bradley. The last section deals with the way 'structures are used to predetermine meaning by unifying divergent material inside largely implicit cultural assumptions'. Throughout the book the author's concern is to deploy historical and other knowledge in the interests of illuminating individual plays, though he seems more sensitive to nuances of text than of performance. The solidity of the scholarship eliminates any charge of superficiality and the resoluteness of the author's concern with critical questions

[1] *Shakespeare: The Poet in his World* (Weidenfeld & Nicolson, 1978).
[2] *Dramatic Identities and Cultural Tradition* (Liverpool University Press, 1978).

eliminates that of irrelevance. This is a collection to which I shall return with pleasure and profit in the future as I have to one or two individual essays in it in the past.

Among studies with a more restricted focus, Ernest B. Gilman's *The Curious Perspective*[1] is interesting both for its subject-matter and its method of approach, though only about a third of the book (two out of seven chapters) deals with Shakespeare. Gilman discusses the relations between Albertian or 'standard' perspective and distorted perspective on the one hand and logical rules and seventeenth-century wit on the other. Wit is to logical rules as 'the curious perspective' to the Albertian. He is not unaware of the methodological problems involved in drawing analogies between the arts but deals with them briskly, not to say summarily, by discussing the reader–viewer's experiences, which are comparable in a way art-objects themselves are not, at least not directly. The plays discussed are *Richard II*, *Twelfth Night* and *A Midsummer Night's Dream*. As to the former, we are asked to see the play itself as a kind of perspective device, not just as a local metaphor but a conceptual model. What it seems to amount to is that we are offered historical support for the 'double vision' which others have noted before in the history plays. Gilman's analysis is subtle and suggestive but not without its occasional over-simplifications and crudities, such as the reference to the 'vigorous heroics and unclouded patriotism' of the early Histories, or the suggestion that the Gardener should extend his arms to make a living emblem of the scales to 'embody' his metaphor. *Twelfth Night* is seen, fairly predictably perhaps, as 'a natural perspective that is and is not' while *A Midsummer Night's Dream* 'undermin[es] the stable frames of reference that usually separate the audience from the work of art'. If that's what the *Dream* does, I wonder what happens in *The Tempest*. In fact, as Mr Gilman makes clear

elsewhere, *A Midsummer Night's Dream* never seriously discomfits the audience, which is always sure of *its* perspective.

Two books on the theatrical background call for attention next, though they have hardly anything in common. Michael Shapiro's substantial study[2] is a careful investigation into the origins of the children's companies, the nature and composition of their audiences and the effect of these on the plays and their performance. I found the chapters on audience behaviour and acting styles especially stimulating. Inevitably there is a certain amount of conjecture (Shapiro disagrees with Foakes's view that Marston's plays were done in a parodic style *throughout*, for instance), but the conjecture is informed and responsible, respecting both established facts and ordinary rules of argument. This is a good deal more than can be said for Martin Holmes's new book[3] which purports to discuss 'the sound of Shakespeare as devised to suit the voice and talents of his principal player'. Mr Holmes occasionally almost deserves the extravagant compliment delivered by J. C. Trewin on his 'infallible ear for a cadence' and has many good things to say about sound effects in individual passages, although there is too much loose babble about sneering vowels and shuddering consonants. But the Burbage he conjures up is a creature of his own imagination; his connection with the historical personage (of whom, in all conscience, we know little enough) is tenuous to the point of invisibility. A lot more is needed to give this wraith colour and credibility than the airy thinness of Mr Holmes's suppositions.

Klaus Peter Jochum has devoted nearly 300 closely printed pages to elaborating and developing the notion of 'discrepant awareness'

[1] *The Curious Perspective* (Yale University Press, 1978).
[2] *Children of the Revels* (Columbia University Press, 1977).
[3] *Shakespeare and Burbage* (Phillimore, 1978).

applied to the comedies some years ago by Bertrand Evans. The consoling chimera of 'objective interpretation' is relentlessly pursued through medieval mysteries and Robert Greene to Ford and Shirley, taking in Shakespeare's Histories and Tragedies on the way. No new insights were forthcoming by the time I guiltily gave up reading (around p. 207); my blood remained strangely unstirred by the revelation that '*Hamlet* (c. 1599–1601) represents an unsurpassed climax in the development of the revenge tragedy as regards the use of informational discrepancies in this genre' and I remain unconvinced that the 'real achievement of the drama [*Love's Sacrifice*] is Ford's early elimination of discrepant awareness after he has carefully built it up to its customary climax'. My awareness of Shakespeare and drama generally remains irredeemably discrepant from Dr Jochum's, and a nagging sense of the otiosity of the topic, at least on this scale, survives even the realisation of the awesome exigencies of the *Habilitationsschrift*.[1]

A wide variety of runners have trotted forth in recent years from the Salzburg stables of the Institut für Anglistik und Amerikanistik (formerly the Institut für Englische Sprache), some swift and sturdy, some short- (or long-) winded and spavined. In the current string, we have a whole issue devoted to Shakespeare's use of Plutarch in *Antony and Cleopatra* and *Coriolanus*.[2] David C. Green treads on slippery ground in arguing that what Shakespeare did *not* use from Plutarch can often help us to understand better what he did but he argues his case well, if sometimes too emphatically, and notes some hitherto unrecognised borrowings, a few of which I feel will continue to be unrecognised. More than once I found his critical comments less than pellucid, as when he remarks (of Shakespeare's choice of the opening of *Antony and Cleopatra*): 'But his choice is not so much his own originality as it is evidence of a clever playwright making the right dramaturgical

decision'. John Dean contributes six expendable pages on Herodotus's alleged impact on the late plays[3] in a volume most of which is taken up by James Henke's discussion of the *Henry VI* trilogy in terms of Jungian archetypes, specifically those of the 'shadow', the 'temptress' and 'the child'.[4] Henke is aware of the reductivism inherent in this kind of approach (though not sufficiently protected against it) and is concerned with patterns of action rather than words but on occasions his notion of the trilogy as psychomachia has a curiously appealing force. In another Salzburg volume Henke argues for an ego-gratifying Faustus who resists the 'temptation' to repent and seizes on his end with as much triumph as fear.[5] In the same volume Richard Corballis discusses Machiavellism in *Sejanus* and two plays by Chapman[6] and Dorothy E. Nameri reflects on correspondences between *As You Like It* and de Musset's *Fantasio*,[7] especially those between the latter's eponymous hero and Jaques.

Before turning to periodical publications, two useful bibliographies must be briefly noted. One is a selective guide to recent work in English on plays by twenty-five Elizabethan and Jacobean dramatists, excluding Shakespeare. Brief summaries of each item are provided and there is a helpful analytical index.[8] The guide was compiled by Brownell Salomon.

[1] *Discrepant Awareness: Studies in English Renaissance Drama* (Peter Lang, 1979).

[2] *Jacobean Drama Studies 78: Plutarch Revisited* (Salzburg, 1978).

[3] *Jacobean Drama Studies 74:* 'Shakespeare's Romances and Herodotus's Histories' (Salzburg, 1977).

[4] *Ibid.*, 'The Ego-King'.

[5] *Elizabethan and Renaissance Studies 71:* 'The Devil Within' (Salzburg, 1978).

[6] *Ibid.*, 'Some Machiavellian Moments in English Renaissance Drama'.

[7] *Ibid.*, '*As You Like It/Fantasio:* A Comparative Study'.

[8] *Critical Analyses in English Renaissance Drama* (Bowling Green University Popular Press, 1979).

The other offers six bibliographical essays on specific dramatists as well as one on eighteen anonymous plays and another on thirty-seven minor dramatists. The critical period covered is 1941–75. This is the last of a four-volume series and is edited by Terence P. Logan and Denzell S. Smith.[1]

Among longer articles devoted to general topics associated with Shakespeare's life and times, Alan C. Dessen provides an interesting guide to some recent studies on the morality background (though he does not mention Emrys Jones's important book on *The Origins of Shakespeare*) and ends with a plea which will provoke a fervent amen: 'future scholars treating dramatic history should continue to provide us with Good Counsel about the complex legacy of the morality play and lead us away from that insidious Vice, Oversimplification'.[2] In the same annual volume of *Shakespeare Studies*, Martha Andresen-Thom takes Juliet Dusinberre mildly to task for taking insufficient account of Shakespeare's own distinctive use of traditional female stereotypes and points out the long ancestry of 'my Lady Tongue' the spiritedly eloquent woman, as much a male ideal as the silent submissive Grissell. She also has pertinent things to say about the significance of certain typical plot structures.[3] Robert E. Burkhart argues the case for Shakespeare joining an acting company within a year or two after 1585, probably after Leicester's men visited Stratford in 1586–7.[4] Bernard Beckerman discusses the problem of *speaking* about Shakespeare in the light of the fact that 'far from being supplemental and peripheral as in the past, the analysis of Shakespeare through performance is now conceded to be a proper and perhaps central way of approaching Shakespeare'.[5] In 'Shakespeare's View of Language: An Historical Perspective'[6] Margreta de Grazia challenges the view put forward by Anne Barton and others that Shakespeare, especially in his later works, implied any scepticism about the inherent capacity of language to articulate human motives, aspirations and emotions. She considers the way that what the sixteenth century considered a moral problem about the speaker's defects (Adam's fall) becomes in the seventeenth a philosophical one about the defects of language, with the possibility of philosophical solutions (hence the proliferation of attempts to devise a 'philosophical language'). She argues that Shakespeare held the earlier view that language is adequate if the speaker's will is correct and attempts to enforce her view through a discussion of *Coriolanus*, *Lear*, and Sonnets 127–54. I find her argument less convincing in relation to *Lear* than to the other two subjects. Of real but peripheral interest is Kent Cartwright's conclusive demonstration that the so-called 'Folger 1560' view of London, which Richard Hosley described as both hitherto unreproduced and an independent source of cartographic evidence, is in fact derived from Agas via an eighteenth-century engraving by George Vertue reproduced in Maitland's (1739) *History of London*.[7] John Orrell gives reasons for believing that the Inigo Jones theatre drawings at Worcester College are probably for the Cockpit in Drury Lane, built in 1616.[8] Finally, John Hazel Smith quotes extensively from the Shakespearian marginalia of Styan Thirlby, Theobald's (unwilling?)

[1] *The Later Jacobean and Caroline Dramatists* (University of Nebraska Press, 1978).

[2] 'Homilies and Anomalies: The Legacy of the Morality Play to the Age of Shakespeare', *Shakespeare Studies*, XI (1978), 243–58.

[3] 'Thinking about Women and Their Prosperous Art,' *ibid.*, 259–76.

[4] 'Finding Shakespeare's Lost Years', *Shakespeare Quarterly*, XXIX, 1 (1978), 77–9.

[5] 'Explorations in Shakespeare's Drama', *ibid.*, XXIX, 2 (1978), 133–45.

[6] *Ibid.*, XXIX, 3 (1978), 374–88.

[7] *Ibid.*, XXIX, 1 (1978), 67–76.

[8] 'Inigo Jones at the Cockpit', *Shakespeare Survey* 30 (Cambridge University Press, 1977), 157–68.

assistant and provides some new information about the relevant manuscript material.[1]

Shakespeare's non-dramatic works have produced, among other things, a persuasive reading of Sonnet 94 by Lorena Stookey and Robert Merrill, in which the aptness of either a literal or an ironic reading of the poem is discounted and it is argued that the sonnet is about the inability of some of those most naturally gifted to participate in human mutuality. The sonnet is climactic rather than part of a continuing dramatic action.[2] Less persuasively, Paul Bates attempts to draw parallels between the sonnets and the plays in terms of plot, character, scene and so on, but his sense of a parallel is far too loose and wayward to provide any useful insights.[3] Wayne A. Rebhorn analyses the complexity of Shakespeare's portrayal of Venus in relation to the ambivalence towards women inherent in the courtly love tradition, and of Adonis in terms of the connection with the heroic tradition from antiquity to the Renaissance.[4] I may also briefly note here Sara van den Berg's close and sympathetic but somewhat inconclusive look at Jonson's commendatory poem for the First Folio.[5]

The articles I have read in the various periodicals have not made me sharply aware of any dominant trend in Shakespeare studies or any particularly favoured plays. A variety of axes are being ground and very few hatchets seem to have been buried. Taking the Comedies first, there is a long account of the historical background to the events of *Love's Labour's Lost* in which Hugh M. Richmond argues, reasonably enough, that the immediate context of the play is Shakespeare's knowledge of the historical Henri IV and his court, both through the spate of pamphlets on French matters then being translated and through men like Southampton who had personal knowledge of Navarre's Court. Readers who accept the general argument (Richard David remarked a long time ago on the fidelity of the play to historical fact) may

still feel that Richmond overstates his case when, for instance, he traces Benedick and Beatrice to the *Heptameron* of Margaret of Navarre.[6] Donald K. Hedrick uses a rejected reading in *As You Like It* as the basis of a plea for 'a richer critical apparatus than is normally used in such disputes'. One can see the force of his claim that the value of critical comment can lie in helping us to see in what way a reading is good, rather than in settling what the correct reading is, without being convinced that the argument is either enriched or clarified by the suggested importation of the terminology of 'discourse pragmatics'.[7] Joan Ozark Holmer argues, by an examination of Shakespeare's principal sources for the casket scene in *The Merchant of Venice* and of echoes of it in the trial scene (some very faint indeed) for a closer dramatic connection between the two episodes than, she claims, is generally allowed.[8] Source study is also at the centre of Robert F. Fleissner's comparison of *The Merry Wives of Windsor* and Boccaccio's tale of Friar Alberto and the Angel Gabriel. The weight to be allowed to the 'eight major correlations' identified by the author can perhaps be gauged from one example: 'In the course of their

[1] 'Styan Thirlby's Shakespearean Commentaries: A Corrective Analysis', *Shakespeare Studies*, XI (1978), 219–41.

[2] 'They that have power to hurt', *Modern Language Quarterly* (March 1978), 27–37.

[3] 'Shakespeare's Sonnets and the Growth of his Dramatic Art,' *Shakespeare Jahrbuch*, 114 (Weimar, 1978), 70–4.

[4] 'Mother Venus: Temptation in Shakespeare's *Venus and Adonis*', *Shakespeare Studies*, XI (1978), 1–19.

[5] '"The Paths I Meant unto thy Praise": Jonson's poem for Shakespeare', *ibid.*, pp. 207–18.

[6] 'Shakespeare's Navarre', *Huntington Library Quarterly*, XLII, 3 (1979), 193–216.

[7] 'Merry and Weary Conversation: Textual Uncertainty in *As You Like It*, II, iv', *English Literary History*, XLVI, 1(1979), 21–34.

[8] 'Loving Wisely and the Casket Test: Symbolic and Structural Unity in *The Merchant of Venice*', *Shakespeare Studies*, XI (1978), 53–76.

analogous escapades, the two varlets don not just one disguise but several.'[1] In 'Shakespeare, Lyly and Ovid: The Influence of *Gallathea* on *A Midsummer Night's Dream*' Leah Scragg argues that the affinities between Shakespeare's play and Lyly's are remarkable enough to suggest conscious influence; Ovid remains something of a grace-note in her piece.[2]

Eugene Waith's substantial essay on *King John* surveys some noteworthy productions of the past and suggests that an approach through the pattern of ideas may obscure what is vitally dramatic in the play – 'the stories the play has presented of John, Constance, Arthur, Hubert and the Bastard'.[3]

In his essay on *King John*, Eamon Grennan sees the play as a 'dramatic broom with which Shakespeare sweeps away many of the no longer convincing or functional props of the historico-dramatic world of his Yorkist plays'.[4] Like Waith he succeeds in making the play seem more interesting than it is usually taken to be, though sometimes at the expense of making the other early Histories, especially *Richard III*, less so. Discussing the latter play Paul N. Siegel isolates a strand of imagery derived from the idiom of business and commerce, asserts that Shakespeare identified the feudal Yorkists with the Elizabethan bourgeoisie and applauds the prophetic Marxmanship by which the bard 'anticipates the bourgeoisie's behaviour when it gained world domination'.[5] The affinity between *Henry VIII* and masque has been noted before but John D. Cox offers a detailed and sensitive account of the play as an 'experiment in adopting the principles of court masque to the traditions of the public theatre, in particular the undercutting of the masque emphasis on the monarch's divine body with the theatrical tradition which stressed the king's mortality'.[6] Tom McBride's essay on the same play dallies half-heartedly with analogies between Machiavelli's Italy and Shakespeare's England and suggests, more relevantly, the fate of Arabella

Stuart as an example of Jacobean Machiavellianism contemporaneous with the play.[7] Virginia M. Carr's essay on the Henriad doesn't seem to me to go much beyond the 'ambivalence' identified by Rossiter, and she seems to believe that traditional Christian political theology unequivocally denied the right of subjects to rise against an unjust king.[8] Andrew Gurr considers the significance of Shakespeare's alteration in *Henry V*, I, ii, 187–204 of the fable of the bees in Erasmus's *Institutio*.[9]

In 'The Dignity of Mortality' Robert E. Wood compares the juxtaposition of satirical, burlesque and serious elements in *Troilus and Cressida* and Marlowe's *Dido* and concludes that Shakespeare's use of satire in tragedy was not unprecedented, presumably because somebody somewhere maintains that it was.[10] T. S. Dorsch's essay on *Measure for Measure* addresses itself to the question of how far a Jacobean audience would have been puzzled by the same things we are in this puzzling play and concludes that Isabella's response to Angelo's proposal would have been no 'problem' to the Jacobeans, also that they would have expected mercy from Angelo while accepting his technical correctness and that they would have expected the disguised

[1] 'The Malleable Knight and the Unfettered Friar: *The Merry Wives of Windsor* and *Boccaccio*', *ibid.*, pp. 77–93.

[2] *Shakespeare Survey 30* (Cambridge University Press, 1977), pp. 125–34.

[3] 'King John and the Drama of History', *Shakespeare Quarterly*, XXIX, 2 (1978), 172–211.

[4] 'Shakespeare's Satirical History: A Reading of *King John*', *Shakespeare Studies*, XI (1978), 21–35.

[5] 'Richard III as Businessman', *Shakespeare Jahrbuch*, 114 (Weimar, 1978), 101–6.

[6] '*Henry VIII* and Masque', *English Literary History*, XLV, 3 (1978), 390–409.

[7] '*Henry VIII* as Machiavellian Romance' *JEGP*, LXXVI, 1 (1977), 26–39.

[8] 'Once More Into the Henriad: A "Two-Eyed" View', *ibid.*, LXXVII, 4 (1978), 530–45.

[9] '*Henry V* and the Bees' Commonwealth', *Shakespeare Survey 30* (Cambridge University Press, 1977), pp. 61–72.

[10] *Shakespeare Studies*, XI (1978), 95–106.

ruler to sort things out in the end. He also points out, *pace* Hunter, Lever, *et al.*, that in 1604 the bed-trick would *not* have been familiar to theatregoers, whatever might have been the case with educated readers.[1] Ruth Levitsky sees *Timon of Athens* as a kind of secular morality like Skelton's *Magnyfycence* in which all virtues are subsumed under the grand virtue of Magnificence, here rather emaciated to signify moderate liberality, resisting temptation and enduring adversity.[2] Gail Kern Paster draws attention to the inevitability of the community devouring its best product, the hero, in *Coriolanus*. For Rome the end is comic, for the audience tragic/ironic.[3]

I turn now to the major Tragedies. James P. Hammersmith in a somewhat repetitive and occasionally opaque essay which owes a good deal to Nigel Alexander's study of *Hamlet*, argues that the hero, dedicating himself entirely to the act of remembering, 'abolishes' time which is now measured in events, rather than in hours and days. Memory is embodied in language and remembering unifies past and present.[4] Jason P. Rosenblatt approaches the topic of incest in the play in terms of a tension between conflicting Biblical texts (Leviticus, xviii, 16 and Deuteronomy, xxv, 5–6). The opposition between the true levirate relationship where the survivor 'represents' the dead brother and the earlier and more primitive function of widow-inheritance where the survivor supplants the deceased provides the dramatic space in which Claudius exists. Rosenblatt amply documents the fact that the finer shades of the problem were the subject of debate in the controversy over the legality of Henry VIII's divorce from his dead brother's wife. (The encyclopaedic reading of Shakespeare's audience never ceases to amaze me; it seems to be as great as that of all the exegetical critics put together.) Our sense of Claudius's role-playing is perhaps sharpened by this painstaking exegesis, but only by making Claudius's character more schematic. As

with most such exercises I suspect that this one will help the reader most when it sinks into the hinterland of his awareness as, fortunately, it will.[5] R. M. Frye documents the existence of a long and popular visual tradition of the young man contemplating the skull and suggests that the successful structural transition from the earlier to the later Hamlet is made largely through iconographic allusions to this tradition in the graveyard scene.[6] Philip Brockbank's illuminating comparison and contrast between *Hamlet* and *Oedipus Rex* establishes the presence in Shakespeare's play of 'the old mysteries of sin and death' which are flattened out or swept aside by the revenge play paradigm.[7]

Developing in detail a point about *Macbeth* made by Emrys Jones in *Scenic Form in Shakespeare*, Robert F. Willson Jr discusses the banquet scene as a play within a play that goes awry.[8] Vincent F. Petronella's examination of 'The Role of Macduff in *Macbeth*' points out the three aspects of Macduff as parallel figure, respondent to death and perceiver of central truths, but does not inquire how, if at all, the three are connected.[9]

D. Aberbach puts forward six specific points of comparison between *Lear* and the Book of

[1] '*Measure for Measure* and its Contemporary Audience', *Shakespeare Jahrbuch* (*West*) (1978–9), 202–17.

[2] '*Timon*: Shakespeare's *Magnyfycence* and an Embryonic *Lear*', *Shakespeare Studies*, XI (1978), 107–21.

[3] 'To Starve with Feeding: The City in *Coriolanus*', *ibid.*, pp. 123–44.

[4] '*Hamlet* and the Myth of Memory', *English Literary History*, XLV, 4 (1978), 597–605.

[5] 'Aspects of the Incest Problem in *Hamlet*', *Shakespeare Quarterly*, XXIX, 3 (1978), 349–64.

[6] 'Ladies, Gentlemen and Skulls: *Hamlet* and the Iconographic Tradition', *Shakespeare Quarterly*, XXX, 1 (1979), 15–28.

[7] 'Hamlet the Bone-setter', *Shakespeare Survey 30* (Cambridge, 1977), pp. 103–14.

[8] 'Macbeth the Player King: The Banquet Scene as Frustrated Play within the Play', *Shakespeare Jahrbuch*, 114 (Weimar, 1978), 107–14.

[9] *Etudes Anglaises*, Jan–March 1979, pp. 11–19.

Job to strengthen the general view that the Biblical story influenced Shakespeare's play.[1] Some of these are helpful but others, such as the fact that both heroes begin with comfort and security and lose everything, would appear to be common to more works than the two in question – to most if not all tragedies, in fact.

In his book on *Lear*, S. L. Goldberg propounded the view that the violent assault on both the characters and the sensibility of the audience in the play is to be understood in terms of recognition of complicity between audience and character. In a careful essay 'On the Blinding of Gloucester' Edward Pechter elaborates this view, pointing out that it is not enough to respond to the blinding merely as the sign of a horrible world where power is in the wrong hands. Gloucester, replacing Kent as the choric figure through whom our experience of the play is mediated, is made to respond in a particular way, then punished for his response – like the audience itself. While the essay is a necessary and often persuasive counter-balance to the 'redemptivist' reading of *Lear*, it comes perilously close to emptying its categories of significance with statements like 'The hand that reaches out to help another is – inevitably it seems – the same hand that would crush the other's torturers, and – whether it would or no – that crushes the self.' The larger the terms of the argument, the less convincing it sounds.[2]

Robert F. Fleissner argues, though not to my satisfaction, that Othello's base Indian was dark brown, not red. Since he also accepts that Nashe's reference in *Pierce Pennilesse* (unmistakably to a Red Indian) was one of Shakespeare's primary sources, a good deal of tricky footnote-work is involved in explaining Shakespeare's 'geographical transformation'.[3] Bryan F. Tyson sees 'not merely echoes but parodic overtones' of *Othello* in *Volpone*. Among other links he points out the common Venetian background, the contemporary setting, the importance of gulling and the similarity in rank between Volpone and the duke. And there is handkerchiefs in both.[4]

According to Joan Carr *Cymbeline* shows Shakespeare probing, principally through a fully human heroine in a world of myth, 'into the mythic habit of thought and its ability to make sense of the human condition'. The parallels between the central events of the play and Orphic and other resurrection myths, as well as the idea of Cloten as the Pauline 'body of death' which Posthumus discards, yield some genuine insights, but it is surely misleading to compare Imogen's dependence on Posthumus to that of fruit on a tree when Posthumus himself uses the metaphor with the roles exactly reversed.[5] Carolyn Asp in her essay on *The Winter's Tale* notes Paulina's unique position as a female counsellor to a male in relation to conventional Renaissance expectations and suggests analogies with female figures in medieval literature such as Boethius's Lady Philosophy. Regrettably the consolations of philosophy as summarised at the end are of the usual mind-numbing banality.[6] Irene G. Dash comments on Warburton's edition of the play in the context of the emerging vogue for nature and rural scenes.[7] Charles Frey discusses *The Tempest* on lines similar to those developed by Leslie Fiedler in *The Stranger in Shakespeare*.[8]

[1] 'The Job Motif in *King Lear*', *Notes and Queries*, n.s. XXVI, 2 (1979), 129–32.

[2] *English Literary History*, XLV, 2 (1978), 181–200.

[3] 'Othello as the Indigent Indian; Old World, New World or Third World?', *Shakespeare Jahrbuch*, 114 (Weimar, 1978), 92–100.

[4] 'Ben Jonson's Black Comedy: A Connection between *Othello* and *Volpone*', *Shakespeare Quarterly*, XXX, 1 (1979), 60–6.

[5] '*Cymbeline* and the Validity of Myth', *Studies in Philology*, LXXV, 3 (1978), 316–30.

[6] 'Shakespeare's Paulina and the *Consolatio* Tradition', *Shakespeare Studies*, XI (1978), 145–57.

[7] 'A Glimpse of the Sublime in Warburton's Edition of *The Winter's Tale*', *ibid.*, pp. 159–74.

[8] '*The Tempest* and the New World', *Shakespeare Quarterly*, XXX, 1 (1979), 29–41.

Lack of space compels me to stuff all the short notes into a trailing rag bag at the end, beginning with notes on general topics. R. J. P. Kuin offers firmer identification than that hitherto available for both the writer and the recipient of Robert Langham's (or Laneham's) letter.[1] M. E. Smith gives some new biographical details about three members of the second Blackfriars Company.[2] R. A. L. Burnet argues, on the basis of three quite plausible examples, that Shakespeare not only knew the text of the Geneva Bible but had read and remembered the marginalia.[3] H. J. Oliver guesses that in Greene's notorious reference to 'the only Shake-scene in a countrey', 'shake' might mean 'steal' as it still does in Australian slang and did in early nineteenth-century English if not earlier.[4] Donald S. Lawless provides some new information on the actor Philip Kingman[5] and the playwright Robert Daborne.[6] Wayne H. Phelps draws attention to a baptismal entry which may refer to Edmund Shakespeare's bastard son, assuming that the parish clerk of both St Leonard's, Shoreditch and St Giles, Cripplegate got 'Edmund' mixed up with 'Edward'.[7]

Two curiosities relating to early plays: F. C. Morgan notes an early-seventeenth-century holograph occurrence of 'honorificabilitudinitatibus' and records a fragment of a letter beginning 'Good Mrs Shakespeare' as well as mentioning a 'Bott' (who may or may not have been the Bott who owned New Place; the fragment has no date).[8] W. L. Godshalk suggests that Webster borrowed 'honey-dew' in The Duchess from the 'honey-stalks' of Titus.[9]

Bottom is well and truly translated by Thomas B. Stroup who derives his name not, as generally, from the weaver's term for the base on which thread is wound, but from a passage (1 Cor., xi, 9) which refers to 'the bottom of God's secrets'. Stroup's affectation certainly has an unknown Bottom, since he twice refers to Bottom as a tailor.[10] Alan Brissenden argues the case for Balthasar rather than Borachio being Margaret's dancing partner in Much Ado.[11]

As usual Hamlet has produced a crop of bright and bouncing offerings. H. E. Kavros suggests, on the basis of a New Testament reference to a red dawn presaging doom, that Horatio's 'the morn in russet mantle clad' implies similar foreboding.[12] He is little perturbed by the consideration (which he concedes) that 'russet' does not quite mean 'red'. Similarly Karl P. Wentersdorf is unperturbed by the fact that he can find no evidence for the arum maculatum, his candidate for Gertrude's 'long purples', ever being called by that name (or dead men's fingers), though the pictorial evidence is tempting.[13] David Haley tells me more than I wish to know about 'sleaded pollax' (studded pole-axe) though once again the pictures are persuasive as is the Spenser reference (deriving from Olaus Magnus).[14]

[1] 'Robert Langham and his "Letter"', Notes and Queries, n.s. xxv, 5 (1978), 426–7.

[2] 'Personnel at the Second Globe: Some Biographical Notes', ibid., 441–4.

[3] 'Shakespeare and the Marginalia of the Geneva Bible', ibid., xxvi, 2 (1979), 113–14.

[4] 'Shakespeare the Shake-scene', ibid., p. 115.

[5] 'Philip Kingman: Some New Information', ibid., pp. 141–2.

[6] 'Some New Light on Robert Daborne', ibid., pp. 142–3.

[7] 'Edmund Shakespeare at St Leonard's, Shoreditch', Shakespeare Quarterly, xxix, 3 (1978), 422.

[8] 'Honorificabilitudinitatibus', Notes and Queries, n.s. xxv, 5 (1978), 445.

[9] 'Shakespeare's "Honey-Stalks": Webster's "Honey-Dew"', ibid., xxvi, 2 (1979), 114–15.

[10] 'Bottom's Name and his Epiphany', Shakespeare Quarterly, xxix, 1 (1978), 79–82.

[11] 'Much Ado, II, i, 86–96: The Case for Balthasar', Notes and Queries, n.s. xxvi, 2 (1979), 116–17.

[12] 'The Morn in Russet Mantle Clad', ibid., pp. 119–20.

[13] 'Ophelia's Long Purples', Shakespeare Quarterly xxx, 3 (1979), 397–402.

[14] 'Gothic Armaments and King Hamlet's Poleaxe', ibid., xxix, 3 (1978), pp. 407–13.

R. W. Dent challenges Fredson Bowers's influential view that 'scourge' and 'minister' are or were opposites, necessarily connected with 'evil' and 'good' respectively.[1] S. Viswanathan suggests a visual reminiscence such as the well-known one by Ralph Willis in *Mount Tabor* as the origin of 'This fell sergeant, Death'.[2] Vittorio Gabrieli finds a reminiscence from Thomas More in the doom of the Ghost[3] and Kenneth Muir discusses a possible borrowing from *Hamlet* in *Locrine*.[4]

The main emphasis of June Winter's essay is on the elucidation of Milton's *Lycidas*, but a genuine glow of illumination is cast backward on the preoccupation with time in *Macbeth*.[5] Sarah Carpenter points out parallels between Lear's Fool and Handy Dandy in *Godly Queen Hester*,[6] while D. L. D'Avray notes the appearance of the Lear story in a thirteenth-century collection of sermons, coming to the wholly unarguable conclusion that 'there is quite a distance between this "exemplum optimum" and *King Lear*'.[7] G. Watson is tempted to think that three of the four references to Cleopatra's crown in the final scene of *Antony and Cleopatra* come from Galen's *Theriake*; on the evidence offered I find the temptation totally resistible.[8]

In 'The Two French Lords of *All's Well That Ends Well*' Richard A. Levin attempts, on the whole convincingly, to clarify the dramatic identity of this troublesome pair and argues for their presence throughout the play.[9] Gary Taylor is concerned to defend the usually amended Folio attribution of dialogue in *Measure for Measure*, IV, ii, 41–6.[10] Ann Thompson notes a plot parallel between Book IV, Chapter One of the *Arcadia* and *The Two Noble Kinsmen*, V, ii.[11]

Two notes on two of the last plays to conclude this survey: Rowena Davies suggests a possible nostalgic allusion to the memory of the Virgin Queen in the characterisation of Imogen, the Phoenix image being applied to both,[12] and Stanton J. Linden thinks Perdita's objection to gillyvors may be due not only to the commonly noted association between streakiness and painting (and therefore, to the Elizabethans, harlotry) but also to the current belief in the aphrodisiac properties of gillyvors.[13] Perhaps Perdita's innocence is a plant hardy enough to thrive in the soil of such knowledge. I wonder.

[1] 'Hamlet: Scourge and Minister', *ibid.*, XXIX, 1 (1978), 82–4.

[2] '"This Fell Sergeant, Death" Once More', *ibid.*, pp. 84–5.

[3] '*Hamlet* and The Supplication of Souls', *Notes and Queries*, n.s. XXVI, 2 (1979), 120–1.

[4] 'Sabrina and Ophelia', *ibid.*, pp. 121–2.

[5] 'The Two-Handed Engine and the Fatal Bellman: *Lycidas* and *Macbeth*', *ibid.*, pp. 126–8.

[6] 'Lear's Fool: Another Proverb', *ibid.*, pp. 128–9.

[7] 'The King Lear Story in a Sermon to Wives by Guibertus de Tornaco', *ibid.*, pp. 132–3.

[8] 'The Death of Cleopatra', *ibid.*, XXV, 5 (1978), 409–14.

[9] *Notes and Queries*, n.s. XXVI, 2 (1979), 122–5.

[10] '*Measure for Measure*, IV, ii, 41–6', *Shakespeare Quarterly*, XXIX, 3 (1978), 419–21.

[11] 'Jailers' Daughters in the *Arcadia* and *The Two Noble Kinsmen*', *Notes and Queries*, n.s. XXVI, 2 (1979), 140–1.

[12] '"Alone Th'Arabian Bird" – Imogen as Elizabeth I?', *ibid.*, pp. 137–40.

[13] 'Perdita and the Gillyvors: *The Winter's Tale*, IV, iv, 79–103', *ibid.*, p. 140.

3. TEXTUAL STUDIES

reviewed by GEORGE WALTON WILLIAMS

While some scholars hold that the production of articles on the habits of the compositors of Shakespeare's plays is of questionable value, other scholars continue to produce such articles; the past year seems to have been generously supplied with provocative studies of the busy typesetters of Folio and Quartos. Jaggard's Compositor B of the First Folio has received the closest scrutiny.

In articles on the texts of *All's Well that Ends Well* and of *Julius Caesar*, Fredson Bowers addresses the fidelity of B in the formal detail of copying speech prefixes. Though this quality of B's work is not the primary concern of these studies, it is of interest that Bowers depends on that fidelity for the conclusions of both of them: 'Compositor B..., would not be likely to go against copy [for a prefix] except perhaps in mechanical matters of abbreviation...[or] in the establishment of a favorite short form of the same prefix' (p. 68).[1] In the *Julius Caesar* paper, Bowers repeats Brents Stirling's suggestion that variant prefixes in two passages (II, i, 86–228; IV, iii, 123–64) disclose not compositorial vagary but post-compositional revision; he adds to this suggestion Dover Wilson's that the same lean actor doubled the parts of Ligarius and Cassius; and he concludes on the basis of the doubling that the revisions took place during rehearsal.[2] He demonstrates that the copy behind the Folio text is a clean scribal transcript of Shakespeare's foul papers (in which the scribe had deliberately chosen the prefix 'Cassi.' to avoid confusion), and he sees the revised passages as having been added to the transcript later in another hand (in which the writer – possibly Shakespeare – had used the prefix 'Cass.'). The scribal variation tends to support the hypothesis of compositorial

fidelity. Writing in 1962, Stirling betrayed some hesitancy in suggesting the possibility of revision for purely 'literary' reasons, but he felt that the bibliographical evidence made a good case for *Julius Caesar*; Bowers expresses no concern for the matter. Stirling's hesitancy is surely not justified; in *Julius Caesar* there is strong historical supposition that Shakespeare did in fact revise. Ben Jonson quoted a line from the play which is not now in the text and, as Kittredge believed, the removal of which has evidently left a half-line of pentameter. It is no strained hypothesis that Jonson heard the line during rehearsal and that Shakespeare corrected that error as he made other improvements. Bowers's article on *All's Well* builds on this demonstration of compositorial fidelity to argue from the unusually varied prefix patterns in the play that the copy behind the Folio is Shakespeare's working papers. In setting these papers Compositors B, C, and D in very large part followed the vagaries of authorial practice in the use of different prefixes and different kinds of prefixes. Bowers proposes that these differences in form be attributed to successive stages in composition. He gives particular attention to the prefixes for the Countess, for Bertram, and for Lafeu, and he explains the three examples of a duplicated prefix within a single speech (I, iii, 119; II, ii, 39; II, iv, 34) as evidence of marginal additions made in the reworking. Though he admits the influences of the abbreviation and the 'favorite short form' (as quoted above) and of a tendency to repeat in

[1] 'Foul Papers, Compositor B, and the Speech-Prefixes of *All's Well that Ends Well*', *Studies in Bibliography*, XXXII (1979), 60–81.

[2] 'The Copy for Shakespeare's *Julius Caesar*', *South Atlantic Bulletin*, XLIII, 4 (1978), 23–36.

the prefix a different form found in the direction immediately preceding, Bowers concludes that variations in prefix form can be attributed 'with some confidence' to the underlying copy, not to the compositors' predilections (p. 81).[1]

Paul Werstine argues for the fidelity of B in general terms. Against Alice Walker's examination of B in setting 1795 lines of *1 Henry IV*, he offers his own examination of B elsewhere in the Folio similarly setting 2360 lines from 'largely uncorrected quarto copy'.[2] (How much the Quartos were uncorrected is arguable; some of the stage directions that Werstine lists as B's 'corrections' seem to this reviewer likely to be the work of a playhouse annotator – e.g., '*The Lion roares . . .*', '*Musicke ceases*', '*Flourish*' – correctly copied by the Compositor in setting F from Q.) On the basis of Walker's figures from *1 Henry IV*, we should expect 215 errors in the six plays; we find instead only 134. In attempting to explain 'the remarkable variation in Compositor B's error rate', Werstine considers and rejects the possibility of another compositor; he then concludes by explaining the abnormally high rate of error in *1 Henry IV* as a result of constraints of cast-off copy and difficulties in justification of lines in that play.

In a comparable examination of a compositor of plays in quarto, Alan E. Craven presents new evidence on the reliability of Valentine Simmes's Compositor A, expanding and refining his 1973 study.[3] Unfortunately, he has not been able (one supposes) to consider the penetrating observations of Peter Davison on the same compositor (published in *AEB*, 1 (1977)). Craven's earlier study concentrated on Simmes's reprint (Q2) of *Richard II* (1598); the present study examines the reprint (Q2) of *The First Part of the Contention* (1600) and the reprint (Q3) of *1 Henry IV* (1604). It reveals that in the six-year period embraced by these reprints Compositor A's work improved but that his rate of accuracy was never so high as could

have been hoped. Compositor A was 'especially prone to errors of substitution' and 'frequently' guilty of omission (pp. 194–5). Craven warns against the assumption that because a text is clean and uncluttered typographically it is also correct. 'The dramatic quartos set by Compositor A [and they include five substantive Shakespearian texts] present a less satisfactory reproduction of what stood in the copy than has hitherto been supposed' (p. 196).

The composition of the first quarto of *Love's Labour's Lost* has been the subject of three articles. The bibliographer must always hope that scholars working independently on the identification of a compositor will reach the same conclusions, i.e. that the data are exact. Paul Werstine[4] and George R. Price[5] have both analysed the composition of William White's Quarto of 1598 and have both concluded that three compositors were at work, but Werstine's Compositors R, S, and T bear no relationship to Price's I, II, and III. Werstine bases his conclusions on the spelling patterns of the compositors as they are found in prints from White's shop in the years 1598–1600; Price bases his on practices in the Quarto: formal treatment of stage directions, prefixes, indentation, capitalization; fullness of directions; spellings; number of gross errors

[1] See also Richard A. Levin, 'The Two French Lords of *All's Well that Ends Well*', *Notes and Queries*, 26 (1979), 122–5.

[2] 'Compositor B of the Shakespeare First Folio', *Analytical and Enumerative Bibliography*, 2 (1978), 241–63.

[3] 'The Reliability of Simmes's Compositor A', *Studies in Bibliography*, XXXII (1979), 186–97.

[4] 'Editorial Uses of Compositor Study', *Analytical and Enumerative Bibliography*, 2 (1978), 153–65; Werstine cites his unpublished dissertation 'William White's Printing Shop and the Printing of *Love's Labour's Lost* Q1 (1598)' (University of South Carolina, 1976).

[5] 'The Printing of *Love's Labour's Lost* (1598)', *Papers of the Bibliographical Society of America*, 72 (1978), 405–34.

per page. The disagreement between the two examinations must discourage the seeker after truth (and this reviewer). To a question perhaps of more significance, the nature of the copy for the Quarto, the two scholars again reach opposing conclusions. Werstine argues on the basis of mixed spelling patterns intruding into their normal patterns that his compositors were setting from a now lost quarto; Price argues on the familiar bases of Shakespearian spellings, the irregularities common to foul papers, and the difficulties of casting off that his compositors were setting from a manuscript. It appears that Werstine is more likely to be right about the compositors than Price, and Price more likely to be right about the copy than Werstine.[1] Werstine also argues that because White's compositors could and did set foreign languages correctly elsewhere, the corruption of the languages in the mouths of the Curate and the Pedant cannot be blamed on the printers but must be attributed to Shakespeare's deliberate efforts to mock the assumed learning of the worthies. Price provides a running title analysis and a collation of the press variants ('Stop-Press Corrections') of the Quarto; this last is the most valuable part of his article. The critics agree in supposing the Quarto to have been set by formes.

In his second article, Price discusses the argument for two 'layers' of composition in Shakespeare's manuscript.[2] Here he becomes venturesome: 'From Shakespeare's Additions to *The Play of Sir Thomas More* we know [!] that he wrote a legible Secretary hand.... But he does not seem to have used italic habitually. Yet he probably believed italic script to be the appropriate medium for a poetic work.... No doubt he intended his final draft of *LLL* to serve a dual purpose.... The scribe was first to copy it on folio sheets as a promptbook, in Secretary hand.... Then, if after the performance someone requested a copy [the scribe could easily transcribe] Shakespeare's final draft into italic hand...on quarto pages' (p. 6). Much of this article considers the position of Dover Wilson (in the edition of 1923), accepting Wilson's 'basic elements...', but with considerable changes in detail as dictated by the participation of the compositors' (p. 9).

Two hypotheses concerning Shakespearian manuscripts are more modest in scope than those relevant to *Love's Labour's Lost* and perhaps more persuasive. Kenneth Muir observes that two passages in Folio *Troilus and Cressida* are virtually identical to the text in the Quarto (II, ii, 106–209; III, iii, 1–100) and were probably reprinted from the Quarto because leaves of the manuscript of the Folio copy were missing.[3] As it is commonly accepted that Shakespeare wrote about fifty lines to a page and, as these two sections are each approximately 100 lines long, Muir is almost certainly correct in this suggestion; clearly each passage reflects the loss of a single leaf, written on both sides. Mary Hobbs, noticing that several manuscripts of 'Sonnet II' concur in a group of readings that vary from the printed text, concludes that they probably derive from a common original.[4] As the manuscript in the Folger, one of this family, heads this poem 'A Song' and numbers the quatrains (it is not 'divided into stanzas', for a sonnet has no stanzas), Hobbs suggests that the common original may have been a musical setting from a now lost song-

---

[1] To prove an hypothesis of derivation, it will be necessary to show that a particular pattern in the later version, meaningless in that version, reflects a pattern in the earlier version, meaningful in that version, as, for example, a variation of compositorial or scribal habits that can be explained by a system of units of 35 lines (a quarto page) or 50 lines (a manuscript page).

[2] 'Textual Notes on *Love's Labour's Lost*, 1598', *Analytical and Enumerative Bibliography*, 3 (1979), 3–38.

[3] 'A Note on the Text of *Troilus and Cressida*', *The Library*, 1 (1979), 168.

[4] 'Shakespeare's Sonnet II – "A Sugred Sonnet"?', *Notes and Queries*, 26 (1979), 112–13.

book by Wilson or Lawes. This is a reasonable suggestion.

Using the 1609 *Sonnets* as his raw material, Randall McLeod presents a new bibliographical technique, 'photographic collation'.[1] The technique of superimposing a photoprint of one exemplar on another to detect changes or identities has been known since the discovery of the nature of the Pavier Quartos (1911), but a new copying paper ('Xerox Transparencies') brings the technique handily within the reach of the individual researcher. McLeod demonstrates by the imposition of transparent copies of the title page of the *Sonnets* that when the imprint was changed, two other alterations were made also – vertical and horizontal: the type for 'SONNETS.' is higher on the page in the Aspley imprint than in the Wright; two 'E' sorts (of different width) have been interchanged in 'SHAKE-SPEARES'. Both of these changes might have been detected by the unaided eye – had man but had the wit to look for them – but it is clear that the technique makes the process easy and straightforward. McLeod's second example of photographic collation will be generally more useful than the first. By photocopying the headlines of all the pages of a forme it is possible by cutting and pasting the transparencies to reconstitute the forme. McLeod demonstrates how this technique identifies variants in types and in spacing; it will be particularly useful in books where the headlines are short and set in small or badly inked type, e.g., 'SHAKESPEARES/SONNETS.'. He also uses his collation to present new evidence on the sequence of printing of sheets K and L. The technique is indeed a useful one and will undoubtedly prove to be of great value in textual studies.

Using the 'traditional' method of collation, the industrious Paul Werstine has collated *Comedy of Errors* in the Folger copies of the Folio that Hinman omitted and has found one semi-substantive variant.[2] As all editions follow the correctly corrected state, the discovery adds no new textual information, but Werstine draws interesting bibliographical deductions from his discovery. The fact that he has extracted only one variant from his labors suggests that Hinman's 'sample' was sufficiently broad and that not much more is to be mined from the Folio field. We must be grateful, however, for even this small favor.

In one of the more interesting theoretical papers of the year, Michael J. Warren confronts head-on the problem of the 'ideal' text and concludes forthrightly that for *King Lear* there is none, that in fact there are two final versions, one reflected in the Quarto and one in the Folio, and that conflation of these two yields a text written by the editor, not by Shakespeare – a play that never was.[3] As a simple example of editorial conflation resulting in a non-dramatic text he cites the short dialogue between Lear

[1] 'A Technique of Headline Analysis, with Application to *Shakespeare's Sonnets*, 1609', *Studies in Bibliography*, XXXII (1979), 197–210.
[2] 'An Unrecorded Variant in the Shakespeare First Folio', *Papers of the Bibliographical Society of America*, 72 (1978), 329–30.
[3] 'Quarto and Folio *King Lear* and the Interpretation of Albany and Edgar' in *Shakespeare: Pattern of Excelling Nature*, ed. David Bevington and Jay L. Halio (University of Delaware, Newark; Associated Universities Press, London, 1978), pp. 95–107. Warren's article may be the harbinger of a royal progress: a section of the 1980 meeting of the Shakespeare Association of America will discuss the text of *King Lear* under the direction of G. B. Evans, and forthcoming volumes from the Cambridge University Press, Princeton, and Scolar will present exhaustive (and no doubt conflicting) studies of its many problems.

This volume of papers and abstracts from the International Shakespeare Association Congress (Washington, U.S.A., 1976) contains also a review by S. W. Reid of the Seminar: Toward the Definitive Text (pp. 242–3). From the welter of comments made at the seminar, Reid has extracted the idea that 'Editions, not texts, may be definitive in a limited sense . . . and thus analytical bibliography may still have some contributions to make in producing a definitive edition with a critical text.'

and Kent at II, iv, 14–21. Quarto and Folio provide three interchanges each (with differing ripostes), yet all editions conflate the two versions to provide four interchanges. 'In each text the climax on the third exchange is powerful...they are both probably "what Shakespeare wrote"; and so respect for the theatrical proportions of the play dictates that conflation cannot be other than textual tinkering.... Either Q or F; *not* both together' (p. 98). In the light of this clear example, Warren proceeds to analyse the characters of Albany and Edgar in the two versions; 'the differences...indicate that a substantial and consistent recasting of certain aspects of the play has taken place' (p. 99). In Q, Albany is well developed, and 'he closes the play a mature and victorious duke assuming responsibility for the Kingdom'; Edgar 'ends the play a young man overwhelmed by his experience'. In F, Albany is a weak character, 'avoiding responsibility'; Edgar is 'a young man who has learned a great deal, and who is emerging as the new leader of the ravaged society. Q and F embody two different artistic visions...they must be treated as separate versions.' Though 'conflated texts... may give their readers all of "what Shakespeare wrote," they do not give them [either version] of Shakespeare's play of *King Lear*.... The principle that more is better, that all is good, has no foundation' (pp. 99, 105). Though one may wonder why such a revision seemed necessary or advisable and why, if it did so, major changes seem to have been made in these two parts only, this provocative paper will no doubt become the basis for a fresh evaluation of *Lear*, of other plays extant in two versions, and of the concept of the 'ideal' text.

Thomas L. Berger discusses three aspects of the printing history of the 'bad' Quarto of *Henry V*: the composition and presswork, the 'staying entry' of 4 August 1600, and the puzzle of the address in the imprint.[1] From his careful and thorough analysis of the Quarto, Berger concludes that it is the work of one compositor, setting by formes; he offers an interesting explanation for the anomalous 'Lord' prefixes on D4ᵛ. His comments on the staying entry supplement the full account by Knowles in the New Variorum *As You Like It*, but his observations on the address in the imprint – a problem apparently unnoticed before now – though intriguing, are inconclusive.

Three articles on the editing of Shakespeare in the eighteenth century remind us that editors of that enlightened age, though they were troubled with matters that seem less technical than those of today, had their difficulties too. John Hazel Smith describes the extensive marginalia that Styan Thirlby entered in three editions of Shakespeare's works – Pope's (1725), Theobald's (1733), and Warburton's (1747).[2] He also records the association between Thirlby and Theobald, to whom Thirlby made his notes available in 1728–9; but his chief contribution lies no doubt in explaining the 'shorthand' in which Thirlby made his comments (mostly in abbreviated Latin). Though Thirlby evidently projected an edition of Shakespeare, he never undertook it; and his place in the editorial tradition must depend on his assembling of critical materials and the assistance he gave to Theobald, who on certain occasions acknowledged that assistance graciously and on other occasions – so Thirlby felt – did not. Thirlby's 'work reveals him to have been more than an "ingenious" emender: his editorial philosophy was well ahead of most contemporaries" (p. 235). 'His judgments were flawed at times by personal considerations; his reputation for...unfinished work seems to have been deserved; but there is also no doubt that he was a scholar of great weight' (p. 236).

[1] 'The Printing of *Henry V*, Q1', *The Library*, 1 (1979), 114–25.
[2] 'Styan Thirlby's Shakespearean Commentaries: A Corrective Analysis', *Shakespeare Studies*, XI (1978), 219–41.

Responding to the note of William Woodson on the 1785 Variorum (*Studies in Bibliography*, XXVIII (1975); see also XXXI (1978)), Arthur Sherbo defines the shares of Steevens, Reed, Malone, and others in the preparation of that edition.[1] He seeks also to clarify the extent of the disagreement between Steevens and Malone, pointing out that though there were editorial differences between them, sharpened perhaps by the work on the 1785 Variorum, the 'relations between the two men, while they probably were not cordial, were not marked by open hostility' (p. 243). 'While it is true...that Steevens succeeded in hurting and angering the courteous Malone, it was not until publication of the 1793 *Shakespeare* that he did so – decidedly not in the 1785 variorum' (p. 246).

Irene G. Dash elevates the tone of this trio of articles by examining Warburton's editing of *The Winter's Tale* in the context of the changing sensibilities of critics and poets towards the simple, the natural, and the sublime.[2] Warburton's critical comments on the play and his 'preferred passages' concentrate on simple characters, external nature, and wildness, paralleling also the emphasis on the sublime and the picturesque in the illustrations for this play in the editions of Theobald and Hanmer. Warburton's 'beauties' 'link contemporary aesthetic theories to new attitudes towards Shakespeare's plays' (p. 170). His edition also was the first to include in the footnotes character analysis, thus anticipating 'the later flowering of psychological analysis of... character' (p. 171) and reflecting the growing interest in the professional training of the actor. The edition deserves a place in the growth of critical sensitivity that the disputatiousness of its editor would seem to have made unlikely.

Four critics suggest emendations or variant readings for four plays; they achieve varying degrees of success in convincing this reviewer of the necessity of accepting their emendations. M. R. Golding proposes that the Fool's quip at his departure at the end of act 1 in *King Lear* should follow the Quarto 'maide' rather than the Folio 'a maid'.[3] The omission of the indefinite article allows a pun on 'made', 'triumphantly successful'. Though this is surely a possible emendation of the accepted text, it does not seem that following the Quarto provides a meaning sufficiently superior to justify departing here from the Folio. Karl P. Wentersdorf attacks three of the most troublesome and problematic of the cruxes in *Hamlet*.[4] For 'the dram of ev'l/Doth...of a doubt/To his own scandal' (I, iv, 37–8) he supports Leon Kellner's 'oft adaunt'; for 'Are of a most select and generous *chief* in that' (I, iii, 74) he supports Steevens's 'choice'; for 'either *the devil* or throw him out' (III, iv, 169) he supports Malone's 'curb the devil'. All of these emendations are based on exact paleographical arguments and close studies of meaning and of the associations of image clusters. They are persuasive. Alan Brissenden notes the five prefixes for Margaret's partner in the dance at *Much Ado About Nothing*, II, i, 86–96, of which in the Folio three are for Benedick and two for Balthasar.[5] All critics dismiss the notions that the prefixes are for two speakers and that Benedick is one of them. Brissenden rejects the emendation to Borachio (suggested by Hinman and Sisson) claiming all the speeches for Balthasar, the appropriate partner for Margaret. Though his conclusion is probably correct, Brissenden would have been helpful if he had suggested how the error came about. Gary Taylor argues convincingly that for the Folio

[1] 'George Steevens's 1785 Variorum *Shakespeare*', *Studies in Bibliography*, XXXII (1979), 241–6.

[2] 'A Glimpse of the Sublime in Warburton's Edition of *The Winter's Tale*', *Shakespeare Studies*, XI (1978), 159–74.

[3] '*King Lear*, I, v, 49–50: A Word for the Quarto Reading', *Notes and Queries*, 26 (1979), 128.

[4] '*Hamlet*: Notes on Three Cruxes', *Studia Neophilologica*, 50 (1978), 179–83.

[5] '*Much Ado About Nothing*, II, i, 86–96: The Case for Balthasar', *Notes and Queries*, 26 (1979), 116–17.

and traditional 'Pandar' in *Henry V*, IV, v, 14, we should read with the 'bad' Quarto 'Leno'.[1] The word *Leno* is used by Thomas Nashe in 1594 and 1596. As it is unthinkable that the reporters of the corrupt memorial Quarto should have inserted this rare word, so it is thinkable that Compositor B, who set this passage in the Folio replaced a word he did not know with one that he and the generality of readers did. Taylor's argument restores a Shakespearian word to Shakespeare's text.

The present writer contributes to the continuing discussion of the spelling of Falstaff's name, noting that on two occasions (of 19) in Qo (1598) of *1 Henry IV*, the speech prefix '*Fast.*' occurs, evidently an abbreviation for Fastolfe; from these aberrant vestigial forms he concludes that Shakespeare devised the anagram 'Falstaff' from the name of the hero Fastolfe.[2]

[1] 'Shakespeare's Leno: *Henry V*, IV, v, 14', *ibid.*, pp. 117–18.
[2] 'Second Thoughts on Falstaff's Name', *Shakespeare Quarterly*, 30 (1979), 82–4.

© GEORGE WALTON WILLIAMS 1980

Thanks to the backing of the Modern Language Association of America, the New Variorum edition of the works of Shakespeare has recently resumed publication. A New Variorum *As You Like It* appeared in 1977, *Measure for Measure* is now in press, and twenty-two other titles are in preparation. Much work remains to be done, however. *Pericles, The Taming of the Shrew, The Two Gentlemen of Verona*, and *The Two Noble Kinsmen* have never appeared in the series and are at present unassigned. The New Variorum editions of *Cymbeline, Hamlet, King John, Love's Labour's Lost, Much Ado About Nothing, Richard III, Sonnets*, and *The Tempest* are antiquated and require replacement; these too are unassigned.

The New Variorum committee invites applications from experienced literary and textual critics interested in undertaking one of these editions. Because of the considerable work involved, the committee favors the appointment of teams to each edition, two or more scholars of approximately equal stature as co-editors or one well-qualified person as editor aided by several who are less experienced as associates or assistants. Inquiries or applications with résumés may be sent to Robert K. Turner, Jr, English Department, University of Wisconsin–Milwaukee, Milwaukee, Wisconsin 53201, USA.

INDEX